Collins

Websters

175 YEARS OF DICTIONARY PUBLISHING

easy learning

ENGLISH
IDIOMS

HarperCollins Publishers
Westerhill Road
Bishopbriggs
Glasgow
G64 2QT

First edition 2011

Reprint 10 9 8 7 6 5 4 3 2 1 0

© HarperCollins Publishers 2011

ISBN 978-0-00-736384-1

www.collinslanguage.com

A catalogue record for this book is
available from the British Library

Typeset by Davidson Publishing
Solutions, Glasgow

Printed in Great Britain by Clays Ltd,
St Ives plc

Editorial staff

American English consultant:
Orin Hargraves

Project manager: Lisa Sutherland

Senior editors:
Penny Hands
Kate Woodford

Contributors:
Sandra Anderson
Katharine Coates
Kate Mohideen

For the publishers:
Lucy Cooper
Kerry Ferguson
Elaine Higgleton

introduction

Collins Webster's Easy Learning English Idioms is designed for anyone who wants to improve their knowledge of English. Whether you are preparing for exams, need a quick look-up guide to English idioms, or you simply want to browse and bring some fun and color into your English, *Collins Webster's Easy Learning English Idioms* offers you the information you require in a clear and accessible format.

What is an idiom?

An idiom is a special type of phrase. It is a group of words that can be difficult to understand even if you know all the words contained in it. In some cases, you can make a good guess at the meaning, because the idiom creates an image that represents an idea in our head. For example, it is easy to see that someone who is described as *a pain in the neck* is annoying; however, in many other cases, it is almost impossible to work out the meaning of an expression.

How to find an idiom

Idioms are listed under headwords, which are ordered alphabetically. In order to find the idiom you are looking for, you will first need to see if the idiom contains a noun. If it does, the idiom will be found under the headword for the *first noun* that occurs within it. So, for example, *call it a day* will appear at **day**, and *the life and soul of the party* will appear at **life**.

If there is no noun in the idiom, look for the *first adjective* or *first adverb*. Examples of these types of idioms would be *drop dead* (found under **dead**), or *leave someone cold* (found under **cold**).

Finally, if there is no noun, adjective, or adverb, look for the *first verb*. An example of this type of idiom would be *give it up for someone*, which appears under **give**.

Remember, then, that the ordering system works as follows:

- first noun
- first adjective
- first adverb
- first verb

introduction

One exception to this rule is that idioms like *hard as nails* or *fresh as a daisy* (called 'similes') are found under their **first adjective** rather than their noun. This is because there are often several nouns that can go with the adjective, and so it is more useful to see them all together in the same place.

Finally, please note that idioms are always placed under their headword in the form in which they appear in the idiom. So, for example, *pick holes in something* will be found under **holes**, not **hole**.

We hope you enjoy finding out more about this fascinating area of the English language. For more information about Collins dictionaries, visit us at **www.collinslanguage.com**.

guide to entries

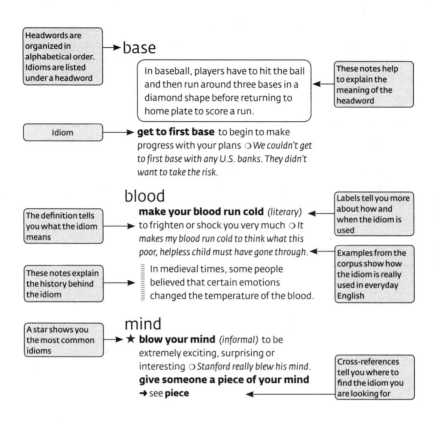

Headwords are organized in alphabetical order. Idioms are listed under a headword

base

In baseball, players have to hit the ball and then run around three bases in a diamond shape before returning to home plate to score a run.

These notes help to explain the meaning of the headword

Idiom

get to first base to begin to make progress with your plans ○ *We couldn't get to first base with any U.S. banks. They didn't want to take the risk.*

blood

make your blood run cold (*literary*) to frighten or shock you very much ○ *It makes my blood run cold to think what this poor, helpless child must have gone through.*

Labels tell you more about how and when the idiom is used

The definition tells you what the idiom means

Examples from the corpus show how the idiom is really used in everyday English

These notes explain the history behind the idiom

In medieval times, some people believed that certain emotions changed the temperature of the blood.

mind

A star shows you the most common idioms

★ **blow your mind** (*informal*) to be extremely exciting, surprising or interesting ○ *Stanford really blew his mind.*
give someone a piece of your mind
→ see **piece**

Cross-references tell you where to find the idiom you are looking for

Idioms

accounting

there's no accounting for taste said when you think that what someone likes is unpleasant or strange ○ *Daisy ordered her favorite pepperoni and pineapple pizza (there's no accounting for taste).*

ace

have an ace in the hole to have something that you can use to gain an advantage ○ *He doesn't usually risk that much unless he thinks he has an ace in the hole.*

In one kind of poker game, you have an ace in the hole when you have an ace as your "hole" card: see "hole card" at **hole**.

play your ace to do something clever and unexpected to give yourself an advantage ○ *Just as the race was nearly over, Hackett played his ace and pulled ahead.*

aces

hold all the aces to have all the power or advantages in a situation ○ *When I was an adolescent, I thought girls held all the aces.*

In many card games, the ace is the card with the highest score.

acid

★ **the acid test** an experience or situation that proves how skillful or effective someone or something is ○ *My first really stressful day when things go wrong: that will be the real acid test.*

Nitric acid can be used to test whether a metal is pure gold because it corrodes most metals but does not affect gold.

acquaintance

a passing acquaintance or **a nodding acquaintance**

1 someone you know, but only slightly ○ *After a while a man came in who was evidently a passing acquaintance of the family and stopped at their table to chat.*
2 slight knowledge of something ○ *We chatted for a little about poetry, with which he showed considerably more than a nodding acquaintance.*

act

The metaphors in these expressions often relate to performers entertaining audiences.

★ **a balancing act** a situation in which you try to satisfy two or more opposing groups or sets of ideals ○ *Mr. Alia is performing a delicate balancing act. He talks of reform, but clings to old certainties.*

★ **be caught in the act** to be seen doing something secret or wrong ○ *The men were caught in the act of digging up buried explosives.*

In this expression, "act" refers to the act of doing something.

★ **clean up your act** to improve your behavior and start to act in a more socially responsible way ○ *He plays a crooked patriarch of a family of petty crooks trying to clean up their act after he's sent to the slammer.*

★ **get in on the act** or **be in on the act** to start doing something that someone else was doing first, so that you share their success or win an advantage ○ *The company's reputation has reached the United States, and*

American investors have been trying to get in on the act.

★ **get your act together** to take control of yourself and organize your activities more effectively in order to be more successful ○ *We're going to be 22 points down by Monday, and we've got to get our act together.*

★ **a hard act to follow** someone who is so impressive or effective that it is difficult for anyone else who comes after them to be as good ○ *He was a hard act to follow – a brilliant intellectual with long experience as an observer of the economic scene.*

action

★ **fight a rearguard action** to try hard to stop something happening, without much hope of success ○ *National telephone companies are fighting a rearguard action against competition from beyond their frontiers.*

> The rearguard of a retreating army is a unit that separates from the rest and acts as a defense while the rest of the army is getting away.

★ **a piece of the action** involvement in an activity that seems exciting and likely to succeed or make money ○ *The airlines may be tipping into profitability, and the unions are going to want a piece of the action.*

actions

actions speak louder than words used to emphasize that people show what they really think and feel by what they do, rather than by what they say ○ *The government needs to understand that actions speak louder than words.*

Adam

not know someone from Adam to not know someone at all, and be completely unable to recognize them ○ *The man greeted me like an old friend, but I didn't know him from Adam.*

> According to the Bible, Adam was the first human being.

ado

much ado about nothing (*journalism*) a lot of fuss about something that is not important ○ *French newspapers described the international uproar as much ado about nothing.*

> "Much Ado About Nothing" is the title of a play by Shakespeare.

agenda

★ **a hidden agenda** a situation in which someone secretly tries to achieve a particular thing while they appear to be doing something else ○ *The unions fear these tactics are part of a hidden agenda to reduce pay and conditions throughout the company.*

> An agenda is a list of things that need to be dealt with, for example, at a meeting.

air

★ **be left hanging in the air** if a question or remark is left hanging in the air, people avoid discussing it because they do not want to deal with it or the issues involved ○ *The moderator made intelligent points but never challenged anybody, so we were left with a lot of questions hanging in the air.*

be walking on air or
be floating on air to feel very happy or excited because something good has happened to you ○ *I can't believe that I've won. I'm floating on air!*

★ **clear the air** to deal openly with misunderstandings, problems, or jealousy, and try to get rid of them ○ *I get angry and frustrated with Hannah's temper, but I'm a great believer in expressing my feelings to clear the air.*

★ **disappear into thin air** or
vanish into thin air to disappear

completely ○ *Her husband disappeared into thin air for years.*

★ **hot air** false claims and promises ○ *In a sense, all the rhetoric about heightened cooperation can be seen as just so much hot air. There are still endless disputes.*

★ **in the air** if a change, idea, or feeling is in the air, people are aware of it or think it is going to happen even though it is not talked about directly ○ *Great excitement was in the air that week in Miami.*

★ **out of thin air** or
from thin air if something appears out of thin air, it appears suddenly and unexpectedly ○ *A crisis had materialized out of thin air.*

pull something out of the air to suddenly state something without considering it carefully or using correct information ○ *She pulled a figure out of the air, an amount she thought would cover several months' rent on an office.*

★ **up in the air** not yet decided or settled ○ *At the moment, the fate of the Hungarian people is still up in the air.*

aisles

roll in the aisles to laugh so much that it is hard to stop ○ *This unpredictable screwball comedy will leave the audience rolling in the aisles.*

≡ The aisles in a theater or cinema are the gaps between the blocks of seats.

aleck

a smart aleck someone who thinks they are very clever and has an answer for everything ○ *"Eventually, I hope to see legions of Arab American smart alecks like myself writing for newspapers," says the columnist.*

≡ Alec or Aleck is a shortened form of the name Alexander.

alive

★ **alive and kicking** if someone or something is alive and kicking, they are

still active or still exist, even though a lot of people might have expected them to have stopped or disappeared a long time ago ○ *Romance is still alive and kicking for a couple who will be celebrating their 50th wedding anniversary this week.*

eat someone alive

1 to cause someone great pain or distress ○ *The pain ate him alive; the world was nothing but fire and pain.*

2 to repeatedly bite someone ○ *"Can we go out?" "Outside? The mosquitoes will eat us alive!"*

skin someone alive

1 to make someone suffer a lot in order to get an advantage for yourself ○ *They are fiercely competitive. If they can skin us alive in business, they will.*

2 to punish someone severely ○ *Who let the cat out? You catch that animal, Ernie, or I'll skin you alive!*

someone will eat someone alive said when you think that someone will completely defeat someone else ○ *Sid will be eaten alive by the hardened criminals in the jail.*

all

go all out → see **go**
that's all she wrote used when you want to indicate that there is no more to be said or that something is finished ○ *He got hurt, and he didn't play much anymore. That's all she wrote.*

alley

be right up someone's alley to be exactly what someone likes or knows about ○ *I thought this little problem would be right up your alley.*

★ **a blind alley** something that is useless and will not lead to anything worthwhile ○ *Sooner or later they will have to realize that this is a blind alley and that they need to rethink their own strategies.*

≡ A blind alley is a street that is closed at one end.

altar

be sacrificed on the altar of something to suffer unfairly or be harmed because of a particular set of ideas or an activity ○ *They agreed that the interests of twelve million farmers could not be sacrificed on the altar of free trade.*

Long ago, an altar was a large stone on which animals were killed during the worship of a god or goddess. The killing of an animal in this way was called a sacrifice.

ambulance

ambulance chaser a lawyer who is eager to make money by defending someone who has been injured ○ *There are more and more ambulance chasers who encourage workers to sue their bosses for accidents in the workplace.*

This expression suggests colorfully that a lawyer would chase an ambulance carrying an injured person, in order to get the opportunity to represent them.

American

American as apple pie typical of American culture or the American way of life ○ *Jeans are as American as apple pie and old jeans show a touch of class.*

Apple pie is a traditional dessert that is thought of as typically American.

angel

a fallen angel someone once good or successful who has become bad or unsuccessful ○ *I consider Taiwan to be a fallen angel in the emerging markets.*

angels

be on the side of the angels to be trying to do what is morally right ○ *The President is on the side of the angels when it comes to racial tolerance, the environment, and Indian rights.*

answer

★ **not take no for an answer** to continue trying to make someone agree to something, despite their refusals ○ *Gerry, whose persistence has been known to wear down the resistance of many executives, refused to take no for an answer.*

ante

In card games such as poker, the ante is the amount of money that each player must place on the table before the game begins.

★ **up the ante** or **raise the ante**
1 to make greater demands or take greater risks in a dispute or contest, and so increase the amount that you will eventually lose or win ○ *Whenever they reached their goal, they upped the ante, setting increasingly difficult challenges for themselves.*
2 to offer a higher gambling stake or financial investment ○ *Its network television division upped the ante by paying an estimated $2 million a year for a deal.*

ants

have ants in your pants to be very restless or impatient ○ *Before, there would be no way I would sit down and take it easy. It was like I had ants in my pants.*

ape

go ape (informal) to become extremely angry or very excited about something and start shouting or behaving in an uncontrolled way ○ *I was in the kitchen preparing the evening meal when Rex ran down the stairs and went ape.*

People who behave in a violent or uncontrolled way are being compared with apes.

appetite

★ **whet someone's appetite** to make someone start to want something very much ○ *Winning the World Championship whetted his appetite for more success.*

≣ To whet a knife means to sharpen it.

apple

the apple of your eye the person that you like more than anyone else ○ *I was the apple of my father's eye.*

≣ In the past, the pupil in the eye was sometimes called the apple.

★ **a bad apple** or
a rotten apple a dishonest, immoral, or unpleasant person who has a bad influence on those around them ○ *They made it clear that they were not going to tolerate a bad apple in the United States Senate.*

≣ If a rotten apple is stored with good apples, it causes the good ones to rot.

applecart

upset the applecart to cause trouble or spoil something ○ *His departure at this critical stage could upset the whole applecart.*

apples

apples and oranges two completely different things that it is useless to compare ○ *To compare one with the other is to compare apples and oranges.*

apron

apron strings
1 the feelings that keep you dependent on your mother after the age when you should be independent ○ *At 21, I just had to get away, to cut those apron strings.*
2 the control that one country or institution has over another even though it should be independent ○ *Isn't it about time Canada cut the apron strings to the monarchy like others have done years ago?*

≣ This expression was originally used to refer to a child, especially a boy, who remained too much under the influence of his mother at an age when he should have become independent.

area

★ **a gray area** a situation or subject that is nor clear or understood and that nobody really knows how to deal with ○ *The court case highlighted the many gray areas in the law affecting stolen animals.*

arm

★ **at arm's length** if one person or organization is at arm's length from another, they are not closely connected, for example, because it would be wrong for them to influence each other ○ *Relations between the bank and the committee will be at arm's length until the report is delivered in July.*

cost an arm and a leg to cost a lot of money ○ *It cost us an arm and a leg to get here. But it has been worth it.*

keep someone at arm's length to avoid being friendly with someone or getting emotionally involved with them ○ *Brian had tried to get close, but his father had kept him at arm's length.*

the long arm of the law the very great power of the police and the legal system to find and punish criminals ○ *He knew that the long arm of the law would soon catch up with him.*

someone would give their right arm to do something or
someone would give their right arm for something someone wants something so much that they would do almost anything to get it ○ *I would give my right arm to be able to start again.*

≣ Most people are right-handed, and so consider their right arm to be more important than their left.

twist someone's arm to try hard to persuade someone to do something ○ *I didn't twist your arm to make you come. You wanted to because you sensed a story.*

armpit

the armpit of a place the least desirable area or aspect of something ○ *The station is the armpit of the city – we need to clean it up.*

> Your armpit is the place under your shoulder where your arm joins your body and is associated with unpleasant smells.

arms

★ **be up in arms** to be angry and protesting strongly about something ○ *The new documentary has the natural gas industry up in arms.*

> "Arms" in this expression means weapons.

★ **with open arms**
1 if you greet or welcome someone with open arms, you show that you are very pleased to see them or meet them ○ *We got out of the trucks to greet them with open arms. We had gifts ready, we were high on the idea of the meeting.*
2 if you welcome an event or new development with open arms, you are very pleased that it has happened ○ *Watchdog organizations welcomed today's guidelines with open arms.*

arrow

a straight arrow someone who is very conventional, honest, and moral ○ *I was very much a product of my environment. I was very traditional, a real straight arrow in lots of ways.*

art

have something down to a fine art to know the best way of doing something because you have practiced it a lot and have tried many different methods

○ *They've got fruit selling down to a fine art. You can be sure that your pears will ripen in a day.*

article

★ **the genuine article** the real or original thing or person, and not a copy or imitation ○ *The decoy tanks are indistinguishable from the genuine article.*

ask

a lot to ask (for) used when what you have asked someone to do or what you have been asked to do is very difficult or demanding ○ *It's a lot to ask to run faster in the second half of the race.*

atmosphere

you could cut the atmosphere with a knife said when you feel that the atmosphere in a place is extremely tense or unfriendly ○ *As soon as we entered the house, you could cut the atmosphere with a knife.*

attitude

with attitude showing a lot of confidence ○ *The Falcons came out with attitude against New London in the match on Saturday.*

awakening

★ **a rude awakening** a situation in which you suddenly realize the unpleasant truth about something ○ *Instead of quick profits, Johnson got a rude awakening.*

ax

an ax is hanging over someone used when someone is likely to lose their job soon ○ *There's an ax hanging over him – he's got one month to put everything right.*
an ax is hanging over something used when something is likely to be destroyed or ended soon ○ *The ax was hanging over 600.*
get the ax or
be given the ax
1 to lose your job ○ *This time, it's the*

business managers, executives and technical staff who are getting the ax.

2 to be canceled or ended suddenly

○ There will be cuts of $170 billion in defense, and almost $120 billion in domestic spending. Do you have any idea what specific programs will get the ax?

★ **have an ax to grind** to have particular attitudes and prejudices about something, often for selfish reasons

○ The senator believed cases should be referred by an independent agency that does not have an ax to grind.

There are several explanations for the origin of this expression. One is a story told by Benjamin Franklin about a man who managed to get his own ax sharpened by asking a boy to show him how his father's grindstone worked.

Bb

babe

a babe in arms someone who is very young ○ *The family has always enjoyed camping, and Chris has been sleeping in tents since he was a babe in arms.*

a babe in the woods an innocent person with no experience who is involved in a complicated situation that they do not understand ○ *By this time I wasn't such a babe in the woods, and one thing I insisted on was that they sign a contract.*

"Babe" is an old-fashioned word for a baby or small child. An old story tells of two young orphans who were left in the care of their uncle. If the children died, the uncle would inherit the family fortune. The uncle ordered a servant to take them into the woods where they died and their bodies were covered with leaves by the birds.

baby

throw the baby out with the bath water to reject something completely, the good parts as well as the bad ○ *Even if we don't necessarily like that, we're not going to throw the baby out with the bath water.*

back

the back of beyond a place that is a long way from any other towns, houses, etc. ○ *He was born in a little village in the back of beyond.*

be on someone's back to annoy someone by criticizing them and putting a lot of pressure on them ○ *The crowd isn't forgiving, and as soon as you make a mistake they are on your back.*

break the back of something
1 to deal with the most difficult parts or the main part of a task ○ *The new administration hopes to have broken the back of the economic crisis by the middle of this year.*
2 to do something in order to make something weaker so that it is destroyed after a time ○ *The government made a big effort late last year to break the back of the black market.*

break your back to work extremely hard to try to do something ○ *When you're breaking your back to make an enterprise work, it's going to cut into your time with family.*

cover your back to do something to protect yourself, for example, against criticism or against accusations of doing something wrong ○ *"Perhaps the greatest singer of his generation." A well-placed "perhaps" always covers your back.*

do something behind someone's back to do something secretly in order to harm someone ○ *He had discovered that it was safer to have the press on his side than to have correspondents sneaking around behind his back.*

get off someone's back to stop criticizing someone and leave them alone ○ *He kept bugging me to such an extent that occasionally I wished he would get off my back.*

★ **have your back to the wall** to have very serious problems or be in a very difficult situation that will be hard to deal with ○ *The European Union has its back to the wall: it must choose between a reform of its working methods or its dilution into a large free trade area.*

off the back of a truck if something has fallen off the back of a truck, or you got something off the back of a truck, you have bought something that was stolen ○ *The only evidence of any criminal tendencies is that Pete once bought the boys a bicycle cheap off the back of a truck.*

on the back of an envelope quickly and without very much thought or planning ○ *But the screenplay sounds as if it has been written on the back of an envelope and the whole thing has an improvised air about it.*

on the back of a postage stamp if eveything that someone knows about something could be put on the back of a postage stamp, they know very little about it ○ *What she knew about children would have fit on the back of a postage stamp.*

put your back into something to start to work very hard in order to do something successfully ○ *Eighty miles across the mountains could be done in six days walking, if she put her back into it.*

★ **say something behind someone's back** to say unkind and unpleasant things about someone to other people ○ *I knew behind his back his friends were saying, "How can he possibly put up with that awful woman?"*

★ **stab someone in the back** to do something that hurts and betrays someone ○ *She seemed to be incredibly disloyal. She would be your friend to your face, and then stab you in the back.* ○ *People begin to avoid one another, take sides, be drawn into gossip and back-stabbing.*

★ **turn your back on someone** to ignore someone and refuse to help them ○ *We appeal to this conference – do not turn your back on the poor. Do not turn your back on the unemployed.*

★ **turn your back on something** to stop thinking about something and paying attention to it, or to reject it ○ *Twilight heartthrob Robert Pattinson has turned his back on fans of the series.*

when your back is turned when you are away or involved with something else ○ *They are quite happy to question you, though, and are not averse to having a look through your personal items when your back is turned.*

you scratch my back and I'll scratch yours used to describe a situation in which one person helps another on the condition that the second person helps them in return ○ *The man knew his business and, willing to play the game of "you scratch my back and I'll scratch yours," charged Eve for only the ingredients he used.*

backs

live off the backs of someone to use the money and resources of another group of people to survive, and give nothing in return ○ *For too long the fat and decadent rich have lived off the backs of the working poor.*

backwards

★ **bend over backwards** to try very hard to do something and to help or please someone, even if it causes you trouble ○ *We are bending over backwards to ensure that the safeguards are kept in place.*

know something backwards and forwards to know something very well ○ *I thoroughly enjoy lecturing and I know my subject backwards and forwards.*

backyard

not in my backyard used to show that someone strongly opposes something being built or developed near where they live ○ *The community is objecting to the development. It's a case of "not in my backyard".*

bacon

bring home the bacon to make enough money to support your family ○ *As a hard-working mom, Danielle has to figure out a way to bring home the bacon.*

bag

★ **in the bag** certain to be obtained or achieved ○ *After being 23-16 up at the break, it seemed victory was in the bag for Ponty.*

> The bag referred to here is a hunting bag, in which hunters carry home the animals and birds they have shot.

leave someone holding the bag to make someone responsible for a problem that nobody else wants to deal with. The usual British expression is **leave someone holding the baby**. ○ *If a project goes bust, investors are left holding the bag.*

★ **a mixed bag** something that contains things that are of very different kinds or qualities ○ *Today's papers carry a mixed bag of stories on their front pages.*

> The bag referred to here is a hunting bag containing the different kinds of animals and birds that the hunter has shot.

someone's bag of tricks a set of special techniques or methods that someone uses in their work ○ *The album is a delightful offering with Griffin going through his bag of tricks to great effect.*

> This expression refers to the bag in which magicians carry the equipment they need for their performances.

something is not someone's bag (*informal*) used to mean that someone is not very interested in something or not very good at it ○ *"Being an umpire is not my bag," Mr. Anders says. "I'd rather be a player."*

> This expression may have originated in the slang spoken by American jazz musicians. They sometimes referred to the type of jazz they played, or to their own distinctive style of jazz, as their bag.

bags

★ **pack your bags** to suddenly leave where you live or work, usually because of a disagreement ○ *If things go wrong and our conditions are not met, we will simply pack our bags and leave.*

bail

jump bail or
skip bail if an accused person jumps bail or skips bail, they fail to appear for a hearing or trial in a court ○ *A background check revealed that Cohen had skipped bail in Tarrytown over six years ago.*

> Bail is money paid to an official in exchange for freedom until a court appearance.

bait

bait and switch a trick in which a business attracts customers with what appears to be a good offer but then gives them goods of a lower quality ○ *The government used the bait and switch technique of telling voters they're voting for a tax that will pay for one thing and then using the money for something else.*

fish or cut bait used to express that someone should do something or get out of the way so others can act ○ *Justice John Paul Stevens has acknowledged it's time to "fish or cut bait" and says he will decide soon whether he will retire.*

> The literal meaning behind this expression is that it is time for someone to make a definite decision either to start fishing, or else to prepare the bait so that other people can fish.

take the bait or
rise to the bait to react to something that someone has said or done in exactly the way that they wanted you to react, usually by getting angry ○ *It's important not to rise to the bait and get mad.*

> In fly-fishing, the fish rise to the surface of the water to take the bait, and so they get caught.

baker

a baker's dozen (old-fashioned) thirteen ○ *Alan Else, series coordinator, has picked out a baker's dozen of top events between April and September.*

≡ Bakers in medieval England had a bad reputation for cheating their customers by selling underweight loaves. After regulations were introduced to fix the standard weight of loaves, bakers began to add a thirteenth loaf to each dozen to make sure they were not breaking the law.

balance

★ **in the balance** if a situation is in the balance, it is not clear what is going to happen ○ *One of the judges had died unexpectedly and the choice of his successor was in the balance.*

≡ A balance is a set of scales that consists of two dishes suspended from a horizontal bar.

★ **throw someone off balance** to suddenly confuse or surprise someone ○ *She was trying to behave as if his visit hadn't thrown her off balance.*

ball

a ball and chain someone or something that limits your freedom to do what you want ○ *Our national debt is an economic ball and chain dragging us down, keeping longer term interest rates high.*

≡ In the past, prisoners were sometimes chained by the leg to a heavy metal ball to prevent them from escaping.

★ **the ball is in someone's court** used to suggest that it is someone's responsibility to decide what to do next in a particular situation ○ *The ball is now in his court. I, and indeed others, have told him quite clearly what we think. He has to decide.*

≡ This expression refers to the game of tennis.

behind the eight ball in trouble or in a difficult situation ○ *If a child doesn't get the basics in primary school they are way behind the eight ball.*

≡ In the game of pool, the "eight ball" is a ball with a number 8 on it, which players have to "sink" (hit into a pocket) last. If the eight ball is between the cue ball and the ball which the player is trying to hit, the player is likely to hit the eight ball first, which is a foul shot.

be on the ball to be quick to notice what is happening and quick to respond to things ○ *You can't bumble along in this business. You have to be on the ball.*

≡ This expression originated with baseball and was said of pitchers who had complete control of the ball.

★ **a crystal ball** a way of saying what will happen in the future ○ *What you need to help you select your new car is a crystal ball to tell you how much it will be worth a few years down the road.*

≡ A crystal ball is a glass ball used by some traditional fortunetellers to predict the future. They say that they can see visions of future events within the ball.

drop the ball to do something stupid or something that shows you have no skill ○ *There are people who'd like to see me fail, I know that. But I'm not afraid. I won't drop the ball.*

★ **have a ball** to enjoy yourself very much ○ *Why not go out and see if there's some place we can dance? Let's go and have a ball.*

≡ In this expression, a "ball" is a formal dance.

★ **play ball** to do what someone has asked you to do, or to work with them in order to achieve something that you both want ○ *The underwriters have threatened to withdraw their support if the banks refuse to play ball.*

★ **set the ball rolling** or
start the ball rolling to start an activity or do something that other people will join in with later ○ *The big supermarket rivals are all cutting prices. Safeway set the ball rolling last week with 30 per cent discounts on a wide range of brands.*

take the ball and run with it to take an idea or plan that someone else has started and develop it in order to see if it will be successful or useful ○ *It's up to him. If he studies, fine. If not, there's nothing we can do. He's the one who has to take the ball and run with it.*

> This expression originated in football, in which a quarterback or receiver can run toward the goal with the ball.

a whole new ball game or
a different ball game a situation that has changed so much that people will have to change the way they deal with it or consider it ○ *If military force were to be used, then that could be a completely different ball game.*

> "Ball game" is often used to refer to a game of baseball.

the whole ball of wax the whole of something. ○ *Perry wanted it all, the whole ball of wax. He wanted the Society for himself.*

ballistic

go ballistic to get extremely angry and start shouting or behaving in an uncontrolled way ○ *The singer went ballistic after one member of his band failed to show for a sound check on the recent tour.*

> This expression uses the image of a ballistic missile, and the powerful explosion that it causes.

balloon

★ **a trial balloon** → see **trial**

ballpark

> A ballpark is a park or stadium where baseball is played.

a ballpark figure or
a ballpark estimate an approximate figure or quantity ○ *But what are we talking about here – a few thousand, millions, two bucks? Give me a ballpark figure.*

be in the same ballpark as someone or something to be as good or important as another person or thing ○ *As a general investigative agency, they're not in the same ballpark as the FBI.*

in the ballpark or
in the right ballpark approximately right ○ *A piece of subtle surgical equipment costs about $5 – an underestimate, maybe, but in the right ballpark.*

balls

keep balls in the air to deal with many different things at the same time ○ *They had trouble keeping all their balls in the air. They were trying to do too much and things were starting to break down.*

> This expression uses the image of juggling, where someone has to keep throwing and catching a number of balls at the same time.

bananas

go bananas over something
1 to become extremely enthusiastic about something ○ *Investors may soon go bananas over this company.*
2 to become completely unreasonable about something ○ *Why is the world going bananas over a harmless movie?*

band

★ **a one-man band** someone who does every part of an activity themselves, without help from anyone else ○ *The chef was a one-man band, taking orders, and cooking and serving at table.*

A one-man band is a street entertainer who plays several different instruments at the same time.

bandwagon

★ **jump on the bandwagon** to get involved in an activity or idea because it is likely to succeed or it is fashionable at the time ○ *There will always be inexperienced people ready to jump on the bandwagon and start teaching classes in whatever is fashionable.*

In elections in the past, political rallies were often publicized by a band playing on a horse-drawn wagon which was driven through the streets. Politicians sat on the wagon and those who wished to show their support climbed on board.

bang

more bang for your buck a bigger quantity or better quality of something for the same amount of money ○ *With this program you get more bang for your buck.*

not with a bang but a whimper if something happens not with a bang but a whimper, it is less effective or exciting than people expected or intended ○ *The festival finished yesterday not with a bang but a whimper, as thousands of disappointed festival-goers left early.*

This is the last line of T. S. Eliot's poem "The Hollow Men" (1925): "This is the way the world ends Not with a bang but a whimper."

bank

★ **break the bank** to cost too much money ○ *Porto Cervo is expensive, but there are restaurants and bars that won't break the bank.*

If one gambler wins all the money that a casino has set aside to pay all the winning bets, they are said to have broken the bank.

laugh all the way to the bank to make a lot of money very easily or very quickly ○ *Investors who followed our New Year stock tips are laughing all the way to the bank.*

This expression was used by the 20th-century entertainer Liberace to describe how he felt when he read bad reviews of his shows.

baptism

★ **baptism by fire** a first experience of a new situation that is very difficult or unpleasant ○ *He certainly has had a baptism by fire as a young union leader.*

This expression originally referred to the deaths of martyrs by burning. It was later used by the French Emperors Napoleon Bonaparte and Napoleon III to refer to someone's first experience of battle.

bark

someone's bark is worse than their bite used when you think that someone seems to be much more severe or unfriendly than they really are ○ *My bark is definitely worse than my bite. When people get to know me, they'll tell you I'm just a big softie.*

barn

closing the barn door after the horse has gone → see **door**

barrel

have someone over a barrel to have someone in a position in which they are forced to do what you want ○ *Local small business owners are saying newly required auditing practices have them over a barrel.*

This expression may refer to a method used in the past to save someone who had almost drowned. The person was placed face down over a barrel, which was then rocked gently backwards and forwards until all the water had drained from their lungs.

scrape the bottom of the barrel or **scrape the barrel** to use something or do something that is not very good, because you cannot think of anything better to use or do ○ *The game designers were scraping the bottom of the barrel for ideas when they came up with this one.*

barrelhead

on the barrelhead or **on the barrel** if you pay cash on the barrelhead or on the barrel for something, you pay for it immediately and in cash. ○ *Customers usually pay cash on the barrelhead, so bad debts aren't much of a problem.*

The most likely explanation for this expression comes from the days when settlers first started living in the American West. Saloons often consisted of just a room with a barrel of drink in it, and customers who wanted to drink had to put their money on the top of the barrel before being served, as credit was not given.

barrels

give someone both barrels or **let someone have it with both barrels** to attack or criticize someone fiercely and aggressively ○ *Let him have it with both barrels and then get out of the situation while you can.*

This expression refers to the firing of both barrels of a double-barreled gun.

base

In baseball, players have to hit the ball and then run around three bases in a diamond shape before returning to home plate to score a run.

get to first base to begin to make progress with your plans ○ *We couldn't get to first base with any U.S. banks. They didn't want to take the risk.*

★ **off base** mistaken or wrong ○ *I don't think the church is off base at all in taking a moral stand on this.*

In baseball, if a player is off base, he is in danger of being put out.

touch base to speak or write to someone, often when you have not spoken to them or seen before ○ *Being there gave me a chance to touch base with the staff members as their new team leader.*

In baseball, batters have to touch the first, second, and third bases to score a run.

bases

cover all the bases or **touch all the bases** to deal with or take care of all the different things that you should ○ *He has managed to cover all the bases, and trade goes on.*

In baseball, batters have to touch the first, second, and third bases to score a run.

basket

★ **a basket case**

1 (informal) a crazy or mentally ill person ○ *You're going to think I'm a basket case when I tell you this, but we used to play with toys when we were about twenty.*

2 a country or organization whose economy or finances are in a very bad state ○ *The popular image about Latin America a few years ago was that it was a basket case.*

This expression was originally used to describe someone, especially a soldier, who had lost all four limbs. It may have come about because some of these people had to be carried around in baskets.

bat

go to bat for someone to give someone a lot of your support or help

○ She was just fabulous in going to bat for me, in not being judgmental and helping me work it out.

This expression refers to a baseball player who joins in the game and takes the place of another batter.

like a bat out of hell very quickly ○ He said "Thank you, sir," and departed like a bat out of hell.

In this expression, "bat" refers to a small, flying mammal. Bats are often associated with the devil, probably because they usually fly at night.

right off the bat immediately or at the very beginning of a process or event ○ He learned right off the bat that you can't count on anything in this business.

The image here is of a ball bouncing quickly off a baseball bat.

bath

take a bath to lose a lot of money on an investment ○ Investors in the company took a 35 million dollar bath on the company, which entered bankruptcy proceedings 18 months ago.

baton

pass the baton to give responsibility for something to someone else ○ Does this mean that the baton of leadership is going to be passed to other nations?

pick up the baton to take over responsibility for something ○ Somebody has to pick up the baton from the beleaguered consumer in this dreadful economy.

In a relay race, team members pass on a baton as they finish running their stage of the race.

bats

have bats in the belfry (informal) to be crazy ○ What nonsense! Don't say that to anyone else or they'll think you've got bats in the belfry.

The belfry is the top part of a church tower where the bells are kept, and bats resting there would fly about wildly when disturbed by the bells being rung. In this expression, the belfry represents the person's head.

batteries

★ **recharge your batteries** to stop working or doing an activity for a period and relax so that you feel better when you start working or doing the activity again ○ After playing in the divisional championship, I took a long break from the game to recharge my batteries.

When people recharge batteries, they put an electrical charge back into the batteries by connecting them to a machine that draws power from another source of electricity.

battle

★ **the battle lines are drawn** used when opposing groups or people are ready to start fighting or arguing, and it has become clear what the main points of disagreement are ○ The battle lines were drawn yesterday for the fiercest contest in the history of local radio.

a battle of nerves → see **nerves**

a battle of wills an argument or conflict in which the people involved are refusing to accept each other's demands ○ It was a battle of wills, and Grace's was the stronger.

a battle of wits a competition or disagreement in which each person involved uses their intelligence and mental ability to beat their opponents ○ With chess you're involved in a battle of wits from start to finish.

★ **fight a losing battle** to try to achieve something when you are very unlikely to succeed ○ Miss Bennett fought a losing battle against her depression.

★ **a running battle** an argument or fight with someone that continues over a long period of time ○ *For the past year, customers have inspired a running battle between the two cellular phone companies.* **someone has won the battle, but lost the war** used when someone has gained one small thing but lost something that is much more important in a long struggle ○ *The strikers may have won the battle, but they lost the war.*

bay

★ **keep something at bay** or **hold something at bay** to stop something from attacking you or affecting you badly ○ *By salting the meat, bacteria were kept at bay, preserving the meat for future use.*

When a hunted animal is at bay, it is trapped by the hounds and forced to turn and face them to defend itself. However, if the animal is successfully defending itself in this position, you can say that it is holding the hounds at bay. This second use seems the most likely origin of the expression.

bead

draw a bead on something to aim your weapon at someone or something ○ *There was only one spot where the light through the trees would have enabled him to draw a bead on his target.*

The bead is the small marker on top of the end of the barrel on some guns, which is used to aim at the target.

be-all

★ **not the be-all and end-all** not the only thing that is important in a particular situation ○ *Grades are not the be-all and end-all of education.*

bean

There are several slang meanings for bean. In the following expression, it means money.

a bean counter someone whose job or whose only interest is how much money a business makes ○ *The reason for America's failure is that we have bean counters running our companies.*

beans

full of beans happy, excited, and full of energy ○ *Jem was among them, pink-cheeked and full of beans after a far longer sleep than anybody else had gotten.*

This originally referred to a horse that was well-fed and therefore full of energy.

★ **spill the beans** to reveal the truth about something secret or private ○ *He always seemed scared to death I was going to spill the beans to the cops.*

This expression has a number of possible explanations. One is derived from an ancient practice of voting by placing colored beans in one of a number of jars or pots, then pouring the beans out and counting them. Another is an informal description of vomiting.

bear

loaded for bear ready and eager to do something, especially something that involves or will cause trouble ○ *We could notify the mainland police, and they could go charging in there with guns and bullhorns, loaded for bear.*

Someone who is loaded for bear has ammunition that is powerful enough to kill a bear, even though they may be hunting smaller animals.

beat

★ **beat your breast** or **beat your chest** to show regret or anger very publicly about something that has gone wrong in a way that is usually not sincere ○ *He is very thoughtful with the* players. He doesn't go around beating his chest all the time. He knows when a quiet chat is what's needed. ○ *His pious breast-beating on behalf of the workingman was transparently bogus, but it was a clever public relations job.*

not miss a beat to always know what is happening and so be able to take advantage of every situation ○ *This time we played like machines. The longer the game went the stronger we got, and we never missed a beat.*

≡ The "beat" referred to here is probably a heartbeat, although it may refer to a beat in music.

without missing a beat without pausing or hesitating ○ *She was asked point-blank whether she should bow out. But, without missing a beat, she replied: "I do not believe it is appropriate for me to withdraw my nomination."*

beaver

an eager beaver someone who is very enthusiastic about work or very anxious to please other people ○ *George was an eager beaver without the ability to live up to his promises.*

≡ Beavers are often associated with hard work, as they spend a lot of time building shelters and dams out of mud and wood.

beck

at someone's beck and call always ready to do what someone tells you to do, even when their orders are unreasonable ○ *Your child must understand that you can't always be at his beck and call for every little thing.*

≡ "Beck" is an old word meaning a gesture, such as a nod or a movement of the hand or forefinger, which represents a command such as "Come here."

bed

get into bed with someone to make an agreement to work with another person or group. This expression is usually used showing disapproval. ○ *The bigger and more complex government is, the more incentive corporations have to politicize themselves and get in bed with Washington.*

not a bed of roses not all pleasant, having some difficult or unpleasant aspects ○ *Life as a graduate is not a bed of roses.*

≡ The bed referred to here is a flower bed.

put something to bed to achieve a plan or task or complete it successfully ○ *Before putting the agreement to bed, we still had to satisfy Fran Murray.*

≡ On an old-style printing press, the bed is the flat part that holds the type. If journalists talk about putting a newspaper or magazine to bed, they are talking about making the final changes before printing.

someone has made their bed and will have to lie on it used to suggest that someone has to accept the unpleasant results of an earlier decision that they made ○ *For Sara, marriage was for life – in her eyes she had made her bed and would have to lie in it.*

someone woke up on the wrong side of the bed or
someone got out of bed on the wrong side used when someone is in a very bad mood without there seeming to be any obvious reason for it ○ *Guys like him sometimes wake up on the wrong side of the bed and say things they don't really mean.*

≡ This relates to the old superstition that it was unlucky to put your left foot on the ground first when getting out of bed. "Get off on the wrong foot" is based on a similar belief.

bee

the bee's knees something or someone that you like very much ○ *Back in the '80s it was the bee's knees but now it looks really out of date.*

Some people believe that this expression refers to the way in which bees transfer pollen from their bodies to pollen sacs on their back legs. However, it seems more likely that it dates from the 1920s, when other similar expressions such as "the cat's pajamas" began to be used.

have a bee in your bonnet to feel very strongly about something and keep talking or thinking about it. ○ *I've got a bee in my bonnet about the confusion between education and training.*

Two images are suggested by this expression. The first is of thoughts buzzing inside someone's head like bees. The second is of someone who has a bee trapped in their hat and is anxious to get it out before they are stung.

beeline

make a beeline for something to go straight to something without any hesitation or delay ○ *The boys headed for computer games while the girls made a beeline for the dolls.*

It used to be believed that bees, having collected the pollen, flew back to the hive in a straight line. In fact, this belief has been proved to be incorrect. "As the crow flies" is based on a similar idea.

beer

make someone cry into their beer to get a sad emotional reaction from someone who is usually very calm ○ *The result was enough to make fans cry into their beer.*

This expression is often used of men, since they typically don't cry very much and may enjoy drinking beer.

small beer something that is not important when compared with another thing ○ *The present political scandal is small beer compared to Watergate.*

"Small beer" originally meant weak beer.

beggars

beggars can't be choosers said when someone must accept an offer or a particular course of action, because it is the only one that is available ○ *"So would you be happy to work wherever you got a job?" "Yes. You've got to take anything that comes around because beggars can't be choosers."*

begging

be going begging to be available to be used or bought because other people are not interested ○ *Nearly half a million vacation packages for the busiest six weeks of the year are still going begging.*

bell

ring someone's bell (informal) to be very attractive, exciting, or satisfying to someone ○ *After a couple of comedies that didn't exactly ring my bell, I thought I'd like to do something different.*

saved by the bell saved from a difficult situation at the last possible moment because of something that happened ○ *There was another period of silence. It was broken by the sound of Eleanor's car pulling up outside the front door. "Saved by the bell," I said.*

This expression refers to the bell that signals the end of a round in a boxing match.

something rings a bell something that someone mentions is slightly familiar to you and you are aware that you have heard it before, although you do not remember it fully ○ *"Who?" he queried, "Passing Clouds? I simply don't remember them. Their name doesn't ring a bell."*

bells

bells and whistles special features or other things that are not necessary parts of something, but that are added to make it more attractive or interesting ○ *People are still buying luxury cars with all the bells and whistles, but cheaper systems are becoming more popular.*

> In the past, organs were used in cinemas to accompany silent films. Some of these organs had devices attached to them which produced sound effects such as bells and whistles.

★ **set alarm bells ringing** or **set warning bells ringing** to cause people to begin to be aware of a problem in a situation ○ *The islanders' fight for compensation has set alarm bells ringing around the world.*

bellyful

have had a bellyful of something (*informal*) to find something very irritating or boring, and not want to experience it any longer ○ *I have had a bellyful of excuses. It's always someone else's fault.*

belly-up

★ **go belly-up** if a company goes belly-up, it fails and does not have enough money to pay its debts ○ *Factories and farms went belly-up because of the debt crisis.*

> This expression may refer to dead fish floating upside down near the surface of the water.

belt

below the belt unfair or cruel ○ *These kinds of blows below the belt are the surest way to destroy a friendship or love affair.*

> In boxing, it is against the rules to hit an opponent below the level of their belt.

★ **have something under your belt** to have already achieved or done something ○ *After a few years, I had enough recipes under my belt to put them into a book.*

★ **tighten your belt** to spend less and live more carefully because you have less money than you had before ○ *Clearly, if you are spending more than your income, you'll need to tighten your belt.*

bend

★ **around the bend** crazy ○ *If anyone told me a few months ago that I'd meet a marvelous person like you I'd have said they were around the bend.*

drive someone around the bend (*informal*) to annoy someone so much that they feel they are becoming crazy ○ *Can you finish that puzzle before your fidgeting drives me completely around the bend?*

benefit

★ **give someone the benefit of the doubt** to decide to believe that what someone is saying or doing is honest and right, even though it is possible that they are not telling the truth or that they are doing something wrong ○ *I am basically a trusting person. I make it a practice to give everyone the benefit of the doubt.*

berth

give someone or something a wide berth to deliberately avoid someone or something ○ *Having lived all my adult life in Africa I have a very healthy respect for snakes and have always tried to give them a wide berth.*

> A berth is the amount of space that a sailing ship needs to maneuver safely.

best

the best of both worlds → see **worlds**

bet

★ **a good bet** or
a safe bet
1 a sensible or useful thing to do ○ *When you're unfamiliar with your guests' likes and dislikes, chicken is a safe bet for the main course.* ○ *If you really want to keep your home safe from robbery, your best bet is still to buy a burglar alarm.*
2 something that is very likely to happen or someone who is very likely to do something ○ *But they will not enjoy reading this book; it is a safe bet that few will read more than 100 pages.*

bets

★ **all bets are off** used when it is impossible to say how a particular situation may develop ○ *This election year all bets seem to be off. In fact, even the folks who make a living predicting what the voters will do find themselves on shaky ground.*

★ **hedge your bets** to decide on more than one thing, so that you will not make a mistake whichever way the situation develops ○ *Political forecasters are hedging their bets about the likely outcome of this Saturday's Louisiana governor's race.*

When bookmakers accept a large bet, they often try to protect themselves against heavy losses by laying bets with other bookmakers. This practice is called hedging.

better

better safe than sorry → see **safe**

bill

★ **be given a clean bill of health**
1 to be told by a doctor that you are completely healthy and not ill in any way ○ *He had a full medical late last year and was given a clean bill of health.*
2 to be examined or considered and then judged to be in a satisfactory condition ○ *Fourteen seaside resorts failed to meet the environmental and safety standards, while 43*

were given a clean bill of health.

A bill of health was a certificate that was given to a ship's master to present at the next port the ship arrived at. It stated whether or not there was an infectious disease aboard the ship or in the port it was departing from.

fit the bill
★ **fill the bill** to be exactly the right person or thing that is needed in a particular situation ○ *I wanted someone who really knew their way around film-making and I knew that Richard would fit the bill.*

The "bill" in this expression is a public notice advertising something such as a show or a play.

★ **foot the bill** to pay for something ○ *Police will have to foot the bill for the slight damage to both cars.*

This expression may come from the practice of someone paying a bill and signing it at the bottom, or "foot."

★ **sell someone a bill of goods** to deceive someone or cheat them out of money or property ○ *McChrystal used the brass on his chest to sell the nation a bill of goods – that the war in Afghanistan could be "won."*

bind

be in a double bind to be in a very difficult situation, because you have problems that cannot be solved easily or without causing more problems ○ *Women are in a double bind: they are expected to act like men, but they are criticized when they do.*

bird

the bird has flown used when someone has escaped or disappeared ○ *He was supposed to follow the woman to work. Instead he'd wandered off, come back a hour later, and found the bird had flown.*
a bird in the hand or
a bird in the hand is worth two in

the bush used to emphasize that it is better to keep something you have than to try to get something better and risk having nothing at all ○ *Another temporary discount may not be what you want, but at least it is a bird in the hand.*

a bird of passage someone who never stays in one place for long ○ *Most of these emigrants were birds of passage who returned to Spain after a relatively short stay.*

an early bird someone who gets up early in the morning or who does something before other people ○ *We've always been early birds, up at 5:30 or 6 am.* ○ *An early-bird discount is sometimes available at the beginning of the season.*

the early bird gets the worm used to suggest that someone who starts immediately has an advantage over others and is likely to succeed ○ *If you're going to make it to the Senate, you need to start right now. The early bird gets the worm.*

eat like a bird to eat very little ○ *She always orders two larger chops and one smaller chop because her daughter eats like a bird and her husband eats a lot.*

a little bird told me an expression that you use to indicate that you will not tell who gave you certain information ○ *Incidentally, a little bird told me that your birthday's coming up.*

a rare bird someone or something that is different from most other people or things ○ *Diane Johnson's book is that rare bird, an American novel of manners.*

≡ "A rare bird" is a translation of the Latin expression *rara avis*, which was used by the Roman writer Juvenal in the 2nd century AD to describe a black swan. At the time, black swans were unknown, although they were later discovered in Australia.

birds

the birds and the bees the facts about sex and sexual reproduction, as told to a child ○ *At the age of 13, I remember having a discussion about the birds and the bees with my father.*

≡ People sometimes explain sex and sexual reproduction to children by telling them how animals reproduce.

birds of a feather two or more people who are very similar in many ways ○ *She and my mother were birds of a feather. You felt something special between them that left you out.*

birds of a feather flock together used when you notice that people from the same group or with the same interests like to be with each other ○ *Birds of a feather flock together. Basically, people seek out neighborhoods that are most congenial to them.*

for the birds stupid, boring, or worthless ○ *This journal business is for the birds. It's a waste of time.*

≡ This expression refers to horse manure, which is of use only to small birds in search of nest material or food such as seeds.

kill two birds with one stone to manage to achieve two things at the same time ○ *The new diabetic weight-loss drug is designed to kill two birds with one stone.*

birthday

in your birthday suit not wearing any clothes; naked ○ *In the upcoming film she may be shown in nothing but her birthday suit.*

≡ This humorous expression refers to the fact that when you are born, on your birthday, you are not wearing any clothes.

bit

A bit is a piece of metal that is held in a horse's mouth by the bridle and reins.

chomp at the bit or
champ at the bit to want to do something very much, but be prevented from doing it, usually by a situation that you have no control over ○ *Foremen had been chomping at the bit to strike before next week's meeting.*

get the bit between your teeth to become very enthusiastic and determined about doing a particular job or task ○ *You're persistent when you get the bit between your teeth, I'll give you that.*

The bit should be positioned at the back of a horse's mouth, behind its back teeth. When a horse bolts, it sometimes takes the bit between its teeth, which makes it very difficult for a rider or driver to use the reins to control it.

bite

bite off more than you can chew to try to do too much ○ *Don't bite off more than you can chew simply because everything is going so well.*

take a bite out of something to take away a part of a sum of money or other quantity ○ *The government is going to be taking a bigger bite out of people's income than ever before.*

bitten

once bitten, twice shy used when a recent and unpleasant experience has made someone not want to get involved in similar situations in the future ○ *I'm certainly not looking for new boyfriends or thinking of having any more kids. Once bitten, twice shy.*

black

★ **black and blue** badly bruised ○ *I spent that night in the hospital and was released the next day with minor head and neck injuries. My face was black and blue.*

★ **black and white** a way of considering things that is too simple, judging things either as right or wrong ○ *That is not an accurate portrait of industrial relations in France. People do not see these things purely in black and white.* ○ *It's just not a black and white issue.*

★ **in black and white** written down ○ *We have a strict, clear rule in black and white, that sexual harassment will lead to expulsion.*

★ **in the black** not owing anyone money ○ *Last year, the company was back in the black, showing a modest pre-tax surplus of $4.6 million.*

This expression comes from the practice in the past of using black ink to fill in entries on the credit side of a book of accounts.

blank

Originally, to draw a blank meant to be given a losing ticket in a lottery.

★ **draw a blank**
1 to not be able to find someone or something or find out about something ○ *I searched among the bottles and under and behind and inside everything I could think of and drew a blank.*
2 to be unable to remember something or to answer a question you are asked. ○ *Why do we recognize a face, but sometimes draw a blank when it comes to the name?*

blanket

a wet blanket
1 someone who spoils other people's fun because they are boring or miserable ○ *"Hey," said Thack, looking at Michael. "Stop being such a wet blanket."*
2 something that makes an event or situation less successful or enjoyable than it would otherwise have been ○ *The weather threw a wet blanket over the championship final yesterday.*

blast

a blast from the past something from the past that you see, hear, or experience

○ It was really a blast from the past to suddenly see her in that video clip.

(at) full blast as loud, hard, or energetically as possible ○ He uses Tchaikovsky's music at full blast for some of the battle scenes.

blaze

★ **a blaze of glory** a lot of attention and interest, especially from newspapers and television ○ The new Bay Theater is ready to open with a blaze of glory tonight.

go out in a blaze of glory or **go down in a blaze of glory** to make one last, often defiant attempt to do or accomplish something, even though it is likely to fail ○ They know they'll never get away with it, so they may as well go out in a blaze of glory.

blessing

★ **a blessing in disguise** an event that causes problems and difficulties at first, but later brings advantages ○ Franklin's illness proved a blessing in disguise, for it gave him strength and courage which he had not had before.

blind

blind as a bat unable to see well ○ Without my glasses I was blind as a bat.

≣ Most bats are active only at night and find their way by sending out sounds and sensing objects from the echoes, rather than by using their eyesight.

the blind leading the blind used to describe a situation in which the person in charge is just as incapable of doing a task as the person who they are meant to be helping or guiding ○ I'm afraid it's the blind leading the blind as I've never actually used this software before myself.

≣ This expression comes from one of the stories that Jesus tells in the Bible (Matthew 15:14). He says that if a blind person tries to guide another

blind person, they are not likely to be successful in getting what they want.

fly blind to be in a situation where you have nothing to help or guide you ○ The business owner who thinks he or she is suddenly a marketing expert is essentially electing to fly blind.

≣ A pilot is flying blind when they are piloting an aircraft without using visual navigation, but relying solely on their instruments.

blink

on the blink not working properly ○ We had to go to the Laundromat because our washing machine was on the blink.

block

★ **on the block** offered for sale at auction. The British expression is **under the hammer**. ○ Last week, after months of rumors, the company officially put itself on the block.

put your head on the block or **put your neck on the block** to risk your reputation or job by taking a particular course of action ○ He really put his head on the block there and it's great to see his bravery being rewarded.

≣ The "block" here is a special piece of wood on which a prisoner was made to place his or her head before being beheaded.

★ **a stumbling block** a problem that stops you from achieving something ○ Your inability to choose between material security and emotional needs is a major stumbling block to your happiness.

≣ This expression comes from the Bible (Romans 14:13), where people are advised not to do anything that might stop other people from being successful.

blocks

These expressions come from track and field, where sprinters put their feet against pieces of equipment called starting blocks to help them start quickly when the race begins.

off the blocks or
off the starting blocks
1 used for describing how quickly someone starts to do something ○ *the higher price of the Porsche is justified as the Porsche is faster off the blocks.*
2 succeeding in starting to do something, often despite difficulties ○ *People thought I was totally crazy, but if you think like that, then you just can't get off the starting blocks.*

blood

★ **bad blood** feelings of anger or hatred between two people or groups because of arguments they have had in the past ○ *The situation has reached a crisis because of the bad blood between the two.*

People used to think that feelings such as anger and resentment were carried in the blood.

be after someone's blood to want to harm or punish someone, because they have harmed you or made you angry ○ *Adam has upset Broderick, who is after his blood.*

blood and thunder full of exaggerated feelings or behavior ○ *In a blood and thunder speech, he called for sacrifice from everyone.*

★ **blood is shed** or
blood is spilled
1 (*journalism, literary*) used to say that people are being killed in fighting ○ *All the signs are that if blood is spilled the countries will be at war.*
2 used to say that trouble or suffering is caused as a result of a change taking place ○ *Given the political blood that was*

spilled over the deficit reduction package, few observers believe the president will start spending more.

blood is thicker than water used to emphasize or express that people are more loyal to their family than to people who are not related to them ○ *Families have their problems and jealousies, but blood is thicker than water.*

blood on the carpet serious trouble as a result of a struggle between people or groups inside a company or other organization ○ *The issue is highly emotional and will cause a lot of blood on the carpet.*

★ **blood, sweat, and tears** great effort or suffering that is involved in a task or project ○ *It's almost as if the end product – the songs themselves – are less important than the blood, sweat, and tears that went into them.*

This expression is originally derived from a wartime speech by the British Prime Minister Winston Churchill, in which he said, "I have nothing to offer but blood, toil, tears and sweat." He used the expression several times in other wartime speeches.

have blood on your hands to be responsible for a death, or for the deaths of several people ○ *I want him to know he has my son's blood on his hands.*

★ **in cold blood** in a calm and deliberate way, rather than in anger or self-defense. People often use this expression to express shock or horror at a killing. ○ *They murdered my brother. They shot him down in cold blood.* ○ *This is just another attempt to excuse the cold-blooded murder of an innocent woman.*

In medieval times, some people believed that certain emotions changed the temperature of the blood.

★ **in your blood** used for describing something that is a very important part of you and seems natural to you, for example, because it is traditional in your family or culture ○ *Trilok has music in his blood. "I was born into a family of musicians."*

it is first blood to someone or **someone draws first blood** (journalism) someone has had a success at the beginning of a competition or conflict ○ *Nigeria's Super Eagles drew first blood with a goal in the 12th minute by Kalu Uche.*

like getting blood out of a stone or **like getting blood out of a turnip** extremely difficult. This expression is used when you are trying to persuade someone to give you money or information. ○ *The goods have to be returned to their rightful owner and getting money back from the seller is like getting blood out of a stone.*

★ **make your blood boil** to make you very angry ○ *This statement is untrue and makes my blood boil.*

In medieval times, some people believed that certain emotions changed the temperature of the blood.

make your blood run cold (literary) to frighten or shock you very much ○ *It makes my blood run cold to think what this poor, helpless child must have gone through.*

In medieval times, some people believed that certain emotions changed the temperature of the blood.

★ **new blood** new people who are brought into a company or organization in order to improve it ○ *Most members of Congress do not deserve to be re-elected because they have been there too long and there is a need for new blood.*

out for blood intending to attack someone, or to make them suffer in some other way ○ *They seem to be out for blood, and they're attacking everywhere where their enemy is*

scent blood to sense a weakness in your opponent and take advantage of it ○ *Currency speculators scenting blood in the Eurozone set off a frenzy of trading today.*

sweat blood to work very hard to achieve something ○ *I sweat blood to write songs with tunes that you can remember.*

taste blood to have a small victory that encourages you to think that you can defeat your opponent completely ○ *Back on his feet and having tasted blood, Zu had one thing on his mind.*

young blood young people who are brought into a company or organization in order to provide new ideas or new talent ○ *The selectors have at last shown some bravery and forward thinking and gone for some young blood, picking a team whose average age is just 26.*

bloodied

bloodied but unbowed (literary) not defeated or destroyed after a bad experience ○ *He went out there and worked for every single vote. It was a narrow victory but an important one. He is bloodied but unbowed.*

Unbowed means standing upright without showing fear or pain. This expression is probably inspired by a line from the poem "Invictus," by William Ernest Henley.

blot

a blot on the landscape a building or some other structure that is ugly and spoils a place which would otherwise be very attractive ○ *The power station is both a blot on the landscape and a smear on the environment.*

blow

★ **soften the blow** or **cushion the blow** to make an unpleasant change or piece of news seem less unpleasant and easier to accept ○ *Although attempts were made to soften the blow, by reducing what some* people had to pay, the tax still met with widespread opposition.

★ **strike a blow for something** to do something that supports a cause or principle, or makes it more likely to succeed ○ *Her appointment would strike a blow for women's rights in Poland.*

blows

★ **come to blows** to disagree so strongly about something that you start to fight ○ *Some residents nearly came to blows over this proposal.*

blue

★ **out of the blue** unexpectedly ○ *Then suddenly, out of the blue, he received a letter from his brother.*

This expression compares an unexpected event to a bolt of lightning from a blue sky. The expressions "out of a clear blue sky" and "a bolt from the blue" are based on a similar idea.

bluff

★ **call someone's bluff** to put someone in a position in which they are forced to do what they have been threatening to do because you do not believe that they will really do it ○ *Mr. Lukanov warned that he would deal severely with any protest actions in the universities. Now, the students have called his bluff.*

In poker, a player who is bluffing is playing as if they have a strong hand when in fact they have a weak one. If another player calls the first player's bluff, they increase their stake to the required amount and ask the first player to show their cards.

board

★ **above board** honest and legal ○ *Anyone who wants to inspect our books can see for themselves that we are totally above board.*

This expression comes from card games in which players place their

bets on a board or table. Anything that takes place under the table is likely to be against the rules, whereas actions above the table, where other players can see them, are probably fair.

★ **across the board** if a policy or development applies across the board, it applies equally to all the people or areas of business connected with it ○ *The compromise proposal reduces funding across the board.*

This expression was used originally in horse racing. If someone bet across the board, they bet on a horse to win or to come second, third, or fourth.

★ **go back to the drawing board** to start again or try another idea because something you have done has not been successful ○ *It's back to the drawing board for an ordinance being developed for regulating wind turbines and solar panels in the city of Astoria.*

Drawing boards are large flat boards, on which designers or architects place their paper when drawing plans or designs.

★ **take something on board**
1 to understand or accept an idea, suggestion, or fact ○ *I listened to them, took their comments on board and then made the decision.*
2 to accept responsibility for a task or problem and start dealing with it ○ *All you have to do is call us. Our coordinator will take your problem on board and solve it.*

The literal meaning of this expression is to take something onto a boat or ship.

boards

go by the boards to be abandoned and forgotten ○ *You may find that all your efforts go by the boards when he is away in college.*

To "go by the boards" originally meant to fall or be thrown over the side of a ship.

boat

float someone's boat (*informal*) to seem exciting, attractive, or interesting to someone ○ *I can see its appeal. But it doesn't float my boat.*

★ **in the same boat** in the same unpleasant or difficult situation ○ *If baldness is creeping up on you, take heart – 40 percent of men under 35 are in the same boat.*

★ **miss the boat** to fail to act in time to take advantage of an opportunity ○ *Critics would say that both Congress and the White House have seriously missed the boat on this set of issues over the last few years.*

★ **rock the boat** to do something that might cause trouble in a situation ○ *Diplomats are expecting so much instability in a power struggle after his death that they argue it's unwise to rock the boat now.*

Bob

Bob's your uncle said at the end of a process or series of events to show that they have ended exactly as expected or in exactly the right way ○ *If the boiler ever gets too hot, the safety valve releases all the excess steam, and Bob's your uncle. No problem.*

This expression dates back to a political scandal in Britain in 1886. The Prime Minister Robert Cecil gave his nephew the position of Chief Secretary for Ireland, and many people criticized him for this. The name "Bob" is short for "Robert."

body

★ **body and soul** with all your energy or skill; completely and without holding back ○ *The whole cast fling themselves into the production, body and soul.*

★ **a body blow** something that causes you great disappointment or difficulty ○ *The failed measure comes as a body blow to President Obama's plan.*

In boxing, a body blow is a punch between the breast-bone and the navel.

keep body and soul together to earn enough money to buy the basic things that you need to live ○ *20-year-old Rafael says he's selling firewood to keep body and soul together.*

over my dead body under no circumstances. You say this to show that you dislike a plan or action that has been suggested, and will do everything you can to prevent it. ○ *They will get Penbrook Farm only over my dead body.*

boil

come to a boil if anger comes to a boil, it increases until it reaches a very high level ○ *Their anger came to a boil last week when they protested at a media campaign against them.*

bold

bold as brass not ashamed or embarrassed, although your behavior is shocking or annoying to other people ○ *Their leader, bold as brass, came improperly dressed, while all the others were wearing black ties.*

This expression may be based on an incident that occurred in Britain in 1770, when the London Evening Post illegally published a report of Parliamentary proceedings. As a result, the printer was put in prison. The Lord Mayor, Brass Crosby, released him and was punished by being imprisoned himself. There were public protests and Crosby was soon released.

bolt

★ **a bolt from the blue** or
a bolt out of the blue an event or

piece of news that surprises you because it was completely unexpected ○ *Mrs. Thomas says the arrest had come "like a bolt out of the blue."*

This expression compares an unexpected event to a bolt of lightning from a blue sky. The expressions "out of a clear blue sky" and "out of the blue" are based on a similar idea.

bomb

be the bomb to be extremely attractive, admired, exciting, etc. ○ *That girl is gorgeous. I mean seriously, she's the bomb.*

bombshell

★ **drop a bombshell** to suddenly tell someone a piece of bad news which they were not expecting ○ *My ex-wife is on the phone and she drops a bombshell. Sue, our beloved daughter, is leaving the country to live in Ecuador.*

bone

★ **a bone of contention** a problem that people have been arguing about for a long time ○ *Pay, of course, is not the only bone of contention.*

close to the bone or
near to the bone if a remark or piece of writing is close to the bone, it makes people uncomfortable, because it deals with subjects that they prefer not to be discussed ○ *This isn't strictly satire, it's far too close to the bone to be funny.*

★ **cut something to the bone** to reduce resources or costs as much as possible ○ *We managed to break even by cutting costs to the bone.*

have a bone to pick with someone to be annoyed with someone about something, and want to talk to them about it ○ *"I have a bone to pick with you."* *She felt justified in bringing up a matter that she had been afraid to discuss before.*

This expression may refer to the fact that dogs often fight over bones.

bones

★ **the bare bones** the most basic parts or details of something ○ *We worked out the bare bones of a deal.*

feel something in your bones to feel very strongly that you are right about something, although you cannot explain why ○ *Joe, I have a hunch you're going to lose tonight. I just feel it in my bones.*

★ **make no bones about something** to not hesitate to express your thoughts or feelings about something, even though other people will not like what you say ○ *There will be changes in the starting lineup until we get it right. I make no bones about that.*

This expression may refer to gambling. "Bones" is an old word for dice, so a gambler who "makes no bones" throws the dice after just one shake, rather than performing an elaborate ritual.

book

★ **bring someone to book** to punish someone officially for something wrong that they have done ○ *No one has yet been brought to book for a crime that outraged Italy.*

Originally, if someone was brought to book, they were ordered to prove that something they had said or done was in keeping with a written rule or agreement.

close the book on something to cause something to end, especially a difficult or unpleasant situation ○ *Lawyers say they are happy to close the book on one of the most frustrating chapters of the company's history.*

a closed book something or someone that you know or understand very little about ○ *Economics was a closed book to him. It constituted a strange, illogical territory where two and two didn't always make four.*

★ **do something by the book** or
go by the book to do something
correctly and strictly, following all the
rules ○ *Modern man is often dull, studious,
careful, safe. He does everything by the book.*

★ **in someone's book** according to
someone's own belief or opinion,
especially when it is different from the
beliefs or opinions of other people
○ *People can say what they like, but in my
book he's not at all a bad guy.*

an open book a person's life or
character that you can find out
everything about, because nothing is
kept secret ○ *Her long life is not a
completely open book, but it is full of
anecdotes and insights into her part in
Hollywood history.*

read someone like a book to know
exactly what someone is thinking and
planning ○ *There are a number of books on
the market that suggest that it is possible to
learn to read a person like a book.*

throw the book at someone to give
someone the greatest punishment that
is possible for the offense that they have
committed ○ *"If this is found to be true,
then we will throw the book at the teams
involved," the chairman of the league said
yesterday.*

≡ This expression refers to a book in
which laws are written down.

you can't judge a book by its cover
used to suggest that someone should
wait until they have more information,
because first opinions may be wrong
○ *You can't judge a book by its cover. Just
because someone looks strange doesn't mean
they're not a nice person.*

books

be in someone's bad books to have
done something that has annoyed
someone ○ *The officers said Samba was in
the bad books of the two powerful officials*

be in someone's good books to have

done something that has pleased
someone ○ *I was never really that
concerned about being in the teacher's good
books.*

cook the books to dishonestly change
the figures in your financial accounts in
order to deceive people ○ *She knew that
when the auditors looked over the accounts
there would be no hiding the fact that she had
cooked the books and $3 million was missing.*

≡ The "books" in this expression are
books of accounts.

boot

★ **get the boot** or
be given the boot (*informal*) to lose
your job ○ *The chief reason he got the boot
was because the governor didn't trust him any
more.*

boots

die with your boots on to die while
you are still actively involved in your work
○ *Unlike some businesspeople who die with
their boots on, he has left the entire running
of Seamark to his son.*

≡ This expression was originally used to
refer to a soldier who died in battle.

lick someone's boots to do everything
you can to please someone, often
because they are powerful or influential
and you want something from them
○ *Even if you didn't have an official position,
you'd still be a big shot locally. everybody
would be licking your boots.*

quake in your boots to be very
frightened or anxious about something
that is about to happen ○ *If you stand up
straight, you'll give an impression of self
confidence even if you're quaking in your
boots.*

bootstraps

Bootstraps are straps attached to a
boot which you use for pulling it on.

pull yourself up by your bootstraps to improve your situation by your own efforts, without help from anyone else ○ *It was his ability to pull himself up by his bootstraps that appealed to his boss.*

bored

bored to death or
bored to tears or
bored stiff extremely bored ○ *There are no jobs, there's nothing to do; these young people are bored to death.*

boss

show someone who's boss to prove to someone that you have more power or control than they do ○ *It was a classic strategy: show new students who's boss at the very beginning and everything will then go smoothly.*

bottle

hit the bottle to start drinking too much alcohol, usually because something very unpleasant or upsetting has happened to you ○ *One newspaper even said I'd started hitting the bottle.*

bottom

at the bottom of the heap or
at the bottom of the pile → see **heap**
→ see **pile**
be at the bottom of something or
lie at the bottom of something to be the real cause of an undesirable attitude or situation ○ *Remember that pride is at the bottom of all great mistakes.*
the bottom falls out of something or
the bottom drops out of something if the bottom falls out of a market or industry, people stop buying its products in as large quantities as they did before ○ *But just as quickly, the bottom fell out of the American home video game market.*
from the bottom of your heart if you mean something from the bottom of your heart, you mean it very sincerely ○ *I*

want to thank everyone from the bottom of my heart. So many people have helped me.

★ **get to the bottom of something** to solve a problem or mystery by discovering the truth about it ○ *The attack was quite severe. We intend to get to the bottom of things and, if need be, ensure that action is brought against those responsible for it.*

scrape the bottom of the barrel
→ see **barrel**

bounds

★ **out of bounds**

1 if a place is out of bounds, you are not allowed to go there ○ *The area has been out of bounds to foreigners for more than a month.*

2 if a subject is out of bounds, you are not allowed to discuss it ○ *The private lives of public figures should be out of bounds to the press and public.*

bow

> "Bow" is pronounced with the same vowel sound as the word "how."

bow and scrape to be too respectful toward a powerful or famous person ○ *Winning this kind of award can be a drawback because some people feel they have to bow and scrape.*

> If you bow, you bend your body toward someone as a formal way of greeting them or showing respect. In the past, "scraping" was a form of bowing which involved drawing back one leg and bending the other.

take a bow written or said before or after a person's name to congratulate that person or show admiration for them ○ *When you've got the best camerawork and the best commentators – Martin Tyler, take a bow – it's hard to go wrong.*

box

a black box a process or system that

produces a particular result although it is not understood how it works ○ *Only a decade ago cancer was a black box about which we knew nothing at the molecular level.*

≣ In an electronic or computer system, a black box is a self-contained part. You can understand its function without knowing anything about how it works.

out of the box if you come out of the box in a particular way, you begin an activity in that way. If you are first out of the box, you are the first person to do something ○ *Arco is definitely first out of the box with an alternative gas for cars without catalytic converters.*

≣ This refers to the game of baseball. A player runs out of the box, which is the marked area where the batter stands, towards first base after hitting the ball.

think outside the box to think about something in a way that is new or different and shows imagination, especially in business ○ *She goes on to urge companies to think outside the box and challenge the old ways of working.*

boy

someone's blue-eyed boy or **someone's fair-haired boy** or **someone's golden boy** a man who someone has a very high opinion of and gives special treatment to ○ *He'd lost interest in Willy by that time – I was the new golden boy.*

a whipping boy someone or something that people blame when things go wrong, even though they may not be responsible for what has happened ○ *Businessmen fear that they and the hard-won free-market reforms will be the whipping boys for the economic ills that confront the new administration.*

≣ A whipping boy was a boy who was educated with a prince and was punished for the prince's mistakes because tutors were not allowed to hit the prince.

★ **you can take the boy out of the country but you can't take the country out of the boy** said to mean someone from the countryside keeps their country values and ideas, even if they live in a city ○ *You can take the boy out of the country, but you can't take the country out of the boy. That describes my husband perfectly. He still loves fishing and shooting.*

≣ This expression is usually used with "boy," but people substitute other nouns if the context requires it.

boys

boys will be boys used to explain that the noisy or rough way that a boy or man is behaving is normal and so should not be punished or cause a reaction ○ *"Your troubles are just beginning," they would say, shaking their heads. "Boys will be boys."*

★ **one of the boys** a man who is accepted as belonging to a group of men who behave in ways that are considered typically masculine ○ *His overly enthusiastic efforts to seem just one of the boys were sometimes embarrassing.*

brain

get your brain into gear (*informal*) to start thinking clearly about something, so that you can achieve what needs to be done ○ *All I want is to get my brain into gear and get back to the top.*

have a brain like a sieve to have a bad memory and often forget things ○ *Grandpa lost his car keys again – his brain's like a sieve.*

brains

pick someone's brains to ask someone for advice or information, because they know more about a subject than you do ○ *I'd like to pick your brains about something.*

★ **rack your brains** or **rack your brain** to think very hard about something or try very hard to remember it. The old-fashioned spelling "wrack" is occasionally used instead of "rack" in this expression. ○ *Reformers are racking their brains for a way to slow down these processes.*

brakes

★ **put the brakes on**
put on the brakes to slow down or stop a process or development ○ *The governor has put the brakes on the tunnel until he has a clearer idea of what the final costs will be.*

brass

the brass ring success or a big reward or profit ○ *There are good and bad features to living among people who are all young, on the make, and going for the brass ring professionally.*

On some merry-go-rounds, a brass ring was placed just out of the reach of the riders. If a rider managed to grab it, they won a free ride.

get down to brass tacks to begin to discuss the basic, most important aspects of a situation ○ *The convention was due to get down to brass tacks today with a debate on the party's performance during the last five years.*

The origins of this phrase are disputed but it may have come about from a way that fabric was once measured, according to the distance between brass tacks, on the counter in a store.

breach

step into the breach to help by doing work that someone else would normally do ○ *When there aren't enough teachers, parents must step into the breach.*

A breach is a gap, and may refer specifically to a gap in a line of soldiers. This expression suggests the action of someone who quickly steps in to take the place of a soldier who has been shot.

bread

the best thing since sliced bread or **the greatest thing since sliced bread** something that someone thinks is very good, original, and exciting ○ *When your program first started I thought it was the best thing since sliced bread. But over the last three months I think you have adopted an arrogant attitude.*

bread-and-butter most basic or important ○ *On major bread-and-butter issues, there's little difference between the two candidates.*

bread and circuses used to describe a situation in which a government tries to take attention away from real problems or issues by providing people with things that seem to make their lives more enjoyable ○ *Metternich proceeded to neutralize political dissent through a policy of bread and circuses.*

This is a translation of a phrase in a satire by the Roman poet Juvenal. It refers to the fact that, in ancient Rome, the authorities provided the people with public amusements and food in order to prevent possible rebellion.

cast your bread upon the waters (*literary*) to do something good or take a risk, usually without expecting very much in return ○ *You should make time to offer assistance to others. It's a case of casting your bread upon the waters – who knows how the favor will be repaid.*

This expression comes from the Bible (Ecclesiastes 11:1), where people are advised that if they are generous and helpful (by "throwing their bread to the waters"), they will be rewarded, but possibly only after a long time.

know which side your bread is buttered on to understand fully how you are likely to benefit from a situation, and know what to do or who to please in order to put yourself in the best possible situation ○ *Donald was a man who knew with utter clarity which side his bread was buttered on.*

★ **your bread and butter** the main way that you earn money ○ *"Who's your audience?" "We play maybe a hundred colleges a year. That is our bread and butter."*

breadline

live on the breadline or
be on the breadline to be extremely poor ○ *They should be stripped of everything they own but the bare essentials. Let them feel what it is like to be on the breadline.*

In times of hardship, particularly in the last century in the United States, poor people used to line up outside bakeries or soup kitchens for free or very cheap bread.

break

★ **give me a break** (informal)
1 said to show that you think that someone is being very annoying or ridiculous ○ *Give me a break! Why quote feminists on a decision that concerns the rights of all women? Why can't they quote mothers, teachers, nurses, or dancers?*
2 said to tell someone to stop criticizing or annoying you and leave you alone ○ *Anxious families yesterday begged youngsters, "Give us a break," after dozens of cars were wrecked by the gangs.*

never be given an even break or
never get an even break to not get the same chances or opportunities to do something as other people ○ *He kept talking about how she never got an even break from the family.*

"Never Give a Sucker an Even Break" is an old movie starring W. C. Fields (1941).

breakfast

eat someone or something for breakfast to deal with, get rid of, or defeat someone or something very easily ○ *The European Central Bank will eat Irish debt for breakfast and the euro will rise as a result.*

breast

beat your breast → see **beat**
make a clean breast of something to start to be completely truthful about something, so that you can begin to deal properly with a problem ○ *If you make a clean breast of your problems, creditors, whether secured or unsecured, are much more likely to deal fairly and leniently with you.*

breath

★ **a breath of fresh air** someone or something that is pleasantly different from what you are used to ○ *Basically, I was bored. So Mike, my husband, was a breath of fresh air.*

★ **hold your breath** to wait in an anxious or excited way to see what happens next ○ *She had been holding her breath and hoping that the agreement would be signed.*

★ **in the same breath** if someone says one thing and then in the same breath says something different, they are saying two things that do not agree with each other ○ *For politicians to demand firm immigration controls and argue against racism in the same breath is a deep contradiction.*

someone is wasting their breath used when there is no point in someone continuing with what they are saying, because it will not have any effect ○ *He wanted to protest again, but the tone of her voice told him he was wasting his breath.*

★ **take your breath away** to amaze and impress you ○ *"Tell me again about the* movie." "It's beautiful. It's so beautiful it takes your breath away."

★ **with bated breath** feeling anxious or excited to see what happens next ○ *They got the people in the villages interested in what was going to happen, so they were then watching with bated breath as the experiment began.*

> "Bate" is an old form of "abate," which in this context means "control" or "hold back."

breeze

shoot the breeze to talk with other people in an informal and friendly way ○ *Goldie does what she likes doing best: shooting the breeze about life, love, and her bad reputation.*

> The sense of "shoot" used here is presumably the same as "shoot the rapids," suggesting riding or being carried along by the flow of a conversation.

brick

come up against a brick wall to arrive at a situation in which something is stopping you from doing what you want and preventing you from making any progress ○ *I was tired, I had been working real hard for a long time and I felt that I'd come up against a brick wall.*

drop a brick to say something that upsets or offends other people, or that embarrasses you ○ *After his comments on the live TV program, Mr. Freeman was immediately aware that he had dropped a political brick of the worst kind.*

drop someone or something like a hot brick → see **drop**

bricks

make bricks without straw to do a job, or try to do it, without the proper resources that are needed for it ○ *His job was apparently to make education bricks*

without straw – that is to say, to be inspiring without having much money.

> This expression is from the Bible (Exodus 5:7), and refers to Pharaoh's order that the captive Israelites should not be given any straw to make bricks.

bridge

someone will cross that bridge when they get to it someone intends to deal with a problem when, or if, it happens, rather than worrying about the possibility of it happening ○ *"You can't make me talk to you." "No, but the police can." "I'll cross that bridge when I get to it."*

bridges

★ **build bridges** to do something to help opposing groups of people to understand each other or behave well towards each other ○ *We look for ways to build bridges between our two organizations.*

★ **burn bridges** to do something that forces you to continue with a particular course of action, and makes it impossible for you to return to an earlier situation ○ *I didn't sell it because I didn't know how long I would be here. I didn't want to burn all my bridges.*

> During invasions, Roman generals sometimes burned their boats or any bridges they had crossed, so that their soldiers could not retreat but were forced to fight on.

brief

in brief in a few words; briefly ○ *Only volunteer that information if asked, and do so in brief.*

bright

bright and early early in the morning ○ *I woke up bright and early and did the weeding before it got too hot.*

bright-eyed

bright-eyed and bushy-tailed lively,

enthusiastic, and full of energy ○ *But for now, go and sleep awhile. I need you bright-eyed and bushy-tailed tomorrow.*

≡ The comparison in this expression is to a squirrel.

britches

get too big for your britches to behave as if you are much smarter or more important than you really are ○ *Nobody on the board will ever allow us to get too big for our britches.*

≡ Britches are pants which reach as far as your knees.

broke

★ **go for broke** to decide to take a risk and put all your efforts or resources into one plan or idea in the hope that it will be successful ○ *TheWildcats played in desperation mode, going for broke and bringing everyone on the attack.*

≡ If a gambler goes for broke, they put all their money on one game or on one hand of cards.

★ **if it ain't broke, don't fix it** used to emphasize that things should only be changed if they are wrong. The word "ain't" is a form of "isn't" that is used in informal or nonstandard English. ○ *With regard to proposals for some grand reorganization of the intelligence community: If it ain't broke, don't fix it. And I believe it is not broke.*

≡ The first recorded use of this modern proverb is by the American Bert Lance, President Carter's Director of the Office of Management and Budget (1977). He was referring to governmental reorganization.

Bronx

a Bronx cheer a rude noise that you make by holding your lips together and forcing your breath out through them

○ *The plans received a Bronx cheer from the public.*

broom

a new broom someone who has just started a new job in an important position and is expected to make a lot of changes ○ *We had a new, exceptionally young principal and he was a very active new broom.*

brown

brown as a berry having a very dark skin from being in the sun ○ *Steve Hobbs had just come back from his vacation, brown as a berry.*

≡ The reference may be to juniper or cedar berries, which are brown, as most other berries are red, purple, or blue.

brownie

★ **brownie points** a reward or congratulations for doing something good ○ *Mr. Stein would almost certainly win extra brownie points for taking an ultra-cautious view and removing uncertainty from the share price.*

≡ The Brownies is an organization for young girls. Members are expected to be well-behaved and helpful.

brunt

★ **bear the brunt of something** or **take the brunt of something** to experience the main consequences of a problem or situation ○ *Two other highways that run west to east will bear the brunt of the excess traffic when the bridge is closed.*

brush

tar someone with the same brush to assume that someone behaves as badly as other people in a particular group ○ *Backing up and apologizing, the mayor said he never meant to tar everyone with the same brush.*

This expression comes from the use of tar to mark all the sheep in one flock to distinguish them from another flock.

bubble

★ **the bubble has burst** used when a situation or idea that was very successful has suddenly stopped being successful ○ *The bubble has burst. Crowds at the team's World League games are down from last year's 40,000 average to 22,000.*

The bubble referred to in this expression is the South Sea Bubble, a financial disaster which took its name from The South Sea Company. In the early 18th century, this company took over the British national debt in return for a monopoly of trade with the South Seas. A lot of people invested in the company, but it crashed in 1720 and many investors became bankrupt.

on the bubble in a difficult situation and at risk of failure or exclusion ○ *Hewlett was on the bubble after a difficult round yesterday.*

The reference may be to a bubble which is about to burst, or to the bubble in a level, which will move off center if the level is not kept exactly horizontal.

buck

In poker, the buck was a marker or object which was passed to the person whose turn it was to deal the next hand. This person could either keep the marker or pass it on, in order to avoid dealing and being responsible for declaring the first stake.

★ **the buck stops here** or **the buck stops with me** used to make it clear that a problem is your responsibility, and you are not expecting anyone else to deal with it ○ *If you are going to blame anyone, it must be the man in charge and that's me. The buck stops here.*

This expression is often associated with U.S. President Harry S. Truman, who had it written on a sign on his desk in the Oval Office to remind him of his responsibilities.

★ **pass the buck** to fail to take responsibility for a problem, and to expect someone else to deal with it instead ○ *He is our responsibility. Canada is the only place he has ever known and to deport him is simply passing the buck because of a legal loophole.*

bucket

kick the bucket to die. This expression is used to refer to someone's death in a light-hearted or humorous way. ○ *All the money goes to her when the old man kicks the bucket.*

The origins of this expression are uncertain. It may refer to someone committing suicide by standing on a bucket, tying a rope around their neck, then kicking the bucket away.

bud

★ **nip something in the bud** to stop a bad situation or bad behavior at an early stage, before it can develop and become worse ○ *It is important to recognize jealousy as soon as possible and to nip it in the bud before it gets out of hand.*

This expression may refer to extremely cold weather damaging a plant and stopping it flowering. Alternatively, it may refer to a gardener pruning a plant in bud to prevent it flowering.

bug

★ **be bitten by the bug** to become very enthusiastic about something, and start doing it a lot ○ *Bitten by the travel bug, he then set off for a working vacation in Australia.*

bull

a bull in a china shop someone who says or does things that offend or upset people in situations where they should be more careful ○ *In confrontational situations I am like a bull in a china shop.*

grab the bull by the horns or **take the bull by the horns** to take definite and determined action in order to deal with a difficult situation ○ *This is the time to take the bull by the horns and tackle the complex issues of finance.*

In bullfighting, the matador sometimes grasps the bull's horns before killing it.

bullet

★ **bite the bullet** to accept a difficult or unpleasant situation ○ *The same stressful event might make one person utterly miserable, while another will bite the bullet and make the best of it.*

During battles in the past, wounded men were sometimes given a bullet to bite on while the doctor operated on them without any anesthetic or painkillers.

bum

a bum steer *(informal)* information that is wrong and misleading ○ *Did you give me a bum steer about your name and address?*

This expression may refer to a worthless bullock. Alternatively, it may refer to someone being given directions that are not correct.

get the bum's rush *(informal)* to be completely ignored or rejected in an unexpected and upsetting way ○ *He turned up there at 2:45 and sat down to lunch with European royalty, while we got the bum's rush.*

A bum is a person who has no permanent home or job, and very little money. This expression refers to a bum being thrown out of a place by force.

bundle

a bundle of joy a baby, especially one just born ○ *Sofia and Thomas have a new little bundle of joy at home, a baby girl named Cosima.*

a bundle of nerves someone who is extremely nervous, worried, or tense ○ *What's the matter? You're a bundle of nerves.*

burn

★ **do a slow burn** to become very angry over a period of time and not resolve the problem that causes this ○ *Mario has been treated badly at work for weeks now, and he's been doing a slow burn.*

burner

★ **put something on the back burner** to decide not to do anything about a situation or project until a later date, because you do not consider it to be important at the time ○ *She put her career on the back burner after marrying co-star Paul Hogan two years ago, spending her time making a home for them in Australia.*

A burner is one of the rings or plates on the top of a stove.

bush

not beat around the bush to say what you want to say clearly and directly, even though it is not pleasant ○ *I decided not to beat around the bush. "I'm at Sam's," I told her. "Eddie didn't come back from his paper route yet. Nobody knows where he is."*

In hunting, beaters drive birds or small animals out of the undergrowth by beating it with sticks. They may have to do this cautiously as they do not know exactly where the birds or animals are.

bushel

hide your light under a bushel
to say little about your skills and good features, instead of being confident and telling other people about them ○ *Don't be tempted to hide your light under a bushel for fear of upsetting other people.*

This is from the Bible (Matthew 5:15), where Jesus says that no one lights a lamp and then hides it under something; instead, they put it on a stand so that it can give light to everyone.

bushes

beat the bushes to try very hard to get or achieve something ○ *He was tired of beating the bushes for work, and he did not want to ask for help or accept charity.*

business

be in business (spoken) to be able to start doing something because everything is ready for it ○ *It plugs in here, right? Okay, we're in business. Let's see how it works, guys.*

business as usual used to show that everything is continuing in the normal way, even though something unpleasant or unexpected has happened ○ *Mr. Fitzwater told reporters: It is business as usual; this isn't the kind of crisis that requires us to drop everything else.*

do the business (informal) to do what is needed to achieve a result. Compare with **do the trick**. ○ *Now I could be judged solely on my achievements as a player, and I was absolutely determined to prove I could still do the business.*

do something like nobody's business to do something a lot or very well ○ *I mean Jeff can talk like nobody's business.*

★ **mean business** to be serious and determined about what you are doing ○ *One of them poked a shotgun at me. I could see he meant business.*

busman

a busman's holiday a situation in which someone spends part of their holiday or vacation doing or experiencing something that forms part of their normal job or everyday life ○ *A fire crew's Christmas outing turned into a busman's holiday when their bus caught fire.*

This expression may refer to bus drivers at the beginning of the 20th century when buses were horse-drawn. Drivers sometimes spent their day off riding on their own bus to make sure that the relief drivers were treating the horses properly.

busy

a busy bee or
busy as a bee if someone is a busy bee or busy as a bee, they enjoy doing a lot of things and always keep themselves busy ○ *He is busy as a bee designing every production on Broadway.*

butter

butter wouldn't melt in someone's mouth used to suggest that someone who looks completely innocent is actually capable of something unexpected ○ *Little Kirsten Leroy looks like butter wouldn't melt in her mouth but put her in a taekwondo square and she's one of the most talented youngsters around.*

butterflies

have butterflies in your stomach to feel very nervous about something that you have to do ○ *He seemed so full of enthusiasm that I felt foolish still having butterflies in my stomach.*

button

★ **a hot button** a subject or problem that everyone is interested in or arguing over ○ *If crime is the city's issue most known to outsiders, rent control is the city's hot button for its residents.*

on the button exactly ○ *He said he'd meet us at 10 on the button.*

press the right button or
press all the right buttons to cleverly or skillfully do the things that are necessary to get what you want in a particular situation ○ *In what it describes as a well-judged performance, the newspaper says he pressed all the right buttons to please the representatives.*

right on the button correct about something ○ *"Am I right?" "Right on the button."*

butts

butts in seats or
butts on seats If a performer or performance puts butts on seats, they are very popular and succeed in attracting large audiences ○ *He's always* been like that and will never change. That's why he gets butts on seats – he's a showman.

buzz

★ **a buzz kill** an event, person, or piece of information that spoils a good time or a good mood ○ *They let a goal in during the last minute. What a buzz kill.*

> In this expression, "buzz" refers to the pleasant sensation that you get from alcohol or just from being in a happy mood.

bygones

let bygones be bygones to forget about a disagreement in the past in order to improve a relationship ○ *Norton was eager to return, so it would've been great if Marvel could've just let bygones be bygones too.*

Cc

cage

rattle someone's cage to do or say something that upsets or annoys someone ○ *I don't rattle their cages and they don't rattle mine.*

cahoots

in cahoots with someone secretly working or cooperating with someone to do something dishonest ○ *They accused him of being in cahoots with smugglers.*

Cain

raise Cain to get very angry about something ○ *I figure she'd raise Cain if we tried to stop her.*

⁝ The reference here is to the Bible story in which Cain murdered his brother, Abel, in a fit of rage. (Genesis 4:1-9).

cake

★ **have your cake and eat it (too)** to get the benefits of two different situations or things, when you should only get the benefit of one of them ○ *The Fed can't have its cake and eat it too: interest rates will go up, but tax revenues will go down.*

⁝ Although "have your cake and eat it too" is now the most common form of the expression, the original was "eat your cake and have it." Some people consider the recent version illogical, since it is certainly possible to have a cake and then eat it but not the other way around.

take the cake to be the most extreme or outrageous example of something bad ○ *Officers say they get to see some pretty odd things but that just about takes the cake.*

⁝ Cakes have been awarded as prizes in competitions since classical times but this expression is thought to have its origin among African Americans in the southern United States in the time of slavery. The competitors walked or danced around a cake in pairs, and the cake was awarded to the couple who moved the most gracefully.

cakes

cakes and ale a time or activity when you enjoy yourself greatly and have no troubles ○ *You can't deny other people cakes and ale just because you've never enjoyed them yourself.*

⁝ This expression is used in Shakespeare's "Twelfth Night." Sir Toby Belch says to Malvolio, "Dost thou think, because thou art virtuous, there shall be no more cakes and ale?" (Act 2, Scene 3). "Cakes and Ale" is also the title of a novel by Somerset Maugham, which was published in 1930.

calf

kill the fatted calf to celebrate and do everything possible to welcome a person ○ *He went off to make movies, and when he returned, his record company didn't exactly kill the fatted calf.*

⁝ This expression comes from the story of "the prodigal son" (Luke 5:3-32), which is told by Jesus in the Bible. In this story, a young man returns home after wasting all the money his father has given him. However, his father is so pleased to see him that he celebrates his return by killing a calf and preparing a feast.

call

★ **a close call** a situation in which someone barely manages to avoid an accident or disaster ○ *"That was a close call," Bess gasped, as the boat steadied and got under way.*

calm

★ **the calm before the storm** a very quiet period that it is likely to be followed, or was followed, by a period of trouble or intense activity ○ *Things are relatively calm at the moment, but I think this is probably the calm before the storm.*

camp

a camp follower a person who likes to be seen with a particular person or group, either because they admire them, or because they hope to gain advantages from them ○ *Even in my day as a player, we had our camp followers.*

Originally, camp followers were civilians who traveled with an army and who made their living selling goods or services to the soldiers.

pitch camp to settle somewhere or have control of a certain area for a period of time ○ *As reporters pitched camp outside their home, the family's political differences became a public concern.*

camper

not a happy camper annoyed or unhappy about something. You use this expression to be humorous or ironic. ○ *He's just been suspended. It's safe to say he's not a happy camper right now.*

can

a can of worms → see **worms**
in the can successfully completed ○ *We've got the interview in the can.*

Old movie film is stored in circular metal containers called cans.

candle

burn the candle at both ends to try to do too much, by regularly going to bed very late and getting up early in the morning ○ *Most people need six or seven hours each night and you're burning the candle at both ends if you regularly sleep for less than five.*

someone can't hold a candle to someone used to say that the first person mentioned is not in any way as good as the second ○ *There are football players now valued in the $10m bracket who can't hold a candle to Mark in terms of ability.*

This expression implies that the first person is not worthy even to hold a light to help the other person to see.

candy

like taking candy from a baby very easy ○ *Stealing the stuff was like taking candy from a baby.*

cannon

★ **cannon fodder** soldiers who are considered unimportant by their officers and are sent to fight in the most dangerous areas, where they are likely to be killed ○ *The fifty-five to sixty-five year-olds would be sent to the front as cannon-fodder. They were to attack ahead of the regular troops and absorb the enemy's fire.*

Fodder is cheap food such as hay or straw that is used to feed animals.

★ **a loose cannon** a person who could cause problems because they are not in control of themselves and act wrecklessly ○ *There is a widespread worry that the military command has turned into a loose cannon beyond the control of the government.*

This expression refers to the cannons that used to be carried on the decks of warships. If one of the cannons was not properly fastened down, it could spin around and make a hole in the ship.

canoe

paddle your own canoe to control what you want to do without anyone else's help or influence ○ *As far as the rest of Europe is concerned we've just got to paddle our own canoe.*

cap

put your thinking cap on or **get your thinking cap on** to try hard to solve a problem by thinking about it ○ *She decided to put her thinking cap on: there must be a job somewhere that she could do.*

This expression may refer to the cap that judges used to wear when passing sentence or judgment.

capital

★ **with a capital ___** said when you want to draw attention to a particular word and emphasize its importance ○ *Students thought studying psychology would tell them something about Life with a capital L.*

carbon

★ **a carbon copy** a person or thing that is very similar to someone or something else ○ *She's always been quiet. She's a carbon copy of her mother – her mother always hated making a fuss.*

A carbon copy of a document is an exact copy of it which is made using carbon paper.

card

a calling card something that someone possesses or has achieved, that gives them a lot of opportunities ○ *The actor used the New York magazine cover story about him as "his calling card."*

A calling card is an old-fashioned card similar to a business card, printed with your name and other personal information. People used to leave their calling cards when they went to visit someone.

a wild card someone or something that causes doubt, because nobody knows how they will behave or what effects they will have ○ *I was always a bit uneasy about him; I liked him, but he was a bit of a wild card.*

In games such as poker, a wild card is a card that can have any value a player chooses.

cards

★ **in the cards** or **on the cards** very likely to happen. ○ *There's no need to look so surprised. This has been in the cards for a long time.*

This is a reference to Tarot cards, or to other cards used to predict the future.

keep your cards close to your chest or **play your cards close to your chest** to not tell anyone about your plans or thoughts ○ *The President was said yesterday to be keeping his cards close to his chest after an informal discussion at cabinet on Thursday.*

This is a reference to card-players holding their cards close to their chest so that nobody else can see them.

lay your cards on the table or **put your cards on the table** to tell someone the truth about your feelings and plans ○ *Put your cards on the table and be very clear about your complaints. This should clear the air.*

The reference here is to players in a card game laying their cards face up for the other players to see.

play your cards right to use your skills to do all the things that are necessary in order to succeed or gain an advantage ○ *Soon, if she played her cards right, she would be head of the Omaha office.*

The reference here is to a player in a card game who can win the game if they use their cards well enough.

carpet

called on the carpet in trouble for doing something wrong. ○ *City staffers often are called on the carpet by disgruntled council members during meetings.*

This expression may refer to a piece of carpet in front of a desk where someone stands while being reprimanded. Alternatively, it could refer to an employer calling a servant into one of the best rooms in the house, which would have a carpet, in order to reprimand them.

roll out the red carpet to give someone a special welcome and treat them very well ○ *The museum staff rolled out the red carpet; although it was a Sunday, the deputy director came in especially to show us around.*

It is customary to lay out a strip of red carpet for royalty or other important guests to walk on when they arrive for an official visit.

carrot

★ **carrot and stick** rewards and threats that are offered in order to persuade someone to do something ○ *But Congress also wants to use a carrot and stick approach to force both sides to negotiate.*

The idea behind this expression is that an animal such as a donkey can be encouraged to move forward either by dangling a carrot in front of it or by hitting it with a stick. The carrot represents the tempting offer and the stick represents the threat.

★ **offer someone a carrot** or **use something as a carrot** to try to persuade someone to do something by offering them a reward if they do it ○ *It has used a relatively small pot of money as a carrot, but what if the federal government offered something more important to states?*

The image here is of someone encouraging a donkey to move forward by holding a carrot in front of it.

cart

put the cart before the horse to do things in the wrong order ○ *Creating large numbers of schools before improving school management is putting the cart before the horse.*

case

In these expressions, a case is one that is being dealt with by a lawyer or doctor, not a box or suitcase.

be on someone's case or **get on someone's case** (*informal*) to keep criticizing someone in an annoying way, because you think that they have behaved badly ○ *I don't need my friends getting on my case and telling me what to do as well.*

a case in point an example of the thing you are talking about ○ *The problem in the past with electric cars was that they were too expensive. One model which cost $100,000 is a case in point.*

make a federal case (out) of something to give something far more importance than it deserves ○ *They determined that the sign had been vandalized and they wanted to make a federal case of it.*

on the case dealing with a particular problem or situation ○ *I am on the case, and as soon as I have a solution to the problem, I'll let you know.*

cash

a cash cow a source of money that continues to produce a large amount of profit over a long period, without needing a lot of funding. ○ *The park has been a cash cow for the city. Sales taxes there account for approximately 15 per cent of the city's general fund.*

The reference is to something that produces money as freely as a cow produces milk.

castles

castles in the air unrealistic plans or hopes for the future ○ *"Along the way I have to become very, very rich." He shook his head in wonder at her. "You're building castles in the air, Anne."*

cat

★ **cat and mouse** or
a game of cat and mouse a situation in which a person tries to confuse or deceive another in order to defeat them ○ *He would play cat-and-mouse with other riders, sometimes waiting until the fourth lap to come from behind and win.*

The reference here is to a cat playing with a mouse before killing it.

Cat got your tongue? used to express the idea that someone who is silent should speak ○ *'Where were you last night?' I didn't say anything. "What's the matter, cat got your tongue?"*

the cat's meow or
the cat's pajamas (old-fashioned) the very best person or thing ○ *She had this great dress on and she thought she was the cat's meow as she came out along the gallery.*

★ **a fat cat** a person who uses their great wealth and power in a way that seems unfair ○ *They want higher taxes for the bulk of the population, not just the fat cats.*

grin like a Cheshire cat → see **Cheshire**

let the cat out of the bag to reveal something secret or private, often without intending to ○ *"The Mosses didn't tell the cops my name, did they?" "Of course not," he said. "They wouldn't want to let the cat out of the bag."*

like a cat on a hot tin roof very nervous or restless ○ *He's like a cat on a hot tin roof before a game.*

"Cat on a Hot Tin Roof" is the title of a play by Tennessee Williams.

like the cat that got the cream or
like the cat that ate the canary looking very satisfied and happy ○ *The 26-year-old Canadian looked like the cat that got the cream as he smooched pretty Jessica Spillas in Toronto.*

look like something the cat dragged in to look very messy ○ *It is quite possible to be an intelligent and successful woman and look like something the cat has dragged in.*

look what the cat's dragged in said when someone arrives to express your dislike or disapproval of them, or as a light-hearted way of greeting them ○ *In strolls Babs. "Now look what the cat's dragged in," says Jeanie, with a nod.*

there isn't room to swing a cat used to express that a place is very small and has very little space ○ *Inside, there isn't room to swing a cat, and everything you see and touch is the most basic junk.*

The "cat" in this expression is probably a "cat-o'-nine-tails," a whip with nine lashes which was used in the past for punishing offenders in the army and navy. However, the expression could be connected with the practice in the past of swinging cats by their tails as targets for archers.

there's more than one way to skin a cat there are several ways to achieve something ○ *There is more than one way to skin a cat; keep positive and try another method of reaching your goal.*

when the cat's away, the mice will play used when you notice that people misbehave when their boss or another person in authority is away ○ *While the bosses are out of the room, the workers watch the game – a case of while the cat's away the mice will play.*

catbird

in the catbird seat in an important or powerful position ○ *If I can run around the world and buy that particular group, then I'll be in the catbird seat.*

⫶ This expression became widely known in the 1940s and 1950s, when it was used by the baseball commentator Red Barber. Catbirds are North American songbirds. The expression may be explained by the fact that catbirds often sit very high up in trees.

Catch

a Catch 22 an extremely frustrating situation in which one thing cannot happen until another thing has happened, but the other thing cannot happen until the first thing has happened ○ *There's a Catch 22 in social work. You need experience to get work and you need work to get experience.*

⫶ This expression comes from the novel "Catch 22" (1961), by the American author Joseph Heller, which is about bomber pilots in the World War II. Their "Catch 22" situation was that any sane person would ask if they could stop flying. However, the authorities would only allow people to stop flying if they were insane.

cats

fight like cats and dogs to frequently have violent arguments ○ *They had fought like cats and dogs ever since he could remember, and he wondered how they'd gotten together in the first place.*
it's raining cats and dogs it is raining very heavily ○ *"Could you see how he looked?" "Not really. It was raining cats and dogs by then."*

⫶ There are several possible explanations for this expression, but none of them can be proved. It may refer to the days when drainage in towns was so poor that cats and dogs sometimes drowned in heavy rainfall. Alternatively, "cats and dogs" could be a corruption or misunderstanding of the Greek word "catadupe," meaning "waterfall," so the expression would originally have been "it's raining like a waterfall." The origin may also be in Norse mythology, where cats and dogs were sometimes associated with the spirit of the storm.

cause

a lost cause something that has failed or is sure to fail ○ *The party has begun depicting his campaign as a lost cause.*

caution

★ **throw caution to the wind** or **throw caution to the winds** to do something without worrying about the risks and danger involved ○ *This was no time to think, he decided. He threw caution to the wind and rang the bell of the apartment.*

ceiling

★ **go through the ceiling**
1 to suddenly increase very rapidly ○ *Sales went through the ceiling and pharmacists began reporting shortages of the drug.*
2 to suddenly become very angry and start shouting ○ *If he did what she said, she was happy, but if he didn't, she went through the ceiling.*

cent

★ **not have a cent to your name** → see **name**
a red cent the smallest possible amount of money ○ *Investors have to remember that with many shows they won't get a red cent back.*

⫶ Cent is another name for penny in this expression, which is almost always used with "not."

center

★ **center stage** the position in which someone or something gets the most attention ○ *The summit is the first time he has occupied center stage at an important international gathering since coming to power last year.*

> The stage referred to is in the theater. The center of the stage is the position where actors are most prominent. "Center stage," "stage left" and "stage right" are used in theater directions for actors, along with "up stage" and "down stage."

cents

someone's two cents someone's expressed opinion. ○ *He'd give the rest of us a chance to put in our two cents, but we usually followed his lead.*

ceremony

not stand on ceremony (old-fashioned) to be direct and say or do the things you think and feel, rather than doing what is expected of you or what would be most appropriate in the situation ○ *The fact that she said that shows that she thinks the relationship is comfortable enough that she doesn't need to stand on ceremony.*

chain

yank someone's chain (informal) to say something that is untrue, either to annoy or to play a joke on someone ○ *When would I learn to smarten up and ignore her when she yanked my chain?*

chalice

a poisoned chalice a job or an opportunity that seems to be very attractive but may in fact lead to failure or a very unpleasant situation ○ *The contract may yet prove to be a poisoned chalice.*

> A chalice is an old-fashioned cup, usually made of metal and shaped like a wine glass.

chance

fat chance (informal) used to express the opinion that something is very unlikely or will not succeed ○ *You want me to do your laundry? Fat chance!*

not a chance in hell or
not a snowball's chance in hell used to express the opinion that something is very unlikely or will not succeed ○ *This plane doesn't have a snowball's chance in hell of taking off within an hour.*

★ **stand a chance** to have a possibility of winning or succeeding ○ *I applied for the scholarship but I knew I didn't stand a chance.*

> This expression is often used negatively.

change

and some change and a small additional amount of money ○ *Some agents earn $118,000 and some change.*

★ **a change of heart** a new and different attitude toward something ○ *At the last minute, she had a change of heart about selling it. It had been in her family for generations.*

changes

★ **ring the changes** to make changes to the way something is organized or done in order to vary or improve it ○ *The different varieties enable you to ring the changes so that your cat never gets bored with his food.*

> In bell-ringing, to "ring the changes" means to ring a number of church bells, each of which gives a different note, one after the other in every possible combination.

chapter

chapter and verse full and accurate

information about something ○ *I explained everything to Lapiere. I gave him chapter and verse.*

≣ This expression refers to the practice of giving precise chapter and verse numbers when quoting passages from the Bible.

charity

charity begins at home used to emphasize that people should deal with the needs of people close to them before thinking about helping other people further away ○ *Charity begins at home. There are many tasks right here on campus that need volunteers as well.*

charm

work like a charm to be extremely effective or successful ○ *We found that it took a few seconds for the connection to kick in but then it worked like a charm.*

≣ In this expression, "charm" refers to an object or spell used by someone with magical powers to achieve something that is otherwise not possible.

chase

cut to the chase to start talking about what is really important ○ *He talked about the need to see all points of view, then he cut to the chase: "Well, it looks like there is nothing here for me. I'm planning to fly back."*

≣ In movies, when one scene ends and another begins the action is said to "cut" from one scene to the next. If a movie "cuts to the chase," it moves on to a scene featuring a chase, which most viewers find exciting.

check

★ **a blank check** complete authority to do whatever you think is best ○ *De Klerk had, in a sense, been given a blank check to negotiate the new South Africa.*

≣ This expression is often used literally to mean that someone gives another person a check without an amount of money written on it.

checks

checks and balances a way of organizing a system so that no part of it has too much influence over the others ○ *A final report issued by the grand jury states that the district lacks adequate checks and balances.*

≣ This expression orginated during the period in which the US constitution was written, to apply to the powers held by the three branches of government. It is still often used to talk about balancing powers within parts of a government.

cheek

★ **cheek by jowl** very close together ○ *After about seven years, all this living cheek by jowl began to irritate people.*

≣ "Jowl" is an old-fashioned word for "cheek."

★ **turn the other cheek** to decide not to take any action against someone who harms or insults you ○ *It's better to learn how to avoid a situation where you have either to defend yourself or turn the other cheek.*

≣ This expression comes from Jesus's words to His followers in the Bible (Matthew 5:39). He tells them that they should not fight against bad people, and that if a bad person hits them on the cheek, they should simply offer the other cheek.

cheese

a big cheese (*informal*) a person who has an important and powerful position in an organization ○ *During the conference big cheeses from the State Department were dropping in and out all the time.*

The word "cheese" in this expression may be a corruption or misunderstanding of the Urdu word "chiz" or "cheez," meaning "thing." This started being used in English in about 1840 because of the British presence in India. Later the word came to refer to a person or boss.

Cheshire

grin like a Cheshire cat to make a big smile, often because you are pleased with yourself ○ *Charles was sitting in his place, grinning like a Cheshire cat, when I joined him.*

The Cheshire cat is a character from "Alice in Wonderland" (1865) by the English writer Lewis Carroll. This cat gradually disappears until only its huge grin remains.

chest

beat your chest → see **beat**

★ **get something off your chest** to talk about a problem that has been worrying you for a long time, and to feel better after doing this ○ *My sister gave me the opportunity to talk and get things off my chest.*

chestnut

★ **an old chestnut** a statement, story, or idea that has been repeated so often that it is no longer interesting ○ *The feminist struggle is too important to become an old chestnut over which people groan.*

chicken

chicken and egg

1 a situation where you cannot decide which of two related things happened first and caused the other ○ *It's a chicken-and-egg argument about which comes first: Do people create this lifestyle? Or does the environment influence how people live?*
2 a problem that is impossible to solve because the solution is also the cause of the problem ○ *It's a chicken and egg problem, where the cost per mile is decried because too few people use the trails, while too few people use them because they are poorly maintained.*

This expression comes from the unanswerable question, "Which came first, the chicken or the egg?"

chicken feed

1 a very small amount of money ○ *The $70,000-a-year that we receive from our sponsors is chicken feed compared to the $20m budgets available to some of our rivals.*
2 something unimportant, especially in comparison to another thing ○ *Ordinarily, this late in the campaign, presidential candidates don't play around with chicken feed like this.*

★ **like a chicken with its head cut off** in an uncontrolled or disorganized way, and not calmly or logically ○ *In almost every movie he's in there's always a scene that features him running like a chicken with its head cut off.*

Chickens have been known to run around for a short time after they have had their heads cut off.

chickens

don't count your chickens or **don't count your chickens before they hatch** said to warn someone that they should not make plans for the future because they do not know for certain how a particular situation will develop ○ *When dealing with important financial arrangements, it is imperative that you do not count your chickens before they hatch.*

chiefs

too many chiefs and not enough Indians said to mean that too many people are giving orders and not enough people are obeying them. This expression is often shortened to "too many chiefs." ○ *It did not take long to find out there were* *too many chiefs trying to run that restaurant.*

≡ A chief is the leader of a tribe of Native Americans.

child

★ **child's play** something that is very easy to deal with ○ *He thought the work would be child's play.*

chills

send chills down your spine or **send a chill down your spine** to scare you ○ *This is a movie that sends chills down your spine, because of the powerful acting, or maybe the powerful soundtrack.*

chin

keep your chin up to remain calm or cheerful in a difficult or unpleasant situation ○ *Richards was keeping his chin up yesterday despite the continued setbacks.*

★ **take it on the chin** to bravely accept criticism and not get upset about it ○ *When the police arrived, he took it on the chin, apologizing for the trouble he'd caused them.*

≡ This refers to someone being punched on the jaw but not falling down.

chink

a chink in someone's armor a person's weakness that you can take advantage of, although they appear to be very strong and successful ○ *Stolen or misplaced USB flash drives are but one possible chink in the armor against information loss.*

≡ A chink is a small hole or opening.

chip

a chip off the old block a person who is very similar to one of their parents in appearance, character or behavior ○ *Lewis's lawyer said "He is a chip off the old block – a hothead and a bully just like his dad."*

≡ The "chip" in this expression is a small piece that has been cut off a block of wood.

★ **a chip on your shoulder** a feeling of anger and resentment because you think that you have been treated unfairly in the past ○ *My father had a chip on his shoulder; he thought people didn't like him because of the way he looked.*

≡ A possible explanation for this expression is that in the past, men were said to balance a small piece of wood on one shoulder in the hope that someone would knock it off and give them an excuse to start a fight.

chips

In the following expressions "chips" are the colored tokens or counters that are used to represent money in casinos.

cash in your chips
1 to sell something such as your investments, in order to raise money ○ *ICI was small in over-the-counter drugs in the States. It decided to cash in its chips at a surprisingly good price.*
2 to die ○ *The Senate's oldest member has cashed in his chips at age 92.*

≡ In a casino, if you cash in your chips, you exchange them for money at the end of a gambling session.

★ **when the chips are down** in a particularly difficult or dangerous situation ○ *There will be no panic. We are at our best when the chips are down.*

≡ In a casino, the players lay their chips down on the table to make their bets.

choice

of choice used after a noun for describing something that is chosen most often by a particular group of people or for a particular purpose

○ *Now we have conclusive evidence that oat bran is the fiber of choice for those who want to keep their cholesterol levels out of the risk zone.*

chord

★ **strike a chord** to make you respond in an emotional way, for example, by feeling sympathy or pleasure ○ *It is a case that has shocked the country – and one that has struck a chord with every family with teenagers.*

chunk

a chunk of change a large amount of money ○ *To defend, educate, and build a nation of 300 million requires a good chunk of change.*

cigar

close but no cigar said to someone to express that they have failed in what they were trying to achieve or make you believe ○ *It was a case of close but no cigar for a group of illegal immigrants intercepted by customs officials on their way to the train station.*

In the past, cigars were sometimes given as prizes at fairs. This expression may have been used if someone did not quite manage to win a prize.

circle

★ **come full circle** to return to an earlier situation or condition, although there has been a long period of changes ○ *Her life had now come full circle and she was back where she started, in misery, alone.*

This may refer to the medieval idea of the wheel of fortune which is constantly turning, so that people who have good luck at one time in their lives will have bad luck at another time.

★ **a vicious circle** a situation where one problem has caused other problems which, in turn, have made the original

problem even worse ○ *The economy has been caught in a vicious circle: the economy couldn't create large numbers of jobs because consumers weren't spending; consumers weren't spending because the economy wasn't creating jobs.*

This refers to the error in logic of trying to prove the truth of one statement by a second statement, which in turn relies on the first for proof. The expression is a translation of the Latin *circulus vitiosus*, meaning "a flawed circular argument."

circles

go around in circles or **run around in circles** to try hard to achieve something but have very little success because you are disorganized ○ *She wastes a lot of energy running around in circles, whereas more careful planning could save a lot of effort and achieve a great deal.*

run circles around someone to be much better at a particular activity than someone else, and be able to beat them completely ○ *My sister's basketball team could run circles around us boys when I was a kid.*

circus

a three-ring circus a lot of noisy or very chaotic activity ○ *They might fight among themselves, but grief was a private thing, not something to be turned into a three-ring circus by newspaper reporters.*

clam

happy as a clam ➔ see **happy**

class

a class act a person or group who is admired for their performance or other qualities ○ *I think Nebraska is the class act of the Big 12 and moving to the Big Ten brings a lot of special credit.*

claws

get your claws into someone to control or influence someone in a selfish way ○ *These people had gotten their claws into him and he didn't know how to get rid of them.*

clean

clean as a whistle

1 having done nothing wrong ○ *There are no scandals. His private life is as clean as a whistle.*

2 completely free from dirt ○ *It leaves your face feeling clean as a whistle but not bone-dry.*

★ **come clean** to tell the truth about something ○ *I had expected her to come clean and confess that she only wrote these books for the money. But, no, she insists that she takes them all very seriously.*

★ **squeaky clean** morally very good, with no character faults ○ *As a country-dweller myself, I can truthfully say that not all people living in the countryside are as squeaky clean as they like to think.*

⯀ Clean surfaces sometimes squeak when you wipe or rub them.

cleaners

take someone to the cleaners to make someone lose a lot of money in an unfair or dishonest way ○ *Just for a change, the insurers discovered that they had been taken to the cleaners.*

⯀ This developed from the expression "to clean someone out," which has been used since the 19th century. People say that they have been "cleaned out" when they have lost all their money and valuables, for example, through being robbed or cheated.

clear

clear as a bell very easy to hear and often understand ○ *Her words, when she finally spoke, were as clear as a bell.*

clear as day in a way that is very easy to see, or very obvious and easy to understand ○ *Suddenly she stepped out from behind a tree less than ten yards from me. I saw her face as clear as day.*

clear as mud confusing and difficult to understand ○ *"It's all written down there! Self-explanatory! Clearly." "Clear as mud. Even I can't understand it, and I'm pretty smart."*

in the clear

1 free from blame or suspicion ○ *Their possessions had not been searched so they were not officially in the clear.*

2 no longer in danger or trouble ○ *She and her husband underwent an agonizing 48-hour wait for the results of tests before discovering he was in the clear.*

3 ahead of other people in a competition or contest ○ *The Huskies were 11 points in the clear at halftime, but that all changed in the first minutes of the third quarter.*

★ **steer clear** to deliberately avoid someone or something ○ *Steer clear of foods made from artificial preservatives.*

cloak

★ **cloak-and-dagger** done in secret ○ *They met in classic cloak-and-dagger style beside the lake in Central Park, both tossing snacks to the ducks.*

⯀ This expression is taken from the name of a type of 17th century Spanish drama, in which characters typically wore cloaks and fought with daggers or swords.

clock

★ **around the clock** continuously, throughout the day and night ○ *Fire crews were working around the clock to bring the huge blazes under control.*

★ **turn back the clock** to return to an earlier period, usually because you think it was a very good time or because you would like the chance to live your life differently ○ *He said if he could turn back the clock, he would act differently.*

clockwork

★ **like clockwork**

1 very smoothly and exactly as expected
○ *The journey there went like clockwork – flying out on Friday from Gatwick it took seven hours door-to-door.*

2 regularly, always at the same time
○ *They would arrive like clockwork just before dawn.*

close

cut it close to not leave much time to get somewhere or do something and so to be nearly late ○ *They didn't plan to get here until six o'clock, and that's cutting it a little close.*

★ **something is too close to call** it is impossible to say who will win in a particular competition ○ *The presidential race is too close to call.*

closet

come out of the closet when someone comes out of the closet, they openly admit something about themselves that other people may not approve of, especially that they are gay ○ *There are so many men who have been married and had children, and then come out of the closet later in life.*

cloth

cut from the same cloth very similar in character, attitudes or behavior ○ *As a whole, Clevelanders are cut from the same cloth. They are hard working, gritty people.*

cut your cloth to make plans and decisions that are based on what you have and not what you would like ○ *The board have made it no secret that they are having to cut their cloth to fit their budget.*

out of whole cloth or
made of whole cloth completely untrue and not based on fact ○ *There are those who say that story was made of whole cloth.*

clothes

clothes make the man used to say that the way a person is dressed gives you an accurate idea about their character or chance of success ○ *Jason was wearing an immaculate blue three-piece suit. Clothes make the man, Linda thought.*

cloud

★ **every cloud has a silver lining** used to express that there is always a good or pleasant side-effect of a bad or unpleasant situation ○ *As they say, every cloud has a silver lining. If we hadn't missed the plane, we would never have met you.*

★ **on cloud nine** very happy because something very good has happened to you ○ *I never expected to win, so I'm on cloud nine.*

This expression may be derived from the numbered cloud categories used by the US Weather Bureau. Cloud nine, cumulonimbus, is the highest and occurs at about 30,000 ft. At this height and above, clouds consist of ice crystals rather than water vapor.

★ **under a cloud** suffering from disapproval or criticism because of something that you have done or are believed to have done ○ *He was under a cloud after his men failed to find who had placed the bomb in the office.*

clover

in clover happy because you have a lot of money and are enjoying a luxurious lifestyle ○ *For the next ten days I was in clover at Vicky and Allen's house. They took me to all the town's attractions and its restaurants.*

Clover is a plant that often grows in fields of grass. Cows are said to enjoy grazing in fields that contain a lot of clover.

club

join the club or
welcome to the club used to express that you have had the same experiences or feelings as someone who has been telling you about their problems or how they feel ○ *Confused? Then join the club.*

clue

★ **not have a clue** *(informal)* to not know anything about something or to have no idea what to do about something ○ *I don't have a clue what will happen now.*

coals

rake someone over the coals to speak to someone very severely about something wrong that they have done ○ *I heard later that Uncle Jim had been raked over the coals for not letting anyone know where we were.*

coast

the coast is clear
1 used to indicate that someone can do what they want to do because others who oppose it are not there to see it ○ *Midge stepped aside, nodding that the coast was clear, and Lettie ran through the lobby and up the main staircase.*
2 there is no traffic to stop someone from proceeding ○ *Wait till this blue SUV passes, then the coast is clear.*

This expression may refer to smugglers sending messages that there were no coastguards around and it was safe to land or set sail.

coattails

★ **on the coattails of someone** because of the success or popularity of another person or activity, and not because of your own efforts ○ *She was looking for fame and glory on the coattails of her husband.*

A tail coat is a man's coat with the front covering only the top half of the body and the back reaching down to the knees in a pointed "tail." It is now usually worn only for formal weddings, or as part of formal evening dress.

cobwebs

blow away the cobwebs to make you feel more alert and lively, when you have previously felt tired or dull ○ *We have a cabin in Vermont, and getting back there after a few days in New York really blows the cobwebs away.*

cock

a cock and bull story a story that you do not believe ○ *They'll be believed, no matter what kind of a cock and bull story they tell.*

This expression may come from old fables in which animals such as cocks (that is, roosters) and bulls could talk. Alternatively, it may come from the names of inns, such as "The Cock" and "The Bull," where people gathered and told each other stories and jokes.

cock of the walk a very proud and confident man who considers himself to be smarter or more important than other people around him ○ *Boyd strutted around telling people what to do – the cock of the walk, so to speak.*

This expression is from the idea of a rooster who is the only male among many hens.

cockles

warm the cockles of your heart to make you feel happy and contented ○ *In the bold black and white setting, the sunny yellow color of the house warmed the cockles of my heart.*

Cockles are a type of shellfish. They are associated with the heart because they have a similar shape. The zoological name for cockles is "Cardium," which comes from the

Greek word for "heart." This expression is a little old-fashioned and people often use it humorously today.

coffee

wake up and smell the coffee to start paying attention and become more practical or realistic ○ *It would really serve you well to wake up and smell the coffee and quit acting like a teenager!*

coin

a coin toss a situation that is or will be decided by chance ○ *Gregory calls a possible interest rate increase a coin toss.*

This expression comes from the practice of deciding small matters by tossing a coin, having decided that one course of action will be taken if the coin comes up "heads," and another course if "tails."

★ **the other side of the coin** the other, very different, aspect of a situation ○ *Of course, I get lonely at times. But the other side of the coin is the amazing freedom I have.*

pay someone back in their own coin to treat someone in exactly the same bad way that they have treated you ○ *We need to tell them that if they don't actually cease their attacks they could face the prospect of being paid back in their own coin.*

"Coin" is an old-fashioned word for currency.

cold

cold as ice acting in a very unfriendly way ○ *He sat cold as ice through breakfast, ignoring Claire's hand on his shoulder as she passed his chair.*

★ **come in from the cold** to become popular, accepted, or active again after a period of unpopularity or lack of involvement ○ *Over the past two years, Swedish investors have come in from the cold.*

"The Spy who Came in from the Cold" is the title of a novel by the English writer John Le Carré, published in 1963.

★ **leave someone cold** to not excite or interest someone at all ○ *Given the world situation, chat about shopping and hairdos leaves you cold.*

★ **leave someone out in the cold** to ignore someone and not ask them to take part in activities with you ○ *The developing countries must not be left out in the cold in current world trade talks.*

out cold unconscious ○ *He was out cold and there was blood everywhere.*

when one person sneezes, another catches cold used to express that the things that happen to one country or person have a great effect or influence on other countries or people ○ *And when the American economy sneezes, the City of London catches cold.*

collar

hot under the collar annoyed about something ○ *Judges are hot under the collar about proposals to alter their terms and appointment rules.*

college

give something the old college try (old-fashioned) to make your best effort to succeed, even if you cannot be successful ○ *The actress playing Hannah gives her lines the old college try, but the movie is terrible.*

color

the color of someone's money proof that a person has enough money to pay for something ○ *He made a mental note never to enter into conversation with a customer until he'd at least seen the color of his money.*

colors

A ship's colors are its national flag.

sail under false colors to deliberately deceive people ○ *This report sails under* *false colors. The author had reached his basic conclusions long before he even began gathering any fresh evidence.*

▤ When pirate ships spotted a treasure ship, they often took down their own flag and raised the flag of a friendly nation, in order to get close enough to the ship to attack it.

★ **see someone in their true colors** to suddenly become aware that a person is not as moral or honest as you thought they were ○ *When my boyfriend was involved in a road rage incident it was as if I was seeing him in his true colors for the first time.*

▤ Once a pirate ship had got close to a treasure ship by "sailing under false colors," it then revealed its true identity by raising its own flag.

★ **show your true colors** to do something that makes it clear you were not being entirely honest with people before ○ *The new packaging is a transparent attempt to mislead consumers. Once again, the company is showing its true colors.*

▤ This expression has the same origin as the previous one, and has a similar meaning.

★ **with flying colors** very successfully ○ *She thought she was on a fast track to a good job as a medical assistant when she passed the entrance exam with flying colors.*

▤ The image here is of a victorious battleship sailing back into port with its national flag flying.

comb

with a fine-tooth comb or **with a fine-toothed comb** very carefully and with great attention to detail ○ *I have taken the responsibility of going through Ed's personal papers and letters with a fine-tooth comb.*

▤ A fine-tooth comb is a comb with very thin teeth set very close together. It is used to remove nits and lice from people's hair.

come

★ **come out fighting** to be prepared to do everything possible in order to win ○ *The crude oil producers have come out fighting, claiming the West is using environmental issues as a way of cutting back on oil.*

▤ If boxers come out fighting, they leave their corner as soon as the bell rings and attack their opponent immediately.

where someone is coming from the reasons for someone's behavior, opinions, or comments ○ *I do see where he's coming from – as a company, we're not great at innovation.*

comfort

★ **cold comfort** encouragement that does not in fact make a difficult or unpleasant situation better ○ *Finding out more about this disease can be cold comfort, as no cure and virtually no treatment are available.*

commando

go commando to wear no underwear under your normal clothes ○ *The singer has been known to go commando on videos.*

common

common as dirt extremely common; not at all special ○ *Genius is common as dirt, John Taylor Gatto has said.*

concrete

set in concrete fixed and impossible to change ○ *With expenditure plans now set in concrete for three years, slower growth would mean higher taxes.*

converted

preach to the converted to present

an opinion or argument to people who already agree with it ○ *While I was encouraged by the positive reception we had received in August I was essentially preaching to the converted then.*

> The converted are people who have converted, or changed their religious beliefs and become Christians. Preaching is the activity of speaking to non-Christians to persuade them to convert.

cookie

be caught with your hand in the cookie jar to be caught stealing or doing something wrong. ○ *The banker had been caught with his hand in the cookie jar. Had my client not been aggressive he would have lost $35,000.*

a smart cookie a clever person who has good ideas ○ *As soon as movie film had been invented, around 1890, smart cookies started thinking about how to accompany pictures with sound.*

that's the way the cookie crumbles used to express the idea that you should accept the way that things happen because there will always be some undesirable results ○ *Even after he failed, he didn't give up. "That's the way the cookie crumbles," he said.*

a tough cookie a person who is very determined to get what they want ○ *Behind that sweet smile, there lies one tough cookie.*

cooks

too many cooks or
too many cooks spoil the broth used when it appears that something may not be successful because too many people are involved in it ○ *So far nothing had worked. It was simply a case of too many cooks.*

> This expression comes from the proverb **too many cooks spoil the broth**.

cool

cool as a cucumber very relaxed, calm, and not emotional ○ *Never once did she gasp for air or mop her brow. She was as cool as a cucumber.*

★ **keep your cool** to control your temper and stay calm in a difficult situation ○ *The manager has kept the pressure off the players by keeping his cool and it has paid off.*

★ **lose your cool** to suddenly get angry and behave in a bad-tempered or uncontrolled way ○ *At this I lost my cool and shouted "for goodness sake, stop!"*

coop

fly the coop to leave a situation, for example, because you do not like it or because you want to have more freedom ○ *It should be a proud moment when a senior stylist flies the coop to set up in a salon of his or her own.*

> A coop is a small cage in which chickens or small animals are kept. "Coop" is also slang for a prison.

cord

cut the umbilical cord or
cut the cord to start acting independently ○ *I'll never forget all you've done for me, but it's time to cut the umbilical cord. I want you to go away. I need time alone to think.*

> An unborn baby's umbilical cord is the tube connecting it to its mother, through which it receives oxygen and nutrients.

core

★ **to the core** very much; deeply ○ *Father Carney said the community was shocked to the core.*

corner

★ **in a tight corner** or
in a corner in a situation that is difficult to deal with or escape from ○ *I was horrified at what I had done and knew I was in*

a tight corner and that everything depended upon my keeping my head.

in your corner supporting you and helping you ○ *Harry and I were encouraged. We felt we already had Bob in our corner.*

In a boxing match, each boxer is given a corner of the ring. Trainers and helpers come into a boxer's corner between rounds and give help and encouragement.

★ **just around the corner** about to happen ○ *With summer just around the corner, there couldn't be a better time to treat your home to a bright new look.*

paint yourself into a corner to put yourself in a difficult situation in which you have almost no choices ○ *I've been watching her these last few years. She's painted herself into a corner. She is trapped.*

"Paint yourself into a corner" refers to someone who is painting a floor and ends up in a corner of the room with wet paint all round them.

turn the corner to begin to recover from a serious illness or a difficult situation ○ *At last, Joe turned the corner.*

corners

★ **cut corners** to save time, money, or effort by not following the correct procedure or rules for doing something ○ *Don't try to cut any corners as you'll only be making work for yourself later on.*

four corners of the world or **four corners of the earth** all the different parts of the world ○ *A foreign correspondent makes friends in all four corners of the world.*

cost

★ **count the cost** to consider how much damage or harm has been caused ○ *Did Arizona politicians judiciously count the cost of the new immigration law?*

couch

★ **a couch potato** a person who spends

most of their time sitting around watching television ○ *In fact, we sit like a pair of couch potatoes in front of the television and watch her eat.*

This expression is a complicated pun based on the American slang term "boob tube" meaning the TV, and the fact that a potato is a variety of "tuber" (root vegetable).

count

The following expressions refer to a "count" in boxing. If a boxer is knocked to the ground and does not get up before the referee has counted to ten, they lose the contest.

down for the count unable to recover from a failure ○ *Without this business, our little town was down for the count.*

out for the count asleep or unconscious ○ *At 10:30 am he was still out for the count after another night disturbed by the crying baby.*

country

★ **you can take the boy out of the country but you can't take the country out of the boy** → see **boy**

courage

Dutch courage a sense of false confidence that comes from drinking alcohol ○ *The survey also noted how some performers used a little Dutch courage to overcome inhibitions.*

In the past, the Dutch had a reputation for drinking a lot of alcohol.

course

★ **on course for something** likely to achieve something ○ *Germany's blend of players from different cultures has put it on course for a fourth World Cup title.*

★ **run its course** or **take its course** to develop gradually and come to a natural end ○ *The real* recovery for the auto industry won't come until the recession runs its course.

★ **stay the course** to finish a difficult or unpleasant task, even though you have found it hard ○ *In Canada, where the infantry is open to women, very few have stayed the course.*

court

★ **hold court** to be surrounded by people who pay you a lot of attention because they consider you interesting or important ○ *She used to hold court in the student union with a host of admirers who hung on her every word.*

> "Court" in this expression refers to the court of a king or queen.

laughed out of court not taken seriously ○ *When one London architect suggested a similar idea to a British developer he was laughed out of court.*

> A plaintiff who is "out of court" has lost the right to be heard in a court of law.

pay court to someone to try to win the affection, approval, or favor of someone ○ *The rabbi's lawyer revealed that Katz's brother paid court to the rabbi's wife in a shocking manner.*

rule something out of court to make something impossible because of a situation ○ *I was going to start studying medicine in September but then in August I caught polio which clearly ruled it out of court.*

cover

blow someone's cover to reveal someone's secret identity or intentions ○ *Although the informant believed Barlow blew her cover, she says she still respects him as a police officer and viewed him as a friend.*

cow

have a cow to become very upset or angry ○ *Don't tell Dad; he'll have a cow if he ever finds out.*

a sacred cow a belief, opinion or tradition that people are not willing to criticize, question or change ○ *Israel's most sacred cow, its nuclear weapons, is under pressure from unexpected quarter.*

> In the Hindu religion, cows are regarded as sacred.

cows

until the cows come home for a very long time ○ *Your child will enjoy this lively DVD until the cows come home!*

> The full form of this expression is "until the cows come home unbidden" or without being asked.

crack

at the crack of dawn very early in the morning ○ *He was scheduled to get up at the crack of dawn for an interview on "Good Morning America."*

★ **have a crack at something** to try to do something difficult ○ *I've decided now to have a crack at the world cross-country race.*

cracked

★ **not all it's cracked up to be** not as good as many people say ○ *Resort package vacations are not always all they're cracked up to be.*

cracking

get cracking *(informal)* to start doing something immediately and quickly ○ *I realized that if we got cracking, we could make the last 700 miles to St. Lucia within our deadline.*

cracks

fall through the cracks or **slip through the cracks** to not be helped by a system which is supposed to help you. ○ *This family slipped through the cracks in the system so they are not eligible for aid.*

★ **paper over the cracks** to try to hide

the fact that something has gone badly wrong ○ *Accepting the mayor's resignation will only serve to paper over the cracks of a much more serious problem.*

cradle

cradle-snatching or
cradle-robbing having a relationship with a person who is very much younger. ○ *His uncle said: "His dad and I just can't believe it. The woman is even older than his mother. It's cradle snatching."*

from the cradle to the grave or
cradle-to-grave throughout all of a person's life ○ *The bloated oil resources at the disposal of the various ruling families have allowed the creation of gold-plated cradle-to-grave welfare states, where the locals want for little.*

rob the cradle to have a relationship with a person who is much younger. ○ *"I'll always be younger," he said, "and there'll always be those who might accuse you of robbing the cradle."*

crash

crash and burn to suddenly fail badly as a result of extreme tiredness or a big mistake ○ *Stress can cause over-achievers to crash and burn, and they can end up suffering from emotional disorders.*

≡ This may be a reference to a plane crashing into the ground and bursting into flames.

craw

something sticks in someone's craw said to mean that something that has happened or been said is upsetting to someone and they cannot accept it ○ *The one thing that really stuck in my craw was a remark that DW made.*

≡ "Craw" is an old word for a bird's throat, so the idea here is of something you have tried to swallow that gets stuck in your throat.

crazy

crazy as a bedbug or
crazy as a loon *(informal)* not at all sensible or practical ○ *By now she'd concluded that Skolnick was crazy as a bedbug.*

cream

the cream of the crop the best people or things in a particular set or group ○ *The first arts center show features the cream of the crop of this year's graduates in photography, film, and video.*

creature

creature comforts modern sleeping, eating and washing facilities ○ *Each room has its own patio or balcony and provides guests with all modern creature comforts.*

≡ This expression includes humans in the category of "creature" (any living being).

creek

up the creek or
up the creek without a paddle *(informal)* in a very difficult situation ○ *We're up the creek because we don't know where to go from here.*

≡ A creek is a small river. The idea is of being in a boat such as a canoe without being able to control it.

creeps

★ **give someone the creeps** to make someone feel nervous, afraid, or uncomfortable ○ *The possibility of beetle parts in the baby formula gives her the creeps.*

crest

on the crest of a wave very successful at what you are doing ○ *They are on the crest of a wave, winning games even when they don't play well*

≡ The crest of a wave is its highest point.

cricket

it's not cricket (British) used to say that someone's behavior is unfair or unreasonable ○ *The bank puts thousands of pounds a year into cricket – yet their treatment of staff is definitely not cricket.*

> Cricket is traditionally associated with the values of fairness and respect for other players.

crisp

burned to a crisp or
burnt to a crisp badly burned ○ *Customers who insist on having their food burnt to a crisp should get it that way.*

crocodile

shed crocodile tears to pretend to be sad or to sympathize with someone without really caring about them ○ *The rumor spread like wild fire that an eyewitness has seen how Chris shed "crocodile tears" during his performance.*

> There was an ancient belief that crocodiles sighed and groaned to attract their prey, and wept while they were eating it. This expression is often used without the verb "shed."

cropper

★ **come a cropper** (mainly British) to suffer a sudden and embarrassing failure ○ *Scott must concentrate on learning his new trade. He will come a cropper if he thinks he knows it all before he starts.*

> "Cropper" may come from the expression "to fall neck and crop," meaning to fall heavily. A bird's "crop" is a pouch in its throat where it keeps food before digesting it.

cross

a cross to bear a responsibility or an unpleasant situation that you must live with, because you cannot change it ○ *"My children are much smarter than me, it is a cross I have to bear," he quips at one point in the interview.*

> The reference here is to Jesus being made to carry the cross on which He was to die to the place of execution.

crossfire

caught in the crossfire suffering the unpleasant effects of a disagreement between other people even though you are not involved in it yourself ○ *But even before the reviews came in, Shyamalan was on the defensive, caught in the crossfire of a debate over ethnicity and authenticity.*

> This expression is more commonly used literally to talk about a situation where someone is in the way of two sets of people who are firing guns, and so is shot by mistake.

crow

as the crow flies in a straight line ○ *Although not distant as the crow flies from Tehran, this mountainous area has always been and still is remote.*

> It used to be believed that crows always traveled to their destination by the most direct route possible. "Make a beeline" is based on a similar idea.

eat crow to admit that you have been wrong and apologize, especially in a situation where this makes you feel ashamed. ○ *But by the end of the year, Safire showed he was willing to eat crow. His first judgments of Watergate, he wrote, had been "really wrong."*

> This expression is said to relate to an incident during the War of 1812. An American soldier who had accidentally entered an area occupied by the British was tricked into handing over his gun. He was then forced by a British officer to take a bite out of a crow which he had shot down. When his gun was returned to him, he forced the British officer to eat the rest of the bird.

crunch

★ **when it comes to the crunch** when a situation reaches a very important or difficult point and you must make a decision on how to progress ○ *When it comes to the crunch, I'd rather have you on my side than anyone else.*

> "Crunch" is the sound used to imitate the sound of something hard being crushed, broken or eaten.

crust

the upper crust the richest people in a society or group from the highest class ○ *Last Tuesday, the upper crust of South Carolina's Republican establishment gathered at the home of the state party chair.*

> Crust is the brownish part of bread on the outside of a loaf. There are several stories about the origin of this expression but none has been proven.

cry

★ **a far cry from something** very different from something mentioned or experienced earlier ○ *It isn't a perfect democracy, but it's a far cry from the authoritarian rule of only a few years ago.*

cudgels

take up the cudgels to speak up or fight in support of someone ○ *The union took up the cudgels for the 367 employees who were made laid off.*

> A cudgel was a short, thick stick that was used as a weapon in the past.

cue

take your cue from someone to copy someone else's behavior or start to have the same opinions ○ *Remember that children will be watching and listening for their parent's reactions and will take their cue from them.*

cuff

★ **off-the-cuff** not prepared or carefully thought out ○ *The singer offered an apology last night, saying: "I'm sorry. I didn't mean any offense. It was a flippant, off-the-cuff remark."*

> One explanation for this expression is that after-dinner speakers used to write notes on the cuffs of their shirts, to remind them of what to say. Another explanation is that in the early days of movies, directors sometimes wrote notes on their cuffs during the filming of a scene, to remind them of what they wanted to say to the actors.

cup

★ **not someone's cup of tea** not very interesting to someone ○ *It's no secret that I've never been the greatest traveler. Sitting for hours on interstates is not my cup of tea.*

cupboard

the cupboard is bare said to mean that everything has been used and there is nothing left ○ *He says the cupboard is bare, but somehow the managers have been paid huge bonuses.*

> The expression comes from a children's nursery rhyme called "Old Mother Hubbard." In it, an old woman goes to a cupboard to get a bone for her dog, "but when she got there, the cupboard was bare," that is, empty.

curiosity

curiosity killed the cat said to warn someone that they will suffer harm or damage if they try to find out about other people's private affairs ○ *"Where are we going?" Calder asked. "Curiosity killed the cat, dear. You'll find out soon enough."*

curtain

★ **bring the curtain down on something** to cause or mark the end of an event or situation ○ *Richardson brings* the curtain down on one of the most amazing managerial careers of all-time this weekend.

In theaters, it is traditional for a curtain to come down in front of the stage at the end of each act and at the end of the play.

curtains

it's curtains used to say that a very undesirable outcome will result ○ *If the vote is yes, it's curtains for us. A way of life will disappear.*

The curtains referred to here are the curtains at the front of the stage in a theater.

curve

throw someone a curve ball to surprise someone by doing something unexpected, sometimes putting them at a disadvantage ○ *Our plan is to go into the winter with our reservoirs full, just in case Mother Nature throws us a curve ball next spring.*

A "curve ball" is a pitched baseball that curves through the air rather than travelling in a straight line.

cut

★ **a cut above (the rest)** much better than other similar people or things ○ *Smith's detective stories are generally agreed to be a cut above the rest.*

★ **cut and dried** clear and definite ○ *Now, this situation is not as cut-and-dried as it may seem.*

One explanation for this expression is that it refers to wood that has been cut and dried and is ready to use. Alternatively, it may refer to herbs that

have been harvested and dried, to be used for cooking and medicine.

cut and run to escape from a difficult situation quickly, rather than dealing with it in a responsible way ○ *He had an unfortunate tendency to cut and run when things didn't go his way.*

In the past, ships' anchors were attached to ropes. If a warship was attacked, rather than causing delay by pulling up the anchor, the sailors would sometimes cut the rope.

★ **the cut and thrust** the aspects of a particular activity or society that make it exciting and challenging ○ *Why does he want to go back into the cut and thrust of business at an age when most men are happily retired?*

This expression comes from sword fighting.

not be cut out for something to lack the right qualities or character for a particular lifestyle or job ○ *As you'll have gathered, I left medicine anyway. I wasn't really cut out for it.*

someone cannot cut it used to say that someone is not good enough at doing something ○ *Many managers can't cut it at the highest level.*

cylinders

★ **fire on all (four) cylinders** to do a task with great enthusiasm and energy ○ *I saw her a few weeks ago and she was firing on all cylinders. I don't think she would know what to do with herself if she didn't work.*

This expression refers to the cylinders in an engine. There are usually four of them.

Dd

dab

a little dab will do ya *(informal)* said to mean that a small quantity is enough ○ *The thing to remember about cooking with shrimp paste is that a little dab will do ya.*

This expression was originally an advertising slogan for hair cream in the 1960s.

daggers

at daggers drawn if two people are at daggers drawn, they are very angry with each other after an argument ○ *The couple have been at daggers drawn since they separated six months ago.*

look daggers at someone *(literary)* to stare at someone in a very angry way ○ *He looked daggers at Mary as if it had all been her fault.*

daisies

pushing up the daisies dead. This expression is used to refer to someone's death in a light-hearted or humorous way. ○ *That was the last time I saw the old rogue. I can only assume he's either in prison or pushing up the daisies.*

damper

★ **put a damper on something** to stop something being as successful or as enjoyable as it might be ○ *The cold weather put a damper on our picnic.*

This expression may refer to either of two meanings of "damper." In a piano, a damper is a device which presses the strings and stops them vibrating, so stopping the sound. In a chimney or flue, a damper is a movable metal plate that controls the amount of air getting to the fire, and so controls how fiercely the fire burns.

dander

get someone's dander up *(old-fashioned)* to annoy someone ○ *His last poll got a lot of people's danders up because he asked them to list the worst Americans in history.*

dark

★ **be in the dark about something** to know nothing about something ○ *The sooner we can find out what has happened, the better for all of us. But at the moment I'm in the dark.*

keep something dark to keep something a secret ○ *She took pleasure in keeping dark the identity of her new boyfriend.*

a leap in the dark a situation in which you do not know what the results of an action will be, usually when you feel you have no other choice but to take this course of action ○ *The couple have taken a leap in the dark, selling their home in Chicago and buying 10 acres of land in the country.*

a shot in the dark a complete guess about something ○ *It was just a shot in the dark but it was the right answer.*

whistle in the dark to try not to show that you are afraid, or to try to believe that a situation is not as bad as it seems ○ *Maggie started telling jokes, trying to keep up everyone's spirits, but we all knew she was just whistling in the dark.*

date

★ **past your sell-by date** no longer useful, successful, or relevant ○ *This type of TV program is well past its sell-by date.*

Most food has a date stamped on its packaging: this is its sell-by date. After this date it is no longer fresh enough to sell.

dawn

★ **a false dawn** (*journalism*) a situation in which you think that something is finally going to improve but it does not ○ *National elections are scheduled for next year, but this country has seen many false dawns before. Is it really heading for democracy and peace this time?*

day

at the end of the day (*spoken*) said just before or after the thing that you think is the most important aspect of a situation ○ *At the end of the day, it's the Germans who will decide.*

★ **call it a day**
1 to decide to stop doing something, usually because you are tired or are bored with it ○ *I searched for the cat for hours but I had to call it a day when darkness fell.*
2 to retire from your job ○ *It's no secret I want his job when he calls it a day.*

★ **carry the day** (*journalism*) if a person or their opinion carries the day in a contest or debate, they win it ○ *Dr. Mead's argument carried the day.*

  This expression was originally used to say which army had won a battle.

the day of reckoning the time when people are forced to deal with an unpleasant situation that they have avoided until now ○ *The president has broken many laws, and his day of reckoning is approaching.*

  According to the Bible, when the world ends, there will be a day of reckoning or day of judgment, when God will judge everyone's actions and send them either to heaven or hell.

day one the first day of something that lasts a considerable amount of time; the very beginning ○ *Our goal is to make sure the bus is ready for the kids from day one.*

don't quit your day job said when you want to suggest that someone should continue to do their normal job rather than trying something new that is difficult or that is not secure. This expression is usually used humorously. ○ *I started my business in the middle of a recession. People thought I was mad and said: "Don't quit your day job."*

have your day in court to have an opportunity to explain your actions or defend yourself ○ *My client wants to have his day in court so that he can prove his innocence.*

★ **late in the day** at the very last moment or in the final stages of a situation, with the result that action may no longer be effective ○ *She feels that it is too late in the day for him to start behaving like a loving husband.*

make my day said when you want to challenge another person to compete or argue with you, so that you can prove that you are stronger and better than they are ○ *"Do you want a fight?" – "Go ahead. Make my day."*

  In the film "Sudden Impact" (1983), Clint Eastwood, playing a detective called Harry, uses this expression to challenge a criminal who is threatening to shoot him.

★ **make someone's day** to do something that makes someone feel very happy ○ *Make your Mom a special card and tell her that you love her. It will make her day.*

save for a rainy day to save some of your money in case there are serious problems in the future ○ *Saving for a rainy day and paying off debts is now a top priority for families.*

seize the day do what is important now, and do not worry about the future ○ *Don't waste your life. Seize the day.*

  This is a translation of the Latin phrase *carpe diem*, which is also sometimes used.

★ **someone has had their day** used to

say that the period during which someone was most successful has now passed ○ *He's done well but, at 60, he has had his day.*

something is all in a day's work something that most people would consider difficult, unusual, or exciting is easy or normal because it is part of your job, or because you often experience this kind of thing ○ *For war reporters, dodging snipers' bullets is all in a day's work.*

daylight

★ **do something in broad daylight** to do something illegal or bad openly in the daytime, when people can see it. This expression is often used to emphasize behavior that is surprising or shocking. ○ *The paintings – valued at $20 million – were stolen in broad daylight by armed men, as some forty visitors looked on.*

daylights

beat the living daylights out of someone

1 to attack someone physically, hitting them many times ○ *The two men were beating the living daylights out of each other.*
2 to defeat someone totally in a competition or contest ○ *He enjoys the money and the fame but his true pleasure comes from walking on to a golf course and beating the living daylights out of everyone else.*

The word "daylights" in this expression may be related to an old threat to "make daylight shine through" someone by stabbing them or shooting them. Alternatively, it may be related to an old meaning of "daylights" referring to someone's eyes or internal organs. If they were badly beaten, their "daylights" would stop working.

scare the living daylights out of someone to frighten someone very much ○ *You scared the living daylights out of me last night. All that screaming.*

days

★ **the good old days** an earlier time, when life was better ○ *They say they want to return the country to the good old days, but what do they mean?*

★ **someone's days are numbered** used to say that someone is not likely to survive or be successful for much longer ○ *As rebels advanced on the capital it became clear that the President's days in power were numbered.*

something has seen better days used to describe something that is old and in poor condition ○ *There was an old brass double bed with a mattress that had seen better days.*

dead

be dead set against something to be completely opposed to something ○ *We are dead set against people keeping chimpanzees as pets.*

be dead set on doing something to be strongly determined to do something ○ *Industries are dead set on blocking the new regulations.*

come back from the dead to become active or successful again after a period of being inactive or unsuccessful ○ *I could not believe I had done it. I had come back from the dead and my career had survived the ultimate test.*

dead as a dodo no longer active or popular ○ *The floppy disk is an invention that is now as dead as a dodo.*

The dodo was a large flightless bird that lived on the islands of Mauritius and Réunion. It became extinct in the late 17th century as a result of hunting and the destruction of its nests by settlers on the islands.

dead as a doornail dead, or no longer active or popular ○ *In 1964, people said the Republican Party was dead as a doornail.*

It is not certain what "doornail" actually refers to. In medieval times, it may have been the plate or knob on a door which was hit by the knocker. It was thought that anything that was struck so often must have been dead. Alternatively, doornails may have been the thick nails which were set into outer doors. It is not clear why these nails should be described as "dead."

drop dead used, usually in anger, to tell someone to go away and leave you alone because you are very angry or annoyed with them ○ *Richard told me to drop dead.*

★ **drop-dead gorgeous** *(informal)* very attractive or beautiful ○ *She's funny, kind, clever -- and drop-dead gorgeous.*

knock 'em dead! *(informal)* said to someone to increase their confidence before they appear or do something in public, especially something formal such as giving a speech in front of a crowd ○ *Just look 'em in the eye and knock 'em dead!*

The word "'em" is a form of "them" used in informal or non-standard English.

★ **someone wouldn't be seen dead** used to say that someone strongly dislikes or disapproves of something ○ *Vincent wouldn't be seen dead in a pair of sneakers and a baseball cap.*

deal

cut a deal to come to an agreement with someone in which each side will benefit ○ *The two companies have finally cut a deal, ensuring that the networks will remain on air.*

a done deal a plan or project that has been completed or arranged and that cannot now be changed ○ *The takeover proposal, however, is not a done deal as the company's shareholders must first approve the plan.*

★ **get a raw deal** to be treated unfairly or badly ○ *We must ask why bank customers get such a raw deal. And then find ways to*

make sure they get treated fairly in future.

This may refer to someone being dealt a bad hand in a game of cards.

death

at death's door seriously ill and likely to die very soon ○ *He has won five golf competitions in three months, a year after being at death's door.*

a death blow an act or event that causes a process, a situation, or an organization to come to an end ○ *They warned that the incidents would be a death blow to the Middle East peace process.*

dice with death to do something very dangerous that could kill you ○ *In their daily lives, fishermen are constantly dicing with death.*

To dice means to play dice, or to gamble.

death and taxes used to talk about things that are completely certain and cannot be avoided in any circumstances ○ *After that, the team's failures became as inevitable as death and taxes.*

★ **fight to the death to do something** to try very hard to achieve something or to keep hold of something, refusing to give up ○ *"I will fight to the death to win – whatever it takes."*

a living death an extremely poor quality of life, such as one due to extreme illness ○ *For nearly four years he has been in a coma, kept alive by medical equipment, but trapped in what one doctor described as a "living death."*

look like death warmed over to look very ill, pale, and tired ○ *You were looking like death warmed over, but you seem a lot better now.*

★ **sign someone's or something's death warrant** to cause the death or end of someone or something ○ *The company's flawed business strategy has signed the death warrants for thousands of jobs.*

A death warrant is an official document that orders that someone is to be executed as a punishment for a crime.

★ **sound the death knell** to be likely to cause the end or failure of an activity or organization ○ *The announcement that the mine would close in March with the loss of more than 980 jobs sounded the death knell for the village.*

A death knell is the ringing of a church bell at a funeral or to announce someone's death.

★ **to death** used after adjectives such as "scared," "worried," and "bored" to mean "very" ○ *She was scared to death that he would leave her.*

deck

all hands on deck said when a particular situation requires everyone to work hard in order to achieve an aim ○ *We had less than three weeks to organize the wedding, so it was all hands on deck*

Members of a ship's crew are sometimes called hands and "deck" refers to the floor of a ship.

hit the deck to suddenly fall to the ground ○ *When we heard the sound of gunfire, we hit the deck and covered our heads with our hands.*

"Deck" normally means the floor of a ship or a raised platform outside a house. Here it means the floor or ground.

not play with a full deck to be slightly crazy or mentally handicapped ○ *I wish her daughters well because they seem so nice and sweet, but clearly their dingbat mother is not playing with a full deck.*

In this expression, "full deck" means a complete set of playing cards and the implication is that someone is missing something important. It would be offensive to use this expression about someone with a known mental disability.

stack the deck to arrange a situation unfairly against someone, or in your own favor ○ *The President is doing everything in his power to stack the deck in his favor and guarantee his regime's return to power.*

The literal meaning of this expression is to cheat when shuffling cards by secretly putting them in an order that is to your advantage.

decks

★ **clear the decks** to make sure that everything that you have been doing is completely finished, so that you are ready to start a more important task ○ *Clear the decks before you think of taking on any more responsibilities.*

In the past, all unnecessary objects were cleared off the decks or floors of a warship before a battle, so that the crew could move around more easily.

deep

★ **deep six someone or something** to get rid of someone or something permanently ○ *Opposition from members may result in the plans being deep sixed.*

This expression originally referred to burial at sea.

★ **run deep** if a feeling or a problem runs deep, it is very serious or strong, often because it has existed for a long time ○ *My allegiance to Kendall and his company ran deep.*

deer

like a deer in the headlights unable to act because of fear or confusion ○ *He's like a deer in headlights. He didn't see this coming and he's unaware of why it came.*

This expression refers to the way a deer will sometimes stand still in the road because it is temporarily blinded by a car's headlights.

degree

give someone the third degree
(informal) to ask someone a lot of
questions in an aggressive way in order
to find out information ○ *My girlfriend
gives me the third degree every time I go out
without her. She wants to know where I've
been and who I've spoken to.*

den

★ **a den of iniquity** a place where people
behave immorally or illegally ○ *Police
have described the dance bar as a den of
iniquity which must be closed down.*

dent

★ **make a dent in something** to reduce
the amount or level of something ○ *The
average family in Dallas spends $200 a week
on food, which makes a big dent in the
household budget.*

department

something is not your department
said to indicate that you are not
responsible for a particular task, or you
do not know much about a particular
subject ○ *The political issues are something
else, but that's not really my department.*

depth

★ **out of your depth** feeling anxious and
inadequate because you have to deal
with a situation or subject which you
know very little about ○ *When I first
started my new job, I felt out of my depth, but
now I love it.*

This expression refers to someone who
is in deep water but cannot swim very
well, or cannot swim at all.

depths

plumb the depths
1 to be an example of extremely bad
behavior ○ *"This crime plumbs the very
depths of the abyss into which it is possible
for the human spirit to sink," the judge said.*
2 to find out everything you can about

something, including things that are
normally secret or hidden ○ *In his writings
Shakespeare plumbed the depths of human
psychology.*
3 to experience an unpleasant or difficult
situation to an extreme degree ○ *They
frequently plumb the depths of loneliness,
humiliation and despair.*

The above expressions relate to sailing
in former times. When a ship was in
shallow water one of the sailors would
find out how deep the water was by
dropping a piece of lead on a string,
called a "plumb," over the side of the
ship.

deserts

The noun "deserts" is related to the
verb "deserve," and it is pronounced
with stress on its second syllable.
"Deserts" is an old-fashioned word
meaning a reward or punishment
which is deserved.

★ **get your just deserts** to deserve the
unpleasant things that have happened to
you, because you have done something
bad ○ *Some people felt sympathy for the
humbled superstar. Others felt she was
getting her just deserts for years of
outrageous behavior.*

designs

have designs on someone to want to
have a relationship with another person,
especially when the second person is not
interested, or is already in a relationship
with someone else ○ *He had a feeling that
Francine had designs on him.*
have designs on something to want
something and to plan to get it,
sometimes in a dishonest way ○ *He has
designs on the top job at the company.*

devices

★ **be left to your own devices** to be left
to do what you want, or to look after

yourself without any help from other people ○ *If left to my own devices, I would eat a chocolate dessert every night.*

≣ An old meaning of "device" was desire
≣ or will.

devil

be between the devil and the deep blue sea to be in a difficult situation where the two possible courses of action or choices that you can take are equally bad ○ *We are between the devil and the deep blue sea: if we pay our rent, we won't have any money for food.*

≣ The origin of this expression is in
≣ shipping, not religion. It is unclear
≣ exactly what the "devil" was, but it is
≣ thought to have been some kind of
≣ seam or plank that was awkward and
≣ dangerous to reach, so a sailor who
≣ had to make it waterproof was in a
≣ very unsafe position, and risked falling
≣ into the water.

better the devil you know used to express the idea that it is better to deal with someone you already know, even if you do not like them, than to deal with someone that you know nothing about, because they may be even worse ○ *It is becoming clearer to them that he is no angel; but better the devil you know.*

have a devil of a job or
have the devil's own job to manage to do something, but only after a lot of difficulty ○ *We got there just in time, but we had a devil of a job finding her in that place.*

speak of the devil or
talk of the devil *(spoken)* said when someone you have just been talking about arrives unexpectedly ○ *"Speak of the devil," she greeted Tom, smiling.*

≣ This expression comes from the
≣ saying "talk of the devil and he will
≣ appear."

diamond

A rough diamond is a diamond that has not yet been cut and polished.

a diamond in the rough *(American)* or
a rough diamond *(mainly British)* someone or something that has a lot of talent or potential but that needs hard work before this talent or potential can be revealed ○ *He may be that diamond in the rough Michigan State fans have looked for since Javon Ringer graduated.*

dibs

(first) dibs on something the right to get or use something before anyone else ○ *She got to the store long before it opened to get first dibs on the sale items.*

≣ This expression comes from an old
≣ children's game in which the pieces
≣ were called dib stones.

dice

the dice are loaded against someone used when everything seems to work to the disadvantage of someone, so that they are unlikely ever to have success ○ *I survived that night on the mountain when all the dice were loaded against me.*

≣ Players who wanted to cheat at dice
≣ games sometimes "loaded" or
≣ weighted the dice so that they tended
≣ to fall in a particular way.

no dice
1 said when you are trying to achieve something but you are having no luck or success with it ○ *I spent part of that time calling everyone I knew to see if I could find another job for him. No dice.*
2 said when you are refusing to do what someone has asked you to do ○ *Nope, sorry, we're not interested, no dice.*

≣ This expression comes from the game
≣ of craps, and means that the player's

last throw is disqualified and not counted.

diddly

★ **not mean diddly** to be completely meaningless or unimportant ○ *Raindrops don't mean diddly to football fans, so bring your rain jackets and have some fun.*

die

the die is cast said when an important decision has been made about the future and it is impossible to change it, even if things go wrong ○ *I have made this decision to get a puppy. In fact, the die is cast: I have already paid for it.*

"Die" is a singular form of the word "dice." Once you have thrown the dice, you cannot do anything to change the way they fall.

★ **to die for** (*informal*) very good or attractive ○ *The food here is to die for, it's heaven on a plate.*

dime

a dime a dozen existing in large numbers and therefore not especially valuable or interesting. In British English, use **two a penny**. ○ *Action movies are a dime a dozen these days.*

in for a dime, in for a dollar said when you are firmly committed to a particular course of action, even though it will probably cost a lot of money or use a lot of resources if you continue ○ *In for a dime, in for a dollar. I took the jacket to the counter.*

turn on a dime to suddenly do something completely different from what you were doing before ○ *Nowadays businesses need to be flexible and to change, and sometimes to turn on a dime in order to stay competitive.*

The idea is of being able to maneuver quickly and easily in a small space, like stopping and changing direction with your foot still on the coin. The expression is also used of cars.

dint

by dint of something because of or as a result of something ○ *He achieved his legendary status by dint of hard work and perfect instincts.*

direction

point someone in the right direction to give someone the information they need to continue with something ○ *If you need help choosing a computer, this guide will point you in the right direction.*

dirt

common as dirt → see **common**

★ **dig up dirt on someone**

★ **dig the dirt on someone** to search for any information about someone that may damage their reputation ○ *They hired a detective firm to dig up dirt on their rival.*

dish the dirt on someone to spread stories about someone, especially things that may embarrass or upset them, or damage their reputation ○ *Many politicians, who protest that their private lives are their own, are quite happy to dish the dirt on a fellow politician.*

do someone dirt or

do the dirt on someone to betray someone or treat them very badly ○ *They tell me you have done me dirt. Tell me it ain't true.*

treat someone like dirt to treat someone very badly ○ *I am in awe of teachers who hang on to their careers even though they are treated like dirt.*

distance

★ **go the distance** to complete what you are doing and reach your goal ○ *Dave Hilton failed to go the distance when he was forced off the field in the second half with a leg injury.*

A boxer who succeeds in fighting until the end of the match is said to "go the distance."

within spitting distance

1 very close to a particular place ○ *Most of the world's biggest financial firms are already established within spitting distance of Wall Street.*

2 very close to achieving an amount, a level, or a goal ○ *We are now within spitting distance of our goal. We've raised $9542.55. Just $457.45 to go.*

★ **within striking distance**

1 very close to a particular place ○ *Hurricane Earl is expected to move within striking distance of the county Friday.*

2 very close to achieving an amount, a level, or a place ○ *He is within striking distance of victory in the election.*

distraction

drive someone to distraction to annoy someone very much ○ *Nothing I said or did would get them to tidy up their bedrooms. It drove me to distraction.*

≣ Distraction is an old word for
≣ madness.

ditch

★ **a last ditch attempt** an action performed when everything else has failed, as a final attempt to avoid disaster, although it too seems likely to fail ○ *The President has been making a last ditch attempt to prevent the rebels taking over the city.*

≣ In this expression, "ditch" means a
≣ trench that has been dug in order to
≣ defend a military position. The
≣ expression refers to soldiers who are
≣ prepared to die in a final effort to
≣ defend the position rather than
≣ surrender.

divide

★ **divide and conquer** a strategy by which someone remains in power by making sure that the people under their control fight among themselves and so cannot unite to achieve their aims and overthrow their leader ○ *Unions are concerned that management may be tempted into a policy of divide and conquer.*

≣ This expression has its origin in the
≣ Latin phrase *divide et impera*. It
≣ describes one of the tactics that the
≣ Romans used to rule their empire.

dividends

★ **pay dividends** to bring a lot of advantages at a later date ○ *Taking time out to get in shape is time well spent and will pay dividends in the long run.*

≣ A dividend is a payment of profits that
≣ is divided among all the shareholders
≣ of a company.

Dixie

someone is not just whistling Dixie used to express that someone is being honest or realistic in what they are saying and that they should therefore not be ignored ○ *"Is that a threat?" "I'm not just whistling Dixie."*

≣ Dixie was the name given to the states
≣ that formed the Confederate side in
≣ the Civil War. The area gave its name to
≣ several songs which were popular as
≣ Confederate war songs.

doctor

just what the doctor ordered extremely pleasant or useful and helping to make you feel better or to improve a situation ○ *"Meatballs in tomato sauce!" Max exclaimed happily. "Just what the doctor ordered."*

dog

a dog and pony show an event with a lot of exciting things happening that has been organized in order to impress someone ○ *We bombarded the management team with charts, graphs, facts, and figures. Our boss responded by dozing off during most of our dog and pony show.*

This expression refers to circus acts involving dogs and horses.

the dog days

1 the hottest days of the year, which occur in July and August in the northern hemisphere ○ *We spent the dog days of summer in the mountains of Arizona.*
2 a period in someone's life or career when they are not having much success or are not making any progress ○ *Those were the dog days of the Neo-Conservative movement.*

The ancient Romans named these days *dies caniculares* or "dog days" because the Dog Star, Sirius, could be seen in the morning sky at this time of year. They believed that the combination of Sirius and the sun produced very hot weather.

dog eat dog used for describing a situation in which everyone wants to succeed and is willing to harm other people or to use dishonest methods in order to do this ○ *In the 1992 campaign, he said that if it was going to be "dog eat dog" he would do anything it took to get himself re-elected.*

dog-in-the-manger (mainly British) wanting to prevent other people from using or enjoying something simply because you cannot use or enjoy it yourself ○ *On the one hand the city council has a high regard for the carnival's tourist benefits, but on the other it does not want it to have too high a profile. It's a dog-in-the-manger attitude which has taken the fun out of a great event.*

One of Aesop's fables tells of a dog that prevented an ox from eating the hay in its manger, even though the dog could not eat the hay itself.

a dog's breakfast or
a dog's dinner (mainly British) a situation, event, or piece of work that is chaotic, badly organized, or very untidy ○ *The government's latest proposals are a dog's breakfast.*

every dog has its day everyone will be successful or lucky at some time in their life. This expression is sometimes used to encourage someone at a time when they are not having any success or luck. ○ *I've been waiting a long time for success – four years – but every dog has its day.*

This proverb has been known in English since at least the 16th century. Shakespeare quotes it in "Hamlet": "Let Hercules himself do what he may, The cat will mew and dog will have his day." (Act 5, Scene 1).

it's a dog's life used to suggest that a job or situation is unpleasant or boring ○ *It's a dog's life being a football coach.*
you can't teach an old dog new tricks used to emphasize that it is often difficult to get people to try new ways of doing things, especially if these people have been doing something in a particular way for a long time ○ *I'm 65 and you can't teach an old dog new tricks.*

doghouse

be in the doghouse to have made people very annoyed with you because of something you have done ○ *Four ambassadors have landed themselves in the doghouse after failing to turn up to a meeting at the White House.*

dogs

call off the dogs to tell someone to stop criticizing, attacking, or damaging another person ○ *After years of persecution, it's time to call off the dogs. He's been punished enough.*

The dogs referred to here are dogs used for hunting.

go to the dogs if a country, organization, or business is going to the dogs, it is becoming less powerful or

successful than it has been in the past
○ *If you ask me, the whole country is going to the dogs.*

let sleeping dogs lie said to warn someone not to disturb or interfere with a situation, because they are likely to cause trouble and problems ○ *Why does she come over here and stir everything up? Why can't she let sleeping dogs lie?*

throw someone to the dogs to allow someone to be criticized severely or treated badly, for example in order to protect yourself from criticism or harm, or because you no longer need them ○ *He will trick you, use you, and throw you to the dogs. He'll do anything to save his own skin.*

≣ The dogs referred to here are dogs used for hunting.

doldrums

★ **be in the doldrums**

1 if an economy or business is in the doldrums, nothing new is happening and it is not doing well ○ *Property prices remain in the doldrums.*

2 to be sad and have no energy or enthusiasm ○ *At that time Freddie had just lost his job and was in the doldrums.*

come out of the doldrums

1 if an economy or business comes out of the doldrums, it improves and becomes stronger after a period of inactivity ○ *Let's hope that the economy may finally be coming out of the doldrums.*

2 to stop being sad and start to feel happier ○ *With the help of my family and friends, I eventually came out of the doldrums.*

≣ The above expressions relate to the Doldrums, which is an area of sea near the equator where there is often little or no wind. This meant that sailing ships could be stuck there for long periods.

dollar

the 64,000 dollar question a very important question that is very difficult to answer ○ *They asked the 64,000 dollar question: "So what makes a good marriage?"*

≣ In the United States in the 1940s, there was a radio quiz show called "Take It or Leave It." Contestants had to answer questions for prizes ranging from two dollars for an easy question to $64 for the hardest. A similar television quiz show in the 1950s increased the prize to $64,000.

you can bet your bottom dollar said to emphasize that you are absolutely certain that something will happen or that something is true ○ *A police insider was quoted as saying of the crime: "You can bet your bottom dollar Sinclair was involved."*

≣ This expression refers to the piles of coins on a poker table. A confident player would bet by pushing a pile of coins to the center of the table using the bottom dollar, on which all the others were resting.

dollars

(bet) dollars to doughnuts said to show that you are certain that something will happen ○ *I'll bet you dollars to doughnuts that, if nothing else, you'll hear back..*

feel a million dollars to feel very healthy and happy ○ *After all my recent problems, I now feel a million dollars.*

look a million dollars to look extremely attractive and well-dressed ○ *She looked a million dollars when she got off the plane.*

domino

★ **a domino effect** a situation in which one event causes another similar event, which in turn causes a further event, and so on ○ *The accident created a domino effect, causing about 10 other cars to crash* *and injuring 14 other people.*

> This expression was first used in the 1950s by an American political commentator to describe what some people thought would happen if one country in a region became Communist: they believed that the other countries in that area would also "fall" to the Communists. The image is of a row of upright dominoes; if one falls, it knocks the next one over and so on, until all of them have fallen over.

dominoes

fall like dominoes to end, be damaged, or be destroyed quickly in large numbers ○ *Personal records fell like dominoes for the girl's cross country team last week.*

done

be done for to be very likely to fail or suffer a bad experience ○ *I knew my diet was done for when they put up a McDonalds right next to the dorm.*

doo-doo

in deep doo-doo in serious trouble ○ *If we can't afford basic civic protections, we are in really deep doo-doo.*

> "Doo-doo" is a children's word for solid bodily waste.

door

be knocking at someone's door to be likely to happen soon, or to be starting to happen ○ *Mike was in terrible trouble but it wasn't long before help was knocking at his door.*

closing the barn door after the horse has gone acting too late, because the problem that the action would have prevented has already occurred ○ *It is good to see the government taking positive action, even though it might look like closing the barn door after the horse has gone.*

door to door calling at every house, apartment, business, etc. in an area ○ *Volunteers go door to door and talk to residents about crime.*

★ **do something by the back door** to do something secretly and unofficially ○ *He said the governor would not allow anyone to sneak in by the back door and seize power by force.*

knock on the door of something to try to join a club or a group, or to try to become part of it ○ *These two players will, I'm sure, soon be knocking on the door of the national team.*

★ **lay something at someone's door** to blame someone for something unpleasant that has happened ○ *We have no doubt about who is responsible for the riot. The blame must be laid at the door of the government.*

one door closes and another one opens said to mean that if one thing you do fails, you will soon have an opportunity to try to succeed at something else. This expression is often used to encourage someone to keep trying after they have had a disappointment or failure. ○ *Robert was philosophical after losing his job. "Obviously, I am disappointed," he explained. "But one door closes and another one opens."*

the revolving door

1 a situation in which the people working in a particular organization do not stay there for very long, and so it is difficult for anything effective to be achieved ○ *The revolving door on the boardroom has continued to turn, with Victoria Jones becoming the sixth chief executive to leave in the past ten years.*

2 a situation in politics in which someone moves from an important position in government to a position in a private company, especially where this may give them an unfair advantage. ○ *Bill Clinton ran a campaign that included a* strong pledge to stop the revolving door between public service and the private sector. **3** a situation where solutions to problems last for only a short time, and then the same problems occur again ○ *These young people are caught in the revolving door of the justice system, ending up back on the streets after serving time in prison.*

doors

★ **do something behind closed doors** (journalism) to do something in private because you want it to be kept secret ○ *The summer I was fourteen and Rita was twelve, our parents started having long talks behind closed doors.*

dos

★ **the dos and don'ts of something** the things that you should and should not do in a particular situation ○ *The publisher produces a detailed booklet full of dos and don'ts for aspiring authors of romantic fiction, stressing that the story must always have a happy ending.*

dot

do something on the dot to do something at exactly the time you are supposed to do it ○ *They have breakfast at nine o'clock on the dot.*

> The minutes on a clock face are often marked by dots.

double

on the double very quickly or immediately ○ *Michael reached for his phone. "Jill? My office, please, on the double."*

> "On the double" is a military expression meaning at twice the normal marching pace.

down

★ **be down to something** to be the cause or reason for something ○ *Much of their success was down to the choice of very*

high-quality players.

be down with something to be in agreement with an idea or suggestion ○ *If you guys want to eat first and then go to the movie, I'm down with that.*

★ **be going down the drain** or **be going down the tubes** to be getting worse or to be being destroyed, with little hope of recovery ○ *Small businesses are going down the drain because of the failed economic policies of this government.*

down and dirty bold, direct, and sometimes rude ○ *The film portrays the rock band at their most down and dirty.*

★ **down and out**
1 having nowhere to live, no job, and no real hope of improving your situation ○ *Having been down and out himself, Barry understands the problems, and he's helped many people to find homes and jobs.* ○ *There are hundreds of down and outs living just a few yards from his palace.*
2 having been beaten, or having lost badly, in a competition or contest ○ *From this newspaper article, you will see that Ted appears to be down and out as candidate for governor.*

> If boxers are down and out, they have been knocked down and have failed to get up before the referee counted to ten, and have therefore lost the contest.

down-at-the-heels or **down-at-heels** untidy and not cared for ○ *The flight to Kathmandu is always full of scruffy, down-at-the-heels people like Hyde.*

> The image here is of a person wearing shoes with worn-down heels because they do not have the money to repair or replace them.

downhill

be (all) downhill from here or **be (all) downhill from there**
1 to be easier because the most difficult

part is now finished ○ *The weather has really improved so the driving should be all downhill from here.*

2 to get much worse because of a sudden change ○ *After that loss his career was all downhill from there.*

drag

★ **drag your feet** or
drag your heels to deliberately delay making a decision about something that is important to you ○ *There's been substantial criticism of the United States for dragging its feet on measures to protect the environment.*

drain

be going down the drain or
go down the drain → see **down**

drawer

★ **top drawer** (*mainly British*) among the best of a particular kind ○ *The Grange Hotel may be top drawer, but it's not pretentious.* ○ *The play has a top-drawer cast including Maria Aitken and Tim Piggot-Smith.*

dream

★ **do something like a dream** to do something very well ○ *She had noticed, from across the dance floor, that he danced like a dream.*

★ **a dream ticket** (*journalism*) two or more well-known people, for example politicians or actors, who are expected to work well together and to have a great deal of success ○ *It should have been Hollywood's dream ticket: husband and wife starring together in a romantic blockbuster movie.*

In the United States, a ticket is a list of candidates that a political party has nominated for election. A "dream ticket" is a pair of candidates that seem to be perfectly matched and who will attract a lot of support.

dreams

★ **beyond your wildest dreams** better than you could have imagined or hoped for ○ *The response of viewers to our charity appeal was beyond our wildest dreams. The money just kept pouring in.*

never in your wildest dreams said to emphasize that you think that something is extremely strange or unlikely ○ *We were told that we had won a lot of money but never in my wildest dreams could I have thought it would be more than £1 million.*

★ **the person or thing of someone's dreams** the person or the thing that someone prefers to all others ○ *It was in Tunisia that they saw the house of their dreams, the most beautiful dwelling imaginable.*

dressed

all dressed up with nowhere to go prepared for something, but with no opportunity to do it ○ *The team were left all dressed up with nowhere to go after their match was called off because of a frozen field.*

dressed to kill wearing very stylish clothes which are intended to attract attention and impress people ○ *She was dressed to kill in a red strapless gown.*

driver

in the driver's seat in control of a situation ○ *Politically, the radicals were in the driver's seat, much to the anxiety of the moderates.*

drop

★ **at the drop of a hat** willingly and without hesitation. This expression is often used to suggest that someone does not think carefully enough about their actions. ○ *People should sort out their own minor problems and not just call the police at the drop of a hat.*

In the early 19th century, boxing matches were often started by someone dropping a hat.

a drop in the bucket something, especially an amount of money, that is very small in comparison with the amount which is needed or expected, so that its effect is insignificant ○ *Unfortunately, this tax won't raise a lot of money. It's a drop in the bucket.*

≡ This expression may come from a line in the Bible in which nations are described as being insignificant, or "a drop of a bucket." (Isaiah 40:15)

★ **drop something or someone like a hot potato** or
drop something or someone like a hot brick to get rid of something or someone as quickly as possible because they are difficult to deal with, or because you do not want them any more ○ *It is a rule of the tourism business that clients must feel happy on holiday. If a place gains a reputation for being unwelcoming, the trade drops it like a hot potato.*

drum

bang the drum for something or someone or
bang the drum about something or someone to support something or someone strongly and publicly ○ *Microsoft has done a lot in recent months to bang the drum about IE9.*

drummer

march to a different drummer (*journalism*) to act in accordance with beliefs or expectations that are different from those of your colleagues or friends ○ *The charter school marches to a different drummer, and I will allow it to continue to do so.*

drunk

drunk as a skunk very drunk ○ *When John arrived here last night, he was drunk as a skunk.*

dry

★ **bleed someone dry** to make someone or something weak by forcing them to use up all their money or resources ○ *He extorted money from me on a regular basis for five years. But he was careful not to bleed me dry.*

≡ In the past, doctors often treated patients by bleeding them, which involved extracting some of their blood.

dry as a bone very dry ○ *By the end of June the pond was as dry as a bone.*

dry as dust
1 very dry ○ *The fields were dry as dust.*
2 very boring ○ *His book is badly written, poorly edited and dry as dust.*

duck

a dead duck someone or something that is a failure ○ *The government is a dead duck.*

★ **a lame duck**
1 someone or something with little real power, for example a politician or a government when their period of office is coming to an end ○ *The government is headed by a president who looks like a lame duck.*
2 someone who is in a very weak position and who needs support ○ *Elizabeth often invites lame ducks to spend Christmas with us.*

★ **a sitting duck** someone who is an obvious target, and whom it is very easy to attack or criticize ○ *They heard the sound of gunfire. "It's a trap," Joe whispered. "And we're sitting ducks! We've got to find somewhere to hide."*

≡ A duck is an easy target for hunters when it is sitting on the water or on the ground.

take to something like a duck to water to discover that you are naturally good at something and that you find it very easy to do ○ *Gilbey became a salesman for BMW. He took to it like a duck to water, quickly becoming Car Salesman of the Year.*

ducks

get your ducks in a row to get everything properly organized and under control ○ *The government needs to get its ducks in a row.*

> The "ducks" in this expression are duckpins. The game of duckpins is a variation of bowling, with ten smaller pins and a smaller ball with no finger holes. The literal meaning of "to get your ducks in a row" is to get your duckpins set up for the next game.

dudgeon

in high dudgeon (*mainly British, literary*) unreasonably angry or annoyed about something ○ *She left the meeting in high dudgeon after learning that the only perk was free coffee.*

dull

dull as ditchwater or
dull as dishwater extremely boring ○ *He's a dull writer and that's a fact. Dull as ditchwater.*

> The expression "dull as ditchwater" is over 200 years old, whereas "dull as dishwater" is a more recent variant. The reference is to the dull dirty color of the water in ditches or in washing-up bowls.

dummy

spit out the dummy (*mainly Australian*) to behave in a bad-tempered and childish way ○ *He spat out the dummy when his wife said that she wanted to go on holiday without him.*

> The image here is of a bad-tempered baby spitting out its dummy (pacifier).

dumps

down in the dumps feeling sad, with no hope ○ *Tom's a bit down in the dumps. Let's try to cheer him up.*

dust

be eating someone's dust to be completely defeated by another person in a competitive situation ○ *We were all eating his dust. I didn't know he could run so fast.*

> If you are riding behind another horse in a race, you have the dust kicked up by the other horse in your face.

★ **bite the dust**
1 to fail or to stop existing ○ *There are thousands of restaurants in and around London. Some make big money. Most break even, and quite a few have bitten the dust.*
2 to die. This expression is used to refer to someone's death in a humorous way. ○ *The climax of most Westerns comes when the villain bites the dust.*

> In stories about the Wild West, cowboys were said to "bite the dust" when they were shot and fell off their horses.

★ **the dust has settled** used when a situation has become calmer and steadier after a series of confusing or chaotic events ○ *Now that the dust has settled, it is clear that nothing much has changed.*

eat someone's dust watch as someone surpasses you in some activity or goes ahead of you ○ *I quickly overtook him, forcing him to eat my dust.*

★ **gather dust** to not be dealt with for a very long time ○ *This project has been gathering dust on the shelves of the Department of Environmental Protection for the last five years.*

shake the dust from your feet to leave a place or a situation, with the intention that you will never return to it ○ *Our job here is done. It's time to shake the dust from our feet and move on.*

This expression occurs in the Bible (Matthew 10:14), where people are advised that if no one welcomes them or listens to their words as they leave a particular place, then they should shake its dust off their feet (= never go back there again).

Dutch

go Dutch *(old-fashioned)* to share the cost of the bill for something, such as a meal or an evening out ○ *Many women are happy to go Dutch with a new boyfriend on the first date.*

Ee

eagle

an eagle eye an ability to find or notice things ○ *No antiques store, flea market, or junk shop escapes her eagle eye.*

Eagles have very good eyesight, and are able to see small animals or objects from a great height.

keep an eagle eye on someone or something to watch a person or thing very carefully ○ *Mr. Grogan kept an eagle eye on everything that was going on in the factory.*

ear

bend someone's ear to keep talking to someone about something, usually in an annoying way ○ *You can't go on bending everyone's ear with this problem.*

go in one ear and out the other if a piece of information goes in one ear and out the other, you pay no attention to it, or forget about it immediately ○ *I'd said it so many times before that it just went in one ear and out the other as far as he was concerned.*

★ **grin from ear to ear** to look very happy ○ *McCarthy was grinning from ear to ear. He absolutely radiated warmth and pride.*

have an ear for something to have the ability to learn and understand the structure of a language or piece of music quickly, and to be able to reproduce the sounds of the language or music easily and accurately. Compare **have a tin ear for** something; see **tin**. ○ *He had an ear for languages, which he enjoyed, and by this time he spoke five fluently.*

have someone's ear to have the attention of a person in power, who listens carefully to your opinions and often follows your advice on important issues ○ *He has been one of Italy's most influential figures, a man who is said to have had the ear of every Italian prime minister.*

keep your ear to the ground to make sure that you find out about all the things that people are doing or talking about ○ *Watch and learn. While you do this, keep your ear to the ground. Know who is coming, who is going: a new vacancy could be an opportunity for you.*

In movies, Native Americans are often shown tracking people or animals by listening carefully to the ground for the sound of their footsteps.

lend an ear to someone to listen carefully and sympathetically to a person who has a problem ○ *Slowly your status at work will improve, and your boss and colleagues will lend a sympathetic ear to your gripes and grievances.*

listen with half an ear to not give your full attention to something ○ *She was listening to the news on the radio with half an ear when she suddenly heard his name mentioned.*

out on your ear (*informal*) suddenly dismissed from a course, job, or group ○ *I'd failed the final exam in History of Art. I had to pass the makeup or I'd be out on my ear.*

play it by ear to deal with things as they happen, rather than following a plan or previous arrangement ○ *"Where will we stay in Georgia?" "Oh, I guess a bed-and-breakfast place. We'll have to play it by ear."*

If someone plays a piece of music by ear, they play it without looking at printed music.

turn a deaf ear to something to refuse to consider a request or an opinion and not pay any attention to it ○ *The Mayor of Paris has long turned a deaf ear to Parisians who want tougher laws to protect the cleanliness of their pavements.*

ears

be all ears to be ready and eager to listen to what someone is saying ○ *"That's a very good question. May I answer it frankly?" "I'm all ears."*

★ **fall on deaf ears** if something you say to someone falls on deaf ears, they take no notice of what you have said ○ *The mayor spoke privately to Gibson yesterday and asked him to resign, but said that his plea fell on deaf ears.*

have nothing between your ears to be stupid ○ *He's good-looking but he has nothing between his ears.*

have something coming out of your ears to have so much of something that you do not want or need any more of it ○ *Everyone who wants to talk to me is talking about football. I have football coming out of my ears. I can't get away from it.*

have steam coming out of your ears to be very angry about something ○ *The team challenge left some designers in tears and others with steam coming out of their ears.*

pin someone's ears back
1 to tell someone off for having done something wrong ○ *Dad was furious about what I'd done and pinned my ears back.*
2 to beat or defeat someone severely ○ *After winning three games in a row, the Reds had their ears pinned back by the Blues.*

prick up your ears to start listening eagerly, because you suddenly hear an interesting sound or piece of information ○ *She stopped talking to prick up her ears – and Kenworthy had heard the same sound.*

≡ When some animals hear a sudden or unfamiliar noise, they literally prick up their ears; that is, their ears become more erect so that they can hear the sound better.

someone's ears are burning someone is being talked about by people in a different place ○ *Howard's ears must have been burning as he was referred to as the "little man in the big house."*

up to your ears very busy with work, or deeply involved in an unpleasant situation ○ *"Why don't you go to the movies with us?" "I can't. I'm up to my ears in reports."*

wet behind the ears new to a situation and therefore inexperienced or naive ○ *Terry was just out of college, with a shapely haircut of medium length that failed to hide the fact that he was wet behind the ears.*

≡ There are two possible origins for this expression. It may refer to a young animal being washed by its mother. Alternatively, it may refer to children forgetting to dry behind their ears after taking a bath.

earth

★ **come down to earth** or
come down to earth with a bump to have to face the reality of everyday life after a period of great excitement ○ *When something good does happen, it's important that it is celebrated. The next day something will happen and you'll come back down to earth.*

★ **down to earth** very realistic and practical. Compare **have your head in the clouds**; see **head**. ○ *They think she's too glamorous and won't want to speak to them. But that's just not true at all. She's very friendly and very down to earth.* ○ *Everyone liked her down-to-earth approach to life.*

earth to someone used humorously to suggest that someone is acting very stupidly or needs to pay attention ○ *Earth to Bob and Kevin: The two cases are in no way comparable.*

This expression is inspired by old science fiction movies, in which people on earth sent messages to those traveling in space to warn them of danger.

promise the earth to promise to give people things that you cannot in fact possibly give them ○ *One voter summed up the mood: "Politicians have lost credibility," he complained. "They promise the earth and don't deliver."*

easier

★ **easier said than done** used to emphasize that something is simple to achieve in theory, but difficult to do in practice ○ *The alternative option is to scrap the unwanted machines, and use the metal for some other purpose. But this, too, is easier said than done.*

easy

In the first idiom below, **ABC** is pronounced "a b c," as if you are spelling it out.

easy as pie or
easy as ABC or
easy as falling off a log very easy to do. Compare **a piece of cake**; see **piece**. ○ *Michael understood at once. "Why, that's easy as pie," he said as the rest of us scratched our heads.*

easy come, easy go used when something comes to you without your making any effort, so it is not important if you lose it ○ *My attitude to money is easy come, easy go. That is to say, I earn a lot, but I also give quite a lot away in different ways.*

go easy on someone to punish or treat someone less severely than might be expected or deserved ○ *They had to go easy on him because he was only thirteen and it was also his first offense.*

go easy on something to not have or use too much of something because you think that it is bad for you ○ *Small meals*

at regular times are important. Go easy on the salt. Don't add extra sugar.

★ **take it easy** or
take things easy
1 to relax and not worry, hurry, or do anything that needs a lot of energy ○ *The seven astronauts aboard the space shuttle Columbia are taking it easy today, following six full days of medical research.*
2 an informal way of saying "goodbye" ○ *"Thanks. See you later." "Take it easy. Don't do anything I wouldn't do."*

ebb

at a low ebb very sad or unsuccessful ○ *When I have been at a low ebb I have found the friendship and Christian love of my fellow churchgoers to be a great strength.*

The ebb tide is one of the regular periods, usually two per day, when the ocean gradually falls to a lower level, as the tide moves away from the land.

★ **ebb and flow** continuous change shown by rising and falling levels or amounts of something ○ *The need for foreign languages in business is increasing, regardless of the ebb and flow of the global economy.*

eclipse

in eclipse (*formal*) much less successful and important than before ○ *Even when her career was temporarily in eclipse she had no financial worries.*

An eclipse of the sun is an occasion when the moon is between the earth and the sun, so that for a short time you cannot see part or all of the sun.

edge

★ **at the cutting edge** or
on the cutting edge involved in the most important, exciting, or advanced developments of a particular subject or activity ○ *Telluride has always prided itself on being on the cutting edge of computer technology.* ○ *These were the men and*

women doing the cutting-edge research.
a cutting edge the ability to be more successful than your opponents ○ *We need a cutting edge and hopefully this product can provide it.*

★ **lose your edge** to no longer have all the advantages and special skills that you had in the past ○ *Its staff disagrees with criticisms that their magazine is out of date or has lost its edge.*

≡ If a sword or knife has lost its edge, it is dull.

★ **on edge** anxious and unable to relax ○ *Brenda had every right to be on edge. Ever since I had left on Saturday morning, she had been bombarded with telephone calls.*
on the edge of your seat very interested and eager to know what happens next, especially in a film, book or sports match ○ *Saturday night's final had the spectators on the edge of their seats.*

★ **take the edge off something** to weaken the effect or intensity of something, especially pain ○ *My head never seemed to clear completely, and the painkillers only took the edge off the pain.*

≡ If something takes the edge off a blade, it makes it dull.

edges
fray at the edges to become weaker, or less certain or stable, to the point of being damaged or destroyed ○ *The government's army has begun to fray at the edges.*

≡ If a piece of cloth or rope frays, its threads or fibers start to come apart.

rough edges
1 small faults in a person's character that affect their behavior towards other people ○ *He had the reputation of sometimes taking himself a little too seriously. Those rough edges have long since worn off.*
2 technical problems in an otherwise

good performance or piece of entertainment ○ *The show, despite some rough edges, was an instant success.*

egg
★ **get egg on your face** to feel embarrassed or ashamed because of something you have done or said ○ *Steve didn't expect to win. He just didn't want to get egg on his face.*

≡ People in crowds sometimes throw eggs at someone such as a politician or performer, to show their anger or dislike for them.

★ **a good egg** a kind and well-liked person ○ *We met Sheila's uncle at the wedding -- he seemed like a good egg.*
lay an egg if something lays an egg, it fails because people are not interested in it or do not want it ○ *Independent studies showed the ad laid an egg.*

≡ This expression is probably derived from the idea of an egg being round and therefore resembling a zero. A "goose egg" is a score of zero in sports.

eggs
★ **put all your eggs in one basket** to put all your efforts or resources into one course of action with the result that you will have no alternatives left if this fails ○ *Don't put your eggs in one basket; study hard at school and always keep an alternative job in mind.*

eggshells
walk on eggshells to be very careful about what you say or do to someone because they are easily upset or offended ○ *Healthy or sick, good days or bad, I felt I was always walking on eggshells around him.*

elbow
elbow grease the energy and strength you need for doing physical work such as cleaning something ○ *Plenty of elbow grease soon moves all the dirt.*

elbow room

1 the freedom to do what you need or want to do in a particular situation ○ *His overall message to governors, though, was that he intends to give them more elbow room to encourage innovation at the state level.*

2 enough space to move freely or feel comfortable, without feeling crowded or cramped ○ *There was not much elbow room in the cockpit.*

elbows

rub elbows with someone to spend time with an important or famous person. A similar expression is **rub shoulders with someone** ○ *At his famous parties, writers, artists, and celebrities rubbed elbows with the ultra-rich and the socially elite.*

element

★ **in your element** doing something that you enjoy or do well ○ *My stepmother was in her element, organizing everything.*

≣ Ancient and medieval philosophers believed that all substances were composed from the four elements: earth, air, fire, and water. To be "in your element" is to be in your natural surroundings, like a bird in air or a fish in water.

elephant

the elephant in the room an obvious truth that is deliberately ignored by everyone in a situation ○ *We both know that we can't carry on like this – it's the elephant in the room.*

★ **a white elephant** something, such as a new building, plan, or project that is a waste of money and completely useless ○ *Will the complex, constructed at some expense but never used, be regarded as a monumental folly, a great white elephant?*

≣ There is a story that the Kings of Siam used to give white elephants, which are very rare, to courtiers who they did not like. The animals cost so much to keep that their owners spent all their money on them and became very poor.

elevator

the elevator doesn't go all the way to the top used humorously to suggest that someone is either stupid or mentally ill ○ *She didn't seem to understand what we were talking about. I think the elevator doesn't go all the way to the top.*

embarrassment

an embarrassment of riches (*literary*) so many good things that you cannot choose among them ○ *Sports fans have an embarrassment of riches to choose from next weekend when three games will be screened live simultaneously.*

empty

run on empty

1 to no longer be as exciting or successful as you once were because you have run out of new ideas or resources ○ *The band's 2008 appearance is widely agreed to be their finest two hours. Certainly, events after this suggest a band running on empty.*

2 to feel tired, confused, and unable to think or work properly because you have not eaten for a long time ○ *If you don't feed your body daily nutrients, you are running on empty – something you can only do for a short time.*

≣ In this expression, the idea is of a car or other vehicle that is still running but has very little fuel left, so the needle of the fuel gauge is pointing to "empty."

enchilada

★ **the whole enchilada** the most extreme, complete, or full version of something ○ *Paul Holmgren and Stan Bowman grabbed their wallets tightly and squeezed so only a few million bucks would come out, not the whole enchilada.*

An enchilada is a Mexican dish consisting of a filled tortilla topped with sauce. The phrase was recorded in a taped conversation of a White House official in the 1960s and became popular after that time.

end

at the end of your rope or **at the end of your tether** feeling desperate because you are in a difficult situation and do not know how to deal with it ○ *Everything is dreadful and I am at the end of my rope.*

The image here is of an animal that cannot move very far because it is tied to something with a length of rope.

★ **be thrown in at the deep end** to start by doing the most difficult part of a job or task, before you have tried to do the easier parts, or to start a job or task without any preparation ○ *Journalist Susan Hocking is being thrown straight in at the deep end when she anchors the evening news next week.*

The deep end is the end of a swimming pool where the water is deepest.

come to a sticky end to die in an unpleasant or violent way ○ *Hassan comes to a sticky end, but so does almost everyone else in the book.*

★ **a dead end** something such as a plan, a project, or a course of action that has no future and will not develop any further ○ *Do you feel you have reached a dead end at work?*

★ **dead-end** boring and unlikely to lead to anything more interesting or successful ○ *He was a dull, nondescript man in a dull, dead-end job.*

A dead end is a street that is closed at one end.

★ **do something to the bitter end** to continue doing something in a determined way and finish it, even

though this becomes increasingly difficult ○ *Despite another crushing defeat, he is determined to see the job through to the bitter end.*

Sailors used to refer to the end of a rope or chain that was securely tied as "the bitter end." Bitts were posts on the ship's deck and ropes would be tied to these to secure the ship in a harbor.

end it all to kill yourself ○ *I desperately wanted to end it all, but I had an adorable little boy who was totally dependent upon me.*

★ **the end of the road**
1 the point where someone or something can no longer continue or survive in a situation ○ *The administration realizes now that they've come to the end of the road of their policy.*
2 the results of someone's actions that cannot be avoided ○ *If she doesn't stop stealing, there's only jail at the end of the road.*

★ **an end run** an action that you do so that you can avoid something ○ *Romney's end run around the finance rules has attracted some bad press.*

In football, an end run is a play in which the man with the ball runs around the end of the defensive line.

★ **end to end** in a row or straight line with ends touching ○ *Lay down the poles end to end along the line where you will build the fence.*

go off the deep end
1 to go crazy, or to behave in a strange or extreme manner ○ *At first they thought that I'd gone off the deep end and had lost my mind.*
2 to become very angry ○ *Dad didn't go off the deep end at all. He just said it wasn't fair to make my mother worry like that.*

The deep end is the end of a swimming pool where the water is deepest.

★ **it's not the end of the world** used to

assure someone that the consequences of an event are not as bad as they might seem at first ○ *If I make a mistake, it's not the end of the world. I can always go back and correct it.*

keep your end up to do what you have said you will do or what you are expected to do in spite of difficult circumstances ○ *The fact of the matter is that we signed a contract and we've worked hard to keep up our end, and they must keep up their end.*

on the wrong end of something unsuccessful in an activity or situation or at some disadvantage because of it ○ *A half-hour after being on the wrong end of a 26-5 loss to the Kansas City Royals, the Detroit Tigers went 8-0 in the second game.*

ends

be at loose ends to lack a plan or goal, and so to feel uncertain ○ *The country is at loose ends with respect to both its internal direction and its place in the world.*

This expression may refer to the ropes on a sailing ship. The ends of the ropes had to be tightly bound to stop them fraying, and sailors were often given this job to do when there was nothing more urgent to be done. Alternatively, the expression may refer to a working horse being untied at the end of the day and released into a field.

★ **loose ends** small details or parts of something that have not been sorted out satisfactorily. ○ *The overall impact of the story is weakened by too many loose ends being left inadequately resolved.*

★ **make ends meet** to be able to pay for the things you need in life, often with very little money ○ *Many people are struggling to make ends meet because wages are failing to keep pace with rising prices.*

Originally, this expression was "make both ends of the year meet," which meant to spend only as much money as you received as income.

play both ends against the middle to pretend to support or favor two opposing people or ideas in order to gain an advantage from a situation ○ *The Irish queen was adept at playing both ends against the middle, sometimes confronting the English, and sometimes co-operating with them.*

enough

enough is enough no more is needed. This expression is used when something continues, even though everyone thinks it should stop. ○ *When will we get our leaders to say enough is enough? The plan is not working.*

envelope

push the envelope to do something to a greater degree or in a more extreme way than it has ever been done before ○ *Each time they flew faster or higher, they regarded that as pushing the envelope.*

Rather than referring to stationery, the sense of envelope here is probably the one used to refer to the shape of a wave in electronics or a curve in mathematics. Pushing or stretching the envelope suggests changing the properties of the wave or curve.

envy

green with envy → see **green**

error

★ **see the error of your ways** to realize or admit that you have made a mistake or behaved badly ○ *I wanted an opportunity to talk some sense into him and try to make him see the error of his ways.*

even

don't get mad, get even → see **mad**

★ **get even** to get your revenge on someone who has hurt or injured you in some way. ○ *He is so incensed by what he considers shabby treatment that he's determined to get even.*

evils

★ **the lesser of two evils** the less unpleasant of two unpleasant options that someone has to choose between ○ *Should she choose the misery of life on the streets or the unhappiness at home? In the end it seemed the street was the lesser of two evils.*

exception

the exception that proves the rule something that does not obey a rule, but shows that the rule exists ○ *To succeed, you must be big and powerful. Osman is neither of these. He is the exception that proves the rule.*

"Prove" here means "to test by experiment or analysis" rather than "to establish as true." So, the meaning is that an exception tests a rule, not that it establishes the rule as true in all other situations.

expense

★ **laugh at someone's expense** to make someone seem foolish by laughing at them ○ *Being fat and bald has ruined my life. I'll never forget the people who laughed at my expense.*

spare no expense to spend as much money as is necessary to achieve or do something ○ *Their stadium is magnificent and the team is ambitious and they plan to spare no expense to catch up with New York once more.*

experience

chalk something up to experience to accept that an undesirable result will prove to be a valuable lesson ○ *You just chalk it up to experience and try to move on. Each day is a new day.*

eye

★ **an eye for an eye** or
an eye for an eye and a tooth for a tooth used to say that the punishment for a crime should be either the same as the crime or equivalent to it ○ *Why do we put people in jail? As an eye for an eye, or to make them realize they did wrong?*

Expressions like this can be found in several parts of the Old Testament of the Bible, which advises that people who do wrong to others should suffer the same punishment as the one that they tried to carry out themselves: "Life shall go for life, eye for eye, tooth for tooth, hand for hand, foot for foot." (Deuteronomy 19:21)

★ **an eye for something** skill at dealing with something or a good understanding of it ○ *With his unerring eye for light, line and color, Greenaway has mounted one of the most beautiful drawing exhibitions ever seen.*

★ **be in the public eye** to be famous and often mentioned or seen on television or in the newspapers ○ *Increasingly, people in the public eye are voicing concern about the effects of their lifestyle on their family life.*

cast an eye on something to examine something carefully and give your opinion about it ○ *"Before the elections I was pessimistic," says Jassem Saddoun, a leading economist who casts a critical eye on domestic affairs.*

★ **cast your eye over something** to look at, consider, or read something very quickly ○ *He cast his eye over the bookcases. She was obviously an avid reader.*

★ **catch someone's eye** if something or someone catches your eye, you notice them because they are very attractive or unusual ○ *He turned the page. The picture caught his eye instantly.* ○ *My mother and my sister love stylish, eye-catching designer hats but cannot afford to buy them.*

the evil eye a harmful force that comes from someone looking at something ○ *She bought an amulet in the market that is supposed to ward off the evil eye.*

In many cultures there is a belief that children must be protected from the evil eye of others who may be envious of them.

give someone a black eye to punish someone severely, but without causing them permanent harm, for something they have done ○ *Whenever the Democratic Party gets too cocky or corrupt, voters tend to give it a black eye.*

A black eye is a dark-colored bruise around a person's eye.

give someone the eye to look at someone in a way that suggests you find them sexually attractive ○ *For flip's sake Mark, calm down: she's not giving you the eye.*

a gleam in someone's eye a plan or project that is only at the earliest planning stage ○ *At present, the plans seem to be no more than a gleam in a developer's eye.*

Words such as gleam, glint and twinkle can be used to describe the way people's eyes shine or reflect the light. They often suggest hidden energy, emotion, or mischievousness and refer to the initial excitement of having a particular idea before putting it into practice.

in the eye of the storm deeply involved in a difficult or controversial situation which affects or interests a lot of people ○ *He was often in the eye of the storm of congressional debates related to U.S. troop withdrawals from Vietnam.*

This expression refers to the center or middle part of a storm. However, in wind storms, such as cyclones and tornados, the eye is in reality a relatively calm area of low pressure in the center.

keep your eye on the ball to continue to pay close attention to what

you are doing. Compare **take your eye off the ball**. ○ *She won widespread praise for her innovation, her tough negotiating skills and her ability to keep things moving, keep her eye on the ball.*

★ **look someone in the eye** to look at someone directly in order to convince them that what you are saying is true, even though you may be lying. ○ *He looked me straight in the eye and said "Paul, I will never lie to you."*

not bat an eye
1 to not be shocked or offended by something that would shock or offend most people ○ *I was totally independent. My mother never batted an eye about the length of time I stayed out at night.*
2 to not be nervous or worried about something that would normally worry most people ○ *Would you believe he ordered them to fill half a tin mug with that stuff and guzzled it without batting an eye, as if it was water?*

Bat is from a French word meaning to beat or flutter and is used of a bird's wings. The idea is that people who do not blink a lot in a given situation appear calm rather than nervous or surprised.

★ **not see eye to eye with someone** to not agree with someone about something ○ *The President did not see eye to eye with him on this issue.*

someone would give their eye teeth for something used when someone wants something very much, and that they would do almost anything to get it ○ *He's the most exciting man I've ever worked with, and I'd give my eye teeth to do something with him again.*

A person's eye teeth are their canine teeth, the pointed teeth near the front of their mouth.

spit in someone's eye to deliberately upset or annoy someone ○ *The mayor spat* *in the eye of small businesses yesterday when he said: "I won't support the weak at the expense of the strong."*

take your eye off the ball to stop paying attention for a moment, with the result that things go wrong for you. Compare **keep your eye on the ball**. ○ *Any reorganization is disruptive. It makes key management take their eye off the only ball.*

★ **there's more to something than meets the eye** used to indicate that something is more complicated or more involved than it appears to be at first ○ *"She is convinced there is more to your friendship than meets the eye." "Well there isn't."*

★ **turn a blind eye to something** to deliberately ignore something because you do not want to take any action over it, even though you know you should ○ *The authorities were turning a blind eye to human rights abuses.*

> This expression was first used to describe the action of Admiral Nelson at the Battle of the Nile in 1798. When told that he was being ordered to withdraw, he put a telescope to his blind eye and said that he could not see the signal. He went on to win the battle.

★ **with the naked eye** with only the eyes, and without the help of instruments such as a telescopes or microscopes ○ *Enough light gets through space for us to see thousands of stars with the naked eye, and millions with an optical telescope.*

eyeball

be eyeball to eyeball if two people who are disagreeing with each other are eyeball to eyeball, they are physically close together, and it seems likely that they will start arguing or fighting ○ *The two of us sat eyeball to eyeball. "Why do you*

hate me?" she asked, without any apparent emotion.

eyeballs

up to your eyeballs in something very deeply involved in an unpleasant situation ○ *The one-time media tycoon is down on his luck, out of a job, and up to his eyeballs in debt.*

eyebrows

★ **raise eyebrows** to surprise, shock, or offend people ○ *Madonna's 13-year-old daughter raised eyebrows at her first day at LaGuardia High School with a flashy accessory: a marijuana leaf-print wristband.*

eyes

★ **all eyes are on someone or something** used when everyone is carefully watching a particular person or thing, often because they are expecting something to happen or develop ○ *All eyes will be on the President tomorrow when he gives his State of the Union Address.*

★ **before your eyes** or **in front of your eyes** if something happens before your eyes, it happens directly in front of you, and you cannot do anything to stop it or change it ○ *With a wrenching crack the stone statue collapsed before my eyes and crumbled to pieces at the bottom of the fountain.*

★ **can't take your eyes off someone or something** if you can't take your eyes off someone or something, you very much want to keep looking at them, often because they are attractive ○ *Anne looked so beautiful no one could take their eyes off her.*

cry your eyes out to cry a lot for a long time ○ *It was a lovely school; I cried my eyes out when I left.*

do something with your eyes closed to do something very easily ○ *He reassembled the gun quickly and expertly. It was something he could do with his eyes closed.*

feast your eyes on something to look at something with a great deal of enjoyment ○ *Billy licked his lips and feasted his eyes on the chocolate cake.*

> The idea is of allowing your eyes to appreciate something visually in the same way that your mouth allows you to enjoy the quantity and quality of food at a feast or large meal.

have eyes in the back of your head to be very good at noticing everything that is happening around you ○ *She has eyes in the back of her head and is always alert to the slightest sign of trouble.*

★ **keep your eyes open** to be aware of things that you can do in a particular situation ○ *Take up any opportunity to increase your knowledge and broaden your horizons. Keep your eyes open for any interesting study courses.*

keep your eyes peeled to watch very carefully for something ○ *They drove there in Charlie's car, so Michael kept his eyes peeled for parking places.*

> This expression refers to not blinking and so not missing anything that happens, however quick. The skin or peel of the eyes are the eyelids.

make eyes at someone (old-fashioned) to try to get someone to notice you because you are attracted to them

○ *He was making eyes at one of the nurses.*

★ **meet someone's eyes** (literary) to look directly into someone's eyes ○ *An uneasy moment of frozen silence passed as Steve looked down and then finally up at me, meeting my eyes with an intense glare.*

only have eyes for someone to only be attracted to one particular person ○ *The 26 year-old model is adored by thousands but only has eyes for one man – her husband.*

only have eyes for something to be determined to have one particular thing ○ *The president came seeking investment in Mexico, but found Western Europe only had eyes for the new democracies to its east.*

★ **open someone's eyes** to cause someone to become aware of a particular situation or fact for the first time ○ *The need for female labor created during two world wars opened many women's eyes to better paid lives in factories and offices.*

up to your eyes in something very busy with work or deeply involved in an unpleasant situation ○ *I'm afraid I shall be late getting back. I'm up to my eyes in work.*

with your eyes glued to something watching something with all your attention ○ *He sat, eyes glued to the TV set with a look usually reserved for a good suspense film.*

face

★ **blow up in your face** if a situation blows up in your face, it unexpectedly goes wrong and destroys your plans or your chances of something ○ *He must have known that having no evidence, this would blow up in his face.*

★ **come face to face with someone** or **meet someone face to face** to meet someone and talk to them directly ○ *When I first heard of his death I didn't want to call her or meet her face to face. I didn't know what to say or how to act.* ○ *The three major vice-presidential candidates took the stage tonight in Atlanta in their only face-to-face confrontation of the campaign.*

★ **come face to face with something** to be forced to experience a problem or the reality of a situation, and have to deal with it or accept it ○ *Before the deal was fully closed, however, Beaverbrook came face to face with a serious problem.*

fall flat on your face to fail or make an embarrassing mistake when you try to do something ○ *I may fall flat on my face or it may be a glorious end to my career.*

★ **fly in the face of something** to be completely against accepted ideas, rules, or practices ○ *The plan to sell rhino horn flies in the face of the international ban.*

get in someone's face (informal) to annoy or upset someone by behaving in a very direct or aggressive way ○ *He pretty much got in my face and told me not to leave or I'd get fired.*

get out of someone's face (informal) to leave someone alone and to stop annoying them or interfering with them ○ *Get out of my face or else I'm going to call the police.*

have a long face to look very serious or unhappy ○ *He came to me with a very long face and admitted there had been an error.*

in the face of something because of or at the same time as a difficulty or problem ○ *Several plans foundered this year in the face of opposition from politicians.*

★ **in-your-face** (informal) unconventional and provocative, and likely to upset or offend some people ○ *Christina James plays Perry's widow, a vivacious, in-your-face woman who is sometimes too honest for her own good.*

★ **keep a straight face** to manage to look serious, even though you really want to laugh or smile ○ *His laugh was hard for Nancy to resist, but she managed to keep a straight face.* ○ *It's the way he tells a joke. He is completely straight-faced and I just fall about laughing.*

look someone in the face to look at someone directly in order to convince them that what you are saying is true, even though you may be lying ○ *He looked me in the face again and repeated, "I swear to you that it wasn't me."*

lose face to be made to look foolish or to do something that damages your reputation ○ *Perhaps the FDA did not want to lose face by reversing its position.*

This is a Chinese expression and refers to the covering of one's face with a fan as a sign of disgrace after revealing one's emotions. "Face" here means the face when wearing an expression of calm.

make a face to show a feeling such as dislike or disgust by twisting your face into an ugly expression, or by sticking out your tongue ○ *She made a face at the musty smell, and hurried to open the windows.*

not just a(nother) pretty face having qualities of intelligence or character, as well as being physically attractive ○ *And don't think he's just a pretty face, even though he has modeled professionally since he was 17.*

★ **put a brave face on something** or **put on a brave face** to try not to let anyone see how upset or disappointed you are with a difficult situation ○ *Dwight was upset by the news, but he put a brave face on it and wrote a note of congratulations.*

★ **save face** to do something so that people continue to respect you and your reputation is not damaged ○ *Most children have an almost obsessive need to save face in front of their peers.* ○ *The change of heart on aid seems to show that officials are looking for a face-saving way to back down.*

> This comes from a Chinese expression that refers to keeping a calm expression and managing to avoid the disgrace of revealing one's emotions. An English equivalent of this might be "to keep a straight face."

★ **say something to someone's face** to say something openly in someone's presence, especially something critical or unpleasant ○ *At school it was hard when people talked about me. No one would ever say anything to my face because they were scared of me.*

show your face

1 if you do not want to show your face somewhere, you do not want to go there, for example, because you are embarrassed or ashamed about something you have done ○ *Louis skulked in his Harlem apartment for three days after his defeat, too ashamed to show his face.*

2 to go somewhere briefly, for example, because you have been invited there and

you feel you should go for a short time ○ *I felt I ought to show my face at her father's funeral.*

someone can do something until they are blue in the face said when you think that however long someone does something or however hard they try, they will still fail ○ *You can speculate till you're blue in the face, but you can't prove a thing.*

someone cannot look someone in the face used about someone who is too ashamed or embarrassed by something that they have done to look at someone else directly ○ *Why did I do that? I can't ever look her in the face again.*

★ **someone will be laughing on the other side of their face** used when someone is happy or successful at the moment, but you think that things are likely to go wrong for them in the future ○ *The league leaders will be laughing on the other side of their faces if they lose tomorrow.*

stare someone in the face to be very obvious, although someone may not yet have realized this ○ *Even when the evidence is staring them in the face, they deliberately misread it.*

★ **stare something in the face** to have to deal with a bad situation that is very likely to occur, or is about to occur ○ *Some of my patients are actually staring death in the face. They've suffered a heart attack, maybe two.*

stuff your face to eat a large amount at one time ○ *The packed buffet was full of people who, like myself, came to stuff their faces.*

take someone at face value to accept the impression that someone gives of themselves, even though this may be completely false ○ *For a while I took him at face value. At that time, I had no reason to suspect him.*

> The face value of a coin or banknote is the amount that is printed on it,

although it may in fact be worth more or less than that amount, for example, because it is very old.

★ **take something at face value** to accept what someone says and believe it without thinking about it very much, even though it may be incorrect or untrue ○ *Clients should know better than to take the advice of a wholesaler at face value.*

throw something back in someone's face to reject something that someone has said or done for you in a way that seems very ungrateful or rude ○ *We extended the hand of friendship and you have thrown it back in our faces.*

written all over your face if an emotion such as relief or misery is written all over your face, it is very obvious to people that you are relieved or miserable, because of your expression ○ *Utter jubilation and relief were written all over the faces of the freed hostages.*

fact

a fact of life a situation that you must accept because it cannot be changed ○ *Turnover and job loss is a fact of life for those who serve in Congress.* ○ *Heartbreak and jealously are facts of life, especially in teenage years.*

fair

fair and square honestly and without cheating or lying ○ *This might start further accusations, but we don't care any more. We won fair and square.*

fairy

a fairy godmother a woman who gives a lot of help to someone when they most need it ○ *She was fairy godmother to Alice, helping with the kids and eventually finding Alice a job.*

This term comes from the fairytale called "Cinderella," in which a fairy godmother appears and uses magical powers to help Cinderella.

fall

be headed for a fall to be doing something which is likely to have unpleasant consequences for you ○ *The Democrats seem to be headed for a fall in midterm elections.*

familiarity

familiarity breeds contempt used to expresss that idea that someone or something that you know very well can easily become boring and irritating to you ○ *Of course, it's often true that familiarity breeds contempt, that we're attracted to those who seem so different from those we know at home.*

farm

buy the farm (*informal*) to die ○ *The plane nosedived into the ground and exploded. He bought the farm.*

A possible explanation for this expression is that, in wartime, American Air Force pilots sometimes said that they wanted to stop flying, buy a farm or ranch, and lead a peaceful life. "Buy the farm" then came to be used when a pilot was killed in a crash.

fashion

after a fashion not very well, or not completely ○ *She was educated, after a fashion, by her aunts at home.*

fast

play fast and loose with something to treat something important without enough care or respect ○ *The banks claim high interest rates are necessary because the government is playing fast and loose with public spending.*

pull a fast one to succeed in tricking someone in order to get an advantage ○ *Someone had pulled a fast one on her over a procedural matter and she was not going to let them get away with it.*

fat

chew the fat to speak with someone in an informal and friendly way about things that interest you ○ *We lounged around, chewing the fat for a couple of hours.*

This may refer to sailors in the past talking to each other while they chewed the fat in the dried meat which they were given to eat.

the fat is in the fire used when someone has said or done something that is going to upset other people and cause a lot of trouble ○ *The senator had broken all the rules, and the fat was in the fire.*

When food is being cooked over a fire, if fat or oil falls into the fire, the flames suddenly burn very fiercely.

someone is living off the fat of the land used about someone who has a rich and comfortable lifestyle without having to work hard for it ○ *The upper echelons of state government will continue to live off the fat of the land.*

This is from the story of Joseph in the Bible. During the famine in Israel, Pharaoh invited Joseph's father and brothers to come to Egypt, where there was plenty of food. He told them that they would be able to eat "the fat of the land" (Genesis 45:18).

fate

★ **seal someone's fate** to make it certain that someone will fail or that something unpleasant will happen to them ○ *The plan removes power from the government, sealing the fate of the unpopular Prime Minister, and transfers it to the President.*

★ **tempt fate** to take unnecessary risks when doing something, or act in a way that may bring you bad luck ○ *Indeed, many experienced yachtsmen charge the organizers with tempting fate in sending so*

many ill-prepared crews into such dangerous waters.

fault

★ **to a fault** more than is usual or necessary ○ *She was generous to a fault and tried to see that we had everything we needed.*

feast

it's feast or famine used to express the idea that sometimes you have too much of something such as money, while at other times you do not have enough ○ *While her life is rich in memories, funds are a problem. "It's feast or famine with me," she says.*

a movable feast something enjoyable that can be found at different times and places, or that is changeable ○ *Their performance venues have tended to be a movable feast.*

This expression originally applied to various religious holidays that are always celebrated at about the same time of year, but not on exactly the same day from year to year.

feather

a feather in someone's cap something that someone has done very well, which deserves admiration ○ *Hauptmann's arrest and conviction had been hailed as a triumph for justice and a feather in the cap of the New Jersey police.*

Traditionally, Native American warriors added feathers to their headdresses as a sign of bravery in battle. Medieval knights in England also wore feathers in their helmets as a sign of their bravery.

you could have knocked me down with a feather (old-fashioned) used to say that you were extremely surprised or shocked by something ○ *I won 54 votes to 48. I was completely overwhelmed; you could have knocked me down with a feather.*

feathers

> If a bird's feathers are ruffled, they stand out from its body, as when the bird is frightened or angry.

★ **ruffle someone's feathers** to say or do something that upsets or annoys someone ○ *The Fed chairman has ruffled a few feathers over Social Security.*

smooth ruffled feathers to make people who are angry or offended by what someone has said feel calmer and happier ○ *Members of the exchange objected to Mr. Rawlins's confrontational style. Mindful of this, Mr. Lawrence has been smoothing ruffled feathers.*

feelers

put out feelers to carefully try to find out about other people's feelings or plans, so that you will know what to do next ○ *"I'm looking to play in Britain at the end of the next Australian season," he said last night. "I've put out feelers for one or two clubs already."*

> Feelers are the long thin sense organs on the heads of insects and certain other creatures such as snails.

feelings

★ **no hard feelings** no feelings of resentment or anger ○ *I have no hard feelings toward anybody. Everything happened the way it happened. You can't change it.*

feet

dead on your feet extremely tired ○ *I'm usually dead on my feet at the end of the game.*

drag your feet to move or work slowly, or to be slow in doing or responding to something ○ *The administration has been accused of dragging its feet on reforms.*

find your feet to become more confident and learn what to do in a new situation ○ *It takes a while for people to find*

their feet at this level and gain the necessary confidence.

> The idea is of finding your sense of balance so you can move around without falling over or needing to support yourself.

★ **get cold feet** or
have cold feet to be unsure whether you want to do something, or to become too nervous and worried to do it ○ *I feel your boyfriend got cold feet about being in a committed relationship. He may even have fallen out of love.*

get itchy feet to become bored with the place or situation that you are in, and want to move somewhere new or start doing something new ○ *I hated living in London, and I started getting itchy feet. Last year, I decided I really wanted to come out to the States.*

get your feet on the ground to become established in a new situation, or become re-established in an old one ○ *They have modest two-room apartments, and until they get their feet on the ground, they take most meals at the institute's cafeteria.*

get your feet wet or
have your feet wet to get involved in something or experience something for the first time ○ *Charlton thinks it's time for me to get my feet wet. He says I'll be able to help the department a lot more if I learn how police actually solve crimes.*

★ **keep your feet on the ground** to continue to act in a sensible and practical way even when new or exciting things are happening or even when you become successful or powerful ○ *He says he keeps his feet on the ground by keeping childhood friends around him.*

land on your feet to find yourself in a good situation, which you think is the result of luck and not your own efforts ○ *He has landed on his feet with a new career set to earn him a fortune.*

This may refer to the belief that when a cat falls, it always lands on its feet without hurting itself.

★ **put your feet up** to have a rest from your work and relax, for example, by lying down or sitting in a comfortable chair ○ *All these dishes can be oven-baked from frozen, while you put your feet up and relax.*

rushed off your feet very busy, often because you are not getting any help or support in your work ○ *Now we have a cut-back in staff in this department, and I'm rushed off my feet.*

someone has feet of clay used when someone who is greatly admired or respected is found to have serious faults or weaknesses that people generally did not know about ○ *When those idols are found to have feet of clay, the pain of disenchantment can be profound.*

According to the Bible (Daniel 2:33), King Nebuchadnezzar asked Daniel to help him to understand a dream he had had about a giant statue. This statue was made of gold, silver, brass, and iron, but it had feet made partly from clay. Daniel told the king that the clay feet were a sign of weakness.

★ **stand on your own two feet** or **stand on your own feet** to show that you are independent and do not need anyone to help you or support you ○ *It now seems clear that foreign aid levels of the 1980s will never be seen again and that these countries will have to stand on their own two feet.*

★ **sweep someone off their feet**
1 to be so attractive, romantic, and exciting that someone falls in love with you almost as soon as they meet you ○ *He is a good fifteen years older than Felicity. He swept her off her feet, though. And I suppose it seemed very romantic.*
2 to be extremely attractive or appealing to someone ○ *Ten British chefs plan to cook a feast they hope will sweep the French off their feet.*

think on your feet to make good decisions and achieve things without having to think about them or plan them first ○ *Being a parent means thinking on your feet and adapting as you go along.*

★ **vote with your feet** to show what you want through your actions, for example, showing your dislike of a place or situation by leaving it ○ *It seems thousands of people are already voting with their feet, and leaving the country in the hope of a better life.*

fellow
a fellow traveler → see **traveler**

fence
★ **sit on the fence** to refuse to state a definite opinion about something or to say who you support in a conflict ○ *The commission has chosen, extraordinarily, to sit on the fence, murmuring that schools must decide for themselves.*

The fence referred to is one that separates two properties or territories and someone sitting on it is unable or unwilling to make a decision about which side to stand on.

fencepost
between you, me, and the fencepost used before a statement to suggest that what you are saying should be kept secret, or would be upsetting to someone ○ *Between you, me, and the fencepost, I don't think there's any chance she'll win.*

fences
★ **mend fences** to do something to try to improve a relationship that has had some problems or disagreements ○ *Yesterday he was publicly criticized for not doing enough to mend fences with his big political rival.*

fever

★ **reach fever pitch** to become very intense and exciting, or very desperate ○ *In the past year, the civil conflict has reached fever pitch.*

fiddle

★ **play second fiddle** to have to accept that you are less important than someone else ○ *The 44-year-old senator will play second fiddle to a man who has been his junior in the Democrat hierarchy.*

> A fiddle is a violin. The expression here refers to the first and second violins in an orchestra.

field

come out of left field to be completely unexpected ○ *All the firms we've talked to have indicated that they don't know. This has really come out of left field to most people.*

> In baseball, left field is part of the outfield. A ball is said to come out of left field when the pitcher throws it in such a way that it seems to come out of nowhere.

★ **have a field day** to take advantage of a situation, especially one which other people find upsetting or difficult ○ *Debt collectors are having a field day in the recession.*

★ **lead the field** to be the best or most successful person in an activity or competition ○ *The Americans continue to lead the field when it comes to child actors.*

left-field (*journalism*) used for describing an unusual and unconventional performer or piece of entertainment ○ *Over the last few years, the most left-field films in world cinema have come from Japan.*

> In baseball, left field is the part of the outfield where the sun and the wind can cause problems with the ball. In addition, the spectators often shout at the fielder in left field, and so players consider it to be a difficult position to play.

out in left field or **out of left field** unusual and unconventional ○ *Most of the business tips are common sense, but others are right out of left field.*

play the field to have many different romantic relationships rather than staying with one person ○ *He gave up playing the field and married a year ago.*

> If gamblers play the field, they bet on all the horses in a race except the one that is considered most likely to win.

fig

a fig leaf something that is intended to hide an embarrassing or awkward situation ○ *In California, medical marijuana has become a fig leaf for those who want to legally smoke pot.*

> According to the Bible (Genesis 3:7), when Adam and Eve ate the apple in the Garden of Eden, they realized that they were naked and felt ashamed, so they covered their genitals with fig leaves.

fight

a knock-down drag-out fight a very emotional, angry, or even violent argument or fight ○ *Nobody had much of a stomach this year for another knock-down drag-out fight over the state budget.*

> This expression refers to a type of boxing match in which a fighter who had been knocked down was dragged out of the ring and replaced by another contestant.

fill

★ **have had your fill of something** to have had as much of something bad as you can manage ○ *They have had their fill of war, poverty, and repression.*

finders

finders keepers used to express the idea that a person has a right to keep something that they have found ○ *Obviously, someone picked up my umbrella and has made no effort to find the owner. Finders, keepers.*

finger

give someone the finger to make an offensive gesture by holding your middle finger up at someone ○ *He told police he had had an argument with someone who cursed at him and gave him the finger.*

have a finger in every pie to be involved in many different activities, often in a way that is disapproved of ○ *He has a finger in every pie and is never short of ideas for making the next buck.*

> The most likely explanation for this expression is that it refers to someone who is involved in making a pie.

★ **have your finger on the pulse** or **keep your finger on the pulse** to know all the latest information about something or have a good understanding of how it works ○ *Although I'm Southern, after all these years in Chicago I think my editors and I have our finger on the pulse of the city.*

> Someone's pulse is the speed and force with which their blood vessels expand and contract as their heart beats. A doctor might feel a patient's pulse by pressing a finger lightly against the large artery in their wrist.

not lay a finger on someone to not hurt someone in any way ○ *One of the men accused of attacking trucker Reginald Denny at the start of the Los Angeles riots says he never laid a finger on him.*

★ **not lift a finger** to not do something or not help someone at all ○ *I'm the one who has to clean it all up. She wouldn't lift a finger if I didn't beg her.*

★ **point the finger at someone** to blame someone for a mistake they have made or accuse them of doing something wrong ○ *One socialist blamed the press for his suicide, but some commentators pointed a finger at the political establishment.*

put the finger on someone (literary) to tell a person in authority that someone has done something wrong or illegal ○ *It's not like we put the finger on anyone real, Janie. Nobody is suffering because of what we told that detective.*

★ **put your finger on something** to understand or say exactly what the cause of a problem or the answer to a question is ○ *He had thought that Houston would have arrived at that solution first; but, no, it was Dr. Stockton who had put his finger on the truth.*

wrap someone around your little finger or

twist someone around your little finger to make someone do anything you want them to ○ *A child who is spoiled is able to wrap her parents around her little finger.*

fingernails

someone is hanging on by their fingernails → see **hang**

fingers

★ **keep your fingers crossed** or **cross your fingers** to hope for luck or success in something ○ *I will be keeping my fingers crossed that everything goes well.*

> People sometimes actually cross their middle finger over their index finger when they use this expression or are wishing someone good luck.

★ **let something slip through your fingers** to fail to get or keep something, especially something good ○ *If your income is greater than your expenses, count yourself lucky – and don't let it slip through your fingers!*

someone can count something on the fingers of one hand used to emphasize that there are surprisingly few of the things mentioned ○ *I could count the jobs advertised each year on the fingers of one hand.*

★ **someone gets their fingers burned**
or
someone burns their fingers used when someone fails or gets a bad result and so is nervous about trying again ○ *The government, after getting its fingers burned so badly, will surely not want to make the same mistake again.*

sticky fingers a tendency to steal ○ *Beverly Cockrell, a rancher, has confronted strangers with sticky fingers on her land.*

work your fingers to the bone to work extremely hard ○ *I have washed, cooked, fetched and carried all my life. I worked my fingers to the bone in this house.*

fingertips

★ **at your fingertips**
1 readily available for you to use or reach ○ *All basic controls are at your fingertips for straightforward, no fuss operation.*
2 if you have facts or information at your fingertips, you know them thoroughly and can refer to them quickly ○ *He wanted to know all about his latest projects, so that the correct answers were at his fingertips when he was questioned by the right people.*

someone is hanging on by their fingertips → see **hang**

fire

breathe fire to be very angry about something ○ *One Democratic legislator who was breathing fire over the Weinberger indictment yesterday was Brooks.*

catch fire to become exciting or entertaining ○ *The play only really catches fire once Aschenbach falls in love.*

★ **come under fire** or
be under fire to be strongly criticized ○ *The president's plan first came under fire from critics who said he didn't include enough spending cuts.*

do something with fire in your belly to do something in a very enthusiastic, energetic, and passionate way ○ *Some people claim he has changed his style, but Ian has played with fire in his belly throughout his career.*

draw someone's fire to do or say something that makes someone strongly criticize you ○ *Their first modern building immediately drew the fire of the architectural establishment.*

≣ "Fire" here means gunfire.

fight fire with fire to use the same methods of fighting and the same amount of force as your opponent ○ *Should liberals adopt those types of aggressive "gotcha" tactics and fight fire with fire or should they take the higher ground?*

hang fire to wait and not do anything for a while ○ *Banks and building societies are hanging fire on interest rates to see how the French vote in their referendum.*

≣ This expression dates from the time when firearms used gunpowder rather than bullets. If a gun hung fire, it did not fire properly because the gunpowder had not caught light. "Flash in the pan" has a similar origin.

hold fire or
hold your fire to delay doing something such as attacking or criticizing someone, because you are waiting to see what will happen ○ *The administration will hold its fire until it sees the details of the bill, but is likely then to oppose it.*

light a fire under someone to force someone to take action or to start behaving in the way you want ○ *They need to crank up their technical research and light a fire under their marketing force.*

There is a story that some American farmers in the early part of the 20th century used to light fires under particularly stubborn mules that were refusing to move, in order to make them do so.

★ **play with fire** to behave in a very risky way that means that you are likely to have problems ○ *Schulte warned government and industrial leaders that those who even venture to think about mass layoffs are playing with fire.*

fish

be like a fish out of water to feel awkward and not relaxed because you are in a situation or surroundings that you are not used to ○ *He thought of himself as a country gentleman; he was like a fish out of water in New York.*

be neither fish nor fowl to seem partly one thing and partly another, and be difficult to identify, classify, or understand ○ *By the mid-1980s, Canada had a constitution that was neither fish nor fowl in terms of political philosophy.*

"Fowl" is an old-fashioned word for a chicken or other bird.

★ **a big fish** an important or powerful person ○ *The four who were arrested here last September were described as really big fish by the U.S. Drug Enforcement Agency.*

a big fish in a small pond one of the most important and influential people in a small organization or social group. You can also talk about **a big frog in a small pond**. ○ *In Rhodesia I was a big fish in a small pond. But here there'd be many lean years before I built up a reputation.*

a cold fish a person who seems unemotional, which makes them appear unfriendly or unsympathetic ○ *He doesn't really show much emotion – he's a kind of a cold fish.*

drink like a fish to regularly drink a lot of alcohol ○ *Her father drank like a fish.*

People used to believe that fish drank constantly because they breathe through open mouths.

have bigger fish to fry or
have other fish to fry to not be interested in something because you have more important, interesting, or profitable things to do ○ *I didn't pursue it in detail because I'm afraid I had other fish to fry at the time.*

something is like shooting fish in a barrel used when one side in a battle or contest is so much stronger than the other that the weaker side has no chance at all of winning ○ *I heard one case where some of the enemy soldiers had come out and they were saying it was like shooting fish in a barrel.*

there are plenty more fish in the sea used to encourage someone that there are still many other people whom they might have a successful relationship with in the future, even though their romance or love affair has ended ○ *If your daughter is upset because her boyfriend left her, telling her that "there are plenty more fish in the sea" won't help.*

fishing

be on a fishing expedition to be trying to find out the truth or the facts about something, often in a secretive way ○ *You know why you're here. You're on a fishing expedition. You're hunting for material.*

fit

fit as a fiddle physically fit and healthy ○ *I'm as fit as a fiddle, I'm never ill, I have an iron constitution.*

This expression may originally have applied to a violin player, or fiddler, rather than to a violin, or fiddle. The fiddler had to be fit in order to play all evening at a festival or party. Alternatively, "fit" could mean "suitable" rather than "healthy," so the original meaning may have been "as suitable for its purpose as a fiddle is for making music."

fit to be tied very angry ○ *Douglas was fit to be tied. He almost killed Harry. He made Harry pay back every last penny.*

"Fit" here means ready or suitable for a particular purpose.

have a fit or
throw a fit to become very angry and upset ○ *She threw a fit when I told her what Jamie had said.*

fits

★ **in fits and starts** not continuously, but regularly stopping and then starting again ○ *Denise's career plans can only proceed in fits and starts.*

A fit is a sudden outburst or attack of a particular emotion.

fix

★ **get a fix on someone or something** to have a clear idea or understanding of someone or something ○ *It's difficult to get a fix on what brokers earn. Their commissions depend on the number and cost of the properties they sell.*

★ **in a fix** in a difficult or dangerous situation that has no easy solution ○ *Growing inflation and oil prices have put the government in a fix.*

★ **there is no quick fix** used to say that there are no simple ways of solving a problem ○ *There can be no quick fix for public spending. If the recovery fails to cut the deficit sharply, a rise in taxes will be needed.* ○ *He warned Congress against any quick fix solutions to get the economy moving.*

flag

★ **fly the flag** to represent your country or a group to which you belong at a sporting event or at some other special occasion, or to do something to show your support for it ○ *It doesn't matter*

whether you are flying the flag for your country, or the Horse Trials Group, or your sponsor, the image you present is all-important.

keep the flag flying to do something to show your support for a group to which you belong, or to show your support for something that you agree with ○ *I would ask members to keep the flag flying by entering some of their plants in both shows.*

a red flag something that gives a warning of a bad or dangerous situation or event ○ *Anyone who raises a red flag could be met by officials when the ship or plane arrives in this country.*

wave a red flag at a bull to try to make someone react angrily ○ *In the South we call that waving a red flag at a bull. How can Sarah not respond to that comment?*

It is a common belief that the color red makes bulls angry. In bullfighting, the matador waves a red cape to make the bull attack.

wrap yourself in the flag or
drape yourself in the flag to try to do something for your own advantage while pretending to do it for the good of your country ○ *Politicians always try to wrap themselves in the flag on Independence Day, but I think most people can see through that.*

flagpole

run something up the flagpole to suggest a new idea to people in order to find out what they think of it ○ *The President should consider running the capital-gains cut back up the flagpole.*

If you run a flag up a flagpole, you pull it to the top using the rope attached to the side of the flagpole.

flak

★ **catch some flak** or
take some flak or
catch a lot of flak to receive strong

criticism about something ○ *McCall, a former cocaine and heroin addict, is catching a lot of flak for comments she made about how to keep her daughter off of drugs.*

flame

★ **an old flame** someone who you had a romantic relationship with in the past ○ *Last week Alec was seen dining with his old flame, Janine Turner, in New York.*

> An old meaning of "flame" was the person that someone was in love with.

flames

be shot down in flames to be criticized strongly or rejected completely ○ *Just six months ago his idea would have been shot down in flames for its sheer lunacy.*

★ **fan the flames** to make a bad situation worse ○ *Extremist organizations in the west were actively fanning the flames in the east, he said.*

> To fan flames means to make them burn more strongly by waving a fan or other flat object next to them.

go up in flames to fail, come to an end, or be destroyed completely ○ *The Hollywood she'd known had gone up in flames the day she left. A new Hollywood and a new Washington had grown up.*

flash

★ **a flash in the pan** an achievement or success that is unlikely to be repeated or to last ○ *Hybrid technology is not just a flash in the pan.*

> This expression has its origins in the way that an old-fashioned flintlock gun worked. Pulling the trigger produced a spark that set light to a small amount of gunpowder held in the "pan." This in turn lit the rest of the gunpowder. However, if it failed to do so there was just a "flash in the pan" and the gun did not fire properly. "Hang fire" has a similar origin.

in a flash very quickly or suddenly ○ *Sam was out of his hiding place in a flash and crossed the space between him and the cliff-foot in a couple of leaps.*

flat

★ **fall flat**
1 if an event or an attempt to do something falls flat, it is completely unsuccessful ○ *The champagne opening of a new art gallery fell flat when the boss's wife fired a cork straight through the most expensive painting on show.*
2 if a joke falls flat, nobody thinks it is funny ○ *He then started trying to tell jokes to the assembled gathering. These too fell flat.*

flat as a pancake very flat ○ *There was barely a breeze and the water was as flat as a pancake.*

flat-footed

be caught flat-footed or **be left flat-footed** to be put at a disadvantage when something happens which you do not expect, with the result that you do not know what to do next and often look foolish ○ *"The people around were caught flat-footed," said Mr. Enko. "Nobody expected floods of such magnitude."*

flavor

★ **flavor of the month** someone or something that is very popular at a particular time ○ *Most stars are likely to declare an unprecedented interest in whatever cause is the latest flavor of the month in celebrity circles.*

> Ice cream parlors sometimes select a particular flavor of the month in order to encourage people to try different flavors of ice cream.

flesh

flesh and blood real and actually existing, rather than being part of someone's imagination ○ *He was the first* writer since Shakespeare to show his readers that the past was peopled by flesh and blood human beings very like themselves.

make your flesh crawl or
make your flesh creep to make you frightened, distressed, or uncomfortable ○ I didn't like him the first time I set eyes on him. He made my flesh crawl and now I know why.

★ **meet someone in the flesh** or
see someone in the flesh to actually meet or see someone, rather than, for example, seeing them in a movie or on television ○ But what does Jamie think of his hero now, having met him in the flesh?

★ **press the flesh** (journalism) to talk to people in a crowd and shake their hands. This expression is often used about politicians, who do this when they are trying to get elected. ○ Royalty's function in the sports arena is generally confined to pressing the flesh and presenting trophies.

put flesh on something or
put flesh on the bones of something to add more detailed information or more substance to something ○ What would a Middle East at peace actually look like? Somebody needs to start putting flesh on those bones.

someone is flesh and blood used to emphasize that someone has human feelings or weaknesses, and that they are not perfect ○ I'm flesh and blood like everyone else and I, too, can be damaged.

★ **someone is your own flesh and blood** said to mean someone is a member of your family that you must help when they are in trouble ○ He's my own flesh and blood; I'll stick by him whatever he does.

flies

be dropping like flies
1 be dying in large numbers within a short period of time ○ Meanwhile Burketown was left without a police officer while people were dropping like flies.

2 be failing in large numbers within a short period of time ○ While other retailers are dropping like flies, supermarkets are making fat profits.

there are no flies on someone used about someone who is quick to understand a situation and is not easily deceived ○ You have to establish that you are an officer with good and tried soldiers: there are no flies on the enemy.

flight

★ **a flight of fancy** an imaginative idea or plan that is pleasant to think about but not at all practical ○ This is no flight of fancy. The prototype is already flying, and production is to begin next year.

flip

the flip side of something the opposite, and usually negative effect of something ○ Humans have many cravings and creature comforts, but the flip side of these for many is addiction, pain and ill health.

The flip side of a coin or of a vinyl record is the opposite side.

floodgates

★ **open the floodgates to something** to make it possible or likely that a particular thing will be done by many people, perhaps in a way that seems undesirable ○ Giving in to the strikers' demands would open the floodgates to demands by workers in other large state-owned industries.

floor

fall through the floor to suddenly decrease to a very low level ○ On the fateful day, Oct. 19, the value of those stocks fell through the floor.

wipe the floor with someone to prove that you are much better than someone else at doing something, or to defeat them totally in a competition, fight, or discussion ○ When you play *against people whose technique is superior and who can match your courage and commitment, they're going to wipe the floor with you.*

flow

★ **go with the flow** to let things happen to you or let other people tell you what to do, rather than trying to control what happens yourself ○ *This year I'm going to take a deep breath, leave my troubles and tension in the departure lounge and go with the flow.*

fly

do something on the fly to do something quickly and automatically, without thinking about it or planning it in advance ○ *This gives architects and designers the power to build an environment, explore it and maybe do some designing on the fly.*

the fly in the ointment the person or thing that prevents a situation from being as successful or enjoyable as it otherwise would be ○ *The only fly in the ointment is the enormous debt portfolios of Marine Midland in Latin America.*

> This expression probably comes from the Bible (Ecclesiastes 10:1), which says that in the same way that dead flies give perfume or ointment a bad smell, a little foolishness spoils great wisdom and honor.

★ **someone would love to be a fly on the wall** used in situations where someone would like to be present when a particular thing happens, and hear what is said or see what happens, although this is actually impossible because it will take place in private ○ *I'd love to be a fly on the wall at their team meetings.* ○ *I'd love to work as the personal photographer of a rock star for a year, documenting their life on the road from a fly-on-the-wall perspective.*

someone wouldn't hurt a fly or **someone wouldn't harm a fly** used

about someone is very kind and gentle ○ *He is, he insists, a pacifist, who would not hurt a fly.*

food

★ **food for thought** something that makes you think very hard about an issue ○ *I am not a religious person, but knowing what a good and faithful servant my friend has been, it has certainly given me food for thought.*

fool

a fool and his money are soon parted used to express the idea that it is easy to persuade someone who is not sensible to spend their money on worthless things ○ *The sad truth is that a fool and his money are soon parted, and even more so, a fool who is in love.*

★ **fool's gold** a plan for making money that is foolish and sure to fail ○ *He dismissed as "pure fool's gold" the idea that devaluing the pound could assist the British economy.*

> Fool's gold is another name for iron pyrite, a gold-colored mineral that is found in rock and that people sometimes mistake for gold.

live in a fool's paradise to believe wrongly and stupidly that your situation is good, when really it is not ○ *Economists have been living in a fool's paradise. The recession has started.*

play someone for a fool to deceive someone and use them for your own advantage ○ *John, do not play me for a fool. You owe me better than that.*

fools

fools rush in where angels fear to tread or
fools rush in used to criticize a person who did something too quickly without thinking clearly about the likely consequences ○ *Sometimes I stop and*

think, how did I get into this? Fools rush in where angels fear to tread.

≡ This proverb comes from Alexander
≡ Pope's "An Essay on Criticism" (1711).

foot

be caught on the wrong foot to be surprised by something that happens quickly and unexpectedly, because you are not ready for it ○ *The supermarket chain seems to have been caught on the wrong foot, still trying to escape its "cheap" past just as it should be capitalizing on that record.* ○ *Again and again European and UN diplomacy has been wrong-footed by events in the Balkans.*

★ **get a foot in the door** to make a small but successful start at something, for example doing business in a new area, and to be likely to do well in the future ○ *The only reason I took the job was because I thought it might help me get a foot in the door.*

get off on the wrong foot to start a relationship or situation badly ○ *Every time I come home on leave, we seem to get off on the wrong foot. We argue a lot.*

≡ The "wrong foot" refers to the left foot.
≡ There is an ancient superstition that
≡ the left side of the body is connected
≡ with bad luck and evil. The Romans
≡ sometimes placed guards at the
≡ entrances to public buildings to ensure
≡ that people entered them with their
≡ right foot first. "Get out of bed on the
≡ wrong side" is based on a similar belief.

have a foot in both camps to support or belong to two different groups, without making a firm commitment to either of them ○ *With an Indian father and an English mother, she had a foot in both camps – or perhaps in neither.*

≡ In this expression, a camp is a place
≡ where an army has put up its tents
≡ during part of a war or battle.

on foot by walking ○ *If it's not raining we can go there on foot.*

★ **put your best foot forward** to work hard and energetically to make sure that something that you are doing is a success ○ *David said that the commission should have put its best foot forward and produced something independent.*

★ **put your foot down**
1 to use your authority in order to stop something from happening ○ *He had planned to go on holiday with his friends, but his father had put his foot down.*
2 to start to drive as fast as you can ○ *Once out of the park and finding a clear stretch of Bay Road, he put his foot down.*

★ **put your foot in your mouth** or **put your foot in it** to say something that embarrasses or offends the person you are with ○ *I put my foot in my mouth right away, referring to folk music. Tom sat forward and glared. "It's not folk music, man. It's heritage music."*

set foot in a place or **set foot on something** to be physically present somewhere ○ *Two of Christopher Columbus's shipmates were the first Africans to set foot in the New World, a study has found.*

★ **shoot yourself in the foot** to do or say something stupid that causes problems for you or harms your chances of success ○ *Unless he shoots himself in the foot, in all probability he will become President.*

someone has one foot in the grave used about someone who is very ill or very old and is likely to die soon. You use this expression when you are talking about illness and death in a light-hearted way. ○ *The guards are completely taken in, they're convinced De Fiore's got one foot in the grave.*

start off on the right foot to immediately have success when you begin to do something ○ *To me this was a man who was prepared to start off on the* *right foot; he was mature with some common sense.*

★ **under foot** in the way ○ *With the kids back in school and out from under foot, now is the time to start cleaning the house.*

footloose

footloose and fancy-free *(old-fashioned)* having very few responsibilities ○ *A divorced man is footloose and fancy-free. He can go to parties on his own, and come and go as he pleases.*

> This term refers to a sail that could move about freely and unpredictably because the ropes holding it at the foot or bottom were loose.

footsie

play footsie

1 to touch or rub someone's foot with your foot under a table, especially as a sign of sexual interest ○ *"Are you trying to play footsie?" she asked.*

2 to try to start a secret relationship that you hope to benefit from ○ *Business leaders have been accused of playing footsie with Congressmen.*

footsteps

★ **follow in someone's footsteps** to do the same thing that someone else did ○ *Rudolph Garvin was a college student, the son of a physician, who wanted to follow in his father's footsteps.*

forest

someone cannot see the forest for the trees someone is so involved in the details of something that they forget or do not realize the real purpose or importance of the thing as a whole ○ *The staff here are working so hard and are so tired that they can't see the forest for the trees.*

forewarned

forewarned is forearmed used to emphasize that if you know about something that is going to happen in the future, you can be ready to deal with it ○ *The authors' idea is that forewarned is forearmed: if we know how persuasion works, perhaps we can resist some of it.*

fort

hold down the fort or

hold the fort to take care of things for someone while they are somewhere else or while they are busy doing something else ○ *Since she was elected to Congress five years ago, her husband has held down the fort at their Norfolk, VA home during the week.*

fortune

★ **a small fortune** a very large amount of money ○ *For almost two years, Hawkins made a small fortune running a drugstore.*

foundations

shake the foundations of something to cause great uncertainty and make people question their most deeply held beliefs ○ *The crisis shook the foundations of the world economy.*

fox

crazy like a fox or

stupid like a fox seemingly crazy or stupid, but actually the opposite ○ *People dismiss him as crazy, but he could be crazy like a fox.*

> The image here is of the fox traditionally viewed as cunning, and thus able to trick people by appearing to act foolish while actually being very clever.

frame

★ **frame of mind** the mood that someone is in, which affects how they experience life ○ *What sense did you get about his frame of mind from your conversations with him?*

in the frame thought to be responsible for a crime or an unpleasant situation, even though this might be untrue ○ *The fact is, there's only ever been one guy in the frame for this killing, and that's the husband.*

> The "frame" referred to here is probably one of the frames, or images, in a reel of film.

frazzle

wear yourself to a frazzle to feel mentally and physically exhausted because you have been working too hard or because you have been constantly worrying about something ○ *Why should I wear myself to a frazzle, trying to save your skin for you?*

free

free as a bird completely free, with no worries or troubles ○ *I have been island-hopping in the Pacific for the past two and a half years, free as a bird.*

freefall

★ **go into freefall** (*journalism*) if the value or level of something goes into freefall, it starts to fall very quickly ○ *Fears are now widespread that the stock market could go into freefall before Christmas.*

> In parachuting, freefall is the part of the jump before the parachute opens.

French

pardon my French used, often humorously, to ask your listeners to excuse you for using an offensive word ○ *Pardon my French, but you're an idiot.*

frenzy

★ **a feeding frenzy** a situation in which a lot of people become very excited about something, often in a destructive or negative way ○ *His statement was unnecessary, and merely served to start a media feeding frenzy.*

> This expression was first used to describe the behavior of groups of sharks when there is blood in the water but not enough food for them all. In this situation the sharks will attack anything that they see, even each other.

fresh

fresh as a daisy very fresh, bright, or alert ○ *She can sleep through anything and emerge fresh as a daisy at the end of it.*

friend

★ **a fair-weather friend** someone who is not helpful to you when you need help ○ *Pulling out of Afghanistan would tell the United States and Britain, another key ally, that Australia was an unreliable ally and a fair-weather friend.*

fritz

on the fritz a piece of machinery that is on the fritz is not working properly ○ *My mother's toaster went on the fritz.*

frog

have a frog in your throat to find it difficult to speak clearly because you have a cough or a sore throat ○ *Even when I was little, other kids would ask if I had a frog in my throat. I just have a raspy voice.*

> In medieval times, there was a belief that if you drank water containing frogspawn, the frogs would grow inside your body. People believed that sore throats and coughing could be caused by the frogs trying to escape from your stomach through your throat.

frosting

★ **frosting on the cake** see **icing**

fruit

★ **bear fruit** to produce good results ○ *People see material conditions getting worse. They don't see the economic reforms championed by the President as bearing fruit.*

forbidden fruit something that you want very much but are not allowed to have ○ *Knowing that from now on you can't eat chocolate or have sugar in your tea can make you want those forbidden fruits even more.*

This expression refers to the story in the Bible in which Eve tempts Adam to eat the fruit of the tree of knowledge, which God had forbidden them to touch.

low-hanging fruit the easiest of a number of things that can be done or obtained ○ *Overtime is low-hanging fruit when it comes to reducing costs; but so many governments haven't managed to tame it.*

frying pan

out of the frying pan into the fire from a bad situation to an even worse one ○ *I was hoping to get my career back on track at Dell, after a bad time at IBM. But as it turned out, I'd gone out of the frying pan into the fire.*

fuel

★ **add fuel to the fire** to make a bad situation worse ○ *You must not take the route of trying to borrow your way out of trouble. This really would be adding fuel to the fire.*

full

be full of yourself to be very proud or conceited, and think only of yourself ○ *I tired of him quite quickly – he's so full of himself.*

fun

poke fun at someone or something to make jokes about someone or something ○ *Tourists, exchange students and expatriates alike enjoy poking fun at the culture they've adopted.*

funeral

it's your funeral said to someone who you think will be affected by bad consequences because they insist on doing something wrong, risky, or dangerous ○ *She'll preview this new material Saturday for Pittsburgh audiences. To those with front row seats, well, it's your funeral.*

fur

the fur is flying said when people are arguing very angrily about something ○ *The world's oldest major championship does not start until tomorrow, yet already the fur is flying thick and fast.*

The image here is of animals tearing out each other's fur during a fight.

furniture

part of the furniture someone or something that has been present somewhere for such a long time that everyone accepts their presence without questioning it or noticing them ○ *In ten years he has become part of the furniture of Washington life, his place on the stage firmly fixed and universally respected.*

fuse

blow a fuse to suddenly lose your temper and not be able to control your anger ○ *For all my experience, I blew a fuse in the quarter-final and could have been sent off.*

A fuse is a safety device found in electrical equipment. If the equipment becomes too hot, the fuse blows, or burns. This breaks the electrical circuit, so that the equipment will stop working.

have a short fuse to lose your temper very easily and be quick to react angrily when something goes wrong ○ *Perhaps he's irritable and has a short fuse, letting you know when he's not pleased.*

See the explanation at "light the fuse."

light the fuse to do something that starts off a new and exciting development, or that makes a situation become dangerous ○ *Ghana's independence in 1957 lit the fuse which led to the rapid freeing of colonial Africa.*

The fuse referred to here is the type that is used to set off a firework or explosive device.

Gg

gains

★ **ill-gotten gains** money or something valuable that somebody gets illegally ○ *These corrupt officials must be forced to give up their ill-gotten gains.*

gallery

play to the gallery to try to impress the public and make yourself popular, instead of dealing seriously with important matters ○ *It took years for Congress to allow TV cameras there, because some members were frightened that others would play to the gallery.*

> The gallery in a theater is a raised area like a large balcony, that usually contains the cheapest seats. In the past, the poorest and least educated people sat there. Actors and other performers found it easier to get applause from them than from the other members of the audience.

game

★ **ahead of the game** well prepared to deal with any change that happens in the activity that you are involved in ○ *We're always looking at new technologies to keep ahead of the game.*

★ **beat someone at their own game** to do something more successfully than someone else, although they have a reputation for doing it very well ○ *The Avalanche beat the Red Wings at their own game: they were more aggressive and equally skilled.*

★ **the game is up** used to say that someone can no longer continue to do something wrong or illegal because people have found out what they are doing ○ *He narrowed his eyes as the red and blue lights of the police car filled the cab. Sensing the game was up, he pulled over.*

a game of cat and mouse → see **cat**

★ **a game plan** the things that someone intends to do in order to achieve a particular aim ○ *So few people stick to their game plan. I stuck to mine. I had always wanted to be a millionaire from a very early age.*

> In football, a game plan is a strategy that the players and coach develop before a game.

★ **give the game away** to reveal something that someone had been trying to keep secret ○ *Johnson had intended to make his announcement in a forthcoming feature in the Times but the paper gave the game away.*

new to the game having no previous experience of an activity that you are taking part in ○ *Don't forget that she's new to this game and will take a while to complete the task, so you need to be very patient.*

not play that game to refuse to do what is expected or what is normally done ○ *Many companies are selling cheap low quality products, but we don't want to play that game.*

the only game in town the only option worth considering ○ *He's the only game in town, and I am hoping that he can show some real leadership strength.*

> This expression may refer to someone being prepared to take part in a game of poker, even if it was dishonest, because it was the only one going on at the time.

★ **play the game** to do things in the

accepted way or in the way that you are told to in order to keep your job or to achieve success ○ *In order to survive in the political system, they have to play the game.*

This is a quotation from the Olympic Creed written by Pierre de Coubertin, founder of the modern Olympics, in 1896. The expression was then used by Sir Henry Newbolt in his poem "Vitaï Lampada" (1898): "But the voice of the schoolboy rallies the ranks: "Play up! Play up! and play the game!"

★ **play a waiting game** to delay making any decisions or taking any action, because you think that it is better to wait and see how things develop ○ *I propose to play a waiting game, and hope that a few of the pieces of this puzzle will soon begin to fit together.*

two can play at this game said when you intend to behave toward someone in the same unfair or unpleasant way that they have been behaving toward you ○ *I never used to get introduced to their clients. So now when I have clients to come and see me, I don't introduce them either. Two can play at this game.*

games

★ **play games** to not be serious enough about a difficult situation ○ *The company says it needs about a week to make a decision on staffing. One employee says he thinks the company is playing games with them.*

gamut

★ **run the gamut** to include a wide range or variety of things ○ *The cast of characters runs the gamut from reality stars to sports stars.*

gangbusters

like gangbusters very energetically and sometimes aggressively ○ *The Lakers, who struggled early, came on like gangbusters at precisely the right time, which is to say, when the playoffs started.*

A gangbuster is someone, especially a police officer, whose job is to break up criminal gangs.

garbage

garbage in, garbage out used to say that if you produce something using poor quality materials, the thing you produce will also be of poor quality ○ *A computer expert, he said he'd learned from computer programming that if you put garbage in, you get garbage out.*

This expression comes from computing. If the wrong information is put into the computer, the output will be useless.

garden

★ **garden variety** very ordinary and of the type that is usually found ○ *The style of the new model sets it apart from garden variety sports cars.*

This expression was originally used to describe the most ordinary variety of a species of plant.

lead someone up the garden path or **lead someone down the garden path** to deceive someone by making them believe something that is not true ○ *He may have led me up the garden path. He said everything was over with Penny but now he seems to be seeing her again.*

gas

run out of gas to suddenly feel very tired or lose interest in what you are doing ○ *Miller, who missed second place by four seconds, said she "ran out of gas" close to the finish.*

The image here is of a car stopping because it has run out of gas.

gasp

★ **last gasp**

1 (*journalism*) achieved at the last possible moment ○ *Last gasp negotiations by the*

National Museum of Photography could ensure major new shows by legendary photographers Richard Avedon and Sebastião Salgado.
2 the very last stage of a long process or period of time ○ Eleven thousand years ago, at the last gasp of the ice age, the area was covered with rich, semi-deciduous forest, not dry grassland.

> These phrases come from 2 Maccabes 7:9 in the Apocrypha of the Bible. Seven brothers and their mother were tortured by King Antiochus, and one of the brothers spoke out defiantly "when he was at his last gasp," or when he was dying.

gauntlet

> Gauntlets are long thick gloves which protect your hands, wrists, and forearms.

★ **run the gauntlet**
1 to have to go through a place where people are trying to harm or humiliate you, for example, by attacking you or shouting insults at you ○ President-elect Chamorro also had to run the gauntlet as bags of water rained down from the Sandinista section of the stadium.
2 to suffer bad treatment from people because of something you are trying to achieve ○ He has run the gauntlet of arrest, police investigation, spells in prison and house detention in connection with his ties to radical groups.

> "Gatlopp" is a Swedish word meaning "lane run." The "gatlopp" was a Swedish military punishment that came into common use in England during the Thirty Years' War (1618-48). The victim had to run between two rows of soldiers who would whip or beat them. In England, the unfamiliar Swedish word "gatlopp" was replaced by the more familiar English word "gauntlet."

take up the gauntlet to respond to a challenge by showing that you accept it ○ We received many letters on the subject, and several said we should ask our readers for nominations. We are taking up the gauntlet. Write to us with your suggestions.

★ **throw down the gauntlet** to do or say something that challenges someone to take action or to compete against you ○ The truckers threw down their gauntlet to the government after an all-night meeting of their strike committee

> In medieval times, a knight would throw one of his gauntlets to the ground as a challenge to another knight to fight. If the second knight picked it up, he accepted the challenge.

gear

> The image in this idiom is of driving a car or riding a motorcycle.

★ **get into gear** to start to deal with something in an effective way ○ The town itself has got into gear with a campaign to improve the environment.
★ **kick into high gear**
★ **shift into high gear** or
move into high gear to start making the greatest effort to achieve something ○ For the two guys who want to be governor, the drive to the state capitol has kicked into high gear.

gears

★ **shift gears** to begin to do something in a different way ○ Companies looking to shift gears and change direction towards other emerging markets will likely find it difficult

genie

the genie is out of the bottle used when something has been done or created that has made a great and permanent change in people's lives, especially a change which people regret ○ *The genie is out of the bottle and all attempts to stop the tide of GM crops are in vain.*

In Arabian mythology, a genie is a mischievous spirit with magical powers. This expression may refer to the story of Aladdin, who rubs a lamp and releases a genie from it.

gentle

gentle as a lamb very kind and calm ○ *Brian was as gentle as a lamb and wouldn't hurt anyone.*

get-go

from the get-go (*informal*) from the beginning of an activity ○ *Borrowing to make distributions was part of the plan from the get-go because of the seasonal nature of the business.*

ghost

give up the ghost
1 to stop trying to do something, because you no longer believe that you can succeed ○ *In Manhattan there was no Memorial Day parade this year. The organizers said they've given up the ghost after so few people turned out last year.*
2 if a machine gives up the ghost, it stops working ○ *A short way off the return ferry, Danny's car gave up the ghost again.*

This expression originally meant "to die," and people still occasionally use it with this meaning.

lay the ghost of something (*mainly British*) to do something that stops you being upset or affected by something bad in your past ○ *Jockey Adrian Maguire laid the ghost of a ghastly week with a comprehensive win in the Champion Hurdle yesterday.*

gift

the gift of the gab or
the gift of gab the ability to speak confidently, clearly and in a persuasive way ○ *He was entertaining company and certainly had the gift of the gab.*

This expression may be related to the Irish and Gaelic word "gab," which means mouth.

gift horse

look a gift horse in the mouth to find faults or difficulties when someone offers you a gift or opportunity ○ *When you're an entrepreneur, you don't look a gift horse in the mouth.*

This expression refers to the fact that you can judge the age of a horse by looking at its teeth.

gills

green around the gills looking as if you are going to be sick ○ *Kenny stumbled out from the washroom. "I'm all right now." He still looked quite green around the gills.*

The gills of a fish are the organs it uses to breathe instead of lungs. This is being used as a humorous term for the mouth.

girl

girl Friday a woman whose job is to help others, especially in an office ○ *Wilma, our solitary girl Friday at the front desk, will answer my incoming calls.*

give

★ **give and take** a situation in which two people or groups do things to help or please each other ○ *I'm in a happy relationship where there's a lot of give and take.*

give it up for someone (*informal*) to cheer or applaud someone ○ *"As a mark of our gratitude for all her effort over the last year, let's give it up for Kath."*

★ **give or take something**
1 used when you want to indicate that a number, especially a large number, is

approximate ○ *The buried crater is 35 kilometers across and dates back 66 million years, give or take a million.*

2 used to mean "except for." It is often used humorously. ○ *We are not in Sydney; this is Schenectady. The two do have a similar feel to them, give or take the odd beach, bridge, harbor and opera house.*

glance

★ **at first glance** said when you are describing your first impression of someone or something, especially when you know that this first impression was wrong or incomplete ○ *The difficulty comes when two people, who appeared at first glance to have so much in common, discover that they have simply grown apart.*

glass

★ **the glass ceiling** the attitudes and traditions that sometimes prevent women, or people from ethnic or religious minorities, from getting the most important jobs ○ *If women are to become part of the core of our military, the glass ceiling must be shattered .*

people who live in glass houses shouldn't throw stones used to emphasize that everyone has faults and so they should not criticize other people for their faults ○ *When will they learn? People in glass houses really shouldn't throw stones.*

glasses

★ **look at something through rose-tinted glasses** to notice only the good things about a situation, so that your opinion is unrealistic ○ *He accused diplomats of looking at the world through rose-tinted glasses.*

gloss

put a gloss on something to try to convince people that things are better than they really are ○ *Garland could see no harm in putting an optimistic gloss on what*

the specialist had actually said.

≣ A gloss is an explanation that is added to a book or other text in order to explain an unfamiliar term. The idea here is that the explanation being given is a misleading one.

glove

fit like a glove to be exactly the right shape or size, or to be exactly right or appropriate in some other way ○ *Surprisingly, she has not sung Leonora for a long time, yet, as I reminded her, she used to say the part fitted her voice like a glove.*

gloves

the gloves are off used to say that people have decided to compete aggressively with each other ○ *In the software price war, the gloves are off.*

≣ The reference here is to boxers fighting with bare fists, which is more dangerous than fighting with gloves on.

glutton

a glutton for punishment a person who keeps on doing something that is unpleasant or difficult for them ○ *What I want to know is why on earth you want anything to do with this confused and angry man. Obviously you're a glutton for punishment.*

≣ A glutton is a greedy person.

gnat

strain at a gnat (literary) to concern yourself with something unimportant, perhaps neglecting something that really is important ○ *When it comes down to distinguishing 1 percent growth from a mild recession, you'd be straining at gnats to tell the difference.*

≣ This expression comes from the Bible (Matthew 23:24). Jesus used it when he was criticizing the scribes and the

Pharisees for being too concerned with unimportant areas of the Jewish law.

go

don't (even) go there (informal) said, often humorously, to suggest that a topic is considered to be too unpleasant or controversial to be mentioned ○ Bloom is romantically linked to Kate Bosworth, but don't even go there. Keeping his private life private is one of the ways he copes with his celebrity status.

go all out to do everything possible in order to achieve something ○ In women's basketball, women play so much harder than guys -- they go all out at all times.

go figure used when you cannot explain something surprising, stupid, or hard to understand, as there seems to be a contradiction ○ "It was certainly unexpected," said Mickelson, who hadn't touched a club for two weeks before the tournament. "I didn't hit it great today and somehow I shot 59. So go figure."

★ **go for it** to make a strong effort to achieve a goal ○ Tonight was the first night I've really seen her step up and just go for it.

what goes around comes around used to emphasize that people's actions will eventually have consequences that they will have to deal with, even though this may not happen for a long time ○ What goes around comes around. If you ignore the other guy when he asks for help, you might just be setting yourself up for a little of the same later on.

goalposts

move the goalposts to change the rules or aims in a situation or activity, in order to gain an advantage and to make things more difficult for the other people involved ○ They seem to move the goalposts every time I meet the conditions that are required.

goat

get someone's goat to annoy someone ○ It was a bad result and a bad performance, but what really got the media's goat was the coach's refusal to share the blame.

This expression may be connected with the early 20th century practice of putting goats in the same stable as racehorses, since the goats seemed to have a calming effect. If someone stole the goat, the horse would be upset and its performance would be affected.

God

God's gift exactly what a particular group of people like or need ○ I can't stand him - he thinks he's God's gift to women.

★ **play God** to behave as if you have complete power and can do anything that you want ○ He insisted that the government should not play God: the market alone should decide what industries should be set up.

take God's name in vain → see **name**

gold

all that glitters is not gold used to express the idea that someone or something may not be as good or as valuable as they first appear ○ All that glitters is not gold and it's a good idea to delay finalizing any important agreements, otherwise you may jeopardize a valuable relationship.

gold in them thar hills a way of making a lot of money ○ Dazzled by the gold in them thar hills, a lot of really smart Americans have gone into the financial world.

This expression refers to the California Gold Rush of the 19th century; the line also appears in the theme song of an old television program about that period.

★ **a pot of gold** a lot of money that

someone hopes to get in the future ○ *When he went to Dallas, he should have said he was going to make his pot of gold. Instead, he said he was going to improve his football.*

strike gold to find, do, or produce something that brings you a lot of money or success ○ *The company has struck gold with its new holiday development.*

good

★ **as good as new** in very good condition and looking new ○ *Manufacturers recommend that carpets should be washed regularly to prolong their life and keep them looking as good as new.*

★ **give as good as you get** to argue, fight or compete as strongly and fiercely as your opponent ○ *Always give as good as you get in discussions and meetings.*

good as gold behaving very well ○ *They were both in the playroom as good as gold.*

good-for-nothing lazy or irresponsible or behaving in a way that is likely to harm or upset other people ○ *Ruth's father was a rich, charming, but good-for-nothing man.*

you can't keep a good man down used to say that if someone is able and determined, they will recover from any difficulties or problems and be successful. You can replace "man" with "woman" or with another word referring to a person. ○ *Rios hit a winning smash from a sitting position before toppling over. You can't keep a good man down, although there are those who would like to try.*

goodbye

★ **kiss something goodbye**
★ **kiss goodbye to something** to accept the fact that you are going to lose something or that you will not be able to have it ○ *After the accident, I felt sure I'd have to kiss my dancing career goodbye.*

goods

★ **deliver the goods** to achieve what is expected or required of you ○ *Is the*

leadership in a position to deliver the goods in two years?*

have the goods on someone to know things about someone that could harm them if these things were made public ○ *He was offering services and materials for about 20 years internationally before anyone had the goods on him and could prove that he was doing it.*

≡ "The goods" here refers to stolen property, which can be used as evidence against the person who is in possession of it.

goose

cook your goose to do something that gets you into trouble or spoils your chances of success ○ *By trying to steal my girlfriend he cooked his goose. After that I just had to sack him.*

≡ There is a story that King Eric XIV of Sweden once arrived at a town to find that the people had hung a goose from a tree. This was intended as an insult, perhaps because geese were associated with stupidity. The King announced that he would "cook their goose," and his soldiers invaded the town and set fire to its main buildings. An alternative theory is that the expression refers to Aesop's fable of the goose which laid golden eggs: see the explanation at "kill the goose that lays the golden egg."

kill the goose that lays the golden egg to destroy something that would have been very profitable or beneficial ○ *It's a classic case of too many tourists loving a place to death. "They're killing the goose that laid the golden egg," said the park manager.*

≡ This expression comes from Aesop's fable about a peasant who owned a goose that laid golden eggs. The peasant was so eager to become rich that he cut the bird open, hoping that he would be able to get all the eggs at once.

someone wouldn't say boo to a goose used about someone who is very quiet, shy or nervous ○ *"If you remember, at college I wouldn't say boo to a goose." "That's right, you were very quiet."*

a wild goose chase a search for something that you have little chance of finding because you have been given wrong information ○ *Every time I've gone to Rome to try to find out if the story could be true, it has turned out to be a wild-goose chase.*

In medieval times, a wild goose chase was an unusual kind of horse race. It started with an ordinary horse race. The winner then rode in any direction they chose and the other riders had to follow. The race may have been called "a wild goose chase" because the movements of wild geese are often irregular and unpredictable, which makes them difficult to hunt.

what's good for the goose is good for the gander or
what's sauce for the goose is sauce for the gander (old-fashioned) used to express the idea that what applies to one person should apply to others, because people should be treated fairly and equally ○ *Unless Washington acknowledges that what's good for the goose is good for the gander, these talks are unlikely to make progress.*

People use this expression especially when they think that men and women are being treated differently for no good reason. A gander is a male goose; a "goose" is a female goose.

gospel

take something as gospel to accept something as being completely true

○ *You will read much advice in books and magazines but you should not take it all as gospel.*

In Christianity, the gospel is the message and teachings of Jesus Christ. The four books of the Bible that describe His life and teachings are called the Gospels.

grabs

★ **something is up for grabs** if something is up for grabs, it is available for anyone who is willing or able to compete for it ○ *Thirty-five Senate seats are up for grabs in tomorrow's election.*

grace

★ **fall from grace** to have made a mistake or done something wrong or immoral, and as a result, to have lost power or influence and spoiled your good reputation ○ *The band later fell from grace when it was discovered that they never sang on their own records.*

★ **a saving grace** a good quality or feature in someone or something that prevents them from being completely bad or worthless ○ *She definitely outshone the so-called "stars" and is one of the film's few saving graces.*

grade

★ **make the grade** to succeed at something, usually by reaching a particular standard ○ *Two public schools failed to make the grade in a new survey of student performance.*

In this expression a grade is a slope. This expression was originally used to refer to a train that succeeded in climbing a steep section of track.

grain

★ **go against the grain**
1 to contradict prevailing trends, beliefs, or principles ○ *Like anyone who goes against the grain, he has paid a price for his beliefs.*

2 to be the opposite of your ideas, beliefs or principles ○ *He would have to take this work, although it went against the grain of everything he believed in and hoped for.*

≣ The grain of a piece of wood is the direction of its fibers. It is easier to cut or plane wood along the direction of the grain, rather than across it.

★ **take something with a grain of salt** to think that a piece of information is not true or not all true ○ *Buyers were warned to take the figures with a grain of salt.*

≣ This very old expression is inspired by a Latin phrase, *cum grano salis*, which had a similar meaning.

grapes

★ **sour grapes** a situation where someone criticizes another person or accuses them of using unfair methods because they are jealous of their success ○ *These accusations have been going on for some time now, but it is just sour grapes.*

≣ In one of Aesop's fables, a fox tries several times unsuccessfully to reach a bunch of delicious-looking grapes. In the end he gives up, telling himself that they are probably sour and inedible anyway.

grapevine

★ **hear something through the grapevine** to hear about something informally, from the people you know ○ *I hear through the grapevine that you are getting ready to sue us. If that's true, I want to hear it from you.*

≣ One of the early telegraph systems in the US was given the nickname "the grapevine telegraph" because the wires often became tangled, so that they reminded people of grapevines. During the Civil War, the telegraph system was used to communicate propaganda and false information, as well as real news about the progress of battles, so that anything heard on the "grapevine" was likely to be unreliable.

grass

the grass is always greener on the other side of the fence used to say that other people often appear to be in a better or more attractive situation than you. This expression is often shortened to "the grass is always greener." ○ *The old saying goes that, to many people, the grass is always greener, and our town's young people are feeling that now.*

★ **the grass roots** the ordinary people who form the main part of an organization or movement, rather than its leaders ○ *The revolution is actually coming from the grass roots and I think eventually the authorities will follow.*

like watching grass grow extremely boring ○ *Some people say that watching a baseball game is like watching grass grow.*

not let the grass grow under your feet to act quickly and efficiently, without delay ○ *Times are still tough for local companies – but they are not letting the grass grow under their feet when it comes to exports.*

grasshopper

knee-high to a grasshopper (old-fashioned) very young ○ *Sue has been drawing since she was knee-high to a grasshopper.*

≣ A grasshopper is a jumping insect.

grave

dig your own grave to put yourself in a difficult situation by doing something wrong or making foolish mistakes ○ *If you go ahead with a private investigation, you'll be digging your own grave professionally.*

★ **turn in your grave** or **roll over in your grave** if someone who is dead would turn in their grave, they would be very angry or upset about something that is happening now if they knew about it ○ *"If Jack Lord could see the new 'Hawaii 5-0' he'd probably turn in his grave," says Manning.*

gravy

★ **a gravy train** a secure and easy way of earning money over a long period, especially by having a job that is easy and well-paid ○ *I keep his salary down because I don't want anyone to think he's riding into work on a gravy train.*

> "Gravy" is an old slang word for money or profit. Railroad workers invented this expression in the early 1920s to describe a regular trip that provided good pay for little work.

Greek

be Greek to someone or
be all Greek to someone to be impossible for someone to understand ○ *Her explanations were Greek to us, and we were left with the feeling that we still had a lot to learn.*

> The idea behind this expression is that Greek is very difficult to learn and understand, especially because it uses a different alphabet from most other European languages.

green

green with envy extremely envious of something that another person has or does ○ *This is the most unexpected discovery I have made in 20 years of digging. Archaeologists in other parts of the world will be green with envy.*

> A greenish-colored complexion was traditionally believed to indicate jealousy.

grin

grin and bear it to have to accept a difficult situation because there is nothing that you can do about it ○ *Severe abdominal pain should always be checked out. Don't just grin and bear it.*

grip

★ **get a grip on something** to take control of a situation so that you can deal with it successfully ○ *So far the country has failed to get a grip on its inflation rate.*
get a grip on yourself or
get a grip to control yourself, so that you can deal with things successfully ○ *I was very frightened and I consciously had to get a grip on myself.*

★ **lose your grip**
1 to lose control over a situation ○ *The opposition feels that the president has lost his grip on the country.*
2 to become less efficient and less confident, and less able to deal with things ○ *He wondered if perhaps he was getting old and losing his grip.*

grips

★ **get to grips with something** to start dealing with a situation seriously, for example, by getting a proper understanding of it ○ *In the front of the van, Julie's still getting to grips with the gears and the brakes and the steering.*

grist

★ **grist for the mill** something that can be put to good use in a particular situation ○ *You are, of course, much better at writing songs when you are completely miserable – it gives you so much more grist for the mill.*

> "Grist" was grain that was brought to a windmill or watermill to be ground. Millers needed regular supplies of grain to keep their businesses in operation.

groove

★ **in the groove** having a continuous series of successes ○ *Sorenstam is back in the groove, shooting a 68 to take the first-round lead.*

This expression may refer to the way the needle fits neatly into the groove on a record.

ground

be thick on the ground to be plentiful ○ *Jobs are not exactly thick on the ground.*

★ **be thin on the ground** to be rare ○ *Ideas are thin on the ground in the film industry.*

break ground to start building something ○ *Simpson and Hurt hope to break ground on a planned outdoor theater at Ten Chimneys next August.*

★ **break new ground** to do something completely different, or to do something in a completely different way. You use this expression to show approval of what is being done. ○ *The program broke new ground in giving women roles traditionally assigned to men.*

cover a lot of ground to deal with many different things ○ *We covered a lot of ground so I decided to present our conversation in two parts to make it more digestible.*

cover the same ground to deal with the same subject or matter again ○ *It feels as if we have covered the same ground many, many times before – and still the same tragedies continue to occur.*

cut the ground from under someone to seriously weaken someone's argument or position, often by doing something unexpected ○ *The scenario is this – you overspend on credit cards; and then a downturn in business cuts the ground from under you.*

fall on stony ground to be ignored ○ *Warnings about the effects on public services fell on stony ground.*

This expression comes from Jesus's story in the Bible (Mark 4:5-6) about a man sowing seed which falls on different kinds of ground. The seed that falls on stony ground dies because the roots cannot grow properly. In the story, the seed represents Christ's teachings and the stony ground represents the people who soon forget or ignore what He has said.

★ **find common ground** to come to an agreement on something ○ *The participants seem unable to find common ground on the issue of agriculture.*

★ **gain ground** to make progress and become more important or more powerful ○ *The idea that the organization ought to change its constitution has been gaining ground for years.*

get in on the ground floor to get involved from the very beginning with something, especially something that is likely to be profitable for you ○ *These smaller companies are getting in on the ground floor of what will be a gigantic industry.*

get something off the ground to put something into operation, often after a lot of hard work getting it organized ○ *Councillor Riley spoke of the dedication and enthusiasm of staff and volunteers in getting the programs off the ground.*

hit the ground running to start a new activity with a lot of energy and enthusiasm, and not to waste any time ○ *She is in excellent shape and in good spirits. She will hit the ground running when she gets back.*

The image here may be of soldiers landing by parachute or helicopter in a battle area and moving off quickly as soon as they reach the ground.

★ **lose ground** to lose some of the power or advantage that you had previously ○ *The United States lost more ground in its trade balance with other countries during the third quarter, running up the biggest trade deficit so far this year.*

★ **the moral high ground** the belief that your policies and actions are morally superior to the policies and actions of your rivals ○ *The party now held the moral high ground and he, as President, could* *defend it in every country in the world.*

> In a battle, the army that is on higher ground has the advantage.

★ **prepare the ground** to do things which will make it easier for something to happen ○ *The talks prepared the ground for the meeting of finance ministers and central bankers in Washington.*

run someone into the ground to make someone work so hard and continuously at something that they become exhausted ○ *Well-trained horses had been starved to death or run into the ground.*

run something into the ground to use something continuously without repairing or replacing it, so that eventually it is destroyed or useless ○ *They're quite good bikes; you can run them into the ground for quite a long time, then just get a new one.*

stomping ground or
stamping ground a place where someone works or goes regularly. People usually say "old stomping grounds" to talk about a place they used to go. ○ *Ford will return to one of his old stomping grounds Tuesday as he visits the Institute of Technology.*

> This expression may refer to the way that stallions stomp while mating. Alternatively, it may come from the dances of male prairie chickens when they gather in spring in order to mate.

suit someone down to the ground to completely meet your needs or requirements ○ *Helen has finally found a method of exercise that suits her outgoing character down to the ground.*

guard

> Your guard is the position that you adopt when you are ready to defend yourself in sports such as boxing or fencing.

★ **catch someone off guard** to completely surprise someone ○ *There was a bright flash, followed a few moments later by a thunderous roar that caught us all off guard.*

★ **lower your guard** to relax when you should be careful or alert, often with unpleasant consequences ○ *The U-boat's crew had made the mistake of relaxing, of lowering their guard just when their sense of danger should have been at its keenest.*

off guard not prepared for something when it happens so that you do not react normally ○ *Taken off guard, he toppled backwards into the arms of his attacker.*

★ **the old guard** a group of people who have worked in an organization or system for a very long time ○ *The company's old guard is stepping aside, making way for a new, more youthful team.*

> The original "Old Guard" consisted of the most experienced regiments of Napoleon Bonaparte's Imperial Guard. These soldiers were considered to be the best in the French army.

★ **on (your) guard** alert and prepared for any attack against you ○ *When Hilton came, he would have to be on his guard each second, for the man was dangerous.*

guess

be anybody's guess to be impossible to know for certain, so that anyone's idea is as good as another's ○ *At this point, it is anybody's guess what impact the decision will have on small businesses.*

guest

be my guest said to someone to mean that you are giving them permission to do something, or inviting them to do something ○ *"Dad," she said. "Tomorrow, I want to go swimming." I indicated the cool, clear water before us. "Be my guest," I said.*

guinea pig

★ **a guinea pig** a person on whom new

ideas or methods are tested ○ *I got the impression they weren't sure of the possible outcome and that I was being used as a guinea pig.*

gums

flap your gums to talk a lot without saying anything important ○ *I suggest you do some research before you start flapping your gums.*

gun

hold a gun to someone's head or **put a gun to someone's head** to force someone to do something by threatening to take extreme action against them if they do not do it ○ *Not a man to have a gun put to his head, Mr. Riordan was soon tearing up the offer and canceling future meetings with the union.*

★ **jump the gun** to do something before the right, proper or expected time ○ *The book wasn't due to be released until September 10th, but some booksellers have jumped the gun and decided to sell it early.*

> If a runner jumps the gun, they begin running before the pistol is fired to start the race.

★ **a smoking gun** evidence that proves that a particular person is responsible for a crime ○ *First of all, there's no smoking gun. In the course of our investigation we did not find a single piece of evidence.*

under the gun under great pressure and in danger of failing completely ○ *Society, in many ways, is under the gun. We have a multitude of problems – medical, health problems, crime problems, educational, literacy.*

guns

be going great guns to be enjoying a period of successful activity ○ *The firm's chairman and managing director is going great guns with his expansion plans.*

★ **the big guns** the most important and powerful people in an organization ○ *She*

is in great demand by the film industry's big guns.

> Cannons used to be referred to as "big guns" or "great guns," while rifles or muskets were called "small guns."

★ **stick to your guns** to refuse to change your decision or opinion about something, even though other people are trying to tell you that you are wrong ○ *He should have stuck to his guns and refused to meet her.*

> The image here is of soldiers remaining in position, even though they are being attacked by the enemy.

with (all) guns blazing with a lot of enthusiasm and energy ○ *The Giants, with guns blazing, beat the Patriots 20-17.*

> Here, blazing means firing continuously.

gut

bust a gut (*informal*) to work very hard at something ○ *I was busting a gut doing horrible jobs – toilet cleaning among other things – to support us.*

a gut feeling an opinion or idea about something that you are sure is right although you cannot explain why ○ *Betty had a gut feeling that the diamond she lost would turn up.*

a gut reaction a response to something that comes automatically, without thinking ○ *My gut reaction was that I never wanted to play baseball again – but I know I will one day.*

guts

spill your guts (*informal*) to tell someone everything about something secret or private ○ *Vincent has spilled his guts. Everything. We got a signed confession from him.*

> Your guts are your intestines or internal organs. The idea is of dramatically revealing something hidden.

play your guts out *(informal)* to compete very hard ○ *A two-touchdown underdog, they played their guts out against a highly ranked favorite at Cougar Stadium.*

guys

nice guys finish last used when you want to suggest that in a competitive situation, there is no benefit in being considerate or fair ○ *Johnson is working to convince his constituents that you don't have to be loud to get results, while Williams is hoping to prove that nice guys finish last.*

Hh

habits

⭐ **old habits die hard** used to emphasize that people are often reluctant to change their way of doing something, especially something that they have been doing for a long time ○ *Despite ideas of equality, old habits die hard and women still carry the main burden of looking after the home and family.*

hackles

⭐ **raise someone's hackles** to make someone angry or annoyed ○ *The taxes will presumably be designed not to raise voters' hackles too much.*

> "Hackles" are feathers on the necks of roosters and some other birds. They rise up when the bird becomes aggressive.

hair

a bad hair day (*informal*) a day when someone's hair does not look attractive ○ *The afternoon winds and choppy waters can whip up more than a bad hair day.*

come within a hair's breadth of doing something to very nearly do something ○ *The parliament came within a hair's breadth of forcing immediate political union between the two countries.*

get in someone's hair to annoy someone and be a nuisance to them ○ *They were very busy and had little time to get in one another's hair.*

get out of someone's hair to stop being a nuisance to someone ○ *Would you like me to get out of your hair and leave you alone?*

a hair of the dog (*spoken*) an alcoholic drink that someone has, usually the day after drinking too much alcohol, because they think it will make them feel less ill ○ *I need a drink, chum. A large hair of the dog.*

keep someone out of your hair to succeed in arranging things so that you are no longer involved with someone who is a nuisance ○ *Just do me a favor, will you? Keep her out of my hair from now on.*

⭐ **let your hair down** to relax and enjoy yourself, without worrying about behaving politely ○ *It is only with friends that most people feel they can let their hair down and be themselves.*

make someone's hair stand on end to make someone very frightened or shocked ○ *The first ten minutes of the film made my hair stand on end.*

make your hair curl to make you very shocked or worried ○ *I could tell you stories that would make your hair curl.*

not a hair out of place used for describing someone whose appearance is very neat and tidy ○ *Not a hair out of place, dressed in navy and white for our photograph, she is clearly a perfectionist.*

not turn a hair to be very calm in an unpleasant or difficult situation, and not show any sign of being afraid or anxious ○ *She started off by accusing him of blackmail but he didn't turn a hair: in fact he more or less ignored her.*

pull your hair out or
tear your hair out to be very angry, upset, or anxious about something ○ *The nation is tearing its hair out over what to do with these child criminals.*

something will put hair on your chest a particular food or drink is very strong ○ *This hearty soup will put hair on your chest.*

wear a hair shirt to deliberately make your own life unpleasant or uncomfortable in a way that is not necessary ○ *No one is asking you to wear a hair shirt and give up all your luxuries.*

> In the past, hair shirts were very rough, uncomfortable shirts made from horsehair. People sometimes wore them for religious reasons, to show that they were truly sorry for their sins.

within a hair's breadth of something very close to something ○ *Sumpa allowed the van to slip to within a hair's breadth of the precipice, then gave the engine full throttle.*

hairs

have someone by the short hairs to have someone completely in your power ○ *The hard fact is that they have got us by the short hairs. We can't do anything without material support from them.*

> "Short hairs" in this expression may refer to a person's pubic hair, to hair on the back of their neck, or to the hair in a beard.

split hairs to make distinctions in a situation where the differences between things are actually very small and unimportant ○ *But once you start splitting hairs like that, where are you going to stop?*

halcyon

halcyon days (*literary*) a time in the past when something was especially successful ○ *When we ask him whether the wool industry will ever see those halcyon days again, he turns away and shakes his head.*

> The seven days before and after the shortest day of the year are sometimes called halcyon days. "Halcyon" comes from the Greek word for kingfisher. According to Greek legend, Halcyone and her husband were turned into kingfishers by the gods. It was believed that these birds built their nests on the sea during the seven days before the shortest day of the year and then sat on their eggs for the next seven days, and that the gods always ensured calm weather during this period.

half

go off half-cocked to be unsuccessful in what you are trying to do, because you have not taken enough care or prepared properly ○ *Remember, don't go off half-cocked when we get there. Stick to the plan.* ○ *In-store guest appearances are usually embarrassing, half-cocked events.*

> If a gun goes off half-cocked, it does not fire properly and so the shot is wasted. This is because the firing mechanism has not been raised high enough to connect with the trigger.

how the other half lives used for describing the lives of people who are very different from you, for example very rich or very poor, or living in a different country ○ *He clearly has little idea how the other half lives, though, carrying a 1,000-dollar bill in his pocket to flourish in small shops that cannot give him change.*

★ **your other half** or **your better half** your husband, wife, or partner ○ *They invited us out to dinner after the election because they said it was high time they met my other half.*

halfway

★ **meet someone halfway** to accept some of a person's opinions or wishes, so that you can come to an agreement with them or have a better relationship with them ○ *Senator Gray said Democrats are willing to meet the president halfway on measures to stimulate the economy.*

halves

not do things by halves to always do everything very well and very thoroughly ○ *In Italy they rarely do things by halves. When designers latch on to a theme, they work it through thoroughly, producing the* *world's most wearable clothes in the most beautiful fabrics.*

hammer

go at it hammer and tongs *(mainly British)*

1 to do something with great energy and enthusiasm ○ *"He loved gardening," sniffed Mrs. Gascoigne. "He went at it hammer and tongs as soon as he got home from work."*
2 to have a noisy argument ○ *"They were going at it hammer and tongs." "What about?" "I'm not very sure, but they were arguing."*

⋮ The image here is of a blacksmith
⋮ holding a piece of heated iron with a
⋮ pair of tongs, and striking the iron
⋮ repeatedly with a hammer.

★ **go under the hammer** *(mainly British)* to be offered for sale at auction. A similar expression is **go on the block**. ○ *The first half of the collection goes under the hammer on Friday and there are some real treasures.*

⋮ In an auction, the auctioneer shows
⋮ that a sale has been made by banging
⋮ a hammer on a table.

hand

be bound hand and foot by something to not be able to act freely or do what you want because something prevents you ○ *These people are still bound hand and foot by tradition.*

be hand in glove with someone or something to be working very closely with another person or organization, often in order to do something dishonest or immoral ○ *Employment on the building sites is controlled by more than 40 gangs, who are believed to be hand in glove with the police.*

⋮ The original form of the expression
⋮ was "hand and glove." It was used to
⋮ say that there was a strong connection
⋮ or similarity between two things.

be waited on hand and foot to be taken care of by someone in every way so that you don't have to do anything for yourself ○ *If you are incapable of lying on a beach and being waited on hand and foot, then La Samanna, on the Caribbean island of St. Martin, is not for you.*

★ **bite the hand that feeds you** to be ungrateful and behave badly toward the person who has helped or supported you ○ *She may be cynical about Hollywood, but ultimately she has no intention of biting the hand that feeds her.*

the dead hand of someone or something used for describing a very negative influence that someone or something has on a situation, for example by preventing change or progress ○ *For too long we have lived under the dead hand of the dieticians and the nutritionists. We have become a society where feasting is frowned on and food faddism is the fashion.*

do something to keep your hand in to do something in order to use the skills which you have developed in the past, so that you do not lose them ○ *I had to wait two years before I was offered another part, and just to keep my hand in, I went on tour with a play that wasn't very good.*

★ **force someone's hand** to force someone to do something that they are not ready to do or do not want to do ○ *Today's move may be a tactical maneuver designed to force the hand of the Speaker of the House.*

⋮ In card games, to force an opponent's
⋮ hand means to force them to play a
⋮ card earlier than they want to.

give someone a big hand to applaud a performer ○ *I'm Hal Morgan and these are the Praise Him Singers from Muncie, Indiana, so let's give them a big hand.*

give with one hand and take away with the other to help someone in one way, but also do something that has the opposite effect, such as harming them or preventing them from achieving what they want ○ *My parents were very supportive, but they gave with one hand and took away with the other, because I never really learned to be independent.*

★ **go hand in hand** if two things go hand in hand, they are closely connected and cannot be considered separately from each other ○ *The principle of the playgroup movement is that play and learning go hand in hand: your child masters new skills and absorbs knowledge while having fun.*

hand-to-mouth if someone is acting in a hand-to-mouth way, they do not plan ahead, but decide what to do from day to day ○ *Unless a government sets its course from the start, it is doomed to spend the rest of its term in hand-to-mouth improvising.*

★ **have a free hand** to have the freedom to make your own decisions on how something should be done ○ *They gave me a free hand to train the squadron as I saw fit.*

★ **have a hand in something** to be one of the people involved in doing or creating something ○ *Peter is a very experienced yachtsman, and had a hand in the design himself.*

have someone eating out of your hand to be in a situation where someone does whatever you want because they admire or love you so much ○ *No one can handle the press like she can and she usually has them eating out of her hand by the time they leave.*

The image here is of an animal that is tame and will take food from a person's hand.

have someone in the palm of your hand

1 to have a group of people, especially an audience, giving you their full attention and responding enthusiastically to everything you say or do ○ *A cursory look at the audience shows that she's got them*

in the palm of her hand.

2 to have complete control over someone so that they will do whatever you want ○ *Boris shrugged off a warning that he is "playing with fire." Barbara's ex-boyfriend said: "She has Boris in the palm of her hand."*

have to do something with one hand tied behind your back to have a disadvantage which makes it difficult for you to succeed in doing something ○ *The team is having to improve with one hand tied behind its back because it has no money to spend on new players.*

have the upper hand to have more power in a competitive situation than the other side and to be able to control things ○ *The changes are by no means revolutionary, but they do suggest that for the first time economic reformers now have the upper hand in the party hierarchy.*

a heavy hand a way of dealing with people that is very harsh or severe, and often unfair ○ *The heavy hand of the military has not prevented their economies from doing very well.*

hold someone's hand to help and support someone in a new or difficult situation ○ *I will support him up to a point but I can't hold his hand forever and there comes a time when John has to take responsibility himself.*

know something like the back of your hand to know something very well ○ *He knows the city like the back of his hand.*

★ **lend a hand** or
lend someone a hand to help someone to do something ○ *If I'd known, I'd have been glad to lend a hand – you should have called me.*

★ **live from hand to mouth** or
live hand to mouth to not have enough money to live comfortably, and to have no money left after you have paid for basic necessities ○ *I have a wife and*

two children and we live from hand to mouth on what I earn. ○ *The village of Cuestecita is typical of the desperate hand-to-mouth economy that exists on the fringes of Cerrejon.*

★ **an old hand** someone who is very skilled at something because they have been doing it for a long time ○ *An old hand at photography, 34-year-old Tim has been shooting British landscapes and wildlife as a hobby for the last 13 years.*

overplay your hand to act more confidently than you should, because you believe you are in a stronger position than you really are ○ *He said the police had overplayed their hand in not accepting the "generous" offer.*

≣ "Hand" in this expression refers to the cards dealt to you in a card game.

★ **reject something out of hand** to reject an idea or suggestion without hesitating and without discussing it first ○ *He has rejected out of hand any suggestion that there can be any compromise over the proposals.*

the right hand doesn't know what the left hand is doing used to describe a situation in which people in one part of an organization do not know what the people in another part are doing and this is causing confusion or difficulties ○ *The right hand doesn't know what the left is doing. One company digs up roads and fills them in, and then another service does the same a few days later.*

≣ This expression comes from the Bible (Matthew 6:3), when Jesus says that if people give money to charity, they should do it without boasting or telling anyone about it. (They should do it so secretly that even their left hand would not know what their right hand is doing.)

show your hand to let other people see what your position is in a competitive situation, and what you intend to do

○ *On domestic politics he seemed unwilling to show his hand too clearly.*

≣ If you show your hand in a card game, you reveal your cards to another player.

someone can do something with one hand tied behind their back said to mean someone who can do something very easily ○ *The Explorer camcorder is so neat and nifty you can operate it with one hand tied behind your back.*

★ **someone or something gets out of hand** used to describe a situation or person that cannot be controlled any longer ○ *We heard a man being abusive. It was getting out of hand so we called the police.*

a steady hand or
a steady hand on the tiller a situation in which someone is keeping good control of a situation ○ *"If ever there was an urgent need for a steady hand on the tiller, it is now," said one European diplomat.*

≣ In a boat, the tiller is the handle with which you steer.

★ **take someone or something in hand** to take control of someone or something, in order to improve them ○ *The feeling is growing that the present administration only reacts to events rather than taking the situation in hand.*

throw in your hand to give up trying to do something ○ *After a brief bounce, Wall Street crashed again, and the financier had to throw in his hand.*

≣ In card games such as poker, if you throw in your hand, you put your cards on the table to show that you accept that you have lost.

★ **try your hand at something** to try doing something in order to see whether you like it or whether you are good at it ○ *In his latest book, he tries his hand at fiction.*

★ **turn your hand to something** to start doing something and do it well, even though you may not be trained to do it ○ *Judy is one of those women who can turn her hand to most things.*

★ **work hand in hand** if two people or organizations work hand in hand, they work closely together, often with a single aim ○ *Steelmakers are working hand in hand with auto makers to slash the cost of producing automotive parts.*

you have to hand it to someone (spoken) said to acknowledge how well someone has done something or how good they are at it, even though you do not like the person or do not approve of their actions ○ *Whatever you thought of his act, you had to hand it to him – he knew how to make money.*

handle

fly off the handle to suddenly become very angry about something and behave in an uncontrolled and irrational way ○ *Unless some decision was reached, they might fly off the handle and do something foolish.*

≡ The reference here is to an ax head that has become loose, and so when someone swings the ax, the head of it flies off.

hands

★ **at the hands of someone** if someone experiences a particular kind of treatment, especially unpleasant treatment, at the hands of a person or organization, they receive it from them ○ *She spoke of the humiliation she endured at the hands of the police.*

be rubbing your hands with glee to be very pleased about something, often something bad which has happened to an enemy or opponent ○ *Some of the cereal producers are rubbing their hands with glee. Lower prices for grain will help them win back a bigger slice of the market in France.*

★ **be wringing your hands** to be expressing sadness or regret about a bad situation, but not taking any action to deal with it ○ *Mr. Ashdown had accused the government of wringing its hands and doing nothing as the country's jobless figures spiraled.*

≡ If you wring something, you squeeze or twist it.

★ **change hands** if something changes hands, one person or organization gets it from another, usually by buying it ○ *The property has changed hands several times recently.*

★ **fall into someone's hands** or **fall into the wrong hands** to be taken or caught by an opponent or enemy ○ *There is a real fear that food supplies could fall into the hands of the Mafia, thus increasing the misery of ordinary citizens.*

★ **get your hands dirty** to get involved with all aspects of your job, including routine, practical, or more junior work, or dealing with people directly. This expression is usually used showing approval. ○ *Getting their hands dirty keeps top managers in touch with the problems of customers, and it shows everybody that serving customers is important.*

★ **get your hands on someone** or **lay your hands on someone** to catch someone who has done something wrong and usually punish them ○ *That's the most likely explanation, they say, but we can't be sure until we get our hands on the culprits.*

★ **get your hands on something** or **lay your hands on something** to succeed in obtaining something you want or need ○ *First of all, how was he able to get his hands on that money so easily?*

★ **have your hands full** to be very busy ○ *The federal government will obviously have its hands full trying to enforce environmental laws while keeping residents happy.*

★ **in safe hands** being cared for by a competent person or organization and therefore not likely to be harmed or damaged ○ *They could get on with their own lives, knowing their girls were in safe hands.*

★ **in someone's hands** in someone's possession or under their control ○ *Some delegates have criticized the move, saying it will leave too much power in the hands of the party leadership.*

★ **off your hands** if someone or something is off your hands, you are no longer responsible for them, because another person has taken responsibility for them instead of you ○ *I can always take the children off your hands for a while, if there's nothing else for me to do.*

★ **on your hands**
  1 if you have a problem or task on your hands, you have to deal with it ○ *What is already clear though is that the local police now have yet another problem on their hands.*
  2 if you have a person on your hands, you are responsible for caring for them or dealing with them, especially when this is difficult or demanding ○ *Those parents who took a lax attitude to family discipline now have delinquent children on their hands.*

★ **out of your hands** if something is out of your hands you are no longer responsible for it ○ *Things were out of our hands now. We could only wait.*

★ **play into someone's hands** to make a foolish mistake or act in the way that someone wants you to act, so that they gain an advantage over you or defeat you ○ *The main opposition parties played into his hands by boycotting the election.*

shake hands on something to conclude a deal or an agreement successfully ○ *So keen were the Russians to shake hands on the deal that they offered to accept palm oil in part payment.*

★ **sit on your hands** to not do something which you should be doing ○ *The pace of*

development in Formula One is so fast that if you sit on your hands you quickly regret it.

someone's hands are clean used about someone who has had no involvement in a crime, mistake, or disaster ○ *Our hands are clean. We have nothing to hide.*

★ **someone's hands are tied** used when something such as a law is preventing someone from acting in the way that they want to ○ *He would like to help but he is powerless because his hands are tied by regulations.*

someone does not get their hands dirty or
someone does not dirty their hands used about someone who avoids doing physical work or the parts of a job that they consider unpleasant or distasteful ○ *These are people who live in the commuter belt around the capital with more secure jobs and who have never had to get their hands dirty earning a living.*

sully your hands (formal) to do something that you find unpleasant or distasteful to do ○ *He had no intention of sullying his hands by playing politics.*

★ **wash your hands of something or someone** to refuse to be involved with a problem or a person who causes problems or to take responsibility for them any longer ○ *The senator said: "We cannot wash our hands of responsibility for the state of the economy."*

> According to the Bible (Matthew 27:24), Pontius Pilate washed his hands in a bowl to show that he would not take responsibility for the death sentence which the public demanded he should pass on Jesus.

★ **win hands down**
  1 to win a contest easily ○ *We have been beaten in some games which we should have won hands down.*
  2 to be clearly the best in a comparison between things ○ *The New Winter Palace*

Hotel wins hands down for both comfort and evocative location, situated a few steps away from the banks of the Nile.

> This expression was originally used in horse racing to describe jockeys who won their races very easily and could cross the winning line with their hands lowered and the reins loose.

★ **with your bare hands** without using any weapons or tools ○ *Rescue workers and residents were digging through tons of mud with shovels and their bare hands yesterday in search of survivors.*

handshake

golden handshake a large amount of money for someone who is asked to retire early ○ *Hill will receive a $500,000 golden handshake when he retires as chairman in July.*

on a handshake if an agreement or contract is made on a handshake, there is no written record of what each person or side must do ○ *As a trader I arranged billion dollar trades, done on a handshake, not with a lawyer sitting on my shoulder.*

handsome

handsome is as handsome does (old-fashioned) used to emphasize that you should judge someone by their actions and not by their appearance ○ *Handsome is as handsome does, my mother and grandmother always said, in order to counter self-admiration.*

handy

★ **come in handy** to be very useful ○ *A penny can come in handy when you have to remove a battery from a toy or a remote and there is no screwdriver to be found.*

hang

★ **get the hang of something** to learn how to do an activity ○ *Once one gets the hang of it, reading a good play can be a delightful and challenging experience.*

hang someone out to dry or

be hung out to dry to be or put someone in a very difficult situation where you or they have been abandoned by the people who previously been supportive ○ *But he's a Democrat, therefore the far right Republicans want to hang him out to dry.* ○ *Once again, the CIA – apparently unable to resist political manipulation by the administration – is in danger of being hung out to dry.*

hang it up to stop playing a sport or retire from a career ○ *Every great player has to hang it up sooner or later and Favre probably should have done it last year.*

someone is hanging on by their fingertips or

someone is hanging on by their fingernails If someone is hanging on by their fingertips or fingernails, they are managing to survive in a difficult situation or to stay in the position they want to, but are always in danger of failing ○ *Their 1-3 conference record leaves Central hanging by their fingertips for any hopes of making a post season appearance.*

happy

happy as a clam very happy ○ *Join the other kids. Do that, and before you know it you'll be happy as a clam.*

happy as a lark very happy ○ *Look at me – eighty-two years old and happy as a lark!*

hard

hard as nails very unsympathetic towards other people ○ *He's a shrewd businessman and hard as nails.*

★ **hard done by** feeling that you have been treated unfairly ○ *Those who felt hard done by made their dissatisfaction clear.*

play hard to get to deliberately make it difficult for someone to obtain something that they need from you, such as your agreement or permission ○ *Anthony has made three huge miscalculations in playing hard to get with the Nuggets.*

hardball

play hardball to do anything that is necessary to achieve or obtain what you want, even if this involves being harsh or unfair ○ *The White House decided to retaliate by taking jobs away from his state, showing they were tough guys who could play hardball.*

Hardball is the same as baseball, and is here being contrasted with softball, in which a larger, softer ball is used and pitches are thrown underarm.

harness

A harness is a set of straps like the one that is fitted to a horse when it pulls a cart.

in harness actually doing a job which you have been appointed to do ○ *They hope to have the Australian Test forward Troy Coker back in harness before the end of the season.*

harvest

reap the harvest to experience the consequences, good or bad, of something done earlier ○ *Sastre felt that the team was unable to reap the harvest of its hard work in the first two weeks.*

hat

all hat and no cattle attractive or impressive in appearance, but lacking anything of real value ○ *He hoped to answer criticisms that he lacked substance, that he was all hat and no cattle.*

This expression comes from the West, where ranchers and other people wear cowboy hats. It is used of someone whose appearance suggests or promises more than they can deliver.

go hat in hand to someone to ask someone very humbly and respectfully for money or help ○ *He won't go hat in*

hand to the White House to ask that sanctions be lifted against his country.

In the past, it was customary for poorer people to remove their hats in front of wealthier people. The expression may also refer to the fact that people sometimes hold out their hats when they are begging, for other people to put money in.

keep something under your hat to not mention to anyone else something that someone has told you ○ *Look, if I tell you something, will you promise to keep it under your hat? Promise now, not a word to anyone.*

This was a slogan used to promote security in Britain during World War II.

★ **old hat** unoriginal or out of date ○ *I think that's a bit old hat now, isn't it? I wanted to do something quite different.*

This expression may have developed because in the times when it was customary for women to wear hats, the fashions in hats used to change very quickly.

pass the hat or
pass the hat around to collect money for someone or something ○ *Airbus will soon be passing the hat around again for an enormous 700-seat aeroplane.*

The image here is of people using a hat to collect money in.

someone will eat their hat if something happens (old-fashioned) used when someone does not believe that a particular thing will happen ○ *I'll eat my hat if anyone under the age of 30 is reading this blog.*

★ **take your hat off to someone** to express admiration for something that someone has done ○ *You have to take your hat off to whoever thought this one up.* ○ *Hats off to them for supporting the homeless*

People sometimes remove their hats as a sign of respect when they meet someone.

talk through your hat to say something that is ridiculous or totally incorrect ○ *He is talking through his hat when he attributes the overcrowding and overuse of parts of the area to its designation as a national park.*

throw your hat into the ring to become one of the people taking part in a competition or contest ○ *He said right away that he would play. I am delighted that he has decided to throw his hat into the ring.*

In the past, prize fighters at showgrounds used to challenge people to fight them. Someone who was willing to accept the challenge would throw their hat into the ring.

hatch

go down the hatch to be eaten or drunk, usually quickly or greedily ○ *A record $4.4 billion worth of candy went down the hatch last year.*

In the 18th century, this expression was used as a toast in the navy. A hatch is an opening in the deck of a ship, through which people and goods can pass.

hatches

batten down the hatches to prepare for a difficult situation by doing everything you can to protect yourself ○ *While most companies are battening down the hatches, fearing recession, Blenheim is leading an assault on the US market.*

Battens are strips of wood used for fastening things down. Hatches are openings in the deck of a ship, or the wooden flaps which cover the openings.

hatchet

A hatchet is a small ax.

bury the hatchet to agree to forget a quarrel and become friends again ○ *One employee said the two men had finally buried the hatchet after their falling-out.*

In the past, when Native American tribes made peace after fighting each other, it was traditional for each tribe to bury a tomahawk or small ax, as a sign of peace.

do a hatchet job on someone or something to say or write a lot of bad things about someone or something in order to harm their reputation ○ *Reporter Malcolm, he says, set out to do a hatchet job on him and succeeded.*

This expression may relate to violent gang warfare in the United States during the early part of the 20th century. See explanation at "a hatchet man."

a hatchet man a man whose job is to destroy things or do unpleasant tasks, often on behalf of someone else ○ *He had to play the hatchet man and it was not pleasant for the many he laid off.*

This expression may relate to violent gang warfare in the United States during the early part of the 20th century. Gangs often hired an assassin or "hatchet man" to hack an important member of a rival gang to death with a hatchet. This work was known as a "hatchet job."

haul

A haul in the following expressions means a trip.

be in something for the long haul to intend to continue doing something until it is finished, even if it is difficult or unpleasant ○ *Impatience is not our* problem. We're in it for the long haul. Five years is the minimum.

★ **a long haul** a task or course of action that will be very difficult to deal with and will need a great deal of effort and time ○ Revitalizing the economy will be a long haul.

★ **over the long haul** over a long period of time in the future ○ The smart economic message for the nation is that prudent leadership, coupled with patience, will accomplish more over the long haul.

hawk

watch someone like a hawk to pay close attention to everything that someone does, usually to make sure that they do not do anything wrong ○ Some guys just sit there and watch her like a hawk, dead sure she's trying to cheat.

≡ Hawks have very good eyesight, and are able to see small animals or objects from a great height.

hay

and that ain't hay used after some amount of money is named to suggest that it is a lot ○ They were $448 million in debt as of the start of the divorce trial–and that ain't hay!

make hay while the sun shines to take advantage of a good situation that is not likely to last ○ Making hay while the sun shines, the Egyptian government has taken radical measures to liberalize the economy.

haywire

go haywire to stop working or operating normally and start behaving in an unpredictable or chaotic way ○ Lauren Ehrlich focuses on T cells that can go haywire, causing childhood leukemia and lymphoma.

head

be banging your head against a wall or
be banging your head against a

brick wall to feel frustrated because someone is stopping you from making progress in what you are trying to do ○ It is a waste of valuable energy banging your head against a brick wall, wishing things were different.

★ **be hanging over someone's head** if something difficult or unpleasant is hanging over someone's head, it worries them because it may cause something bad to happen to them in the future ○ It is unlikely that the governor would want to appoint him if an inquiry was hanging over his head.

≡ This expression may relate to the story of the Sword of Damocles; see explanation at "sword."

★ **be head and shoulders above someone** to be much better than other people or things of the same kind ○ Richards, according to the article, was head and shoulders above any other player at his peak.

bite someone's head off to speak to someone in an unpleasant, angry way, because you are annoyed about something ○ And don't bite my head off just because you're in a bad mood!

build up a head of steam to gradually become more and more angry, anxious, or emotional about something until you can no longer hide your feelings ○ Bob was the most angry, as if in waiting for the other items to be cleared he had built up a greater head of steam.

★ **bury your head in the sand** to deliberately refuse to accept the truth about something unpleasant ○ Don't be an ostrich and bury your head in the sand, hoping your problems will disappear.

≡ People used to think that ostriches buried their heads in the sand when they were in danger.

come to a head or
bring something to a head if a

problem or disagreement comes to a head, it reaches a state where you have to take action to deal with it. You can also say that a particular event or factor brings a problem or disagreement to a head. ○ *These problems came to a head in September when five of the station's journalists were fired.* ○ *The issue that brought things to a head over the weekend was the sudden dip in demand for transatlantic flights across the industry.*

> This expression may refer to farmers waiting for cabbage leaves to grow together and form a head. Alternatively, the reference may be to a boil on a person's body forming a head just before it bursts.

★ **fall head over heels** to fall suddenly and deeply in love with someone ○ *It was obvious that Alan had fallen head over heels in love with Veronica.*

> Until the late 18th century this expression was "heels over head," which refers to someone doing a somersault.

★ **from head to toe** or
from head to foot over the whole of someone's body ○ *She was covered from head to toe with bruises.*

get in over your head or
be in over your head to become or be deeply involved in a situation which is too difficult for you to deal with ○ *He realized that he was in over his head, and that only his family could help him.*

> Here, the reference is to getting into water that is too deep to stand up in.

★ **get into someone's head** to understand what someone is really thinking or feeling ○ *He played the role well – you could really get into his head.*

get your head around something to succeed in understanding or accepting something such as a new idea ○ *He can't get his head around the fact that the children*

born in this country are not "immigrants."

★ **go head-to-head** to compete directly with another person or organization, especially in business and sport ○ *General Motors and Ford are expected to go head-to-head in the markets to buy up rival 15% stakes in Jaguar.* ○ *As top athletes, we should be running against each other whenever possible. Head-to-head competition makes our sport what it is.*

★ **go over someone's head**
1 to appeal to a higher authority than someone in an attempt to get what you want ○ *He was reprimanded for trying to go over the heads of senior officers.*
2 if something that someone says or writes goes over someone's head, they do not understand it because it is too difficult for them ○ *The few books that exist today introduce grammar that goes over young heads.*

★ **go to your head**
1 if someone lets success go to their head, they start to think that they are better or more intelligent than other people, and they begin to behave in an arrogant or silly way ○ *Ford is definitely not a man to let a little success go to his head. He knows he still has a lot to learn.*
2 if alcohol goes to your head, it makes you slightly drunk and perhaps affects your judgement so that you do silly things ○ *He was not accustomed to strong liquor and it went to his head.*

★ **hang your head** to show that you feel shame or regret for something ○ *If anyone expected them to hang their heads following Saturday's season-opening loss, forget about it.*

have your head in the clouds to be out of touch with reality and perhaps have impractical ideas about achieving success ○ *Whether some of them still have their heads in the clouds after our win over the Cowboys, I don't know.*

have your head screwed on to be

sensible and realistic ○ *Good girl! I always knew you had your head screwed on right.*

a head of steam a lot of support for something such as a plan or cause ○ *There's an increasing head of steam behind getting a Tea Party candadate on the ballot this November.*

⠿ A steam engine can only work when the steam has reached a particular pressure level.

head-to-head if two people or groups who are in conflict have head-to-head talks, they meet to discuss the subjects they disagree about ○ *They have just begun a third session of head-to-head talks which are expected to last until late afternoon.* ○ *Next time you have a head-to-head with someone in authority, watch your language.*

★ **keep a cool head** to remain calm in a difficult situation ○ *I have to keep a cool head and try not to let my anger show.*

★ **keep your head** to remain calm in a difficult situation ○ *The most important thing is to keep your head and look to the future.*

★ **keep your head above water** to struggle to survive, for example, by keeping out of debt ○ *Thousands of other small businesses like mine are, at best, struggling to keep their heads above water or, at worst, have gone bust.*

★ **keep your head down**
1 to try to avoid trouble or involvement in a difficult or dangerous situation by behaving in a quiet way, so that people will not notice you ○ *After unity, he had little time for Christian Democrats who had kept their heads down under the old regime.*
2 to continue to concentrate and work hard at something ○ *When he gets a chance of winning, he keeps his head down and really goes for it.*

★ **laugh your head off** or
scream your head off to laugh or scream a great deal ○ *They were probably*

laughing their heads off.

★ **lose your head** to panic and not remain calm in a difficult situation ○ *He warned the party not to lose its head, saying that it was not a "time for panic."*

not right in the head (*spoken*) strange, foolish, or crazy ○ *"According to Great-Aunt Louise," I said, "the grandmother wasn't quite right in the head."*

off the top of your head
1 (*spoken*) if you comment on something off the top of your head, what you say is an immediate reaction and is not a carefully considered opinion, and so it might not be correct ○ *Last year the amount of money we put into development and support was, off the top of my head, about twenty-eight thousand dollars.*
2 if you know something off the top of your head, you know it well and can remember it easily ○ *She can recite all the state capitals in alphabetical order, off the top of her head.*

off your head (*British*) very strange, foolish, or dangerous ○ *It's like working in a war zone. You must be off your head to live in that area.*

out of your head (*informal*) very strange, foolish, or dangerous ○ *If he didn't kill anybody, it was only by luck because he was out of his head and screaming like a maniac.*

put your head above the parapet to do or say something in public that has previously been kept private, and risk being criticized or attacked ○ *This is a policy option that cannot be ignored – although no one is prepared to put their head above the parapet to say so.*

⠿ Parapets are banks of earth or walls which soldiers build for protection against enemy attacks.

put your head in a noose or
stick your head in a noose to deliberately do something which will put you in danger or in a difficult situation

○ If I have to be caught, OK, but I am damned if I will put my head in a noose and walk into that hotel!

> A noose is a loop and knot that is tied in rope in order to hang someone.

put your head into the lion's mouth to deliberately place yourself in a dangerous or difficult situation ○ Put your head into the lion's mouth and just say "I don't know what the hell is going on."

> This expression refers to the traditional circus act where a lion-tamer puts his or her head in a lion's mouth.

put your head on the block → see **block**

★ **scratch your head** to be puzzled and unsure about what to do about a problem or question, or to be unsure what the solution is ○ A lot of people are scratching their heads and saying, "What are we doing? Are we getting our money's worth?"

someone can do something standing on their head If someone can do something standing on their head, they can do it very easily ○ Tom, the cameraman, had won five Oscars during his long working life, and could have directed the whole movie standing on his head while playing a game of cards.

★ **something rears its head** or **something rears its ugly head** used to say that something bad starts to appear or be active ○ Now the same ugly forces of racial hatred are beginning to rear their heads again.

★ **turn something on its head** or **stand something on its head** to use the same facts of an argument or theory to produce a different or opposite conclusion ○ Instead of pleading for women's rights, they should turn the argument on its head and point out the cost of denying women the right to earn.

headlines

grab headlines to get a lot of attention in newspapers or on television news ○ The personal lives of these stars seem to grab more headlines than their careers do!

> Headlines are the titles of stories in newspapers, which usually appear in big type.

heads

★ **heads will roll** used to say that people responsible or in positions of power when something goes wrong will be punished, usually by losing their job or position ○ The widely-held view is that heads will roll over the losses.

> In the past, people in important positions were sometimes beheaded if they were considered responsible for a mistake or problem.

knock people's heads together to force people who are disagreeing to reach an agreement ○ If he's unable to knock everybody's heads together, then questions are going to be raised about his own ability to continue in office.

put your heads together to try to solve a problem together with other people ○ If there's a problem, there's no sense of floundering around. We all just sit down, put our heads together and figure it out.

make heads or tails of something to understand what is happening or how something works ○ We are doing an audit of the books to try to make heads or tails of what happened.

not make heads or tails of something to not be able to understand something at all ○ I couldn't make heads or tails of it myself, but it sounded like some sort of hymn or prayer.

★ **turn heads** to be so beautiful, unusual, or impressive that people are attracted to you and cannot help looking at you or paying attention to you ○ At the age of 20, the dark-haired actress was already turning heads in the right places.

headway

★ **make headway** to make progress in the thing that you are trying to achieve ○ *A spokesman said the two sides have agreed on a timetable for the rest of the talks and have also made headway on some security issues.*

heap

at the bottom of the heap low down in society or in an organization ○ *At the bottom of the heap live at least 1 million people – the rural poor.*

at the top of the heap high up in society or in an organization ○ *While the executive salaries should put Suncorp at the top of the heap in Queensland, they would barely rate in Sydney and Melbourne.*

heart

> The heart is traditionally regarded as the center of the emotions.

★ **a bleeding heart** someone who is too sympathetic towards people who claim to be poor or suffering ○ *This huge leap in crime and the misery it causes can't be blamed on poverty, as the bleeding hearts always insist: we are much richer now than we were then.* ○ *This was precisely the sort of bleeding-heart sentimentality that Charles Lindbergh deplored.*

★ **break someone's heart**
1 to make someone feel extremely upset and unhappy because you end a love affair or close relationship with them ○ *When he left his wife for me, I was appalled. What I'd wanted was a good time, but in the end I broke his heart.*
2 if something breaks someone's heart, the fact that it is happening makes them feel sad and depressed, because they believe that it is bad or wrong ○ *It broke my heart to see this woman break down the way she did.*

★ **a broken heart** if someone has a broken heart, they feel very sad because a love affair or close relationship has ended ○ *We have all read in fiction of people dying of a broken heart, but can this happen in reality?* ○ *Mary is broken-hearted and has spent many nights crying.*

cross my heart *(spoken)* said when you want to assure someone that you are telling the truth. This expression is used mainly by children. ○ *And I won't tell any of the other girls anything you tell me about it. I promise, cross my heart.*

> This expression refers to the Christian practice of moving your hand across your chest in the shape of a cross.

★ **cry your heart out** to cry a great deal. ○ *I threw myself on to the bed and cried my heart out. It took me a long time to get over the emotional damage of that encounter.*

★ **eat your heart out** when you want to draw attention to something you have done, you can say "eat your heart out" and mention the name of a person who is famous for doing the same kind of thing. In the following example, James Bond is a fictional spy. ○ *We just managed to overtake the bus, and smashed through the gate just as it was being closed. James Bond, eat your heart out, I say.*

> This idea is an old one - the Greek philosopher Pythagoras is reputed to have used the saying "do not eat your heart out." meaning "do not waste your life worrying."

from the bottom of your heart → see **bottom**

harden your heart against someone or something to force yourself to feel unfriendly or unsympathetic towards someone or something, even if you do not want to ○ *The most important things for Nicholas now are mobility and Braille lessons. You will have to harden your heart against doing everything for him.*

★ **in your heart of hearts** if you believe,

know, or feel something in your heart of hearts, you believe, know, or feel that it is true, even though you are very reluctant to accept it ○ *But in your heart of hearts, you must know that you're not going to save some of these children?*

★ **lose heart** to start to feel discouraged or to lose interest in something, usually because things are not progressing in the way that you hoped ○ *I suppose I'm less optimistic than I was at first. This disease seems to recur so often you begin to lose heart.*

lose your heart to someone *(literary)* to fall in love with someone ○ *Don't lose your heart to him too soon because he could just be filling in time with you.*

★ **open your heart** or
pour out your heart to tell someone your most private thoughts or feelings ○ *At first my boyfriend was incredibly supportive. I'd phone him up and pour out my heart in a way I couldn't to anyone else.*

★ **set your heart on something** to decide that you want something very much and aim to achieve or obtain it ○ *She decided not to got to college. Instead she set her heart on a career in catering.*

★ **someone has a heart of gold** used about someone who is kind and generous, and enjoys helping other people ○ *He helped all the local sports teams – baseball, basketball, football and hockey. He had a heart of gold.*

someone's heart goes out to someone If someone's heart goes out to someone else, they feel a lot of sympathy for that person because they are suffering ○ *You looked so sad when you walked up the aisle at the funeral. My heart went out to you when I watched it.*

someone's heart hardens against someone or something used to say that someone starts to feel unfriendly or unsympathetic towards someone or something ○ *All of a sudden my heart*

hardened against my beautiful mother and her desire for fun and a rich, handsome husband.

someone's heart is in the right place said when you think someone is kind, considerate, and generous, although they may lack other qualities that you consider to be important ○ *Whether Johnson's professional judgement was good or not, I decided that his heart was in the right place.*

someone's heart is in their mouth used about someone who feels extremely anxious or nervous, because they think something bad may be about to happen ○ *My heart was in my mouth when I walked into her office.*

someone's heart isn't in something used to say that someone is doing something that they are unenthusiastic about and that they are not enjoying ○ *Playing was no longer fun. I lost my competitiveness and my heart wasn't in it.*

someone's heart sinks used when someone suddenly feels very worried or disappointed ○ *There was a police car outside the house. My heart sank.* ○ *I'll never forget that heart-sinking moment when they told me the news.*

★ **something is close to your heart** used to say that a subject is very important to you and that you are concerned about it or interested in it ○ *For presenter Manjeet K. Sandhu the position of Asian women in society is an issue very close to her heart.*

★ **take something to heart** to pay a lot of attention to someone's advice or criticism, and be greatly influenced or upset by it ○ *He could have taken this criticism to heart since he built his reputation on being a good manager.*

wear your heart on your sleeve to allow your feelings to be obvious to everyone around you ○ *She simply doesn't wear her heart on her sleeve so it's sometimes* *difficult to know what she's feeling.*

hearts

★ **win hearts and minds** to persuade people to like or accept something new or different ○ *The strategy of using aid as a weapon has failed to win hearts and minds and is instead fueling further violence.*

heartstrings

★ **tug at the heartstrings** to cause someone to feel a great deal of pity or sadness for someone or something ○ *Miss Cookson knows exactly how to tug at readers' heartstrings.*

  In medieval times, it was believed that "heartstrings" were tendons which supported the heart.

heat

the heat is on used to say that there is a lot of pressure to do or achieve something ○ *To perform well when the heat is on, all you have to do is let it happen.*

if you can't take the heat, get out of the kitchen used to express the idea that someone should either learn to tolerate the difficulty or unpleasantness of an activity, or stop being involved in it ○ *If you are coach of a successful football team and you can't take the heat you should get out of the kitchen.*

  This expression became very widely known when the American President Harry S Truman used it in 1952 to announce that he would not run again for president.

★ **in the heat of the moment** without stopping to think about what you are doing or saying, because you are angry or excited ○ *He said that his comments were made in the heat of the moment and were not supposed to be a personal attack.*

★ **turn up the heat on someone** to put pressure on a person or situation in order to get what you want ○ *The firm will be turning up the heat on its rivals in a highly*

competitive industry now scrapping for a share of the domestic market.

heave-ho

give someone or something the heave-ho to make someone leave their job or to get rid of something ○ *A nationwide protest hit Huntsville on Wednesday, and those attending say they want to give the old heave-ho to the House Speaker.*

heaven

in seventh heaven extremely happy ○ *After I was given my first camera I was in seventh heaven.*

  According to Islam, there are seven heavens. The seventh is the most glorious and is governed by Abraham. In the Jewish religion, the seventh heaven is the dwelling place of God and his angels.

move heaven and earth to do everything you possibly can to make sure that something happens ○ *He had been moving heaven and earth for six weeks in order to prevent the movie being made; and he had failed.*

heavens

the heavens opened (*literary*) used as a way of saying that it began to rain very heavily ○ *As we sat down to eat, the heavens opened for a few minutes and we all crouched under our blue awning holding our plates.*

heel

★ **bring someone to heel** or **call someone to heel** to force or order someone to obey you ○ *In practice it's still not clear how the president will use his power to bring the republics to heel.*

heels

★ **at your heels**
  1 following close behind you ○ *They led the girls away, their mother at their heels.*
  2 threatening or challenging you in some

way ○ *Intel and Motorola may dominate the market for microprocessors but scores of firms are snapping at their heels.*

★ **dig in your heels** or
dig your heels in to refuse to do something such as change your opinions or plans, especially when someone is trying very hard to make you do so ○ *He could dig in his heels and fight stubbornly for what he believed to be right.*

drag your heels → see **drag**

★ **come on the heels of something** to happen very quickly or immediately after another event ○ *The news comes on the heels of the appointment of new chief executive Cedric Walker.*

★ **hard on someone's heels** or
hot on someone's heels
1 doing nearly as well as someone else in a competitive situation, and likely soon to be doing better than them ○ *The next generation of British athletes is pressing hard on the heels of today's champions.*
2 close behind someone, often chasing them ○ *But the law was hard on their heels. Within two weeks gang leader Michael McAvoy and Brian Robinson were behind bars.*

kick up your heels to enjoy yourself a lot, for example at a party ○ *Combine music, culture and good food in Jersey City this month. Kick up your heels at the annual Jersey City Jazz Festival.*

This refers to a horse that has been released into a field; horses commonly do this as they gallop off.

cool your heels to wait somewhere and feel bored or impatient because you have nothing to do, or because someone is deliberately keeping you waiting ○ *The Tunisian authorities wouldn't grant us permission to fly all the way down to Sfax, so I had to cool my heels at Tunis Airport.*

set someone back on their heels to surprise or shock someone, and often put them at a disadvantage ○ *Ireland started*

brightly, only to be set back on their heels by the first error just 10 minutes into the match.
take to your heels (literary) to run away. ○ *He took to his heels and rushed out of the room.*

heights

★ **dizzying heights** or
the dizzy heights a very high level of success in a particular field ○ *Turner had first known such dizzying heights in the 1960s when she became one of the top exponents of black American music.*

hell

★ **all hell breaks loose** used to describe a situation where there is a lot of fuss, arguing, or fighting ○ *In "Jungle Fever," a happily-married black architect begins an affair with his Italian-American secretary, but all hell breaks loose when his wife finds out.*

This expression first appeared in John Milton's "Paradise Lost" (1667), book 4, line 917, when the Archangel Gabriel addresses Satan: "Wherefore with thee Came not all hell broke loose?" (i.e. why did all hell not break loose and come with you?). Here, "broke" means "broken," but the meaning of this expression has since changed.

come hell or high water in spite of the difficulties involved ○ *The chairman of the Senate Judiciary Committee says the all-male panel will have two female members this year, come hell or high water.*

★ **from hell** used after a noun to refer humorously to something or someone extremely unpleasant, or as bad as they can possibly be ○ *A cute family puppy turns into the pet from hell in this comedy starring Charles Grodin.*

give someone hell
1 to make someone's life very unpleasant by behaving badly toward them ○ *She gets teased at school. The children give her hell, particularly the older boys.*
2 to shout at someone or speak to them

angrily because they have done something wrong ○ *When she didn't get off the train at Boston, I phoned the police and they found her in a sleeping compartment. She gave me hell for embarrassing her!*
3 to be very painful ○ *My back's giving me hell, let me tell you! But I'm still going to do some gardening.*

go hell for leather to move or do something very quickly, often without care ○ *The Dutch boys are confident from all their skating and go hell for leather.*

≡ This expression may originally have related to horse riding. "Leather" would refer to a saddle.

★ **go through hell** to have a very difficult or unpleasant time ○ *After the case he made no comment, but his lawyer said that he had gone through 10 months of hell.*

go to hell to be destroyed ○ *This government has to wake up. The country is going to hell and they're just sitting on their backsides.*

hell freezes over if something will not happen until hell freezes over, it will never happen ○ *"Tell them you'll get married when hell freezes over," she says.*

hell hath no fury like a woman scorned used to suggest that women often react to something that hurts or upsets them by behaving very angrily and viciously ○ *Faithless husbands who doubt that hell hath no fury like a woman scorned should read Tolleck Winner's novel "Love With Vengeance" and beware.*

≡ This comes from William Congreve's "The Mourning Bride" (1697): "Heav'n has no rage, like love to hatred turn'd, Nor Hell a fury, like love scorn'd."

hell on earth a place or a situation that is extremely unpleasant or that causes great suffering ○ *Organizing it all has been hell on earth, but it has turned out wonderfully.*

★ **just for the hell of it** for fun or for no particular reason ○ *On the same street, David, aged 10, has been arrested for burglary. Another boy has been caught putting sugar in gas tanks, just for the hell of it.*

★ **a living hell** a situation or a place that is extremely unpleasant or that causes great suffering. ○ *School is a living hell for some children.*

play hell with something to have a bad effect on something or to cause great confusion ○ *Divorce and remarriage play hell with property and inheritance law.*

put someone through hell to give someone a very difficult or unpleasant time ○ *Her family say the girl has put them through hell since the incident.*

★ **raise hell**
1 to cause trouble by behaving badly in public, for example, by making a lot of noise and breaking things or upsetting other people ○ *Are they the type that first thing they want to do is go out and raise hell, or are they here to play football?* ○ *He has had a reputation as a hell-raiser but claims to have now settled down.*
2 to protest strongly and angrily about a situation in order to persuade other people to correct it or improve it ○ *She came in and raised hell. Her son's sports bag was missing.*

there'll be hell to pay used to warn that there will be serious trouble if a particular thing happens or if it does not happen ○ *If I try to get through the kitchen with these muddy boots, there'll be hell to pay. You know what she's like.*

to hell and back if someone has been to hell and back, they have had a terrible experience, although it is now finished ○ *We have been to hell and back but the love of this little boy has kept us going.*

hem

hem and haw to hesitate in speaking, or to fail to commit yourself to a course of action ○ *After much hemming and hawing, they finally came to a decision.*

herd

ride herd on someone to supervise other people or their actions or watch them closely ○ *His departure would undermine state efforts to ride herd on the oil companies.*

> Originally, "riding herd" involved patroling on horseback around a herd of animals, in order to make sure none of them wandered away.

here

★ **neither here nor there** *(spoken)* completely unimportant or irrelevant, and not affecting a situation in any way ○ *"You know John doesn't believe in marriage, mom." "What John believes is neither here nor there."*

herring

★ **a red herring** a piece of information, a suggestion, or an action that is irrelevant and, often deliberately, is taking people's attention away from the main subject or problem that they should be considering ○ *This is a total political red herring and an attempt to divert the public from the main issues in the campaign.*

> A red herring is a herring that has been soaked in salt water for several days, and then dried by smoke. Red herrings were sometimes used when training dogs to follow a scent. They were also sometimes used to distract dogs from the scent they were following during a hunt.

het

★ **be het up** *(old-fashioned)* to be upset, anxious, or irritated ○ *It's not important – don't get het up about it.*

hide

you haven't seen hide nor hair of someone used to express surprise that you haven't seen someone, because you expected to ○ *She said she was driving to New Orleans and I haven't seen hide nor hair of her since.*

> A hide is the skin of an animal, especially the tough skin of a large animal.

high

high as a kite very excited ○ *When I had finished the course I felt as high as a kite. But when my wife asked me what I had learned I could not be specific.*

★ **leave someone high and dry** to leave someone in a difficult situation which they are unable to do anything about ○ *Schools with better reputations will be flooded with applications while poorer schools will be left high and dry.*

> The image here is of a boat that is left on a beach after the tide has gone out.

★ **ride high** to be very popular or successful at the present time ○ *The elections came at a time when the Democrats were riding high, while support for the GOP had slumped.*

> The image here is of a horse rider who sits very straight in their saddle and seems very proud and confident.

search high and low for something or **hunt high and low for something** to look for something very carefully and thoroughly, looking in every possible place that it could be ○ *I've searched high and low for the pictures, but I just can't find them since I moved.*

highway

highway robbery a situation in which you are charged a lot of money for something that should cost a lot less or even nothing at all ○ *They are charging three bucks for the comics, which sounds like highway robbery to us.*

hike

take a hike used for telling someone rudely to go away or stop being involved

○ *But chances are that Truman, in as nice a way as possible, told Koury to take a hike.*

hill

★ **not amount to a hill of beans** to be unimportant or have no influence ○ *Just a change in party majorities won't amount to a hill of beans; we need a clean start.*

★ **over the hill** no longer young, and too old to do a particular thing ○ *It's true some people regard you as probably over the hill at fifty.*

≣ The image is of the top of a hill as the middle of life, so passing over the top of the hill leads downwards to old age and death.

hilt

★ **to the hilt** or
up to the hilt used to emphasize that someone does something to the greatest possible extent ○ *He'll be a good candidate. We'll back him to the hilt.*

≣ The hilt of a sword or knife is its handle. The image here is of a knife or sword being pushed in all the way to the handle.

hip

joined at the hip if two people are joined at the hip, they are very close to each other emotionally and they spend a great deal of time together ○ *Though we often work together, we're not joined at the hip, so we see things differently.*

shoot from the hip or
fire from the hip to give your opinion or react to situations very quickly, without stopping to think it through properly ○ *She specifically declared that she did not shoot from the hip. She liked to think long and hard before making decisions.*

≣ The image here is of a cowboy removing his gun from its holster and firing immediately, without raising it to take aim.

hissy

throw a hissy fit or
have a hissy fit or
pitch a hissy fit to become upset or angry about something trivial, or when you don't get what you want ○ *Kentucky's Insurance Commissioner recently threw a hissy fit that any 2-year-old denied its toy would envy.*

history

★ **be history** (*spoken*) to be no longer important, relevant, or interesting ○ *He sometimes wonders if he made the right choice when he decided to give up football. "I might have made it in football, but that's all history now."*

★ **the rest is history** used when the speaker or writer knows that everyone is familiar with what happened next ○ *A job with the company was advertised in The New York Post. I applied and the rest is history.*

hit

★ **hit or miss** done carelessly or without proper planning, so equally likely to fail or succeed ○ *The acting, however, is hit or miss: it ranges from the highly stylish to the appallingly gauche.*

★ **hit it off** if two people hit it off when they first meet, they find that they like each other or get along well and have many things in common ○ *After their extended two hour talk yesterday, the two leaders actually seem to have hit it off.*

★ **a hit list**
1 a group of people or things that someone intends to take action about, for example, by punishing them or getting rid of them ○ *They published a hit list of countries guilty of unfair trade practices, and called for bilateral negotiations with the offending countries.*
2 a list containing the names of important people who a terrorist or criminal organization intend to kill

○ *The letter, which said the family is on a hit list, has been passed to police for further investigation.*

★ **make a hit** if you make a hit with someone, they like you or are impressed by you when they meet you ○ *Eleanor and Sara made a hit with the whole delegation.*

Hobson

Hobson's choice a decision that forces you to choose between two things which are both bad, and so you cannot possibly be happy ○ *They want rid of him, he is irreplaceable. It really is Hobson's choice for them. Hell with him, or Hell without him.*

> This expression may refer to a man called Thomas Hobson, who earned money by renting out horses at the end of the 16th century. He had a particular system for using each horse in turn, so a customer was given no choice, even if there were many horses available.

hog

> A hog is a pig.

go hog wild to behave in an uncontrolled and excited way ○ *That doesn't mean you should go hog wild and double the recipe's sugar content. Just keep the word "moderation" in mind.*

> Hogs can sometimes become uncontrolled and aggressive.

★ **go whole hog** or **go the whole hog** to do something to the fullest extent possible ○ *The store sells a range of hi-fi speakers costing from $19.99 to $99.99. Or you can go the whole hog and buy a dedicated sound output system for $499.*

live high on the hog to have a good life, with plenty of money ○ *He and Austen were living high on the hog in a penthouse apartment with three servants.*

hold

get hold of something to obtain and take control of something, especially something that is hard to get ○ *The working class cannot simply get hold of the ready-made state machinery and wield it for its own purposes.*

get hold of someone to catch and detain someone ○ *Before any could get hold of him, Sadko jumped from the ship and plunged below the waves.*

★ **put something on hold** to decide not to do, change, or deal with something now, but to leave it until later ○ *Some observers suggest that, as a result of this, he'll just put the project on hold until the political climate changes.*

> This expression is probably from the term used when someone making a telephone call waits for the operator to connect them.

holds

★ **no-holds-barred** used for describing a way of behaving when people act very forcefully or enthusiastically, without paying attention to any limits that may exist ○ *He had a no-holds-barred attitude and just attacked everything.*

> This expression refers to a wrestling match in which many of the usual rules do not apply, and so competitors can hold their opponent in any way they like.

hole

be in the hole to owe money to someone else ○ *The Federal Housing Administration has just been discovered to be $4 billion in the hole.*

> The "hole" referred to here may have been a slot which was cut in the surface of a poker table in a gambling house. The money which the house charged was placed in the slot, and fell into a locked drawer. Gamblers who

owed money to the house were said to be "in the hole."

blow a hole in something

1 to spoil something such as a plan or make it less effective ○ *If schools opted out of school board control, would it blow a hole in the new system?*

2 to reduce an amount of money considerably ○ *A major natural disaster such as an earthquake or hurricane could blow a hole in the fund.*

burn a hole in your pocket

if money is burning a hole in your pocket, you are very eager to spend it as soon as possible, especially on something you do not really need but would like to have ○ *Money always tends to burn a hole in my pocket.*

a hole card something that you keep secret or hidden until you are ready to use it to gain an advantage over other people ○ *The fact that I knew where she was and had in my possession a boxful of evidence were my only two remaining hole cards.*

In "stud" poker, the "hole" card is a card that is dealt to you face down so that the other players cannot see it.

in a hole in a difficult or embarrassing situation ○ *Local Democrats are now in a dreadful hole after last Tuesday's election results.*

someone needs something like a hole in the head used to emphasize that someone does not want something at all, and that it would only add to the problems that they already have ○ *We need an interest rate rise like we need a hole in the head.*

This is said to be a translation of a Yiddish expression. It became more widely known following the play "A Hole in the Head" (1957) by Arnold Schulman, and a film of the same name starring Frank Sinatra (1959).

holes

pick holes in something to find weak points in something such as an argument or theory that show that it is wrong ○ *They say that the great science of the 21st century will be biology. Thus we do not need so many physicists as in the past. It is easy to pick holes in this argument.*

something has more holes than Swiss cheese used to say that something, such as an argument or theory, has so many flaws that it cannot be taken seriously ○ *"The current laws," he says, "have more holes than Swiss cheese."*

Swiss cheese is a pale cheese that has many round holes in it.

hollow

★ **ring hollow** if a statement or promise rings hollow, it seems false, or insincere ○ *Details of his 27-year affair have been revealed to all. His speeches on family values and the stability of marriage ring hollow now.*

The idea is of an object that is meant to be solid making a loud noise when struck, indicating that it is weaker or cheaper than it was believed to be.

holy

the holy of holies something that people think is the most special or important thing of its kind ○ *Last year, his work was performed for the first time at the Aldeburgh Festival, the holy of holies in the contemporary British music scene.*

In a Jewish synagogue, the holy of holies is the inner room that only the chief rabbi may enter.

home

★ **at home**

1 if you feel at home in a particular situation, you feel relaxed, comfortable, and happy ○ *Melanie is equally at home singing oratorio, spirituals, jazz or performing in musical theater.*

2 if someone or something looks at home somewhere, they look as if it is normal, natural, or appropriate for them to be there ○ *The 16-year-old's huge shoulder and arm muscles would look more at home on a male hammer thrower.*

★ **be home free** to have achieved victory or success in a contest or other activity, or to have solved all your problems ○ *We've won, but we aren't home free yet – we've still got two more matches to play.*

be nothing to write home about to be not very interesting, exciting, or special ○ *Yes, there is cheese, bread and meat in the local market and shops, but it's nothing to write home about.*

★ **be on home ground** or **be on home turf** to feel confident and secure because you are in the area where you work or live, or are doing something that is very familiar to you ○ *This is a play where Godber is on home turf, writing about the mining communities of his childhood.*

bring home the bacon

1 to be the person in a family who goes out to work and earns enough money for the family to live on ○ *The question "Who brings up the baby and who brings home the bacon?" has become one of the most important of all political questions.*

2 (journalism) to win or do very well in sports ○ *But Reid and Duffield showed that, given the right horsepower, they are capable of bringing home the bacon in style.*

★ **bring something home to someone** to make someone fully aware of how serious or important something such as a problem, danger, or situation is ○ *This new TV commercial really brings home to people how badly some children are treated.*

close to home if a remark is close to home, it makes people feel uncomfortable or upset because it is about a sensitive or very personal subject ○ *The message the film conveyed struck so hard and so close to home that it moved me to tears.*

★ **come home to roost** if something bad or unacceptable that someone has done comes home to roost, they will now have to deal with the unpleasant results of their actions ○ *You ought to have known that your lies would come home to roost in the end.*

> This expression is taken from the poem "The Curse of Kehama" by the English poet Robert Southey: "Curses are like young chickens, they always come home to roost."

★ **hit home** or **strike home** if a situation or what someone says hits home or strikes home, people realize that it is real or true, even though it may be painful for them to accept it ○ *In many cases the reality of war doesn't hit home with reservists until they're actually called upon to fight.*

hit a home run to do something that is very successful ○ *Bartlett Giamatti hits a home run here with his memoir of encounters with W.H. Auden over many years.*

> In baseball, when a batter hits a home run, they hit the ball a very long way, so that they are able to run around all the bases and score a run before the other team gets the ball back.

the home stretch or **the home straight** the last part or stage of a long or difficult activity ○ *This month, Wales take on the Czech Republic in the home straight of the qualifying competition.*

> The home stretch or home straight is the final part of a horse race.

★ **make yourself at home** to relax and feel comfortable somewhere as if you were in your own home or in a very familiar situation ○ *Arnold and Gwen had found the hidden key, let themselves in and made themselves at home.* ○ *"Sit down," Anne said. "Make yourself at home."*

homework

do your homework to do what is required to be fully prepared for a situation, especially by studying and researching ○ *They did their homework, examined the data, heard from the experts about what was happening and then took action.*

honest

honest as the day is long (old-fashioned) very honest ○ *This boy's hard-working, ambitious, smart, and honest as the day is long. They don't come any better than Russell here.*

hoof

hoof it to walk somewhere ○ *Along the way, I stopped for a bagel and coffee and then hoofed it home.*

hook

do something by hook or by crook to do something even if it is very difficult for you, or you have to use dishonest means ○ *If a man took Antonia's fancy, she would go out of her way to get him by hook or by crook.*

> The hook in this expression is a billhook, which is a cutting tool with a hooked blade. A shepherd's crook is a long stick with a curve at the top. This expression may refer to a medieval law which allowed ordinary people to collect firewood from forests belonging to the King or a lord, so long as they took only dead wood which they could reach with crooks and billhooks.

★ **get off the hook** to manage to get out of the awkward situation you are in without being punished or blamed ○ *We cannot let the government get off the hook for what it has done.*

hook, line, and sinker very intensely, deeply, or fully ○ *I fell for her hook, line and sinker.*

> When fish are caught, they sometimes swallow part of the fishing line and the "sinker" or weight, as well as the hook.

on your own hook alone, without any help ○ *St. Mary's Hospital does not meet incoming flights with its own vehicle. Patients come on their own hook.*

> The reference here is to someone catching a fish using their own equipment and without help from others.

ring off the hook if your telephone is ringing off the hook, so many people are trying to call you that it is ringing all the time ○ *His phone started ringing off the hook as banks and financial institutions begged for his help.*

swallow something hook, line, and sinker to be fooled into believing something completely and being deceived by it ○ *Our president is one heck of a salesman, and people are just swallowing this thing hook, line, and sinker, without knowing what it's all about.*

hookie

★ **play hookie** to be absent without an excuse, especially from school ○ *Next week we have plans to skip town, play hookie on Friday and relax.*

hooks

get your hooks into someone to control or influence someone very strongly, often in a way that is not good for them ○ *The big industries like to get their hooks into the bright young people, to subsidize them through their education and then reap the benefit.*

hoops

make someone jump through hoops or
make someone go through the hoops to make someone prove their ability and willingness to obtain something that they want by forcing

them to do a lot of difficult things first ○ *They basically put a four-year course into three years and made us jump through hoops.*

▤ Circus animals are sometimes trained to jump through hoops that are hung or held above the ground and sometimes set on fire.

hoot

not give a hoot or
not give two hoots to not care about something or someone at all ○ *I'm really disgusted with our politicians. They don't give a hoot about their constituents.*

hop

hopping mad extremely angry ○ *Apparently, the family is hopping mad that she left them nothing in her will.*

a hop, skip, and a jump if one thing is only a hop, skip, and a jump away from another, they are very close together or very closely linked ○ *Of course, the Romanian language is just a hop, skip, and a jump from Italian.*

hopper

★ **in the hopper** in preparation and soon ready to happen or be acted on ○ *Last year we approved four new programs and we have two more in the hopper.*

▤ A hopper is a part of a machine that holds parts or fuel about to enter the machine. Hopper is also used to describe a place where proposed legislation is kept before being debated.

horizon

★ **on the horizon** almost certainly going to happen or be done quite soon ○ *With breast cancer, as with many common diseases, there is no obvious breakthrough on the horizon.*

horn

toot your own horn to boast about

yourself ○ *Maybe I am a superstar right now, but I don't go around tooting my own horn; this is a game that kicks you right back in the face.*

▤ In the past, the arrival of important people in a place was announced by the playing of trumpets.

hornet

stir up a hornet's nest to do something that causes a lot of controversy or produces a situation that is extremely difficult to deal with ○ *According to my brother Paul, this Lonnie Norton was asking a lot of questions and stirring up a hornet's nest around town.*

▤ A hornet is a large wasp with a powerful sting.

horns

lock horns to argue or fight with someone ○ *During his six years in office, Seidman has often locked horns with lawmakers as well as the administration.*

▤ The reference here is to two male animals, such as deer, fighting over a female and getting their horns caught together or "locked."

on the horns of a dilemma having to choose between two or more alternatives, which seem to be equally good or equally bad ○ *I was often caught on the horns of a dilemma. Do I work late in the air-conditioned cool darkness of the office, or retreat to the cafe for a cold lemonade?*

▤ In logic, a dilemma is a situation where an argument leads to two choices which are both undesirable. In the Middle Ages, a dilemma was traditionally represented as an animal with two horns such as a bull.

pull in your horns or
draw in your horns to start behaving more cautiously than you did before, especially by spending less money ○ *The*

world's big spenders have pulled in their horns during the recession and the top designers have felt the pinch.

When snails sense danger, they pull in their "horns," which are the stalks that their eyes are on.

horse

back the wrong horse to support the wrong person in a contest or election ○ *We think they're backing the wrong horse if they support the Mengistu government.*

come down off your high horse or **get down off your high horse** to stop acting in a superior way ○ *It is time for the intellectuals to get down off their high horses and to really take the struggle into the ghettoes.*

In the past, very large horses were a sign of high rank because they were owned and ridden only by knights.

eat like a horse to eat a lot because you have a large appetite ○ *When Kelly is on medication, he eats like a horse and when he is off, he has almost no appetite at all.*

beat a dead horse to waste your time trying to achieve something that cannot be done ○ *They're exhausted. You're beating a dead horse. You have some talented boys but they're playing like run-down machines.*

from the horse's mouth if a piece of information comes from the horse's mouth, it comes directly from the person who knows best or knows most about it, and so you are sure it is true ○ *Most of the book is completely true; it comes from the horse's mouth.*

This expression may refer to the fact that you can tell a horse's age by looking at its teeth. Alternatively, it may simply refer to a racing tip that is so reliable that it is as if the horse itself has told you how well it is going to perform.

get on your high horse to behave as if

you are better than other people, and refuse to accept any criticism of yourself ○ *When Kuwait was occupied, President Bush and Prime Minister John Major lost no time in getting on their high horses.*

a one-horse race a contest in which it is obvious even before it starts that one person or team is much better than the others and will win ○ *Marseille are threatening to turn the French championship into a one-horse race.*

a one-horse town a town that is very small and uninteresting ○ *Lumut is something of a one-horse town, but you can always take a boat across to Pangkor island and look at Dutch ruins.*

★ **someone is a dark horse** if someone is a dark horse they have had success or may be about to have success when not much is known about them ○ *To many people, Atkinson is a dark horse who worked away for many years behind the scenes at British Airways.*

This expression may refer to a horse that people do not know very much about, so that it is difficult to predict how well it will do in a race.

a stalking horse

1 something that is being used to obtain a temporary advantage so that someone can get what they really want at a later date. This expression is usually used to show disapproval. ○ *The development will act as a stalking horse for further exploitation of the surrounding countryside.*

2 someone in politics who stands against the leader of a party to test the strength of any opposition to them. They then withdraw in favor of a stronger challenger, if it looks likely that the leader can be defeated. ○ *There was even talk of one of them putting up for the leadership as a "stalking horse" for the real contender.*

Stalking horses were horses that were used by hunters. They were trained to allow their rider to hide behind them, and so get closer to the birds they were hunting.

★ **a Trojan horse** a policy or activity that seems harmless, but is likely to damage or destroy something important ○ *Apple may well use iTunes as a trojan horse to mount a far reaching assault on Facebook with the release of Ping, a social feature integrated within iTunes.*

This refers to an ancient Greek story. The city of Troy was under siege from the Greeks. The Greeks built a large hollow wooden horse and left it secretly as a gift for the Trojans, who took it into the city. However, Greek soldiers were hiding inside the horse, and they were able to cause the destruction of the city.

you can lead a horse to water but you can't make it drink this expression means you can give someone the opportunity to do something, but you cannot force them to do it if they do not want to ○ *You can't educate kids who aren't interested. You can lead a horse to water but you can't make it drink.*

horses

change horses in midstream to stop using one system and start using another one, or to stop supporting one person and start supporting someone else. ○ *I think we were very wise not to change horses in midstream.*

The American President Abraham Lincoln used this expression in 1864, "I am reminded of the story of an old Dutch farmer, who remarked to a companion that it was best not to swap horses when crossing streams."

hold your horses *(spoken)* said to tell someone to wait, slow down, or stop for a moment, often when you think that they are going to do something silly ○ *Hold your horses a minute, will you, and*

just take another look at this badge.

wild horses wouldn't make someone do something used to say that someone will not do something even if other people try to force them to ○ *Wild horses wouldn't make Nicola sell the yard if she found out it would make me rich.*

hostage

a hostage to fortune someone who cannot control how a situation develops, and so has to accept any bad things that happen ○ *Charles, then nearly 33, had already made himself a hostage to fortune by declaring that 30 was a suitable age to settle down.*

This expression comes from an essay by Francis Bacon, "Of Marriage and Single Life" (1625): "He that hath wife and children hath given hostages to fortune."

hot

be hot to trot to be very eager to get involved in something or start doing something ○ *We're hot to trot to take a road trip and try out this hotel.*

hot and bothered very upset or worried about something ○ *He was astonished that everybody had got so hot and bothered about the affair.*

someone blows hot and cold
1 if someone blows hot and cold, their attitude about something keeps changing, so that sometimes they seem enthusiastic or interested, and sometimes they do not ○ *The media, meanwhile, has blown hot and cold on the affair.*
2 sometimes someone's work or performance is good, and sometimes it is not ○ *They seem to have blown hot and cold in their early matches.*

too hot to handle if someone or something is too hot to handle, you mean that they are so dangerous, difficult, or extreme that people do not want to be involved with them ○ *Even for* *someone of Mr. Hurd's skill and experience, the situation proved too hot to handle.*

hotcakes

sell like hotcakes or
go like hotcakes to be very popular and sell in large numbers very quickly ○ *Their jam was selling like hotcakes.*

"Hotcakes" is another term for pancakes.

hots

★ **have the hots for someone** *(informal)* to be sexually attracted to someone ○ *He will be joining the show later this season as a Columbia teacher Serena has the hots for.*

hour

★ **at the eleventh hour** very late or at the last possible moment ○ *The concert, scheduled for last Saturday, was canceled at the eleventh hour, after the star Peter Gabriel pulled out on Thursday.* ○ *The eleventh hour decision came as the President made it clear he was prepared to gamble his political career if it came to conflict.*

In the Bible, Jesus uses this expression in the story of the laborers in the vineyard (Matthew 20:1-16). In Jesus's time the hours were counted from dawn until dusk, with the twelfth hour bringing darkness, and so the eleventh hour was the last hour before dark.

hours

at all hours at any time of the day or night ○ *In Hollywood, you can shop at all hours, and get almost anything you want.*
wee hours or
small hours the middle of the night, starting at 1 am ○ *In the wee hours of Thursday, doctors at the hospital came out of the operation theater with a sense of triumph.*

This expression comes from the fact that on a clock, small numbers (1, 2, and 3) denote the hours in the middle of the night.

house

bring the house down if a person or their performance brings the house down, the audience claps and cheers loudly for a long time because they liked the performance so much ○ *We had just one rehearsal and I was petrified but, as Lenny predicted, the sketch brought the house down.*

In this expression, the "house" means a theater.

eat someone out of house and home to eat so much food that it costs someone a lot of money to feed you ○ *They eat everybody out of house and home but nobody minds because they provide such first-rate entertainment.*

This expression was used in Shakespeare's play "Henry IV Part II," act 2 scene 1 (1597). When asked why she wants her lodger Sir John Falstaff arrested, the landlady Mistress Quickly replies: "He hath eaten me out of house and home; he hath put all my substance into that fat belly of his."

get on like a house on fire or
get along like a house on fire if two people get on like a house on fire, they quickly become close friends, for example, because they have similar interests ○ *I went over and struck up a conversation, and we got on like a house on fire.*

This expression suggests suddenness and intensity, like an old wooden house that would catch fire and burn easily and quickly.

a halfway house a compromise between two things, or a combination of two things ○ *The option of totally segregating retail and investment banks is in there, but so is an interesting halfway house.*

A halfway house was originally an inn located halfway between two neighboring towns or villages and would have been used by coach passengers. Today "halfway house" also denotes a place where people released from prison or rehabilitation live before returning to society.

★ **a house of cards** a system, organization, or plan that is likely to fail or collapse ○ *This government could fall apart like a house of cards during the first policy discussion.*

> This refers to the building of an elaborate but unstable pyramid structure using playing cards.

★ **put your house in order** or **get your house in order** to make sure that all your affairs are arranged properly and there is nothing wrong with them ○ *The government gives the newspaper industry a twelve-month deadline to put its house in order or face tough statutory controls.*

household

a household name someone or something that is very famous or known by very many people ○ *H1N1 became a household name last year because of its severity.*

hue

a hue and cry a loud protest about something or opposition to it ○ *There probably will be a hue and cry about my suggestion of more power to the police.*

> Until the 19th century, "hue and cry" was the legal name for the cries of someone who had been robbed and who was calling for others to help. It was an offense for anyone to refuse to join the chase, once they heard the cry. "Hue" comes from the Old French "huer," meaning "to shout."

huff

★ **in a huff** behaving in an irritable, bad-tempered, and childish way, because you could not get something you wanted ○ *He stormed off in a huff because he didn't win.*

hump

hump day Wednesday. This expression came from the next idiom, "over the hump," because after Wednesday you are over the hump of the work week. ○ *It's hump day, and we can all use some motivation to get us through the rest of the week.*

over the hump past the worst part of an unpleasant or difficult situation ○ *I think we're basically over the hump in this instance. We've got an economy now that's likely to grow.*

hush

hush money money paid to someone so that they will keep a secret ○ *The firm has been accused of paying $750,000 in hush money to its former finance director as part of an alleged attempt to cover up a conspiracy.*

hymn sheet

sing from the same hymn sheet (mainly British) if two or more people are singing from the same hymn sheet, they agree about something, and are saying the same things in public about it ○ *As she and her husband face a court case, they can be relied upon to sing from the same hymn sheet.*

Ii

i

dot the i's and cross the t's to add the final minor details to a piece of work, plan or arrangement ○ *Unless all the i's are dotted and the t's are crossed, a contract is not likely to be valid.*

This expression refers to the fact that in some handwriting, you write a word with one movement of your pen, and then go back and add the dot to any i's and the cross-stroke to any t's.

ice

★ **break the ice** to say or do something to make people feel relaxed and comfortable at a party or a meeting ○ *Break the ice with tea or coffee and get to know your client a little better.*

This expression refers to the need to break the ice around a ship before it is able to sail.

★ **put something on ice** to postpone something ○ *Plans have been put on ice for a meeting in London of the five permanent members of the United Nations Security Council.*

This expression refers to the use of ice to preserve food and prevent it from decaying.

sell ice to an Eskimo or **sell ice to Eskimos** said to mean that a person is so persuasive they could convince people to buy something they already have plenty of. You can also talk about **selling snow to Eskimos**. ○ *He could sell anything -- even ice to an Eskimo!*

"Eskimo" is an old-fashioned word for the Inuit people of the Arctic regions of North America. Ice and snow are common plentiful there due to long, harsh winters.

★ **skate on thin ice** to get into a difficult situation which may have serious or unpleasant consequences. ○ *All through my career I had skated on thin ice and somehow had, so far, got away with it.*

★ **something cuts no ice** said about something that does not impress you ○ *Flying is dreadful. Statistics cut no ice with anyone scared of going up in the air in a plane.*

This expression refers to ice-skating. In order for the skater to move easily, the blades must be sharp so that they cut into the ice.

icing

★ **the icing on the cake** an extra good thing that happens and makes a situation or activity even better. You can also talk about **the frosting on the cake**. ○ *I was proud to be a member of the Mercedes-Benz Grand Prix team, but to drive their fantastic sports cars as well really was the icing on the cake.*

ignorance

ignorance is bliss said to mean that if you do not have any information about a particular thing or situation, you cannot worry about it ○ *I used to feel that, politically, ignorance is bliss. But something changed this summer.*

inch

come within an inch of doing something to very nearly do something ○ *A driver who comes within an inch of smashing into a tree will nonetheless claim that there is nothing wrong with his eyesight.*

give someone an inch and they'll take a mile if you allow someone to do something small or simple, they will use the opportunity to take advantage of you ○ *Be tough and uncompromising – if you give colleagues an inch, they will take a mile.*

to within an inch of your life very severely ○ *His fists were clenched as if he were going to beat Smythe to within an inch of his life.*

information

too much information (*informal*) said when you do not want to hear any more about something, because it is private or embarrassing. Sometimes people shorten this expression to the initials TMI. ○ *"I've gone to the bathroom twice already." "Too much information!"*

ink

bleed red ink (*journalism*) to have severe financial problems ○ *Even large companies are bleeding red ink. But they are quickly closing plants and axing thousands of jobs to boost performance.*

This expression comes from the practice in the past of using red ink to fill in entries on the debit side of a book of accounts.

ins

★ **the ins and outs** all the complicated details or facts about a situation or system ○ *There are many helpful books now available written by cookery and dietary experts who can advise on the ins and outs of dieting in great detail.*

insult

★ **add insult to injury** to make a bad situation worse by doing something that upsets or harms someone, after you have already done something bad to them ○ *The Council of State opposed the president's suggestion and added insult to injury by leaking its hostile and secret comments to the press.*

iron

pump iron to lift weights for exercise ○ *Shuey spends most of his time in the weight room pumping iron.*

This expression became popular after a 1977 film called "Pumping Iron," about professional weightlifters.

strike while the iron is hot to act immediately, while you have the best chance of succeeding at something ○ *This is the week to get plans off the ground. It's time to strike while the iron is hot.*

A blacksmith can only bend or work iron when it is hot.

★ **with an iron fist** with great force and often violence ○ *The Generals have ruled the nation with an iron fist for more than half of its independent existence.*

irons

have a lot of irons in the fire to be involved in several different activities or have several different plans at the same time, so that it is likely that something will succeed even if other things fail ○ *"I will be earning a lot more money," he says, declining to say how much more. "I also have a number of other irons in the fire."*

ivories

tickle the ivories to play the piano ○ *They don't play in public anymore, but they still enjoy tickling the ivories at home with their grandchildren.*

On older pianos, the tops of the keys are made of ivory, which comes from elephant tusks. Ivory is not used today for this purpose.

ivory

★ **someone lives in an ivory tower** used to suggest that someone's lifestyle or their work prevents them from experiencing the problems experienced by ordinary people, and so they remain

generally unaware of these problems
○ *They're all out of touch – they live up in a little ivory tower, and they don't see what's going on down here.*

≡ This is a translation of a French expression "tour d'ivoire," which was used by the critic Saint-Beuve to describe the way in which the writer Alfred de Vigny isolated himself from the rest of society.

Jj

Jack

★ **before you can say Jack Robinson**
very suddenly and quickly ○ *The pair of them were out of the door and down the steps before you could say Jack Robinson.*

> The identity of Jack Robinson is unknown and the name might have become popular because both elements were once extremely common. The phrase appears in the novel "Evelina" (1778) by Fanny Burnley: "I'll do it as soon as say Jack Robinson."

jack

a jack-of-all-trades
1 someone who has many different skills ○ *He soon caught the theater bug, and became a jack-of-all-trades at the local amateur theater.*
2 someone who can do a lot of different things but who is not very good at doing any of them ○ *His critics sometimes described him as a jack-of-all-trades.*

> The name Jack was used to refer to any man or workman.

jackpot

★ **hit the jackpot**
1 to suddenly be very successful and earn a lot of money ○ *The National Theater hit the jackpot with its first musical, Guys And Dolls.*
2 to suddenly succeed in getting or finding something that you have been trying to get or find ○ *I went through all the people called Lasalles in the Sydney phone book until I hit the jackpot.*

> This expression was originally used in poker. A "jackpot" was a sum of money that increased until someone could start the betting with a pair of jacks or higher.

jazz

and all that jazz and other things of a similar kind. This expression is sometimes used in a slightly disapproving way. ○ *She shops at one of those eco-supermarkets that promotes sustainability and healthy eating and all that jazz.*

Jell-O

like trying to nail Jell-O to the wall
extremely difficult or impossible. **Jell-O** is a trademark. ○ *Right now, it's just about like trying to nail five pounds of Jell-O to the wall.*

> This expression was first used by President Theodore Roosevelt in a letter to William Roscoe Thayer in 1915. He was describing the difficulty of negotiating with Colombia over the Panama Canal.

Jesus

★ **come to Jesus** used to refer to a situation in which someone deals with or resolves a crisis in a dramatic or forceful way ○ *We had a little come to Jesus talk at halftime and I think we became a football team in the second half.* ○ *Five weeks after the crash, Gorelick summoned the FBI brass to a come-to-Jesus meeting in Washington.*

> This expression is based on the activity at a Christian revival meeting, in which a preacher asks those present to "come to Jesus" (that is, start believing in him).

jewel

★ **the jewel in someone's crown** the best thing that someone has, or the achievement that they can be most proud of ○ *His achievement is astonishing and this book is the jewel in his crown.*

≣ This expression was known in Victorian times, but is probably most well known as the title of a novel by Paul Scott, published in 1966, that formed part of a series set in the Raj, or Victorian India. In this title, India is seen as the "jewel," and the "crown" is the British Empire.

job

do a job on someone *(informal)* to defeat or harm someone in some way ○ *Coetzer is a difficult opponent. But I'm equally sure I can do a job on him.*

a full-time job a task that takes a great deal of time and effort ○ *Maintaining a happy home in which a family can thrive is a full-time job, and for many women it becomes their career for life.*

sleeping on the job not attending to responsibilities properly ○ *Summers has been caught yet again sleeping on the job.*

Joe

Joe Public or
Joe Schmoe or
Joe Six-Pack an average man or person ○ *We need to use language that Joe Public can understand.*

John

★ **someone's John Hancock** someone's signature ○ *The promotion was announced today by Best Buy Mobile and allows you to pick up a high-end smartphone with your John Hancock and a new 2 year agreement.*

≣ This expression comes from American statesman John Hancock, first signer of the Declaration of Independence, who wrote his name very large and legibly so that the King could see it.

Johnny

Johnny-come-lately a person who

becomes involved in an activity or organization after it has already started, and who is therefore less reliable or experienced than the people who have been involved since the beginning ○ *Motorola has given Apple a good kicking and reminded Jobs' Mob that it is still a Johnny-come-lately to the mobile scene.*

≣ This name used to be given to new or inexperienced sailors in the American navy.

joker

the joker in the deck someone or something that is different from the other things or people in a situation and does not seem to fit in, or may cause problems ○ *Ray enjoys long walks and the occasional game of golf. He is probably best known as the quiet one who is the joker in the deck.*

≣ The joker in a deck of playing cards is the card that does not belong to any of the four suits.

Joneses

keep up with the Joneses to try to have or do the same things as other people that you know, even if you do not really have enough money to do this, or are not really interested in these things ○ *Her mother was very eager to keep up with the Joneses, and through much of her teens Linda accepted what she now calls "these false values."*

≣ This expression comes from the title of a comic strip by Arthur Momand, which was first published in the New York "Globe" in 1913.

judgment

sit in judgment to criticize other people ○ *I think people should work hard to keep a marriage alive. I don't want to sit in judgment on other people, but if there's anything that's good, try to hold on to it.*

jugular

★ **go for the jugular** to attack an opponent or enemy very decisively at the point where you can cause the greatest damage ○ *The Titans also showed the ability to go for the jugular, blowing open the game in the third quarter.*

> The jugular vein is a large vein in the neck and supplies blood to the neck and face.

juice

let someone stew in their own juice
or
let someone stew to deliberately leave someone to worry about something, such as the consequence of their actions, and to not do anything to comfort or help them ○ *He was very mean to everyone and now no one will speak to him; let him stew in his own juice.*

jump

★ **get a jump on someone** to do something before someone else does and so gain an advantage over them ○ *This year, many stores did try to get a jump on the shopping season by holding promotional sales even before Thanksgiving.*

> This expression refers to a competitor in a running race leaving the starting blocks ahead of the other competitors.

★ **jump up and down** to be very excited, angry or upset about something ○ *He is not someone who jumps up and down. He is a man of quiet determination and firm principles.*

one jump ahead → see **step**

jury

★ **the jury is still out** used to say that people have not yet formed an opinion about something or reached a decision ○ *The jury's still out on what the long-term effects of air pollution are.*

> This refers to the time when the jury in a court case retires from the court room to decide on a verdict.

justice

do justice to someone or something

1 to give someone or something the attention or effort that they deserve ○ *He's an innovative, creative talent who I know will do justice to the tradition and glamour of the Academy Awards.*

2 to properly represent someone or something ○ *"To do justice to this great man and his music is a huge responsibility,"* he said.

poetic justice a good or bad thing that happens to someone who deserves it ○ *He started the Playoffs in the all-important top 5 in the standings, so it would be poetic justice of sorts to see him win from 11th.*

Kk

kahuna

a big kahuna or
a grand kahuna *(informal)* a person who has an important and powerful position in an organization, especially the most powerful position ○ *Anybody who has a protégé knows that sometimes they get a little uppity and want to mess with the big kahuna.*

> The word "kahuna" is from Hawaiian and means "wise man" or "shaman."

kangaroo

a kangaroo court a group of people or an actual court that forms an opinion or judgment without any normal procedure or good reason ○ *The meeting was an open discussion rather than a Kangaroo court.*

> This expression compares a court to a bunch of kangaroos, who "jump" to conclusions.

keel

★ **on an even keel** calm or progressing steadily, especially during or after a period of troubles or difficulties ○ *She sees it as her role to keep the family on an even keel through its time of hardship.*

> The image here is of a ship moving along smoothly and steadily, because it is balanced and not leaning to either side.

keep

something earns its keep
if something earns its keep it is of good value and justifies the amount of money that it costs or the space that it takes up ○ *In Bob's garden everything must earn its keep, with fruits and vegetables given priority over flowers.*

keeper

I am not someone's keeper said when you do not know where someone is and that you cannot be expected to know ○ *"I don't know where he is," Hughes replied, "I'm not his keeper." "No, simply his employer."*
not your brother's keeper not responsible for other people in any way ○ *Part of me wants to help him, but part of me realizes I can't be my brother's keeper.*

> These expressions come from a story in the Bible (Genesis 4:9). Cain has killed his brother, Abel, but he tries to deny it. When he is asked where his brother is, he replies, "I know not: Am I my brother's keeper?"

ken

something is beyond your ken said about something that you do not have much knowledge, understanding or experience of ○ *The subject matter is beyond the ken of the average layman.*

> "Ken" here means the full range of someone's knowledge or understanding. The Scottish verb "ken" means "know."

kettle

★ **a different kettle of fish** something that is completely unlike another thing that you have mentioned ○ *Artistic integrity? Who needs it? Money? Now that's a completely different kettle of fish.*

kibosh

put the kibosh on something to prevent something from happening, continuing, or being successful ○ *The company gave its subscribers access to software that puts the kibosh on pop-up ads if a user doesn't want them.*

> The origin of this expression is uncertain, but some people think that "kibosh" may come from Yiddish.

kick

kick someone upstairs → see **upstairs**

get a kick out of someone or something to enjoy someone or something very much ○ *Hockey fans aren't the only ones who will get a kick out of the book.*

a kick in the pants or
a kick in the butt or
a kick in the ass a negative experience or a punishment, especially when something positive is expected ○ *Arizonans are justifiably angry that the American Dream of my generation has become a kick in the pants.*

kick someone when they are down to hurt, upset or criticize someone when they are already in a weak position or at a disadvantage ○ *Expulsion would be regarded by many people, including many in the party, as going too far in kicking a man when he's down.*

kicks

get your kicks out of something to get enjoyment from something ○ *He gets his kicks out of football and Swedish hot-dogs and doesn't mind doing the chores at home.*

kid

like a kid in a candy store enjoying yourself far too much and not controlling your behavior in any way ○ *A money manager in Chicago, he went on a buying binge and "felt like a kid in a candy store," he recalls.*

treat someone with kid gloves to treat someone very carefully because

they are very important or because they are easily upset ○ *Mr. Sarbutts was treated as a VIP. Everybody was treating him with kid gloves.*

> Kid is very soft leather.

kill

★ **move in for the kill** to act decisively to defeat your enemy or opponent ○ *Nick and I appeared almost unstoppable and we moved in for the kill.*

killing

★ **make a killing** to make a large profit very quickly and easily ○ *The boss of New York's top pizza chain made a killing on the market yesterday by selling off most of his shares.*

kindness

kill someone with kindness to treat someone very kindly even though this is not what they need or want ○ *"He is killing me with kindness," Sallie says. "He's just too attentive."*

king

a king's ransom (old-fashioned) a very large sum of money ○ *Roberts is asking a king's ransom for her next film role.*

live like a king to have a luxurious and very comfortable lifestyle ○ *Company executives lived like kings. The top thirty-one executives were paid a total of 14.2 million dollars, or an average of 458,000 dollars.*

kingdom

blow someone to kingdom come to destroy someone, especially in a very violent way ○ *One false move could blow us all to kingdom come.*

> This comes from the line "Thy kingdom come" in the Lord's Prayer in the Bible. (Matthew 6:10)

kiss

kiss and make up to sort out a disagreement and end a conflict ○ *They* *argue constantly and publicly but always manage to kiss and make up.*

★ **kiss-and-tell** referring to the public story someone tells after they have had a love affair with a famous person ○ *On many occasions we discussed selling details of kiss-and-tell stories.*

> This expression appears in the play "Love for Love" by William Congreve (1695): "Oh, fie, Miss, you must not kiss and tell."

★ **the kiss of death** something that is certain to cause failure or ruin ○ *Relying on cliches is the kiss of death for a decent writer.*

> This expression refers to the Bible story of how Judas betrayed Jesus by kissing him. This identified Jesus to the Romans, and led to his arrest and crucifixion.

kit

the whole kit and caboodle all of something. ○ *I would probably find that I could borrow the whole kit and caboodle.*

> "Caboodle" may come from the Dutch word "boedal," meaning "property."

kitchen

everything but the kitchen sink very many things, many of which are unnecessary ○ *When she goes on a picnic, she always wants to take everything but the kitchen sink.*

> The image of this expression is of a restaurant kitchen serving a dish made with everything in the kitchen (i.e. every available ingredient) except for appliances that are nailed down.

kite

go fly a kite said to someone who is annoying you, so that they will go away ○ *I asked him if he would be willing to do a taped interview and he told me to go fly a kite.*

kittens

have kittens to be extremely worried or upset by something ○ *The boss will have kittens if I don't get that dress back within the hour.*

> In the Middle Ages it was said that if a pregnant woman was having stomach pains she had kittens clawing inside her womb.

knee

knee-high to a grasshopper (old-fashioned) very young ○ *I've lived here since I was knee-high to a grasshopper.*

knees

be on your knees to be extremely weak or tired ○ *Several times this afternoon he had sounded as if he were on his knees.*

★ **bring something to its knees** to cause a country or organization to be in an extremely weak condition ○ *The company was brought to its knees after a wave of paralyzing strikes.*

go down on your knees to beg desperately for something ○ *They won't take the manager back, even if he gets down on his knees and apologizes.*

knell

★ **sound the death knell** see **death**

knickers

get your knickers in a twist (mainly British, informal) to become extremely upset or worried about something. Americans use the equivalent expression **get your panties in a twist**. ○ *Let's not get our knickers in a twist until we see the outcome of those games.*

knife

like a hot knife through butter quickly and without any problems ○ *His voice cut through the noise like a hot knife through butter.*

★ **on a knife edge** in a situation in which nobody knows what is going to happen next ○ *Our finances are on a knife edge at the moment.*

stick the knife in to deliberately do or say things that will upset another person or cause problems for them ○ *Her colleagues, often eager to stick the knife in, defended her yesterday.*

twist the knife to deliberately do or say things that make a situation even worse for someone who is already upset or experiencing problems ○ *Jones then twisted the knife with another goal.*

knight

a knight in shining armor a man who rescues you from a difficult situation ○ *I just felt dizzy and then I collapsed. I am very, very grateful to Tom and he really was my knight in shining armor.*

In stories written or set in the Middle Ages, a knight in shining armor traditionally came to the rescue of a "damsel (or young woman) in distress."

a white knight a company that rescues another company that is about to fail or be taken over ○ *1300 workers are fighting for their jobs, hoping for a white knight to rescue the factory from closure.*

knives

★ **the knives are out** used to describe a situation where people are feeling very angry or resentful towards someone, and are trying to cause problems for them ○ *His book has hit the stores and the knives are out.*

knock

knock someone sideways to make someone feel amazed, confused or very upset ○ *Something like this, a huge shock, completely knocks you sideways.*

knock something sideways to severely damage something so that it may not recover ○ *Confidence in the legal system has been knocked sideways, hasn't it?*

knot

cut the Gordian knot *(literary)* to succeed in solving a very complicated and difficult situation or problem ○ *Scott decided to close the inquiry last year when he concluded that it would be possible to go on for ever. "You have to cut the Gordian knot."*

According to an ancient legend, Gordius, the king of Phrygia, tied a knot that nobody could untie. It was said that if anyone untied it, they would become the next ruler of Asia. When Alexander the Great heard this, he solved the problem by cutting through the knot with a sword.

★ **tie the knot** *(informal)* to get married ○ *The couple tied the knot last year after a 13-year romance.*

Tying knots in items of clothing or ribbons worn by the bride and groom is a traditional feature of many wedding ceremonies, symbolizing their unity.

knots

tie someone in knots to confuse someone by using clever arguments, so that they cannot argue or think clearly any longer ○ *He could tie her in knots in an argument and never once missed an opportunity to prove his intellectual superiority.*

tie yourself in knots to make yourself confused or anxious, and so you are not able to think clearly about things ○ *He was tying himself in knots, trying to sound at once supportive of the president, yet somehow disapproving of the "damage" to the country's "reputation."*

know

★ **know someone or something inside out** to know someone or something extremely well ○ *He knows Washington inside out.*

not know whether you are coming

or going *(spoken)* to feel very confused and unable to think clearly ○ *The truth is I'm so excited that I hardly know whether I'm coming or going.*

knuckles

★ **rap someone on the knuckles** to criticize or blame someone for doing something that you consider to be wrong ○ *If we find the bank made a mistake or was negligent, we will rap them on the knuckles.*

In the past, teachers sometimes punished pupils who behaved badly by hitting them on the knuckles with a ruler or stick.

Ll

labor

★ **a labor of love** a job or task that you do for pleasure or out of duty without expecting a large reward or payment for it ○ *They concentrated on restoring outbuildings such as the Victorian greenhouse, an expensive labor of love.*

This expression appears in the Bible (1 Thessalonians 1:3), which refers to people's "labor of love" (= the work that they do prompted by love), and the strength of people's confidence in Jesus.

ladder

move up the ladder or
climb up the ladder to improve your situation by becoming more important or successful ○ *They made it to the semifinals last weekend and moved back up the ladder to fourth place.*

lady

it isn't over until the fat lady sings or
it ain't over till the fat lady sings used to emphasize that nothing is certain until the end and there is still time for a situation to change ○ *"Who knows, Michael might fall off and break a leg," he joked. "As they say, it isn't over until the fat lady sings."*

The origin of this expression is uncertain but it may refer humorously to the fact that in the final part of an opera there is often a piece sung by the heroine before her death, a part often played by a large soprano singer.

lam

on the lam trying to escape or hide from someone, such as the police or an enemy ○ *He was arrested on Friday, after living on the lam since 1999.*

"Lam" is an American slang word meaning running away.

lamb

like a lamb gentle, quiet, and obedient ○ *She'd followed him like a lamb. She hadn't asked him why he was taking her to a medical research laboratory rather than to a normal hospital or clinic.*

lambs

like lambs to the slaughter if people go somewhere like lambs to the slaughter, they behave quietly and obediently without resisting because they have not realized that it will be dangerous or unpleasant, or because they realize that they are powerless ○ *The record companies have an easy life. We grovel and follow their every word like lambs to the slaughter.*

land

get the lay of the land or
get the lie of the land to find out the details of a situation or problem ○ *I'm not sure what's going to happen. That's why I'm coming in early. I want to get the lay of the land.*

land-office

do a land-office business to be very successful ○ *The Paradiso, one of the capital's newest and most luxurious clubs, was doing a land-office business.*

Before the Civil War, the government opened up land offices that sold rights to pieces of land in the West. So many people wanted to buy land to settle on that there were often long lines outside the offices before they opened in the morning.

lane

★ **the fast lane** a way of living that seems full of activity and excitement but that often involves a lot of pressure as well ○ *Tired of life in the fast lane, Jack, a fifty-ish businessman, decides to give it all up to fulfill a dream of becoming a painter.*

"Fast lane" and "slow lane" refer to the speed of traffic in the different lanes of an expressway.

language

speak the same language to have the same interests, opinions, or goals as someone else ○ *There is hardly any difference now between the so-called moderates and the hard-liners in the Senate, so they are speaking the same language.*

lap

Your lap is the area at the top of your thighs when you are sitting down, where a child would sit.

fall into someone's lap if something good falls into someone's lap, it happens to them without any effort on their part ○ *It would not be safe to assume that victory will fall into our lap at the next election.*

in the lap of the gods if something is in the lap of the gods, it will be decided or affected by luck or chance, rather than anything you can do ○ *Once they had repaired my lung they had to stop the operation. The liver is self-healing anyway, so at that stage, my life was in the lap of the gods.*

The idea here is that nobody knows what blessings will fall from the lap of the gods until they actually appear on earth.

in the lap of luxury in conditions of great comfort and wealth ○ *We don't live in the lap of luxury, but we're comfortable.*

The image is probably of luxury personified as a woman with a small child sitting on her lap whose every need is attended to by her.

land in your lap if a problem lands in someone's lap, they are forced to deal with it although it is not really their responsibility ○ *These problems have landed in the lap of Donald Jackson, an unassuming manager with little international experience.*

the last lap the final part of an activity before it is finished ○ *The proposal was rolled out last Wednesday, during the last lap of the three-day summit.*

In this expression, "lap" means one complete trip around a track or racecourse.

larger

★ **larger than life** used for describing someone who seems more interesting or exciting than other people, for example, because they are very talented, or because they behave in an unusual or interesting way ○ *John Huston was a larger-than-life character, whose temperament was as dramatic as any of the fictional figures in his own films.*

last

last but not least used when you want to show that the person or thing you are mentioning last is not the least important ○ *Last but not least, Bristol Palin and partner Mark Ballas danced the quickstep to You Can't Hurry Love.*

lather

in a lather very worried and upset about something ○ *The truth of the matter is that you have spent the past six months working yourself up into a lather over situations which are really none of your business.*

When horses get very hot, the sweat on their coats sometimes forms a foamy substance called lather.

laugh

★ **have the last laugh** to make your critics or opponents look foolish or wrong, by becoming successful when they said that you would fail ○ *Singer Des O'Connor is expecting to have the last laugh on his critics by soaring to the top of the Christmas hit parade.*

laundry

★ **air your dirty laundry in public** or **wash your dirty linen in public** to talk about unpleasant or personal matters in front of other people, when most people consider that such things should be kept private. ○ *We shouldn't wash our dirty laundry in public and if I was in his position, I'd say nothing at all.*

★ **a laundry list** a large number or long list of things ○ *This document is expected to set out a laundry list of reasons why shareholders should reject the bid.*

→ see **dirty**

laurels

In ancient Greece, the laurel or bay tree was associated with the god Apollo. The winning competitors in the Pythian games, which were held in honor of Apollo, were given crowns or wreaths of laurel.

look to your laurels to work hard or think seriously about what you are doing, in order to make sure that you continue to be successful ○ *The SEC maintains a critical role, but it must now look to its laurels.*

★ **not rest on your laurels** to not rely on previous successes, but to continue working hard to make sure that you have continued success ○ *The trouble with all successful restaurants, however, is the tendency to rest on their laurels and stagnate.*

law

★ **be a law unto yourself** to behave in an independent way, ignoring laws, rules, or conventional ways of doing things ○ *Most athletic departments are pretty much a law unto themselves – unaccountable in terms of where this money goes.*

the law of the jungle a situation where the normal rules and values of civilized life do not exist, and so, for example, strength, power, and aggressiveness have more effect than moral values and legal rights ○ *The streets are subject to the law of the jungle and policing has been entrusted to private law enforcement agencies.*

This phrase became popular from "The Jungle Book" by Rudyard Kipling (1894). "The law of the Jungle, which never orders anything without a reason, forbids every beast to eat Man, except when he is killing to show his children how to..." Instead of encouraging aggression, this law actually places limits on the use of violence in the animal kingdom.

★ **lay down the law** to tell people very forcefully and firmly what to do ○ *They were traditional parents, who believed in laying down the law for their children.*

★ **take the law into your own hands** to punish someone who you believe has done something wrong, even though you have no right to, and even if this means that you yourself break the law ○ *Could we have taken the law into our own hands and thrown the unwanted visitors out?*

lay

get the lay of the land → see **land**

lead

In these expressions, "lead" is pronounced with the same vowel sound as the word "red."

≡ Lead is a very heavy metal.

get the lead out used to tell someone to start working or moving faster ○ *You'd better get the lead out and start producing results.*

≡ The original form of this phrase was "get the lead out of our pants." The idea was that a person was moving slowly because they were carrying some heavy weight.

go down like a lead balloon to be completely unsuccessful and unpopular ○ *A senior source said the memo had gone down like a lead balloon.*

leaf

The "leaf" in these expressions is a page of a book.

shake like a leaf → see **shake**
★ **take a leaf out of someone's book** to copy someone and behave or do something in the same way as them, usually because they were successful when they acted in that way ○ *If he wants a better rapport with the public, it's high time he took a leaf out of Goldberg's book and started doing game shows and interviews.*

★ **turn over a new leaf** to start to behave in a better or more acceptable way than previously ○ *The military leader said he and the king have agreed to turn over a new leaf in their relations with one another.*

leap

take a flying leap or
take a flying leap off a tall building or
take a flying leap through a rolling doughnut said when you want to completely dismiss someone from any association with you ○ *When I first heard about tethering my iPhone's internet service to my computer my first thought was "Now I can tell Comcast to take a flying leap!"*

leaps

by leaps and bounds
★ **in leaps and bounds** rapidly ○ *The U.S. population grew by leaps and bounds.*

lease

a new lease on life If someone or something is given a new lease on life, something makes them successful once again or improves their condition ○ *The old oak table was picked up for just $20 and subsequently given a new lease on life by Kim's mother.*

≡ A lease is a contract by which you can rent property for a fixed period of time.

leash

A "leash" is a long thin piece of leather or chain, which you attach to a dog's collar so that you can keep the dog under control.

give someone a longer leash to allow someone a lot of freedom to do what they want, rather than controlling them very strictly ○ *At the beginning of the 1992 campaign, Dan Quayle was given a longer leash than ever before.*

keep someone on a short leash or **keep someone on a tight leash** to control someone carefully and only allow them a small amount of freedom to do what they want ○ *The government strove to impress the country with its calm reasonableness and kept its troops on a tight leash.*

strain at the leash to be very eager to do something ○ *The players had better realize that we have enough youngsters straining at the leash to take their places if they don't do their jobs.*

least

to say the least used after an adjective or a statement to show that what you think or feel is much stronger than the way you are saying it ○ *The results were surprising, to say the least.*

leave

be left in the dust to be outdone or left far behind by someone or something ○ *The Canadian economy was left in the dust by the torrid pace of expansion in the U. S. economy in the third quarter.*

When a vehicle moves off, or a person runs off, the moving wheels or feet cause dust on the road to rise up behind them.

left

left and right used to emphasize that something is happening or being done a great deal ○ *They're all expecting the state to pay out money left and right.*

leg

break a leg said to a performer who is about to go on stage as a way of wishing them good luck ○ *Jason sent Phillip a fax from the airport before Monday's show, with the greeting: "Break a leg and enjoy yourself."*

There are many superstitions associated with the theater. For example, many performers consider that it is unlucky to say "good luck" directly to anyone. Instead, they pretend to wish them bad luck.

★ **give someone a leg up** to help someone to achieve something and become successful, especially by giving them an advantage that other people do not have ○ *The mother seemed to think that her name had given her boy a leg up on the competition.*

To give a rider a leg up means to help them get on to the horse.

not have a leg to stand on to be in a very weak position, usually because you are unable to prove a claim or statement you have made ○ *I haven't got a leg to stand on. I had no witnesses.*

pull someone's leg to tease someone about something, for example, by telling

them something which is not true ○ *Is he serious or just pulling our legs?*

There are two possible explanations for this expression, although there is no proof for either. One suggestion is that in the past, when someone was being hanged, their friends or family sometimes pulled their legs hard so that they died more quickly and suffered less. Alternatively, the expression may refer to thieves tripping people up before they robbed them.

talk the hind leg off a donkey to talk a lot ○ *He could talk the hind leg off a donkey. It took real perseverance to get through to him on the telephone.*

legs

have legs if an idea, plan, or story has legs, it is likely to work or be true ○ *Mr. Blucher was confident that his concept had legs, so he persisted and pressed Mr. Cooper for a meeting.*

on its last legs no longer as useful, successful, or strong as before, and about to fail altogether ○ *By the mid-1980s, the copper industry in the US was on its last legs.*

leopard

a leopard does not change its spots used to emphasize that it is not possible for someone bad or unpleasant to change and become good and pleasant ○ *Women who believe they have tamed a "wild" man are usually wrong. The cliché that a leopard doesn't change its spots still happens to be true.*

A form of this proverb is used in the Bible (Jeremiah 13:23), by the prophet Jeremiah, to say that wicked people never change. He asks: "Can Ethiopians change the color of their skin or leopards change their spots?" He concludes that people who have been taught to do wrong, or who have always done wrong will find it difficult to become good.

let

let it all hang out to behave in a very informal and relaxed way, without worrying about hiding your emotions or behaving politely ○ *The defense most frequently claimed for the baring of the more dreadful revelations is that of "unburdening"; let it all hang out and you will feel better.*

letter

a dead letter a law or agreement that people do not pay any attention to, although it still exists ○ *In this conflict, international humanitarian law is a dead letter. Unacceptable practices are going on.*

A dead letter is a letter that the post office is unable either to deliver or to return to the sender, because it does not have the right address.

★ **follow something to the letter** to carry out instructions, rules, or advice exactly in every detail ○ *Even if that international agreement is followed to the letter, the ozone layer won't recover fully until the year 2060.*

★ **the letter of the law** what is actually written in the law, rather than the moral principles on which it is based. You usually use this expression to show disapproval. ○ *The Home Office stuck to the letter of the law over the definition of dependants.*

level

on the level honest and truthful ○ *Wait a minute, is this guy on the level or not?*

license

a license to print money a commercial activity that allows people to get a lot of money with little effort or responsibility ○ *The deregulated utilities have become a license to print money at the expense of the consumer.*

lick

a lick and a promise a quick, not very careful action, with the intention that you will do it more thoroughly later ○ *There have been so many competing chores that I've only been able to give this task a lick and a promise this past week.*

lid

blow the lid off something or **take the lid off something** (*journalism*) to reveal the true nature of a difficult or dangerous situation or problem which has previously been hidden ○ *"The Knowledge" is a new documentary series blowing the lid off music business scandals.*

★ **keep the lid on something** to keep the true nature of a particular situation or problem hidden, or to control it and stop it becoming worse ○ *But I understand that Murray was desperately trying to keep the lid on a potential scandal.*

flip your lid (*informal*) to become extremely angry or upset about something, and lose control of yourself ○ *"Boy, you are brave," she said, bathing the bleeding cut. "A lot of grownups flip their lids when you clean a cut like this."*

lie

get the lie of the land → see **land**

give the lie to show that something is definitely not true, though people may believe it ○ *That statement was so dumb that it gave the lie to the long-held notion that top lawyers are all smart negotiators.*

★ **live a lie** to live in a way that is dishonest and false ○ *My mother never told my father the truth about me. We've been living a lie all this time, and now she has taken me from him.*

a white lie something that is untrue, that is often said in order to protect someone or to avoid hurting someone's feelings ○ *I believe that this is a case where a little white lie is really more appropriate than the truth.*

life

★ **fight for your life** to be very seriously ill or injured and be in danger of dying ○ *A boy aged 15 was fighting for his life last night but two younger children were said to be out of danger.*

frighten the life out of someone or **scare the life out of someone** to frighten someone a great deal ○ *Further tests revealed that three of my veins had furred up and I needed triple bypass surgery. It scared the life out of me.*

get a life said to or about someone to express criticism, to ridicule them, or to suggest that they should take an interest in something more important ○ *It was six o'clock in the evening. I was still in my pajamas. Nicole looked at me, said she thought I was deteriorating, and suggested I get a life.*

hold someone's life in your hands to have complete control over what happens to someone ○ *You feel a responsibility to people because sometimes you're holding their life in your hands.*

larger than life → see **larger**

the life of the party someone who is very lively and entertaining on social occasions, and is good at mixing with people ○ *She was having a very enjoyable time and was clearly the life of the party.*

life is a bowl of cherries used to express the idea that life is full of pleasure and enjoyment. This expression is often used negatively to comment on an unpleasant or difficult situation, or to criticize someone for their unrealistic views. ○ *Life's not exactly a bowl of cherries when you're an international champ.*

live the life of Riley to have a very enjoyable time because you have no worries about money or work ○ *He was living the life of Riley, enjoying vacations in Italy and trips to the theater, while we had barely enough to eat.*

This expression probably comes from a song "Is That Mr. Reilly," which was popular in the 1880s and described what Reilly's life would be like if he was rich.

put your life in someone's hands to put yourself in a situation where someone has complete control over what happens to you ○ *After all these years, do you take me for a fool? What makes you think I would put my life in your hands?*

risk life and limb to do something very dangerous that may cause you to die or be seriously injured ○ *He is not prepared to risk life and limb on this dangerous track to clinch the title.*

someone can't do something to save their life (spoken) If someone cannot do something to save their life, they cannot do it at all ○ *He can't sing to save his life but he is a good guitarist.*

take your life in your hands to take a lot of risks when you do something ○ *A rider who does not know the road takes his life in his hands by cycling in the dark.*

you bet your life used for agreeing with someone or saying "yes" in a very emphatic way ○ *Do I want to go to Cancun instead of your sister's wedding? You bet your life I do!*

light

★ **be given the green light** if a plan or action is given the green light, someone in authority says that it can be carried out ○ *Despite local planning opposition he has finally been given the green light to develop a row of 11 derelict houses he owns in east Baltimore.*

in the cold light of day if you think about a problem, feeling, or event in the cold light of day, you think about it some time later and in a calmer or more practical way than was possible at the time it happened ○ *He has to sit down in the cold light of day and analyze what needs to be done to prevent the franchise from being penalized.*

★ **a leading light** someone who is considered to be one of the most important, active, and successful people in an organization or campaign ○ *He is a leading light in the just launched campaign to rid the sport of racism.*

A leading light was a light that was placed at the entrance to a harbor or shallow channel of water, as a guide for ships.

light as a feather weighing very little ○ *It was a monstrous machine as large as a building and as light as a feather.*

★ **the light at the end of the tunnel** something that gives you hope about the future and for the end of a difficult or unpleasant situation ○ *After horrific times we are seeing light at the end of the tunnel.*

light dawns used to say that someone suddenly realizes or understands something that they should have realized or understood before ○ *"Oh!" she said, as if the light had finally dawned on her. "I'm on the wrong floor, huh?"*

out like a light very deeply asleep ○ *Dad gently closed the door again. "She's out like a light," I heard him whisper to my anxious mother.*

★ **see the light** to start to understand or agree with something, especially after a long period when you have not understood or agreed with it ○ *Christianity taught him values that the West preached but largely ignored in practice. But he had seen the light and urged everyone to share it with him.*

★ **see the light of day** to become known by or available to a large number of people ○ *This book might never have seen the light of day without the enthusiasm, support, and friendship of my editor, Daniel Bial.*

lightning

lightning does not strike the same place twice used to suggest that someone who has been exceptionally lucky or unlucky is unlikely to have the same good or bad luck again ○ *Observers reckon he will be very lucky to repeat the performance. Lightning does not strike twice, particularly in big business.*

a lightning rod for something a person who is naturally blamed or criticized by people, although there are other people who are responsible ○ *He told the Palermo court he was an innocent lightning rod for Italy's many crime problems.*

A lightning rod is a long metal strip, one end of which is attached to the roof of a building, with the other end in the ground to protect the building from being damaged by lightning.

like lightning or
like greased lightning extremely quickly or very suddenly and unexpectedly ○ *I ran across that room like lightning and pushed back the curtain.*

lights

the lights are on but nobody is home used to say that although someone seems to be normal or satisfactory, they are in fact very stupid or useless ○ *According to Harrington, many projects are not properly thought through: "You get the feeling that the lights are on but no one's at home."*

like

like it or lump it (informal, mainly British) to have to accept a situation even though you do not like it, because you cannot do anything to change it ○ *If you're a shareholder in the company then you have some sort of say in the way things are run. But as a paying customer you like it or lump it.*

lily

gild the lily to act unnecessarily by trying to improve something which is already very good ○ *Here in Europe I'm* *gilding the lily. There they really need advice.*

This expression may be based on lines in Shakespeare's "King John" (1595): "To gild refined gold, to paint the lily... Is wasteful and ridiculous excess." (Act 4, Scene 2)

limb

go out on a limb to do something risky or extreme, which puts you in a position of weakness ○ *It seems to me that you would prefer to stay in your present situation rather than go out on a limb and try something completely new.*

In this expression, a limb is a branch of a tree. The image here is of someone who climbs out along a limb, away from the main trunk.

★ **out on a limb** in a position of weakness without any help or support ○ *No company wants to be the first to put its rates up. The companies who have tried have found themselves out on a limb.*

tear someone limb from limb if someone threatens to tear you limb from limb, they are extremely angry with you and threaten you with violence ○ *Police were lucky they found him before I did because they would have been arresting me. I would have torn him limb from limb.*

limits

★ **off limits** if an area is off limits, you are not allowed to go there. If a thing is off limits, you are not allowed to use it or do it ○ *The area was kept off limits to foreign journalists until early this year.*

line

all the way down the line or **right down the line** at every stage of a situation or activity, or including all the people or things involved in a situation or activity ○ *It is the government that has fought for reform all the way down the line.*

★ **along the line** or **down the line** during the course of a

situation or activity, often at a point that cannot be exactly identified ○ *And then somewhere along the line I looked at what was really happening.*

be out of line (*spoken*) to be completely wrong to say or do a particular thing ○ *Addressing a fellow officer like that is out of line, and I won't stand for it, hear me?*

The line referred to here is a line of soldiers, who are expected to act as a unit.

★ **the bottom line** the most important and basic part of what you are discussing ○ *The bottom line is that the great majority of our kids are physically unfit.*

This expression refers to the last line in a set of accounts, which states how much money has been made.

★ **cross the line** to start behaving in an unacceptable way, for example, by getting involved in something extreme or antisocial ○ *The show's pretty outrageous, but I don't think it crosses the line.*

The "line" in this expression may refer to boxing matches in the past, when a line was drawn on the ground which neither boxer could cross. "Draw the line" may be based on a similar idea.

★ **down the line**
1 at a later date ○ *Whether that happens further down the line we cannot say.*
2 if something happens a particular number of years or months down the line, it happens after that amount of time ○ *So 25 years down the line, you look back and there's a sense that it was all better back then.*

★ **draw the line**
1 to impose a restriction or limit on a situation or activity ○ *It is difficult for charities to know where to draw the line between acceptable and unacceptable sources of finance.*
2 to not do a particular activity, because you disapprove of it or because it is so

extreme ○ *I'll do virtually anything – although I think I'd draw the line at running naked across the set!*

There are several theories about the origin of this expression. It may come from early versions of tennis, in which the court had no fixed size: players agreed their own limits and drew lines accordingly. Alternatively, it may be connected with the 16th century practice of using a plow to cut a line across a field to indicate a boundary between two plots of land. A third possibility is that it refers to boxing matches in the past, when a line was drawn in the ring which neither boxer could cross. "Cross the line" may be based on a similar idea.

draw a line in the sand to put a stop to or a limit on something ○ *It was time to draw a line in the sand, forget the past, and work together.*

draw a line under something to enable a bad situation to be considered as over, so that people can start again or continue with things more productively ○ *He said the document draws a line under the painful chapters of our past and clears the way for a new beginning.*

★ **a fine line** a point at which it is difficult to distinguish between two different activities or situations, especially when one is acceptable, and the other is not ○ *There is a fine line between being well taken care of and being fussed over too much – so don't overdo it.*

the front line a position in which you play an important part in achieving or defending something ○ *The newest members of staff have been thrust to the front line of the team's rebuilding effort.*

The image here is of soldiers in the front line during a battle.

get a line on someone to get some information about someone ○ *We've been trying to get a line on you, and the more we try, the less we find.*

in the line of fire or
on the firing line in a position where you are likely to be criticized or attacked ○ *There comes a time in their lives when your children begin to test the influence they have over others and, as parents, you are first in the line of fire.*

★ **on line** operating fully ○ *A number of products are coming on line that will change the way oncology is practiced.*

★ **put something on the line** or
lay something on the line
1 to do something that causes you to risk losing something such as your reputation or your job ○ *He had put his career on the line and I wasn't prepared to let people forget that.*
2 to speak truthfully and directly about your feelings ○ *You have to put your emotions on the line with love, but he cannot do this.*

Originally, "lay it on the line" may have been connected with gambling. It meant to lay a bet on the sideline in the game of craps, or on the counter of a betting window at a racecourse.

★ **sign on the dotted line** to formally agree to something by signing an official document. This expression is often used to mean simply that you make a firm commitment about something. ○ *Once you sign on the dotted line you are committed to that property.*

★ **step out of line** to do something that you should not do or to behave in an unacceptable way ○ *Values and traditions were accepted and agreed by everyone. If you stepped out of line, you knew what to expect.*

The line referred to here is a line of soldiers, who are expected to act as a unit.

★ **toe the line** to behave in the way that people in authority expect you to behave

○ Journalists who refuse to toe the line will have to be fired.

At the start of a race, runners stand in a row with their toe just behind the starting line.

linen

wash your dirty linen in public
→ see **laundry**

lines

on the right lines or
along the right lines behaving in a way that is likely to result in success ○ Sometimes all you really require is just a friendly voice to tell you that you are on the right lines.

★ **read between the lines** to understand what someone really means, or what is really happening in a situation, even though it is not stated openly ○ He was reluctant to go into details, but reading between the lines it appears that the bank has vetoed any idea of a merger.

link

★ **a weak link** an unreliable part of a system, which may cause the whole system to fail ○ It was automatically assumed that Edward would be the weak link in the partnership.

lion

fight like a lion to fight bravely ○ She would have fought like a lion to protect her son.

★ **the lion's share** the largest part of something ○ Defense has taken the lion's share of this year's budget.

This refers to Aesop's fable "The Lion and his Fellow Hunters," in which a lion goes hunting with several other animals and takes everything that they catch for himself, instead of sharing it with them.

★ **walk into the lion's den** to deliberately place yourself in a dangerous or difficult situation ○ The senator walked into the lion's den of his press accusers, looked them in the eye, and fought back.

This expression comes from the story in the Bible of Daniel (Daniel 6), who was thrown into a den of lions because he refused to stop praying to God. However, he was protected by God and the lions did not hurt him.

lions

throw someone to the lions to allow someone to be criticized severely or treated badly, without trying to protect them ○ Tanya isn't sure exactly why she's been thrown to the lions. She traces it back to quotes she made about the business that were reproduced out of context.

In Roman times and at other periods in the past, people were sometimes put to death by being thrown into a den of lions.

lip

button your lip to keep silent about something although you would really like to speak ○ He had the grace and good sense to button his lip, even though this clearly caused him personal pain.

★ **keep a stiff upper lip** to hide your emotions and not let other people see what you are feeling ○ I shared my feelings with no one because I had always believed in keeping a stiff upper lip, and putting on my best face for family and friends.

This is supposed to be a national characteristic of the English.

★ **pay lip service to something** or
give lip service to something to appear to be in favor of an idea without doing anything to support it ○ These agreements give lip service to money going back to the people. But there is not even a formula for how it would be determined.

In this expression "service" means the same as respect. A contrast is being made here between what people say and what they really think, based on an idea expressed in various places in the Bible.

lips

lick your lips to look forward eagerly to a future event ○ *Both performed admirably against Central Michigan and they must be licking their lips at the chance to run against Minnesota.*

★ **on people's lips** or **on someone's lips**

1 if something is on people's lips, a lot of people are talking about it and seem to be interested in it ○ *The question on most people's lips was not whether there would be war but when it would it break out.*
2 if a question or comment is on someone's lips, they want to ask or say it or are in the process of asking or saying it ○ *He stopped in the dressing room beside their bedroom, hung his coat over the corner chair, his apology already on his lips.*

read my lips said to tell someone to believe and trust what you are saying ○ *Mr. Bush won the White House in 1988 thanks, in large part, to his now infamous pledge "read my lips: no new taxes."*

someone's lips are sealed used about someone who will keep a secret that someone else has told them ○ *As for anything told to me in confidence, well, my lips are sealed.*

litmus

★ **a litmus test** *(journalism)* an effective and conclusive way of proving or measuring the quality or success of a particular thing ○ *The success of wind power represents a litmus test for renewable energy.*

Litmus paper is used to test the acidity of substances. It turns red in acid conditions and blue in alkaline conditions.

live

live and breathe something to be extremely enthusiastic about a particular subject or activity ○ *Williams lived and breathed motor racing.*

live and let live to accept differences and not interfere with people who behave or think differently ○ *The vast majority of Americans are content to live and let live.*

lives

have nine lives to keep managing to get out of difficult or dangerous situations without being hurt or harmed ○ *I think this is probably going to be the end, although he has shown he is a political cat with far more than nine lives.*

This expression comes from the saying "a cat has nine lives," which people use to say that cats seem to survive a lot of very dangerous situations or events.

loaf

half a loaf is better than none used to emphasize that it is better to take what you can get, even if it is very little, than to risk having nothing at all ○ *In this case, I think a half a loaf is better than no loaf at all .*

lock

★ **lock, stock, and barrel** completely or including every part of something ○ *It would have been much easier for us to have shut the business down lock, stock and barrel, and to have saved our cash and not paid a dividend.*

The three main parts that make up a complete gun are the lock, the stock, and the barrel.

lockstep

in lockstep if two people or things move in lockstep, they are very closely linked and dependent on one another, so that if one changes, the other changes too ○ *Many criminologists argue that support for the death penalty moves in lockstep with the crime rate.*

> Lockstep is a way of marching in which the marchers follow as close behind each other as possible.

loggerheads

★ **be at loggerheads** to strongly disagree about something ○ *Social workers and doctors are at loggerheads over how well the new system will work.*

> In medieval times, loggerheads were implements with long handles and a round bowl on one end. In battles, the bowl was filled with hot tar, and then thrown at the enemy.

loins

gird your loins or
gird up your loins (journalism, literary) to prepare yourself to deal with a difficult or stressful situation ○ *He is girding his loins for another round of high-level meetings.*

> This expression is used several times in the Bible. The Hebrews wore long loose robes which they tied up with a girdle or belt when they were working or traveling.

long

★ **be long on one thing and short on another** to have a lot of one thing but not very much of another ○ *The prime minister's speech was long on words but short on solid action.*

long as your arm very long ○ *The phone's been buzzing non-stop. I've got a list of messages as long as my arm.*

look

give someone a dirty look to look at someone in a way that shows that you are very angry about something ○ *Tony was being a real pain. Michael gave him a dirty look and walked out of the kitchen.*

looked

★ **have never looked back** to have never regretted a decision ○ *He became a professional photographer in 1978, and has never looked back.*

loop

★ **in the loop** part of a group of people who make decisions about important things, or know about these decisions ○ *There are ways that are being worked out to make sure that the Congress is fully in the loop.*

out of the loop not part of a group of people who make decisions about important things, or know about these decisions ○ *He is out of the loop, and it irks him.*

throw someone for a loop or **knock someone for a loop** to shock or surprise someone very much ○ *The banker was surprised to find Johnson in his usual high spirits. If Kravis's offer had thrown him for a loop, Johnson wasn't letting it show.*

loose

★ **cut loose** to become free from the influence or authority of other people ○ *Italy has not cut loose from the ERM as determinedly as Britain.*

hang loose to relax or not to be too serious about something because it is not important ○ *Get something to eat and come back to the office. And hang loose.*

★ **on the loose**
1 free after escaping or not being caught ○ *You have to wake up every day knowing that whoever committed those awful murders is still on the loose.*
2 not being controlled or supervised by anyone and free to behave however you want ○ *The problem is high-spirited youngsters on the loose in the country's leafy lanes.*

Lord

take the Lord's name in vain → see **name**

lose

★ **lose it** (*informal*)
1 to become extremely angry or upset ○ *I completely lost it. I went crazy, berserk. I was shouting and swearing.*
2 to become unable to do something you are usually able to do ○ *He walked on stage, looked out into the audience and just lost it. He forgot the words and started to make up completely different ones.*

loss

★ **at a loss** not knowing what to do or say in a particular situation ○ *These women also face language barriers and are at a loss to know where to go for help.*
at a loss for words → see **words**
a dead loss a completely useless person or thing ○ *Politics is in crisis, and politicians are a dead loss.*

losses

★ **cut your losses** to decide to stop spending time, energy, or money on an activity or situation on which you have already spent a lot without having any success ○ *Only you can decide if you should push on to the end of your degree program or cut your losses and get out.*

lot

all over the lot spread across a large area or over a wide range of things ○ *IBM's investments have been all over the lot – in fiber-optic technology, data-retrieval systems, computer networks and so on.*

≡ In this expression a lot is an area of
≡ land.

someone has a lot to answer for said to mean that someone is responsible for something bad that has happened ○ *Even if economists can explain in hindsight how the recession happened, the profession still has a lot to answer for.*

★ **throw in your lot with someone** or **cast your lot with someone** to decide to join someone and to share

whatever good or bad things happen to them ○ *That does not mean that France is ready to throw in its lot with other Community states on defense matters.*

≡ In the past, "lots" were objects such as
≡ pieces of straw or paper that people
≡ used when making a decision or
≡ choice. Each lot represented, for
≡ example, a different piece of property
≡ or course of action. All the lots were
≡ put together and then chosen at
≡ random to decide who would receive
≡ the different pieces of property or
≡ what action would be taken.

loud

★ **loud and clear** if someone says something loud and clear, they say it openly and forcefully so that it cannot be misunderstood or ignored ○ *The message must come across loud and clear from the manager: No matter how hard I ask you to work, I work as hard or harder.*

love

all's fair in love and war used to express the idea that under difficult circumstances, any kind of behavior is acceptable ○ *He appears to live by the boorish credo that all is fair in love and war. And being cruel to mistresses and wives isn't wrong.*

for love nor money if you cannot get something for love nor money, it is very difficult to get ○ *You won't get a room here, not for love nor money.*

★ **no love lost** or
little love lost if there is no love lost between two people or groups, they do not like each other at all ○ *There was no love lost between the country's two most powerful politicians.*

≡ Originally this expression had the
≡ opposite meaning to its present one.
≡ It used to mean that the two people
≡ liked each other a lot.

luck

down on your luck suffering a period of bad luck ○ *Even when people are down on their luck, they deserve the same human courtesy that any of us would expect.*

the luck of the draw something that depends on chance rather than on the efforts or qualities of the people involved ○ *On better acquaintance, you may decide that there's no basis for a real friendship with a colleague. That's just the luck of the draw.*

This expression refers to the act of drawing a card at random from a deck of playing cards.

push your luck to do something risky that could spoil the success you have already had ○ *With gambling it's definitely best to quit while you're ahead, rather than trying to push your luck.*

lucky

strike it lucky to suddenly have some good luck ○ *I arrived at 12:30 to give myself time to find a parking meter, but struck it lucky immediately.*

This expression has its origins in mining in the 19th century. It refers to someone finding the minerals or oil that they were looking for. "Strike oil" and "strike it rich" are based on the same idea.

lump

★ **a lump in your throat** a tight feeling in your throat because of a strong emotion such as sorrow, nostalgia, or gratitude ○ *Meg felt a lump in her throat. She was going to miss Dot, even though the two of them had never been particularly close.*

lumps

★ **take your lumps** to accept bad results, luck, or events without getting upset ○ *Ben Bernanke has taken his lumps for his stewardship of the Federal Reserve.*

lunch

out to lunch not aware of what is happening around you, or not intelligent or capable ○ *He has failed to fulfill his role as the mayor who could take charge. He is seen as a man who is out to lunch.*

★ **there's no such thing as a free lunch** used to express the idea that you cannot expect to get things for nothing, since most things that are worth having need to be paid for or worked for ○ *The government has spent 14 years telling the nation that there is no such thing as a free lunch and lecturing us on the virtues of sound economics.*

This expression dates back to at least 1840. It became popular again when the American economist Milton Friedman used it in the 1970s.

lurch

★ **leave someone in the lurch** to put someone in a difficult situation by suddenly going away or abandoning them, without giving them very much notice of your plans ○ *My secretary left me in the lurch on Friday and I haven't found a replacement yet.*

In the card game cribbage, a player is left in a position known as the lurch when an opponent has scored 51 points before the player has managed to either score 31 points or move their peg around the first corner of the board that is used to keep the score.

lying

★ **not take something lying down** to complain about or fight against a bad situation ○ *It is clear that he means to push everyone out who does not agree with him, and I for one am not going to take it lying down.*

Mm

mad

don't get mad, get even used to suggest that if someone harms you, you should not waste your energy on being angry, but should concentrate on harming them in return ○ *Use these bad feelings that you have. Don't get mad. Get even.*

≡ This expression is believed to have come from the strong-willed politician Joseph P. Kennedy, father of John F. Kennedy. A book by Alan Abel with this title, described as "a manual for retaliation," was published in 1983.

mad as a hatter very strange, foolish, or crazy ○ *Her sister's as mad as a hatter and if you ask me she's not much better herself.*

≡ In the 19th century, "hatters" or hat-makers used nitrate of mercury to treat fabrics such as felt. This substance is poisonous, and if the hat-makers breathed it in, they often suffered brain damage. As a result, hatters were traditionally thought of as mad.

mad as a hornet extremely angry ○ *Bob grinned. "I'll bet he's as mad as a hornet." "He did not sound at all pleased," Jerry admitted.*

≡ A hornet is a kind of wasp.

make

make something stick → see **stick**

makings

★ **have the makings of something** to have the potential to become a particular thing or develop in a particular way ○ *Even before that win, the team seemed to have the makings for something special this*

season. ○ *I believe La Russa sincerely feels McGwire has the makings of an outstanding coach.*

man

★ **the low man on the totem pole** → see **totem pole**

a man's home is his castle said to mean that people have the right to do what they want in their own home, and other people or the state have no right to interfere in people's private lives ○ *A man's home is his castle, and his recycling habits are his own concern.*

the man on the street an ordinary, average person ○ *The wealthy and powerful don't want the man on the street to know what they're up to.*

man or beast people or animals. This expression is often used to mean anyone at all. ○ *People used to say that this medicine could cure any illness of man or beast.*

★ **someone's right-hand man** someone's close assistant and the person they trust to help and support them in everything they do ○ *He was always by her side, and supported her in everything she did. He was her right-hand man, her business manager, and he traveled with her everywhere.*

≡ There are several possible explanations for this expression. One is that the right side of the body is traditionally associated with skill and strength. Another is that it may refer to the soldier who was responsible for the right side of a troop of horses. Also, in the past, the position on the right of the leader at political or social gatherings was the place of honor.

map

★ **put someone or something on the map** to cause someone or something to become well-known or important ○ *The film which really put Ellen Barkin on the map was The Big Easy.*

marbles

have all your marbles to be completely sane and rational ○ *The producer Mirian Adhtar has found four particularly fearless old ladies; and they have all their marbles.*

lose your marbles (*informal*) to become crazy or senile ○ *At 83 I have not lost my marbles and my memory is, thank God, as clear as it ever was.*

pick up your marbles and go home to leave a situation in which you are involved because you are dissatisfied with the way things are going. The use of this expression suggests that you are acting like a child. ○ *Many people regard a U.S. presence as a desirable counterweight. No one wants the U.S. to pick up its marbles and go home.*

≡ The reference here is to a player in a game of marbles who is annoyed about losing and therefore stops playing and takes the marbles away so that nobody else can play either.

march

★ **steal a march** to do something before someone else and so gain an advantage over them ○ *Investors from other countries will be annoyed that their Japanese competitors have once again stolen a march on them.*

≡ If an army steals a march on the enemy, it moves secretly and takes the enemy by surprise.

Marines

★ **tell that to the Marines** used when you want to emphasize that you don't believe what someone says or thinks ○ *If you think that a passport or a piece of paper says you have to the right to liberty and freedom, please be my guest and go over there and tell that to the marines.*

≡ The Marines are a branch of the armed forces that are considered to be very tough.

mark

★ **a black mark** an expression of disapproval for something that you have done ○ *The poor patient care was a permanent black mark on the doctor's record.*

≡ This expression may refer to a practice in schools in the past. If children misbehaved, the teacher put black marks against their names on a list.

first off the mark acting more quickly than anyone else ○ *The fine art season began yesterday, and Christie's were first off the mark with a collection of seven paintings by Paul Cèzanne.*

get off the mark
1 to start to do an activity quickly ○ *Don't waste time with small talk; get off the mark right away.*
2 to score or win for the first time in a sporting contest ○ *The goal was Atkinson's second of the season, having got off the mark against Chicago on Saturday.*

≡ The "mark" in this expression is the line which runners stand behind at the start of a race.

hit the mark to be very good, and to succeed in pleasing people ○ *As with the rest of the book, the idea is there, but as a whole it doesn't hit the mark.*

≡ The "mark" in this expression is the target used in archery or shooting.

★ **leave your mark** or **leave a mark**
1 to do something important that has a lasting effect ○ *He now has five more years*

in office and would still dearly like to leave his mark on the world.

2 to have an experience that has a lasting effect on you ○ *I lived abroad, in Asia, for four years, and this is an experience that tends to leave its mark.*

★ **make your mark** to do something that causes you to become noticed or famous ○ *The article looks at the new generation of Japanese directors making their mark in world cinema.*

off the mark incorrect or inaccurate ○ *Mussels are sometimes called "Poor Man's Oysters," but I think that name is way off the mark.*

on the mark correct or accurate ○ *Michael is right on the mark about movies being out of step with American culture.*

overshoot the mark to do something to a greater extent than is necessary or desirable ○ *I really overshot the mark, and I still feel embarrassed about it.*

≣ The "mark" in this expression is the
≣ target used in archery or shooting.

overstep the mark to behave in a way that is considered unacceptable ○ *Sometimes newspapers overstep the mark but overall they do more good than harm.*

≣ The "mark" in this expression may be
≣ the line behind which runners stand
≣ before the race. Alternatively, it may
≣ refer to boxing matches in the past,
≣ when a line was drawn in the ground
≣ which neither boxer could cross.

★ **quick off the mark** quick to understand or respond to something, or to take advantage of an opportunity. ○ *The Venezuelan delegation at the United Nations was quick off the mark to call urgent meetings of ambassadors belonging to the Rio Group.*

slow off the mark slow to act or to react to a situation or event ○ *International relief efforts on behalf of the refugees were slow off the mark.*

≣ The "mark" in this expression is the line
≣ which runners stand behind at the
≣ start of a race.

up to the mark of a satisfactory standard or quality ○ *They get rid of those whose work is not up to the mark.*

≣ The "mark" in this expression is a
≣ hallmark, which is an official symbol
≣ put on gold and silver items that reach
≣ a particular standard.

★ **wide of the mark** incorrect or inaccurate ○ *For once, it seems that their figures are not too wide of the mark.*

≣ The "mark" in this expression is the
≣ target used in archery or shooting.

market

★ **in the market for something** interested in buying or getting something ○ *If you're in the market for expensive skin care products, the following list includes some of the most well known.*

marrow

"Marrow" is the fatty substance inside the bones of a person or animal.

chilled to the marrow feeling very cold ○ *An icy wind murmured through the trees. Lenny was chilled to the marrow.*

to the marrow absolutely; completely ○ *I was thrilled to the marrow when the invitation arrived.*

masters

serve two masters to be loyal to two opposing principles, beliefs, or organizations ○ *But there is something more fundamentally wrong: Mr. Nicholas is expected to serve two masters: politics and the law.*

≣ This expression is used in the Bible
≣ (Matthew 6:24, Luke 16:13). In the
≣ Sermon on the Mount, Jesus says that
≣ no man can serve two masters,
≣ because he will hate one of them and
≣ love the other.

mat

go to the mat to fight very fiercely about something ○ *Librarians have gone to the mat for us and I'm determined to do my part to help them meet the demand for the books.*

≡ This expression refers to a wrestler who fights fiercely and is willing to risk a fall.

match

★ **meet your match** to find that you are competing or fighting with someone who is as good as you or is better than you ○ *When I got into the room with Wesley, it was almost like looking into a mirror for me. I had finally met my match in power and intellect.*

a shouting match an angry debate about something ○ *We didn't want to get into a horrible shouting match with the university.*

≡ This expression is commonly used to talk about an argument in which people shout at one another.

the whole shooting match the whole of something ○ *I filled in my donor card, ticking the whole shooting-match, from kidneys to liver.*

≡ This may be a reference to someone winning all the prizes in a shooting contest.

McCoy

the real McCoy something that is genuine, rather than a fake or a copy ○ *You can buy prosciutto anywhere, but if you want the real McCoy, you need to go to Parma.*

≡ It is possible that "McCoy" was originally "Mackay." There was a 19th century liquor manufacturer called Mackay who advertised his product as "the real Mackay" to distinguish it from other brands with similar names.

Alternatively, the expression may come from a dispute between two branches of the MacKay clan over which was older. Eventually the MacKays of Reay, or the "Reay MacKays," won the dispute.

meal

make a meal of something to spend more time or energy on something than is necessary ○ *Alexander has made such a meal out of a mildly mistaken newspaper report.*

a meal ticket a way of getting money on a regular basis and securing a good lifestyle ○ *A degree has never been a meal ticket, but the recession is making life for graduates tougher than ever.*

a square meal a large, filling, nutritious meal ○ *The troops are very tired. They haven't had a square meal for four or five days.*

≡ On sailing ships in the past, sailors ate off square wooden plates.

meaning

someone does not know the meaning of the word said when you want to emphasize that someone does not have a particular quality or never had a particular kind of experience ○ *She is an optimist; Ruthie doesn't even know the meaning of the word depression.*

means

by fair means or foul by any possible method, even if it is dishonest or unfair ○ *She never gave up trying to recover her property, by fair means or foul.*

measure

★ **for good measure** in addition to other things in order to make certain that something is successful or complete ○ *This is a fairly conventional love story, with a murder mystery thrown in for good measure.*

★ **have the measure of someone**
to understand someone or know what
they are like ○ *Lili was the only person I
knew who had the measure of her brother.*

meat

dead meat
1 *(informal)* a person who is in serious
trouble that may result in them being
injured or killed. This expression is often
used in threats. ○ *He's dead meat if he
comes back here.*
2 a person who is in serious trouble which
will have unpleasant consequences for
them, such as losing their job ○ *Anyone
who remembered her said she was dead meat.*

meat and drink to someone
something you find easy to cope with
and enjoy doing ○ *What normal people
considered pressure was meat and drink to
Robert Maxwell.*

meat and potatoes the most
important or basic aspects of something
○ *Before I get to the meat and potatoes of this
column, let me just start out by summarizing
some well-known facts.*

**one man's meat is another man's
poison** used to say that different people
like different things ○ *Art is everywhere.
Because it is a question of personal taste, the
cliché of one man's meat being another's
poison is in this case especially fitting.*

The Roman author Lucretius said in
"De Rerum Natura": "What is food to
one person may be bitter poison to
others."

medicine

**give someone a taste of their own
medicine** to do the same bad thing to
someone that they have done to you
○ *The cowardly thugs who mug old people
should be given a taste of their own medicine
with the return of corporal punishment.*

medium

a happy medium a way of doing
something that avoids extremes or is
acceptable to opposing sides ○ *We need to
find a happy medium between protecting the
environment and promoting tourism.*

men

dead men tell no tales used to
point out that someone who is dead
cannot reveal the truth about what
caused their death ○ *Hanley told police the
gun went off accidentally while Mr. Khan was
playing with it. "These statements were a
cover-up," Mr. Spencer told the jury. "Hanley
killed Mr. Khan. He knows that dead men tell
no tales."*

★ **the men in suits** the men who are in
control of an organization or company
and who have a lot of power ○ *A lot of
young people feel detached from older
politicians – the men in suits.*

separate the men from the boys to
show who is strong and capable and who
is not ○ *This is the game that will sort out
the men from the boys. It is absolutely vital to
win the replay and get to the final.*

messenger

shoot the messenger to unfairly
blame a person who has given you bad
news or information, when you should
instead be angry with the people who are
really responsible for the situation ○ *I
don't make the rules – don't shoot the
messenger!*

Mickey Finn

★ **slip someone a Mickey Finn**
(old-fashioned) to serve someone a drink
to which a drug has been secretly added
which makes them sleep ○ *In the story, he
saves the world by giving the alien a Mickey
Finn, so he oversleeps and misses a meeting
with his alien masters.*

Midas

★ **the Midas touch** the ability to make
money from or be successful in anything
that you do ○ *He had yet to discover the*

Midas touch that would bring his company to prominence.

Midas was a king of Greek mythology who loved gold. He was given the power to turn anything into gold by one of the gods.

middle

★ **in the middle of nowhere** a long way from any other place ○ *When I was 14, my family moved away from Phoenix to a farm in the middle of nowhere.*

★ **middle-of-the-road**
1 politically neither very left-wing nor very right-wing ○ *He is a moderate, middle-of-the-road person who understands both sides of the discussion.*
2 very ordinary, rather than unusual, exciting, or extreme ○ *These are, for the most part, ordinary middle-of-the-road people who want the usual things out of life.*

midnight

burn the midnight oil to stay awake very late at night in order to finish a piece of work ○ *Chris is burning the midnight oil trying to finish his article on the Bosnian situation.*

The image here is of someone working late into the night by the light of an oil lamp.

mile

go the extra mile to be willing to make a special effort to do or achieve something ○ *I discovered that going the extra mile has always been the hallmark of successful people.*

a mile a minute very fast ○ *Susan Berger was attractive, personable and could type a mile a minute.*

a mile away or
a mile off if you say that you can spot something or someone a mile off, you mean they are very obvious and easy to recognize ○ *You can spot undercover cops a mile away.*

run a mile to escape as quickly as possible ○ *He likes the ladies but he'd run a mile if one chased him.*

miles

miles away thinking deeply about something, and not paying attention to what is happening around you ○ *Her mother was pacing up and down and seemed miles away. She hadn't noticed them at all.*

milk

it's no use crying over spilled milk said in order to emphasize that it is pointless to worry or be upset about something that has happened and cannot be changed ○ *But a rueful Mr. Phelps reflected that, for him, "it didn't work, did it? But it's no use crying over spilled milk."*

milk and honey (literary) a situation in which you are very contented and have plenty of money ○ *The days of milk and honey are back – at least for CEOs of the major airlines.*

This expression is used in the Bible to describe the Promised Land of the Israelites. (Exodus 3:8)

milk someone for something to get something from someone by any method possible ○ *Mother and daughter conspired to milk him for everything they could get.*

mill

go through the mill to experience a very difficult situation ○ *"Oh I've been through the mill," said Shirley. "Single parent, no money, and a boyfriend who beat me up."*

The reference here is to grain passing through a mill and being made into flour.

★ **run-of-the-mill** ordinary and unexciting ○ *I was just a very average run-of-the-mill kind of student.*

This expression may be using the image of a watermill making the same movements continuously and regularly so long as the flow of water stays the same. Another suggestion is that it comes from the use of "run-of-the-mill" as a term for timber that has been sawn at a sawmill but has not yet been graded.

million

a chance in a million something that is very unlikely to happen ○ *It is amazing really. He had a chance in a million of surviving. We are so relieved he is all right.*

one in a million very special ○ *At 25, Bernstein was a star. One in a million.*

millstone

★ **a millstone around your neck** a very unpleasant problem or responsibility that you cannot escape from ○ *Long-term illness can make you feel like a millstone around your family's necks.*

A millstone is one of a pair of very heavy round flat stones that are used to grind grain.

mincemeat

make mincemeat of someone to defeat someone completely in a fight, argument, or competition ○ *I remember how Lillian made mincemeat of him at a dinner party without him even realizing.*

Mincemeat is meat or other food that has been cut into very small pieces or that has been forced through the small holes in a machine.

mind

★ **blow your mind** (*informal*) to be extremely exciting, surprising or interesting ○ *Stanford really blew his mind. He loved the feeling of the place, he loved the people.*

★ **cross your mind**
1 if a thought crosses your mind, you suddenly think of it ○ *The thought crossed my mind that she might be lying about her age.*

2 if something never crossed your mind, it never occurred to you or you did not consider that it could happen ○ *It evidently never crossed his mind to enter politics.*

give someone a piece of your mind
→ see **piece**

have a one-track mind to only ever think or talk about one subject ○ *He is the complete modern hitter: powerful, accurate, and with a one-track mind for hitting home runs.*

This probably refers to a single-track railroad, which will only allow trains to move in a single direction.

★ **in your mind's eye** in your imagination or memory ○ *I can often see you in my mind's eye, sitting in your house alone.*

★ **in your right mind** rational and behaving sensibly ○ *Those places are so dangerous that no one in their right mind would go there unless they had to.*

it boggles the mind
the mind boggles said when something is difficult to imagine or understand because it is so amazing, strange, or complicated ○ *It boggles the mind to think what they could eventually achieve.*

★ **keep something in mind** to be careful to remember something important ○ *Go where you like, but keep in mind that some places are more problematic than others for women traveling alone.*

a load off your mind something that you no longer need to worry about ○ *Armstrong heaved a sigh of relief, "That's a load off my mind."*

mind over matter used to describe situations in which someone seems able to control events or solve a physical problem by thinking in a focused way about it ○ *Good health is simply a case of mind over matter.*

mind your p's and q's → see **p**

★ **out of your mind**
1 crazy, foolish, or insane ○ *When her boss told her she would have to reduce her salary, she snapped, "Are you out of your mind?"*
2 extremely worried, jealous, or afraid ○ *I was out of my mind with fear, I didn't know what to do.*

★ **slip your mind** if something slips your mind, you forget it ○ *The reason for my visit had obviously slipped his mind.*

minds

★ **of two minds** hesitant and unable to reach a decision about something ○ *Roche was of two minds about whether to make the trip to Oslo.*

mint

★ **in mint condition** in very good condition; like new ○ *You are looking at a very rare Mercedes Benz SLR 722 in mint condition.*

▤ A mint is a place where money is manufactured and printed so money that comes from a mint is new.

miracles

A miracle is a wonderful event that you cannot explain, or that would not normally be considered possible.

work miracles to achieve very impressive results ○ *This beauty cream really works miracles and freshens up my face.*

misery

put someone out of their misery
1 to end a situation that is causing someone to suffer ○ *Almost 1,000 high school seniors awaiting their SAT scores were today put out of their misery.*
2 to deliberately kill a person who is suffering, for example, because they have an illness that cannot be cured ○ *There were at least a dozen pills in the bottle, surely enough to put her out of her misery.*
3 to kill an animal because it is very old or sick, or because it is badly injured ○ *I carry medicines to relieve sick and injured animals. Some are in such pain that I'm forced to put them out of their misery.*

miss

★ **a miss is as good as a mile** said to mean that almost succeeding is no better than failing badly ○ *Shiftless people generally excuse their laziness by saying, "I am only a little behind" but a little late is much too late, and a miss is as good as a mile.*

mojo

lose your mojo to stop being effective in what you do best, and so lose an advantage ○ *The Patriots have lost seven of their last eight games. What gives? Has Tom Brady lost his mojo?*

▤ The word "mojo" is from an African-American dialect and it refers to witchcraft or magic.

mold

The "mold" in these expressions is a container that is used to make something into a particular shape. Soft or liquid substances are put into the mold, and when they harden they form objects with the shape or pattern of the mold.

★ **break the mold** to completely change the way something has traditionally been done, and do it in a new way ○ *His stated ambition is to create a third party and break the mold of US two-party politics.*
they broke the mold when they made someone or something a particular person or thing is special or unique, and that there is nobody else or nothing else quite like them ○ *He is a most remarkable man. They broke the mold when they made him.*

Monday

a Monday-morning quarterback

a person who gives advice about how something should have been done, after it has already happened ○ *Some Monday-morning quarterbacks said the initial lower bid, without junk bonds, was a factor in his losing the company.*

> The quarterback is the football player who decides the plays and tells the team which moves to make. Many professional football games are played on Sunday, so a "Monday-morning quarterback" is someone, usually a man, who tells people what actions would have resulted in a victory.

money

even money having an equal chance that either of two things will happen ○ *With the next two games at home, Atlanta has to be considered at least even money in this series.*

have money to burn to have more money than you need ○ *With Record profits pouring in even during this recession, oil companies have money to burn.*

make money hand over fist to make a lot of money very quickly ○ *North Carolina National Bank is making money hand over fist in Texas.*

> This is derived from the image of a sailor moving his hands steadily one over the other while pulling in a rope or raising a sail.

money is the root of all evil used to express the idea that greed is the cause of a particular problem or the cause of society's problems in general ○ *I believe the amount involved in this project is a substantial sum, and money is the root of all evil, as they say.*

> This proverb comes from a letter in the Bible from St. Paul to his disciple Timothy. (1 Timothy 6:10)

★ **money talks** used to say that people with a lot of money have power and influence and they can get whatever they want ○ *As far as he is concerned, money talks and he can do what he likes.*

★ **put your money where your mouth is** to give practical support to causes or activities that you believe are right, especially by giving money ○ *If the governor is so keen on the school he should put his money where his mouth is and give us more resources.*

right on the money completely right ○ *His analysis was right on the money.*

> This expression was originally used to describe a bet that turned out to be exactly right.

the smart money if the smart money is on a particular result, then that result is expected by the people who know a lot about it ○ *The smart money is on him losing his seat to the Tea Party challenger.*

spend money like water to spend a lot of money unnecessarily ○ *She spends money like water to create a luxurious home far beyond her means.*

throw good money after bad to spend a lot of money in an attempt to get back money that you have already lost, for example, in a bad investment ○ *We are not offering any more cash; we don't want to throw good money after bad.*

★ **throw money at something** to try to solve or improve a problem by spending a lot of money on it, instead of thinking about it carefully or doing other things ○ *The government's answer to the problem has been to throw money at it.*

monkey

have a monkey on your back to have a serious problem that is making your life difficult or unpleasant ○ *The whole medical system that has become a monkey on the back of people without an adequate income.*

make a monkey out of someone to make someone seem ridiculous or stupid

○ *If it makes any difference, I'm not here to make monkeys out of the police, I'm a cop myself.*

monkey business dishonest or unacceptable behavior ○ *You try any monkey business and you're in trouble, right?*

monkey see, monkey do used to show disapproval of someone who is copying another person's behavior ○ *They saw other players fighting so they did the same. It's monkey see, monkey do.*

throw a monkey wrench in the works → see **wrench**

month

a month of Sundays

1 a very long time ○ *Torrential rain and jet-black skies can make each day seem like a month of Sundays.*

2 if something will not happen in a month of Sundays, it is very unlikely to happen ○ *"I think I know what you're about," he growled, "but it'll never work – not in a month of Sundays."*

monty

the full monty (mainly British) something that is as complete or extreme as possible ○ *Ron sang "My Way" right through, from the simple piano intro to the big orchestral finish, the full monty.*

moon

ask for the moon to ask for something that you cannot possibly have ○ *We're not asking for the moon, but we are asking for some help so that we can continue to progress.*

howl at the moon to waste your time and energy trying to do something which is impossible or trying to get something which you cannot have ○ *You need to adjust your expectations and stop howling at the moon.*

once in a blue moon very rarely ○ *I only get over to Cambridge once in a blue moon, even though I live in Boston.*

In some places, if there are two full moons in a calendar month, the second is called a "blue moon." This is rare.

★ **over the moon** very happy ○ *I'm over the moon about the way this album turned out.*

promise the moon to promise to give people things that you cannot in fact possibly give them ○ *So many banks try to lure customers by promising the moon.*

moth

like a moth to a flame in a way that shows that someone is strongly attracted to something ○ *The bright lights of New York drew Kharin like a moth to a flame.*

motions

★ **go through the motions** to do something that you have to do or are expected to do, but without any real effort or enthusiasm ○ *Many of the students who did attend classes with any regularity were just going through the motions.*

mountain

make a mountain out of a molehill to make a small, unimportant problem seem big and important ○ *It's unlikely that Smith will be punished; you are making a mountain out of a molehill.*

the mountain must come to Mohammed or **Mohammed must go to the mountain** used in a situation in which one person wants to see another, but neither person is immediately willing to go to the other ○ *The mountain must come to Mohammed; we'll send a man tomorrow.*

These expressions are based on a story about the prophet Mohammed, who was asked to show his power by making Mount Safa come to him.

mountains

move mountains to do something that seems impossible, particularly when love or a particular belief makes you feel determined to succeed ○ *We should all repeat five times a day, "It is possible to change!" With this belief, you can move mountains.*

> This expression comes from the proverb "Faith will move mountains," which is based on the words of Jesus to his followers in the Bible (Matthew 17:20). He tells them that if they believe in God, they can make great things happen.

mouth

down in the mouth unhappy or depressed ○ *As for George, I hear he's a bit down in the mouth.*

foam at the mouth

1 to be very angry ○ *Stewart was foaming at the mouth about an incident at the hospital the previous afternoon.*

2 to be very excited about something ○ *At that time the newspaper had foamed at the mouth in favor of agreement with Fascist countries.*

laugh out of the other side of your mouth said to warn someone that although they are happy or successful at the moment, things are likely to go wrong for them in the future ○ *You'll laugh out of the other side of your goddam mouth after this game.*

make your mouth water

1 to look or smell delicious to you ○ *She was bent down getting the casserole from the oven. The fragrant steam made his mouth water.*

2 *(journalism)* to be very attractive or appealing to you ○ *The zoo's site in Lincoln Park would make any developer's mouth water.*

shoot your mouth off

1 to talk loudly and boastfully about

yourself or your opinions ○ *He'd been shooting his mouth off saying he could sing, when of course, he couldn't.*

2 to talk publicly about something that is secret ○ *What if he decides to try for a little more money, or to shoot his mouth off around town?*

talk out of both sides of your mouth to give completely different advice or opinions about something in different situations ○ *One of Larry's problems is that he speaks out of both sides of his mouth. At Harvard he panders to the students with his radical ideas. But then, in the outer world, he has to pull back from these positions.*

move

get a move on to hurry ○ *You'd better get a move on if you're going to make it back in time for the match.*

movers

★ **the movers and shakers** *(journalism)* the people who take an active part in a particular event, organization or movement and who often bring in new developments ○ *She and her husband have become movers and shakers behind the scenes of the Tea Party.*

> This comes from the poem "Ode" by Arthur O'Shaugnessy (1874): "We are the music-makers And we are the dreamers of dreams… We are the movers and shakers Of the world for ever, it seems."

mud

be dragged through the mud to be accused of behaving in an immoral or unacceptable way ○ *People don't like to see an admired institution dragged through the mud like this.*

★ **throw mud**

★ **sling mud** to try to spoil a person's reputation by saying bad things about them or by telling lies ○ *The newspaper* *and magazine articles that followed were especially vicious, with supporters of both stars quick to throw mud.*

murder

★ **get away with murder** to be able to do whatever you like without anyone trying to control, punish, or criticize you ○ *His charm and the fact that he is so likeable often allows him to get away with murder.*

scream bloody murder to make a lot of noise or fuss about something ○ *People are screaming bloody murder about the amount of traffic going through their town.*

muscles

★ **flex your muscles** to behave in a way that is intended to show that you have power and that you are considering using it ○ *It's time to flex your muscles and show the world what you are capable of.*

music

★ **face the music** to accept responsibility for something that you have done wrong and to prepare yourself to be criticized or punished for it ○ *The authorities had found us out and we were about to face the music.*

> The "music" in this expression may refer to the orchestra at an opera or musical. The orchestra sits in front of the stage, so when a performer faces the audience, they also face the orchestra, or "music." Alternatively, the expression may come from an army practice in which a soldier who had been dismissed for dishonorable behavior was sent away with drums beating.

★ **music to your ears** a statement that makes you feel very happy when you hear it, for example, because you have been hoping or waiting to hear it for a long time ○ *The judge's words were music to the ears of the accused.*

mustard

not cut the mustard to not be as good as you should be ○ *You have to be on form every week and people soon start noticing if you're not cutting the mustard.*

> "Mustard" used to be slang for "the best" or "the genuine article."

muster

★ **pass muster** to be satisfactory for a particular purpose or job ○ *Only one country has yet to fulfill all the membership requirements, but it is expected to pass muster soon.*

> In the army and navy, a "muster" is an inspection of the soldiers' or sailors' uniforms and equipment.

mutton

mutton dressed as lamb (*mainly British*) a woman who dresses in a style that is considered suitable only for younger women ○ *This woman is older than me, heavier than me and is mutton dressed as lamb.*

> Mutton is the meat of an adult sheep, and lamb is the meat of a young sheep, as well as being the name of the animal itself.

Nn

nail

★ **another nail in the coffin of something**

★ **another nail in someone's coffin** the latest in a series of events that are seriously harming something or someone ○ *The vote is another nail in the coffin of the one-party system which the country has now largely renounced.*

hit the nail on the head or
hit it on the nail to describe a situation or problem exactly ○ *I agree with Dr. Carey, everything he says. I think he's hit the nail right on the head.* ○ *"It sounds as if he almost depended on you as much as you depended on him." "You just hit it on the nail."*

name

★ **make a name for yourself** to become famous or well-known as a result of doing a particular thing ○ *In a game dominated by boys, one player is making a name for herself.*

★ **the name of the game** the most important aspect of an activity or situation ○ *In the current economic climate, survival is the name of the game.*

not have a penny to your name or
not have a cent to your name to have very little money ○ *He didn't have a penny to his name.*

someone's name is mud used when someone has said or done something that has made them very unpopular with a particular group of people ○ *His name has been mud at the Telegraph since he left to work for a rival newspaper.*

This expression may refer to Dr. Samuel Mudd. John Wilkes Booth, the assassin of Abraham Lincoln, broke his leg while trying to escape and was treated by Dr. Mudd. Although Mudd did not know what his patient had done and acted in good faith, he was put in prison and he and his family were hated for many years.

take God's name in vain or
take the Lord's name in vain to use God's name disrespectfully, especially by swearing ○ *He persevered, and always gently corrected us when we took the Lord's name in vain.*

take someone's or something's name in vain to use another person's or a thing's name for your own purposes in an inappropriate or disrespectful way ○ *Let's remember that what we do from this point is being done in the name of justice. Let's not take her name in vain.*

This is from the second of the Ten Commandments in the Bible. It says that people should never use the name of God carelessly: "Thou shalt not take the name of the Lord thy God in vain." (Exodus 20:7)

names

★ **call someone names** to use insulting words or expressions to describe someone when you are talking to them or about them ○ *At my last school they called me names because I was so slow.*

name names to state publicly who is responsible for or involved in something ○ *A United Nations tribunal investigating the case is preparing to name names.*

napping

be caught napping to not be prepared for something that happens, and perhaps lose an advantage as a result ○ *European firms have been caught napping. As a result,* they now control barely one-tenth of the world market while Japanese firms control nearly half of it.

≡ "Napping" means the same as sleeping or dozing.

nature

the nature of the beast something that is an essential part of the character of the person or thing that you are talking about ○ *Baker likes to say that negotiations always get tougher toward the end. That's the nature of the beast.*

navel

navel-gazing thinking only about yourself and your own problems or activities, rather than concerning yourself with the problems or activities of other people ○ *I'm very good at motivating people to do things, so I'm a doer rather than a thinker. I've never really done much navel-gazing!*

≡ Your navel is your belly button.

near

so near and yet so far said to express regret or sadness when you have gotten very close to achieving what you wanted, but in the end you failed ○ *It was a crushing experience to have victory snatched away in such a desperate manner. It's heartbreaking to be so near and yet so far.*

neck

breathe down someone's neck
1 to be close behind someone in a race, contest, or other competitive situation ○ *No doubt Jones and Armstrong maintain a consistently high standard because both have talented rivals breathing down their necks.*
2 to closely watch and check everything that someone does ○ *Most farmers have loan officers breathing down their necks, so everything has to have an economic reason.*
dead from the neck up stupid ○ *If you want my opinion, your lawyer is dead from the neck up.*

★ **neck and neck** exactly level in a race or contest, so that it is impossible to say who will win ○ *The latest opinion polls show both parties running neck and neck.*

≡ Two horses are said to be neck and neck when they are exactly level and it is impossible to say which one is winning the race.

put your neck on the block → see **block**
put your neck on the line to do something although it is risky and you may lose your reputation or money as a result ○ *Gere put his neck on the line to make Sommersby. It was a gamble, both in terms of his public image and his wallet.*

risk your neck to do something dangerous that could result in your being killed or injured ○ *I won't have him risking his neck on that motorcycle.*

save someone's neck to rescue someone or yourself from harm, injury, or death ○ *They lied to the police to try to save his neck.*

someone could wring someone's neck or
someone would like to wring someone's neck used to say that a person is very angry with someone else ○ *That crazy Dot! He could wring her neck for this! She had no right to tell tales to his mother!*

≡ To wring something means to twist it and squeeze it.

★ **stick your neck out** (*informal*) to say or do something that other people are afraid to say or do, even though this may cause trouble or difficulty for you ○ *At the risk of sticking my neck out, I doubt whether the compensation fund will be needed.*

≡ This expression may come from boxing, where fighters need to keep their necks and chins drawn in or protected in order to avoid being hit by their opponent.

this neck of the woods (*informal*) the place where you are at the moment ○ *What's there to do in this neck of the woods?*

★ **up to your neck in something** (*informal*) very deeply involved in something bad such as debt or corruption ○ *The Prime Minister was up to his neck in scandal.*

your neck of the woods (*informal*) the area that you live in ○ *I discovered, however, that stone troughs were pretty scarce in my neck of the woods and expensive as well.*

> "Neck" in this expression comes from "naiack," which means "point" or "corner" in an Algonquian Native American language.

needle

like looking for a needle in a haystack extremely difficult or even impossible to find ○ *Police have told Mrs. Barrow that searching for the cat will be like looking for a needle in a haystack. The chances of recovering the animal are slim.*

nelly

> "Nelly" is sometimes spelled "nellie."

not on your nelly (*British, old-fashioned*) said in order to indicate that there is no chance at all of something happening. ○ *They finally become adults, thanks to all your hard work, and do they turn up for mom's birthday? Not on your nelly.*

> This expression may come from Cockney rhyming slang. "Not on your Nellie Duff" stands for "not on your puff," which also means "definitely not."

nerve

★ **touch a nerve** or
touch a raw nerve to upset someone by mentioning a subject that they feel strongly about or are very sensitive about

○ *Buchanan's speech touched a raw nerve here at the Capitol.*

nerves

★ **get on someone's nerves** to annoy or irritate someone ○ *The phone used to get on my nerves – people calling him at home as if it was an extension of the office.*

nerves of steel an ability to be very steady and strong in a difficult situation ○ *Driving a local train requires nerves of steel, given how overcrowded and chaotic they are.*

★ **a war of nerves** or
a battle of nerves a situation in which two opposing people or groups are trying to weaken each other psychologically, for example, by frightening each other, in order to get what they want without taking any direct action ○ *In the war of nerves between the two sides, it is becoming more and more difficult to separate their real intentions from their propaganda tactics.*

nest

feather your nest to take advantage of your position in order to get a lot of money, so that you can lead a comfortable life ○ *The politicians seem anxious to feather their nests at the expense of the people.*

> Some birds line their nests with soft feathers which they pluck from their own breasts or gather from the ground.

fly the nest or
leave the nest to leave your parents' home to live on your own ○ *When their children had flown the nest, he and his wife moved to a cabin in the woods.*

foul your own nest (*literary*) to do something that damages your own interests or chances of success ○ *Man has invented a hundred brilliant ways of fouling his own nest – the pollution, the heat, the poisons in the air, the metals in the water.*

★ **a nest egg** a sum of money that you are saving for a particular purpose ○ *All he* wanted was a few months decent money to help him retire. He thought this was his last chance to build a nest egg.

net

★ **cast a wide net** to involve a large number of things or people in what you are doing ○ *The U.S. has cast a wide diplomatic net, asking a variety of other nations to deliver the same message to Iran and to Syria.*

★ **slip through the net**

1 if people slip through the net, the system that is supposed to help or deal with them does not do it properly ○ *It's hard to knock the selection process because the chances of any young talent slipping through the net are so minimal.*

2 if someone who is behaving illegally slips through the net, they avoid being caught by the system or trap that is meant to catch them ○ *Government officials fear some of the criminals identified by police may have slipped through the net.*

new

something is the new something used to announnce that something has become the new fashion or has replaced something else. People are creative with this expression: "brown is the new black/ fish is the new meat, etc." ○ *Forty is the new thirty. Everyone knows that. This is boom time for Middle Youth.*

news

★ **be news to someone** if something someone says is news to you, you did not know about it previously and are surprised by it or think it may not be true ○ *When he was told about the story, the governor said it was news to him.*

★ **break the news** to make something known that was not known before ○ *I'm dreading having to break the news to her about Bob's death.*

no news is good news used to suggest that there is no need to worry, because people normally only send information when something bad has happened ○ *I had heard nothing all week. "Oh well," I thought. "No news is good news."*

niche

★ **carve a niche** or

carve out a niche to create a secure position for yourself, especially at work ○ *He has carved a niche for himself as an ABC television commentator and is certain to be kept on as long as the network continues to broadcast Saturday matches.*

A niche is a hollow area that is made in a wall to display something such as a statue or an ornament.

nick

★ **in the nick of time** at the last possible moment, when it is almost too late ○ *She woke up in the nick of time and raised the alarm.*

nickel

A nickel is a five cent coin and a dime is a ten cent coin.

nickel and dime

1 not very important or only functioning on a small scale ○ *A lot of American kids run similar nickel and dime ventures, selling sweet, cool drinks outside their parents' home in the long, hot summers.*

2 to weaken or exhaust someone or something, for example by continually taking small amounts of money away from them, or by continually making small changes or requests ○ *Oakland, like other cities, has been reeling from financial crisis and consequently has been nickel and diming essential services for years.*

a wooden nickel something completely false or worthless ○ *He looked at the card as though it were a wooden nickel. "That doesn't prove a thing," he said.*

night

a night owl someone who regularly stays up late at night, or prefers to work late at night ○ *The street noise and late-night parties make this hotel a haven for night owls.*

like night and day extremely different or opposite ○ *We're night and day from where we were at the time of the last audit.*

nines

dressed to the nines or **dressed up to the nines** wearing very fashionable or glamorous clothes ○ *Everyone is dressed up to the nines. Huge hats, frills, tight dresses, sequins and high heels.*

There have been many explanations offered for the origin of this expression. Most relate to the number nine in some way, but none has been generally accepted.

nip

nip and tuck used to describe a situation in which it is impossible to say who will win a competition or contest because both sides are performing equally well ○ *It was nip and tuck throughout as the players struck the ball with equal venom.*

One explanation for this expression is that it comes from sword-fighting, where a "nip" is a light touch and a "tuck" a heavier blow. Another is that it comes from horse racing, where it means the same as "neck and neck."

nits

pick nits to point out small problems or faults with something, often ones that seem relatively unimportant ○ *He then spent the second half of his interview picking nits, particularly about the environmental impact on "the beautiful" Bluebell Hill.*

Nits are the sticky eggs laid by the head louse, a small insect that lives and breeds in human hair.

nitty-gritty

the nitty-gritty the most important details or features of something ○ *With seven of the nine weeks of the regular football season behind us we are down to the nitty-gritty.*

nod

get the nod to receive permission from someone to start something, or be promised their support ○ *We'll hold off interviewing Hythe any further until we get the nod from you.*

★ **give someone the nod** to give someone permission to start something, or promise them your support ○ *Of the 15 members of the committee, all seven Republicans are prepared to give him the nod.*

a nod and a wink a situation in which someone communicates something to you by saying it indirectly or by giving you some kind of signal. This expression is usually used to show disapproval, often because something illegal or dishonest is taking place. ○ *A nod and a wink from the chairman is all it takes to move share prices up or down.*

a nod's as good as a wink used to suggest that it is not necessary to explain something further, because you understand what someone has already told you indirectly ○ *Professor Mason was a very shrewd and skilled operator, and if he wanted to get his own way, a nod was as good as a wink.*

This comes from the saying "a nod's as good as a wink to a blind horse," which suggests that both the nod and the wink are equally useless, as the horse would not be able to see either.

noises

★ **make noises** to talk about something in a vague or indirect way ○ *Your credit* card is over the limit and the loan officer is making noises about your overdraft.

make the right noises to say things that suggest that you will deal with a problem or issue in the way that someone wants you to ○ *The President was making all the right noises about multi-party democracy and human rights.*

nook

every nook and cranny all parts of a place or object ○ *I love how he knows every nook and cranny of Venice and can speak such good Italian.*

A nook is a corner or recess in a wall, and a cranny is a narrow opening or gap.

nooks

★ **the nooks and crannies** the smaller or less accessible parts of a place or object which are not normally noticed ○ *In the weeks before Christmas, we would scour the house, searching all the nooks and crannies trying to find our presents.*

nose

cut off your nose to spite your face to do something in order to hurt another person, without realizing or caring that you will hurt yourself just as much or even more ○ *The manager does not want to cut off his nose to spite his face by leaving him on the bench, but he does want the player to realize the error of his ways.*

In this expression, "to spite" means to deliberately annoy or upset.

follow your nose
1 to make decisions and behave in a particular way because you feel instinctively that this is what you should do, rather than because you are following any guidelines or rules ○ *I'd started a bit of journalism, so I had a source of income. And I've just followed my nose doing that ever since.*
2 to go straight ahead, or to follow the

most obvious route ○ *More or less follow your nose till you come to Baltimore Street. Turn right and it's there.*

give someone a bloody nose
1 to defeat someone in a contest or competition in a way that does not cause permanent damage but makes them look foolish or inferior ○ *Most are so fed up with this new tax that they are threatening to give the party more than a bloody nose in the forthcoming election.*
2 to damage the other side in a war or conflict enough to cause it to withdraw, at least for a time ○ *Giving the national army a bloody nose is one thing. Taking on its full might another.*

keep your nose clean to behave well and avoid trouble ○ *The best advice I can give is tell you to keep your nose clean.*

keep your nose out of something to not interfere in something, because it does not concern you ○ *Nancy realized that this was his way of telling her to keep her nose out of his business.*

keep your nose to the grindstone to concentrate on working hard at your job, and not concern yourself with other things ○ *There is more to life than keeping your nose to the grindstone and saving for a rainy day.*

A grindstone is a revolving stone disk which is used to sharpen metal tools. The reference here is to a person bending over the grindstone while they are working, so that their nose is close to it.

lead someone by the nose to control someone completely so that they do whatever you want ○ *The government has let itself be led by the nose by the timber industry into suppressing the report for the narrow commercial advantage of those involved.*

Bulls and other animals sometimes have rings through their noses so that a rope can be tied to the ring in order to lead them along. This expression is used in Shakespeare's play Othello, when Iago says Othello "will as tenderly be led by the nose as asses are." (Act I, Scene 3)

★ **look down your nose at someone or something** to regard a thing or person as inferior and treat them with scorn or disrespect ○ *The professor and his intellectual friends still look down their noses at Disneyworld and other popular tourist destinations.*

★ **a nose for something** a natural talent for finding something ○ *Harry runs his own news agency. He has a well-trained nose for a story.*

not see beyond your nose or **not see beyond the end of your nose** to think only about yourself and your immediate needs, rather than about other people or wider and longer-term issues ○ *Time to act your age. You're too busy thinking about you and about everything to do with you that you don't see beyond the end of your nose.*

on the nose exactly ○ *Starlin Castro came up in early May and batted .300 on the nose while anchoring the Cubs' middle infield.*

The origin of this expression is in broadcasting. When a show was running on time, the producer put a finger on his or her nose to signal this fact to the performers.

pay through the nose for something (*informal*) to pay more for something than you consider fair or reasonable ○ *It looks like those taking out new insurance policies on their houses, cars, boats and planes will be paying through the nose.*

stick your nose into something

★ **poke your nose into something** to interfere in something that does not concern you ○ *If anyone should be apologizing, it should be me for sticking my nose into other people's business.*

put someone's nose out of joint to offend or upset someone, because they think that they have not been treated with the respect that they deserve ○ *Gillian's sons were resentful of their new step-sisters. Barry had his nose put out of joint by Lucy's aloof sophistication, although she was his junior.*

★ **rub someone's nose in it** to embarrass or upset someone by reminding them of something that they do not want to think about, such as a failure or a mistake that they have made ○ *You obviously delight in the defeat of a fellow performer! And proceed to rub his nose in it, don't you?*

★ **thumb your nose at someone or something** to behave in a way that shows disrespect or contempt for someone or something ○ *There is a hard-core of young persistent offenders, and too many of them are simply laughing at authority and thumbing their noses at the court.*

To thumb your nose at someone literally means to make a rude gesture by placing the end of your thumb on the end of your nose, spreading out your fingers, and wiggling them.

★ **turn up your nose at something** to reject something because you think that it is not good enough for you ○ *Some top-flight university graduates turned up their noses at business jobs and tried instead to get into government service.*

★ **under your nose** if something, especially a bad thing, happens under your nose, it happens in your presence or very near to you, and you do not or cannot do anything to stop it ○ *Then suddenly I knew what had been going on here all along, right under our noses.*

nothings

whisper sweet nothings to speak to someone in a romantic or affectionate way ○ *Some women are turned on by romantic men who'll hold their hand in the street and whisper sweet nothings in their ears.*

notice

sit up and take notice to start paying attention to and dealing with a problem ○ *Who is going to sit up and take notice in Washington and shout enough is enough?*

nowhere

★ **from nowhere** or
out of nowhere suddenly or unexpectedly ○ *I remember looking both ways before crossing and seeing nothing. The car came from nowhere and hit me.*

nuclear

go nuclear to get extremely angry and start behaving in a forceful or irrational way as a result ○ *Since I dropped the pictures off, I've been wearing a crash helmet in case you go nuclear. On a scale of ten, how angry are you at me for them?*

number

any number of a large number of different people or things ○ *There could be any number of reasons why he hasn't written.*

do a number on someone (*informal*) to harm someone in some way, for example, by cheating them or by totally defeating them in a game or match ○ *The Irish team are looking to do a number on England in Dublin tomorrow.*

have someone's number to understand what kind of person someone is, so you know how to treat them or deal with them ○ *If they have your number from the start, and it is a small hotel, you are bound to get extra attention.*

look out for number one to selfishly put your own needs and interests before everyone else's ○ *My priority is to look after number one – to create a lifestyle I am happy with.*

someone's number is up used to predict that something unpleasant is going to happen to someone, and that there is nothing that they can do about it ○ *"Oh, Nancy, we're safe!" breathed Bess. "I thought for a while our number was up!"*

This is derived from army or navy life. A soldier or sailor who had been killed or who had died was said to have lost his mess number, or given up his allotted place in the dining hall.

numbers

★ **crunch numbers**
★ **crunch the numbers** to do calculations ○ *The Parks Commission will now crunch the numbers and review the community's opinions before making a final decision at its October meeting.*

★ **play the numbers game** to use amounts or figures to support an argument, often in a way that confuses or misleads people ○ *Since everyone plays the numbers game differently, there is hot debate about the real volume of sales.*

The "numbers game" or "numbers racket" is an illegal lottery. It involves people placing small bets on a series of numbers that appear in particular sections of that day's newspaper, for example, the stock market figures.

nut

a tough nut to crack a problem that is difficult to solve or a person who is difficult to deal with or to defeat in an argument or competition ○ *Despite not having won a title of note, Harrington has taken 17.5 points from a possible 20 in international singles, making him a tough nut to crack.*

nuts

★ **go nuts** to become extremely angry, excited, or mentally ill ○ *I wanted to protect Angelina but these guys went nuts and one punched me in the nose.*

★ **the nuts and bolts of something** the detailed facts and practical aspects of something, as opposed to abstract ideas about it ○ *Surely you have to work out the nuts and bolts of something before you can commit yourself to it?* ○ *I'm a nuts and bolts politician. I always have been.*

nutshell

★ **in a nutshell** used for summarizing something in a brief way ○ *She wants me to leave the company. I want to stay. That's it in a nutshell.*

nutty

nutty as a fruitcake (*informal*) very strange, foolish, or crazy ○ *Despite his maddening fidgeting, the man is a charmer – intense, funny, and nutty as a fruitcake.*

> "Nutty" or "nuts" is an informal word for mad. Nutty can also mean containing a lot of nuts in the way that a fruitcake often does.

Oo

oaks

great oaks from little acorns grow
or
mighty oaks from little acorns grow used to express the idea that something large and successful can begin in a small and insignificant way ○ *Henry Ford did not start his operations by opening hundreds of factories in his first year. Remember, mighty oaks from tiny acorns grow.*

Acorns are the nuts that grow on oak trees.

oats

feel your oats to be full of energy and excitement ○ *Chad is a young up-and-coming player who's starting to feel his oats.*
sow your wild oats or
sow some wild oats to have fun when you are young, before you are married ○ *Randy, I do love you, but sometimes a girl needs to sow some wild oats.*

odds

★ **against all odds** in an extremely bad situation, with very little chance of success ○ *They struggled against all odds to regain apartments and homes occupied by other people during the war.*
★ **at odds with something** not matching or corresponding to another thing ○ *His outlook on life was pessimistic, quite at odds with his wife's out-going personality.*
★ **be at odds with someone** to disagree with someone about something ○ *The region has reportedly been at odds with the central government both militarily and politically.*
by all odds according to most calculations or opinions ○ *By all odds, the horse should have brought $10,000 at the sale.*

off-chance

★ **on the off-chance** in the hope that something good will happen, although that is unlikely ○ *One American visitor had turned up on the off-chance of catching a glimpse of the princess.*

oil

like oil and water two people who are like oil and water are very different from each other ○ *He and the General did not get along. The two were like oil and water together.*
no oil painting unattractive or ugly ○ *I started seeing a guy who was no oil painting but wonderfully bright and interesting.*
pour oil on troubled waters to do or say something to make an angry or tense situation calmer or more peaceful ○ *He is an extremely experienced politician, who some diplomats believe may be able to pour oil on the troubled waters.*

Pouring oil on rough water can calm it. The Greek author Plutarch mentioned it in about 95 AD: "Why does pouring oil on the sea make it still and calm?"

strike oil to suddenly become successful in finding or doing something ○ *A new generation of high-tech billionaires struck oil in the information industries - computers, microchips and software.*

This expression is more commonly used literally to say that someone discovers oil in the ground as a result of drilling.

old

old as the hills very old, and perhaps old-fashioned or very traditional ○ *Their equipment may be modern, but the techniques remain as old as the hills.*

olive

★ **an olive branch** something that indicates that you want to end a disagreement ○ *"We are holding out an olive branch, inviting the landowners to talk. We are trying to break the deadlock."*

> The story of the Flood in the Bible (Genesis 8:11) tells how Noah sent out a dove to see if there was any sign of land. If the dove found some land, it would mean that God had forgiven man. When the dove returned, it had a fresh olive leaf in its beak, so Noah knew that the floodwaters had almost gone.

omelet

you can't make an omelet without breaking eggs it is impossible to achieve something without there being bad or unpleasant side-effects ○ *You can't make an omelet without breaking eggs – you just have to break as few as possible. Even so, it seems wrong to put a major road through such beautiful countryside.*

once-over

give someone the once-over to look at someone or analyze them quickly to get a general impression of their appearance or character ○ *Penny gives me the once-over. I'm wearing a bright jacket that'll go down well with European viewers, she says.*

one

be one up on someone to have an advantage over someone because you have done something that they have not done or because you know something that they do not know ○ *"Just because you met somebody doesn't mean you know anything about them." "No, but you're one up on the person who hasn't met them."*

one and the same the same ○ *Police strongly believe the man the girl described and Billy Balidbid are one and the same.*

put one over on someone to gain a victory or advantage over someone ○ *Clark insisted: "It's nice to put one over on your old boss but I don't hold any grudges."*

open

be wide open if a contest or competition is wide open, it is very difficult to say who will win because the competitors are all equally good ○ *The Democrats breathed a sigh of relief last night as two polls showed the election race was still wide open.*

blow something wide open
1 to change something completely by doing things in a totally different way ○ *Pamela has blown the old news anchor image wide open.*
2 to reveal something secret that other people have been trying to hide ○ *Has it occurred to you that he can blow the operation wide open?*

leave yourself wide open or **lay yourself wide open** if you leave yourself wide open to criticism or ridicule, you make it very easy for other people to criticize or ridicule you, because you behave in a naive or foolish way ○ *The statement leaves us wide open to attack.*

open-and-shut easily decided or solved because the facts are very clear ○ *The prosecution behaved as if they had an open-and-shut case.*

> In this expression, the word "and" means "and then," suggesting that the case being dealt with has been opened and then closed again almost immediately because it was easy to solve or deal with.

operator

a smooth operator someone who is good at getting what they want and persuading people to do things ○ *How do you turn a sheltered, antisocial computer geek into a smooth operator?*

order

the order of the day what usually happens in a particular situation ○ *He goes to a game preserve in Botswana, where the order of the day will be rhinos, hippos and elephants.*

★ **a tall order** a task that will be very difficult ○ *I've got to beat him by four shots tomorrow, and that's a very tall order.*

⋮ An old meaning of "tall" is large or
⋮ excessive.

orders

★ **marching orders** the instructions that you are given in order to carry out a plan or achieve an aim ○ *As one mid-level White House official put it, "We're still waiting for our marching orders."*

⋮ This expression relates to the army.
⋮ When soldiers are given marching
⋮ orders, they are ordered to march
⋮ to a particular place.

out

go all out → see **go**

★ **out-and-out** very clearly and definitely the kind of person or thing mentioned ○ *This was almost certainly an out-and-out lie.*

overdrive

★ **go into overdrive** to begin to work very hard or to perform intensely or very well ○ *When the bodies were discovered, the media went into overdrive.*

⋮ Overdrive is an extra gear on some
⋮ vehicles, which enables them to go
⋮ faster than they can with ordinary
⋮ gears.

overtime

work overtime to work very hard in order to achieve something ○ *This might explain why people sleep longer when the immune mechanisms are working overtime to fight off infections.*

⋮ This expression is more commonly
⋮ used to say that someone is spending
⋮ extra time doing the job that they are
⋮ employed to do.

own

★ **call your own** used to name a thing that you have or would like to have; often used in a negative sentence ○ *Steven never had a dog he could call his own till he bought Puffball.* ○ *Tricia is a 12-year-old girl looking for a family to call her own.*

come into your own to start to get recognition for being good at something ○ *Mendenhall came into his own after starting up his own business.*

★ **hold your own** to be able to defend your position against someone who is attacking you or threatening you ○ *Some areas of heavy industry, such as shipbuilding, were able to hold their own in international markets.*

Pp

p

mind your p's and q's to try to speak and behave politely or to act in an acceptable way, so that you do not offend people ○ *She always put on her best act and minded her p's and q's in front of the queen, but their relationship wasn't that close.*

≣ This expression may originally have been a warning to children not to confuse p's and q's when learning the alphabet. Alternatively, "p's and q's" may stand for "pleases and thank yous," or expressions of politeness.

pace

★ **set the pace** to do something that is regarded as a good example, so that other people then do the same thing ○ *The consensus is that Versace has got it right this season and has set the pace for mainstream fashion.*

≣ This is derived from the fact that a fast runner determines the speed at which all the other competitors in a race have to run.

someone can't stand the pace or **someone can't take the pace** used to indicate that someone does not work or function effectively when they are under pressure, and so they cannot compete or do things as well as other people ○ *They were constantly testing me, as if to prove I couldn't take the pace.*

paces

★ **put someone through their paces** to get someone to show you how well they can do something ○ *The eleven boxers on the team are in the hands of coach Ian Irwin, who is putting them through their paces.*

≣ To put a horse through its paces means to test it to see how well it has been trained.

pack

ahead of the pack more successful than your competitors or rivals ○ *This new management system has kept the company far ahead of the pack in terms of product development.*

≣ A pack here is a group of animals such as hounds or wolves.

page

on the same page in agreement about what you are trying to achieve ○ *We're all on the same page in our careers, we all have the same professional needs.*

turn the page to make a new start after a period of difficulties ○ *Shareholders at Fiat's annual meeting will be looking for signs that the troubled company really does mean to turn the page.*

paid

★ **put paid to something** (mainly British) to completely end or destroy someone's hopes, chances, or plans ○ *Great Britain gave a limp performance here last night that put paid to their chances of reaching the Olympic finals.*

pain

★ **no pain, no gain** used for saying that anything that gives you an advantage will also involve difficulty or suffering ○ *There are lots of activities we enjoy, such as marathon running, where "no pain, no gain" applies.*

★ **a pain in the neck** (informal) someone or something that is very annoying ○ He was a pain in the neck. I was glad when he left my department.

pains

growing pains temporary difficulties and problems in an organization or a relationship as it develops and grows stronger ○ The country is now facing some troublesome growing pains. The economy is still expanding, but at a slower rate than in the recent past.

Growing pains are pains that children sometimes get in their muscles and joints. Many people wrongly think that they are caused by the children growing too fast.

paint

something is like watching paint dry a way of saying that something is extremely boring ○ "We've done one shot since nine this morning," complains Donna, a student who has taken the day off to be an extra. "It's like watching paint dry."

pale

★ **beyond the pale** completely unacceptable ○ There will be no more compromises with people whose views are beyond the pale.

"Pale" comes from the Latin palum, meaning "stake," and in English it came to refer to a territorial boundary marked by a line of stakes. The area inside was regarded as civilized, but the area beyond the pale was seen as barbaric.

palm

grease someone's palm to give money to an official in order to gain an unfair advantage over other people or in order to get something that you want ○ Files do not move in government offices unless you grease the palms of officials.

The idea behind this expression is that grease and oil help machines work smoothly. In the same way, bribing people will make it easier to get what you want.

pan

a flash in the pan → see **flash**

Pandora

★ **open a Pandora's box** to do something that unintentionally causes a lot of problems, which you did not know existed before ○ This latest controversy has opened a Pandora's box of intrigue among the coalition government's different factions.

According to Roman mythology, Prometheus offended the gods and in revenge Jupiter ordered the creation of Pandora, the first woman. Jupiter gave Pandora a box which she was to offer to the man she married. Pandora married Prometheus's brother Epimethius. He opened the box and all the problems and wickedness that now trouble the world flew out and could never be put back.

panties

get your panties in a twist or **get your panties in a bunch** to become extremely upset or worried about something. In Britain the equivalent expression **get your knickers in a twist** is used. ○ Let's not get our panties in a twist until we see the outcome of those games.

pants

beat the pants off someone (informal) to defeat someone completely in a contest or competition ○ Devlin indicated the chess table beside the sofa. "Any excuse to get away from that. He was beating the pants off me."

bore the pants off someone or **scare the pants off someone** or

charm the pants off someone
(*informal*) to bore, scare, or charm someone a lot ○ *When I was a kid, circuses bored the pants off me, but I'd always wanted to be a performer.*

someone is caught with their pants down used when someone is not prepared for what happens and this reveals an embarrassing or shocking fact about them ○ *In 1991, the Department of Transportation was caught with its pants down and took seven months to produce the document needed to change legislation.*

wear the pants to be the person in a couple who makes all the important decisions ○ *She may give the impression that she wears the pants but it's Tim who makes the final decisions.*

paper

not worth the paper it's written on if a promise, agreement, or guarantee is not worth the paper it's written on, it is in fact worthless, although it appears to be official or definite ○ *If consumers do not know they can get compensation when a service breaks down, these service standards will not be worth the paper they are written on.*

a paper tiger a person, country, or organization that seems to be powerful, but does not really have any power ○ *Unless the assembly has the power to fire the mayor, it will prove to be nothing but a paper tiger.*

a paper trail written evidence of someone's activities ○ *The criminal proceedings were raised after investigations found a paper trail of checks that were written on dummy bank accounts.*

★ **something looks good on paper** used when something seems to be a good idea, plan, or argument at the time you read about it, but may not be good in reality ○ *This system looks good on paper but it is expensive and, in my view, still of very limited value.*

papers

get your walking papers or
be given your walking papers to be made to leave something such as a job or a relationship ○ *It was Vogel's turn to get his walking papers from the board of directors.*

> This is derived from the instructions given to infantry soldiers about the length and destination of a march.

par

> In golf, "par" is the number of strokes a good golfer is expected to take for a particular hole or for the whole course.

★ **below par** or
under par
1 below the standard expected ○ *The recession has left sales a little below par in the past two or three years.*
2 tired or ill and unable to perform or work as well as usual ○ *Women who feel below par are unlikely to perform at their best.*

★ **par for the course** normal and to be expected ○ *He said long hours are par for the course. "I'm up every morning at six, or even earlier."*

parade

rain on someone's parade
(*journalism*) to do something that spoils someone's plan, usually a plan that is very important to them ○ *It's irritating that he could rain on my parade by stealing the record before me.*

parker

> "Nosy" is sometimes spelled "nosey."

a nosy parker someone who is interested in things that have nothing to do with them ○ *The towon's resident nosy parker, Olive, likes to spy on her neighbors with binoculars.*

part

★ **do your part** to do what is required of you to make something succeed ○ *Jessica Baker did her part, scoring a goal to keep the score 1-0 going into halftime.*

★ **look the part** to dress or behave in the way that is characteristic of a particular kind of person ○ *You look the part of an English gentleman, so he is half ready to believe you as soon as you meet.*

> This is probably derived from the idea of an actor wearing a costume that suited the role or part that they were playing.

★ **part and parcel** involved or included in something and unable to be separated from it ○ *There comes a time during every player's season when his his game isn't at its peak and he just doesn't make the shots. It's part and parcel of being a professional.*

take someone's part (old-fashioned) to support or defend someone, especially in a dispute with other people ○ *It seemed to me that she should have taken my part, should somehow have defended me from my father.*

partner

a partner in crime someone who cooperates with another person to achieve something ○ *Evgeni Malkin, Crosby's offensive partner in crime, led the league in scoring with 113 points.*

a sparring partner someone with whom you enjoy arguing or debating ○ *They gave the podium to Tony Snow, considered a skillful sparring partner for reporters.*

> The literal meaning of "sparring partner" is a person with whom you practice in the sport of boxing.

party

bring something to the party to make a contribution to a particular activity or situation ○ *Johnson asked,* "What do they bring to the party?" "They bring a lot to the party," Cohen replied, "principally $3 billion in capital."

the party is over said to mean that the most enjoyable or profitable part of an activity has ended ○ *The party is over for Palmer's fans as he announced his retirement last night.*

past

be past it or

be getting past it to no longer be as good as in the past ○ *My husband Eric could do with another second-hand car. The one we've got at the moment is getting a bit past it.*

I wouldn't put it past someone said to express that you would not be surprised if someone did something bad ○ *I wouldn't put it past him to double-cross Schrader, especially after the rumor I heard the other day.*

pasture

put someone out to pasture to make someone retire from their job, or move them to an unimportant job, usually because people think that they are too old to be useful ○ *I'm retiring next month. They're putting me out to pasture.*

> When horses have reached the end of their working lives, they are sometimes released into pastures (that is, fields of grass) to graze.

pastures

greener pastures a new and better situation ○ *There are drawbacks for teachers seeking greener pastures overseas, and many are disuaded by the lengthy process involved in going to work outside the US.*

★ **pastures new** (mainly British) a new situation ○ *If the job doesn't meet my ambitions I'll be off to pastures new. I want to go to the top.*

> This is a quotation from "Lycidas" (1638) by the English poet Milton: "At last he rose, and twitch'd his Mantle blew:

Tomorrow to fresh Woods, and Pastures new." This is sometimes wrongly quoted as "fresh fields and pastures new."

pat

★ **a pat on the back** congratulations or appreciation for something someone has done ○ *Any mail order company that gives such rapid response to a customer's complaint deserves a pat on the back.*

stand pat to not change something or refuse to change your mind about something ○ *There are certain issues on which the US would stand pat and insist on unanimity.*

> In the game of poker, if a player stands pat, they are satisfied with the hand dealt to them and do not exchange any of their cards.

patch

★ **go through a rough patch**

★ **hit a rough patch** to experience or start to experience problems ○ *You can't just abandon what you worked on all during the offseason because you hit a rough patch.*

> This expression may come from sailing, in which an area of sea with high waves is called a "rough patch."

path

beat a path to someone's door to be eager to talk to someone or to do business with them ○ *Fashion editors now beat a path to Mugler's door and thousands of followers flock to get into one of his events.*

> This expression has been attributed to the American writer Ralph Waldo Emerson (1803-82), who used similar words in a lecture: "If a man write a better book, preach a better sermon, or make a better mousetrap than his neighbor, 'tho he build his house in the woods, the world will make a beaten path to his door."

★ **cross someone's path** to meet someone by chance ○ *The book is full of cutting criticisms of the celebrities who crossed her path.*

path-breaking (*journalism*) completely different and new and affecting the way in which things are done or considered in the future ○ *Russia's Parliament today approved a path-breaking measure that gives individual farmers a right to buy and sell their own land.*

pay dirt

"Pay dirt" is often written as "paydirt."

hit pay dirt or
strike pay dirt to find or achieve something important and valuable ○ *"Let's not give up on the courts," Millard says. "We still might hit pay dirt with one of the issues."*

> This expression refers to earth that contains enough valuable minerals to make it financially worthwhile to mine it.

peanuts

if you pay peanuts, you get monkeys used to emphasize that if an employer pays very low wages, they cannot expect to find good workers ○ *The new pay policy will definitely have an effect on quality. The truth of the matter is that if they pay peanuts, they will get monkeys.*

pearls

cast pearls before swine (*literary*) to waste your time by offering something that is helpful or valuable to someone who does not appreciate or understand it ○ *I have wonderful costumes, with feathers and top hats, but it's like casting pearls before swine, they don't care what you wear.*

> This expression comes from the Bible, from the Sermon on the Mount

(Matthew 7:6), when Jesus is giving his followers advice on how they should live. He tells them not to waste things that are holy on the unholy, and not to throw precious things (such as pearls) to the pigs.

pearls of wisdom something that sounds very wise or helpful. People usually use this expression ironically, to suggest that in fact they think the person is saying something very obvious or boring. ○ *I'm sure we're all very grateful for the pearls of wisdom that fall from Mr. Greenberg's lips.*

peas

like two peas in a pod very similar in appearance or character ○ *She is convinced the men are brothers. She said: "It was uncanny. They were like two peas in a pod."*

pecking

★ **the pecking order** the order of importance of the people or things within a group ○ *Offices came in 29 sizes, which varied in accordance with the occupant's place in the corporate pecking order.*

When groups of hens are kept together, a "pecking order" often forms. This means that a stronger bird can peck a weaker bird without being pecked in return.

pedal

★ **put the pedal to the metal** to start making the greatest amount of effort to achieve something ○ *I've got to put the pedal to the metal and achieve as much as I can in 2011, because that's going to be my last year of boxing.*

This expression refers to the accelerator pedal in a car. When you "put the pedal to the metal," you push the pedal all the way down to make the engine go as fast as possible.

pedestal

A pedestal is a base on which something such as a statue stands.

knock someone off their pedestal to show that someone is not as good or talented as people generally think ○ *The tabloids had been trying for several years to knock Jackson off his pedestal.*

★ **put someone on a pedestal** to think someone is extremely good, talented or perfect ○ *I put my own parents on a pedestal. I felt they could do no wrong.*

peg

a peg on which to hang something a way of introducing or drawing attention to your ideas or opinions ○ *He rarely discusses the book, using it as a peg on which to hang his opinions – and not necessarily those related to the book.*

a square peg in a round hole someone who is in a situation or is doing a task that does not suit them at all ○ *Taylor is clearly the wrong man for the job – a square peg in a round hole.*

take someone down a peg or two or **bring someone down a peg or two** to make someone who is behaving in an arrogant and unpleasant way realize that they are not as important or talented as they think ○ *I think he needed to be taken down a peg or two.*

This expression may refer to the tuning of musical instruments such as guitars or violins, where pegs are used to keep the strings tight. Alternatively, it may refer to the game of cribbage, where pegs are used to keep the score.

pegged

have someone pegged to understand completely the way someone is or who they are ○ *Those who have her pegged as fragile singer-songwriter should hear her touring band at full blast playing the Na Na Song.*

pencil

a pencil pusher someone who works in an office in contrast to more active kinds of work ○ *Many of the men who now sit on company boards are pencil pushers with PhDs and MBAs from top schools, but lack operating experience in business.*

pennies

not have two pennies to rub together to have very little money ○ *And from all those interviews her family gave to the Press they sounded as if they didn't have two pennies to rub together.*

pinch pennies to try to spend as little money as possible ○ *States and the federal government are pinching pennies everywhere they can and often cutting arts programs first.*

penny

in for a penny, in for a pound said to express the idea that when you are firmly committed to a particular course of action, you must be prepared to spend whatever it will cost. Americans use this expression and also the equivalent, **in for a dime, in for a dollar**. ○ *In for a penny, in for a pound. I took the jacket to the counter.*

not have a penny to your name → see **name**

★ **a penny for your thoughts** said when you want the opinion of a person who is not saying anything ○ *Anna was gazing out the window when I walked in. "A penny for your thoughts," I said.*

> This expression suggests that you would actually pay someone a penny to hear their opinion, but it is used as a polite way to get someone to speak.

penny-wise and pound-foolish careful in small matters but careless in more important ones ○ *If we had auditors to go out and check on this, we would have saved billions of dollars. In other words, we have been penny-wise and pound-foolish here.*

a pretty penny a large amount of money ○ *As you might imagine, a grand piano costs a pretty penny.*

turn up like a bad penny (old-fashioned) to appear again in a place where you are not welcome or wanted ○ *Her husband was able to trace her, to turn up again on her doorstep like the proverbial bad penny.*

two a penny or
ten a penny (mainly British) used for describing things or people that are not especially valuable or interesting because there are a lot of them. An equivalent expression is **a dime a dozen**. ○ *Gloomy economic forecasts are ten-a-penny in Europe.*

perch

> A perch is a pole, branch or other place where a bird sits to rest.

knock someone off their perch to cause someone to fail, or damage their status or position ○ *The Cardinals were knocked off their perch at home last Saturday by McDaniel College (3-0), 24-14.*

petard

hoist by your own petard (formal) if someone is hoist by their own petard, their plan to benefit themselves or to harm someone else results instead in benefit to the other person or harm to themselves ○ *His plans backfired terribly and in the end he was hoist by his own petard.*

> "Petards" were metal balls filled with gunpowder that were used to blow up walls or gates. The gunpowder was lit by a slow-burning fuse, but there was always a danger that the device would explode too soon and "hoist" the person lighting it, that is, blow them up in the air.

Peter

rob Peter to pay Paul to use money

meant for paying off one debt to pay off a different debt and so still be in debt ○ *He got behind on his mortgage and he borrowed from loan companies. He started robbing Peter to pay Paul.*

phrase

to coin a phrase said when you are making a pun or using a cliché or colloquial expression, in order to show that you realize people might think that it is a silly or boring thing to say, but you think it is relevant in spite of this ○ *Stunned Jackson was, to coin a phrase, "sick as a dog."*

> To coin a new word means to invent it or use it for the first time. In this expression, the term is being used ironically.

picnic

be no picnic be difficult or unpleasant ○ *"Poor little mites," she said of the evacuees. "It's no picnic for them being taken away from their homes."*

picture

★ **get the picture** to understand what another person is trying to explain or describe to you ○ *They smoke, they play pool, they gamble. You get the picture, I'm sure.*

in the picture
1 involved in the situation you are talking about ○ *I was completely in the picture from the beginning.*
2 very likely to get something such as a promotion or success ○ *He told me that Annabella was back in the picture. She was the best one they could find.*

keep someone in the picture
to tell someone about any changes or developments in a situation ○ *He's changed so many things – too many to mention. But he's always kept me in the picture.*

out of the picture
1 no longer involved in the situation you

are talking about ○ *Once Derek was out of the picture, however, Malcolm's visits to the Swires became more frequent.*
2 not one of the people who is being considered for a promotion or place on a team ○ *But they said I'm their fifth choice for quarterback, so I'm totally out of the picture.*

★ **put someone in the picture** to tell someone about a situation that they need to know about ○ *I believe that I could now produce evidence to prove my case, if you are prepared to listen. I brought you here for that reason, to put you in the picture.*

pie

eat humble pie to admit that you have been wrong and apologize, especially in situations where this is humiliating or embarrassing for you ○ *The columnist was forced to eat humble pie and publicly apologize to the Congresspeople involved when the conversation was put in context.*

> "Umbles" is an old word for the guts and offal of deer. When nobles had venison or deer to eat, the "umbles" were made into a pie for their servants. As "umbles" pie was eaten by "humble" people, the two words gradually became confused. "Humble pie" came to be used to refer to something humiliating or unpleasant.

★ **pie in the sky** very unlikely to happen ○ *Ideally what I would like to see would be free childcare, but I think that's pie in the sky at the moment.* ○ *Changes are a real possibility. This is not pie-in-the-sky stuff.*

> This expression comes from the song "The Preacher and the Slave" (1911) by Joe Hill, an American songwriter and workers' organizer: "You'll get pie in the sky when you die. (That's a lie.)"

piece

all of a piece with each part or aspect consistent with the rest ○ *Thus the* *biosphere is all of a piece, an immense, integrated, living system.*

give someone a piece of your mind (old-fashioned) to tell someone that you are angry at them and explain why ○ *Carla was ready to go back in the kitchen and give the chef a piece of her mind but I got her out of there.*

★ **a piece of cake** something that is very easy to do ○ *"It's not exactly a stressful job is it?" "If it's quiet, it's a piece of cake. It's just a bit boring."*

a piece of the action → see **action**

★ **a piece of work** a person who is very exceptional, usually in a shocking or annoying way ○ *Wow, what a piece of work this guy is. He seems to think he can change the facts to suit himself.*

say your piece to give your opinion about a particular matter, although you are aware that other people may not agree with you, or be interested in what you have to say ○ *Each preacher stood for two minutes on a box, said his piece, and stepped down.*

pieces

★ **go to pieces**
1 to be so upset or distressed by something that you cannot control your emotions or cope with the things that you have to do ○ *Every time he's faced with a problem he goes to pieces.*
2 if your work or a relationship goes to pieces, it is no longer as good as it once was and you cannot stop it getting worse ○ *My work is all going to pieces.*

★ **pick up the pieces** to do what you can to get a situation back to normal again after something bad has happened ○ *People in the high desert communities near Palm Springs, California, are picking up the pieces after last night's earthquake.*

shot to pieces completely ruined ○ *When I came here my confidence was shot to pieces.*

pig

buy a pig in a poke to buy or accept something when you have not seen it, or do not know enough about it ○ *We think a lot of people bought a pig in a poke when they voted for the guy and ignored some of the things about his past.*

≡ "Poke" is an old Scots word that means "sack." The idea here is of someone buying a sack that they have been told contains a pig — but they have not seen inside the sack.

eat like a pig to eat a lot of food, usually in a greedy or disgusting manner ○ *She could hear the part of herself that was self-critical say, "You eat like a pig. I can't stand looking at you. You're fat."*

like a greased pig so fast that no one can catch you or stop you ○ *He ran down the road like a greased pig.*

make a pig of yourself (informal) to eat a very large amount at one meal ○ *I'm afraid I made a pig of myself at dinner.*

squeal like a stuck pig to scream very loudly, as though you are in a lot of pain ○ *Alan tried to calm him while Miller continued to scream like a stuck pig.*

sweat like a pig (informal) to be very hot and to sweat a lot ○ *The two officers standing just out of camera shot were sweating like pigs in the studio lights.*

pigs

when pigs fly or
when pigs can fly said to suggest that something is very unlikely to happen or be true ○ *Boyd says the plan will become a reality "when pigs can fly."*

pike

down the pike at a time in the near future ○ *There may be some new treatments coming down the pike. There's a new medicine called tacrine that was recently made available.*

≡ The reference here is to a turnpike or toll road.

pile

at the bottom of the pile or
at the top of the pile low down or
high up in society or in an organization
○ *I'm more concerned about the people at the
bottom of the pile who don't have jobs and
who don't have houses.*

pill

a bitter pill to swallow a difficult or
unpleasant fact or situation that has to
be accepted ○ *Gordon Hodgson, Cowie's
chief executive, said the failure to win was "a
little bit of a bitter pill to swallow."*

sugar-coat the pill to try to make bad
news or an unpleasant situation more
acceptable for someone by giving them
or telling them something good or
pleasant at the same time ○ *Of course,
government economists have been doing their
part as well to try to sugar-coat the pill of tax
increases.*

★ **swallow a bitter pill** to accept a
difficult or unpleasant fact or situation
○ *Our people have swallowed a bitter pill in
accepting this peace agreement.*

pillar

from pillar to post if someone is
moved from pillar to post, they are
moved repeatedly from one place or
position to another, usually in a hurried
or disorganized way so that they suffer as
a result ○ *I didn't want the children pushed
from pillar to post.*

> This expression comes from an early
> form of tennis that was played
> indoors. Players often played shots
> back and forth across the court, from
> the posts supporting the net to the
> pillars at the back of the court.

pillar to post (*journalism*) used for
describing a victory in sports, especially
in horse racing, in which the winner was
in the lead from the start of the race
○ *Sally Prosser held off the best of the Far*
*East to top the Asian circuit, thanks largely to
a pillar to post victory in the JAL Malaysian
Open.*

> This may refer to the posts that mark
> the start and finish of a racecourse.

pilot

★ **on automatic pilot** or
on autopilot acting without thinking
about what you are doing, usually
because you have done something many
times before or because you are very tired
○ *Steve seemed to be on automatic pilot and
able to go on driving without a word of
complaint or apparent fatigue.*

> In aircraft, automatic pilot is a device
> that automatically keeps the plane on
> course without the need for the pilot
> to do much.

pinch

in a pinch if absolutely necessary. ○ *Six
people, and more in a pinch, could be seated
comfortably at the table.*

★ **feel the pinch** to not have as much
money as you used to have, and so be
unable to buy the things you would like
to buy ○ *Poor households were still feeling
the pinch and the electricity price hike made
matters worse.*

pink

in the pink (*old-fashioned*) very fit and
healthy ○ *"Hello. Good evening. How are
you?" "Very well. And you?" "Oh, in the pink."*

> "Pink" here means best, and the word
> is derived from the flower of this name,
> which also gave its name to the color
> pink.

tickled pink extremely pleased about
something ○ *Her dressmaker, Nicole
Marnier, would just be tickled pink if we put
one of her outfits in the magazine.*

> This expression may refer to someone's
> face becoming pink or redder when
> they are being tickled.

pins

be on pins and needles or
sit on pins and needles to be very
anxious or nervous because you are
waiting to see if something happens the
way you want it to ○ *I think we all have
been sitting on pins and needles and anxious
for something to happen.*

pipe

a pipe dream an idea about what you
would like for the future that is probably
impossible ○ *He went on to say that he
doesn't think a relationship is in the cards for
Damon and Elena, that it's just "a pipe dream
for Damon."*

This expression refers to the sort of
idea that someone is likely to have
when they are smoking opium or some
other drug in a pipe.

put that in your pipe and smoke it
said when you want to tell someone that
although they may dislike or disagree
with something you have just said, they
must accept that it is a fact or true ○ *As
for rules, the only person who makes rules in
this house is me. So you can tell Miss
Underwood from me: she can put that in her
pipe and smoke it.*

pipeline

★ **in the pipeline** being planned or in
progress. A similar expression is **in the
works**. ○ *Over 350 major hospital audits
have been completed. There are nearly 300
more in the pipeline.*

piper

**he who pays the piper calls the
tune** used to emphasize that the person
who pays for something has the right to
decide how that thing operates or is
organized ○ *The ancient law that he who
pays the piper calls the tune has not been
repealed even in this permissive democracy.*

This may come from the custom,
dating back to the 17th century, of
hiring traveling musicians to play at
festivals and weddings. The people
who paid for the music were able to
choose the tunes they wanted to hear.

pay the piper to experience the
consequences of an earlier bad action
○ *The former wrestler is finally ready to pay
the piper for his arrest earlier this month.*

This expression suggests that
someone has already enjoyed the
music provided, and now must pay
those who performed it.

pitch

★ **make a pitch**
1 to tell people how good something is
and try to persuade them to support it or
buy it ○ *The president also used his remarks
to make a pitch for further space exploration.*
2 to try to obtain something ○ *So far
Federal Reserve Chairman Alan Greenspan
hasn't made a pitch for the job.*

place

★ **fall into place**
1 if you have been trying to understand
something, and then everything falls into
place, you suddenly understand it and
everything becomes clear ○ *Bits of the
puzzle fell into place. He knew now who had
written the letter summoning Father
Benjamin.*
2 if things fall into place, events happen
naturally to produce the situation you
want ○ *During February everything will
start to fall into place, leaving you with a
satisfied feeling that you're living life to the
full.*

★ **out of place**
1 not in the correct place ○ *Everything
was neatly arranged. There was no sign of
anything out of place.*
2 seeming wrong in a particular
situation ○ *The man seemed somehow out
of place at a gallery opening. He looked more
earnest than elegant.*

a place in the sun a job or situation where someone will be happy and well-off, and have everything that they want ○ *I've done what everybody's done. I've fought my way in. I think I've earned my place in the sun.*

This phrase was used by Bernard von Bulow, the German Chancellor, in a speech to the German parliament in 1897, referring to his country's desire to play a part in the colonization of East Asia: "We do not wish to force anyone into the shade, but demand our own place in the sun."

★ **put someone in their place** to show someone that they are less important or clever than they think they are ○ *In a few words she had not only put him in his place, but delivered a precise and damning assessment of his movie.*

★ **take second place** to be considered to be less important than another thing or person and be given less attention than them ○ *My personal life has had to take second place to my career.*

places

★ **be going places** to be showing a lot of talent or ability and be likely to become very successful ○ *If we can play like that every week, then this team is going places.*

★ **in high places** used for describing people who have powerful and influential positions in a government, society, or an organization ○ *You do not rise so high, so fast, without having a few friends in high places.*

★ **trade places** to be in someone else's situation while they are in your situation ○ *"I would trade places with you in a heartbeat," he told the players, "to be able to do what you're doing."*

plague

avoid someone or something like the plague to deliberately avoid someone or something because you

dislike them so much ○ *I normally avoid cheap Chianti like the plague.*

The plague is bubonic plague, a disease that killed over 50 million people in Europe and Asia during the 14th century and was referred to as the Black Death.

plain

plain as day very easy to see, or very obvious and easy to understand ○ *He was lying there plain as day, a starchy sheet covering the lower half of his hospital gown.*

plain as the nose on your face very obvious or easy to understand ○ *It's plain as the nose on your face that this company is wildly undervalued.*

planet

what planet does someone come from? (*informal*) said to suggest that you think someone has crazy ideas, or behaves in a very strange way, or does not understand something at all ○ *What planet are they from? The Government could easily do something about bank charges, but they won't because that might offend their supporters in the banking industry.*

plank

walk the plank (*journalism*) to accept responsibility for something that has gone wrong and leave your position ○ *If they think that the President is going to lose, they might decide, "OK, why should I walk the plank for him?"*

Many people believe that pirates used to kill their prisoners by forcing them to walk along a plank sticking out from the edge of a ship until they fell into the sea.

plate

★ **have enough on your plate** or **have a lot on your plate** to have a lot of work to do or a lot of things to deal with ○ *He's got enough on his plate without* *worrying about tactics and the performances of others.*

step up to the plate to come forward and take responsibility for something ○ *He's got to step up to the plate and deal with these accusations.*

When baseball players step up to the plate, they move into batting position.

plates

keep plates spinning or
have (a lot of) plates spinning to deal with many different things at the same time ○ *The screenwriters have a lot of plates spinning, and some of the scenes work better than others.*

This expression uses the image of a trick in which a person keeps a number of plates spinning on the top of thin poles.

platter

hand someone something on a silver platter or
hand someone something on a platter to give someone something without them having to work or make an effort to get it ○ *You act like a five-year-old. You expect me to hand you everything on a silver platter, and when you don't get it, you stamp your little foot and cry.*

A platter is a large plate used for serving food.

play

make a play for something to try to get something that you want ○ *Analysts say the company could soon be making a play for properties around the world.*

make a play for someone to try to win the attention or admiration of a person who you find attractive ○ *All the girls made a play for him.*

a play on words an expression or joke in which words suggest more than one meaning or are used in a clever way ○ *The name Net-a-porter is a play on words of "pret-a-porter," the French word for high style ready-to-wear clothing.*

play someone for a fool to deceive someone and use them for your own advantage ○ *John, do not play me for a fool. You owe me better than that.*

playing field

★ **a level playing field** a situation that is fair. You usually use this expression when talking about the fact that a situation is not fair, or when saying that you think it should be fair. ○ *At the moment we are not competing on a level playing field.*

★ **level the playing field** to remove an advantage that someone has, so that everyone may compete or participate equally ○ *Manufacturers view the bill as a move to level the playing field between domestic and foreign manufacturing.*

plea

cop a plea to agree to be found guilty and accept punishment of a crime in order to avoid a trial for a more serious crime ○ *He got caught for the former offense and copped a plea with the Feds to avoid going to prison.*

This sense of "cop" is related to a slang sense that means "steal" or "adopt."

plot

★ **lose the plot** (*journalism*) to become confused and not know what you should do ○ *Vikram's working so many hours as junior doctor he's losing the plot completely and keeps mumbling about the people he's killed by falling asleep on the job.*

the plot thickens used when a complicated situation or series of events starts to become even more complicated or mysterious ○ *At this point the plot thickened further. A link emerged between the attempt to kill the Pope and the kidnapping of the American.*

This phrase was widely used in 19th century melodramas, or popular plays that involved extreme situations and extreme emotions, and is now used humorously.

plug

★ **pull the plug on something** to stop supporting a project or activity, usually with money, so that it fails and has to stop ○ *The government has set out detailed conditions under which it would pull the plug on the sale.*

plunge

★ **take the plunge** to do something that you have been thinking of doing for some time, even though it is difficult or risky ○ *Helen decided to take the plunge and turned professional in 1991.*

pocket

★ **dig into your pocket** or **reach into your pocket** to pay for something with your own money ○ *Potential lenders will need to be persuaded that the government is tackling its economic problems before they dig into their pockets again.*

in someone's pocket if you are in someone's pocket, they control you or have power over you and so you do everything that they tell you ○ *Democrats suffered badly in the election from Republican claims that they were in the pockets of the unions.*

★ **out of pocket** having less money than you should have or than you intended, for example, because something was more expensive than you expected or because of a mistake ○ *The promoter claims he was left $36,000 out of pocket.*

★ **out-of-pocket** used for describing expenses that someone pays out of their own money, and that are normally paid back later ○ *I charge fifty dollars an hour plus out-of-pocket expenses.*

pockets

★ **line your pockets** to make a lot of money in a dishonest or unfair way ○ *He has been lining his pockets for 27 years while his country has festered in poverty.*

live in each other's pockets to spend a great deal of time together, perhaps too much ○ *Just because you're married doesn't mean you have to live in each other's pockets.*

point

★ **be a sore point with someone** if a particular subject is a sore point with someone, it makes them feel angry, embarrassed, or upset ○ *The continuing presence of foreign troops in their country remains a very sore point with these students.*

★ **boiling point** a situation that has become very tense or dangerous because the people involved are so angry that they are likely to go out of control ○ *Tempers were already close to boiling point as the dispute remained deadlocked for the ninth day.*

not to put too fine a point on it used when what you are about to say may sound unpleasant, unkind, or critical ○ *We didn't meet. In fact, not to put too fine a point on it, I was warned off.*

★ **a sticking point** a problem that stops you from achieving something, especially in a series of negotiations or a discussion ○ *Sources say a Republican call for a cut in the capital gains tax is the main sticking point in budget negotiations.*

points

★ **score points**

1 to gain an advantage over someone, especially in a discussion or argument ○ *They're not remotely concerned about the disabled. They're concerned about trying to score points off Willie Brown, the Democratic speaker of the State Assembly.* ○ *We can see our leaders looking shifty in close-up every*

night on television. There is no frankness, only point-scoring.
2 to do something that impresses someone or makes them admire you ○ *Again, Laine paused, clearly confident in his arguments. He was scoring points with the judge and the spectators. The judge kept nodding in agreement.*

poker

★ **a poker face** a blank expression on someone's face that makes it impossible for you to know what they are thinking ○ *The most wanted high school basketball player in San Antonio is keeping a poker face about where he'll go to college.*

In the game of poker it is important to show no emotion on your face so that other players can't guess whether you are holding winning or losing cards.

pole

in pole position in a very strong position in a competition or competitive situation, and likely to win or be successful ○ *They've been favorites all season and are in pole position now.*
someone wouldn't touch something or someone with a ten-foot pole used when someone does not want to have anything to do with someone or something, because they do not trust them or like them ○ *The history of the place kept the price down. No one would touch it with a ten-foot pole.*

poles

★ **poles apart** very different ○ *The East seemed to be poles apart from the capitalist West.*

The reference here is to the north and south poles.

poor

poor as a church mouse (old-fashioned) very poor ○ *I was as poor as a church mouse, but I bought that wreck of a car.*

Mice living in a church are unlikely to find much to eat as there is no kitchen or food cupboard.

port

any port in a storm said to mean that when you are in danger or difficulty, you sometimes cannot choose where you find shelter, comfort or safety ○ *I think he moved in with Mandy because he couldn't face the prospect of having to take care of himself. You know, any port in a storm.*

possum

play possum to try to make people ignore you by pretending to be dead or asleep ○ *"Playing possum, huh?" said Joe. "Right," said Frank. "I figured it might be interesting to hear what they had to say to each other when they thought I was unconscious."*

The possum or opossum is a North American and Australian animal. If it is threatened by another animal it sometimes lies still, as if it is dead, so that the animal will lose interest.

post

The following expression refers to the finishing post in a horse race.

first past the post (mainly British) finishing first or achieving something first in a race or competitive situation ○ *First past the post was Kenyan athlete John Mutai, who pipped Irishman Jerry Healy by just 20 seconds.*

This expression is sometimes used in talking about electoral systems. A first-past-the-post electoral system is one in which the candidate who gets the most votes or the party that wins in the most areas wins the election.

postal

go postal (informal) to become extremely angry ○ *When he saw the sign he went postal.*

posted

★ **keep someone posted** to continue giving someone the latest information about a situation that concerns them ○ *She made me promise to keep her posted on developments.*

poster

poster child (*journalism*) someone who is so typical of a quality, activity, or situation that everyone associates them with it ○ *Eikenberry has led a campaign to make Lowry the poster child for tax increases and everything wrong with government.*

> A poster child is literally a young person who appears on a poster advertising something, typically a charity.

pot

go to pot if something is going to pot, its condition is becoming very bad, because it has not been properly taken care of ○ *The neighborhood really is going to pot.*

keep the pot boiling to make sure that a process does not stop ○ *I threw in a question, just to keep the pot boiling while my brain caught up.*

> This expression may refer to meat that is chopped into pieces and cooked in a pot. Alternatively, the "pot" may have been a melting pot, where metal objects were melted down.

the pot calling the kettle black used to describe a situation in which someone with a particular fault accuses someone else of having the same fault ○ *In a prime case of the pot calling the kettle black, 48-year-old Brian, whose recent loves included two 22-year-olds, asked a friend: "Why must she go for an older man? She should know better than that."*

> In the past, both pots and kettles were hung over fires, and would be burned black.

the pot of gold at the end of the rainbow something that will be very difficult to achieve in reality, although you dream of getting it ○ *I would rather be honest with people than mislead them that there is going to be some pot of gold at the end of the rainbow.*

> There is an old legend that a pot of gold is buried at the point where the end of the rainbow meets the ground.

a watched pot never boils (*old-fashioned*) used to emphasize that if you wait and watch anxiously to see something happen, it will seem to take a very long time, or it will not happen at all ○ *This strategy is doomed from the start because it is far too public: a watched pot never boils.*

potato

drop something or someone like a hot potato → see **drop**

a hot potato a controversial subject or problem that most people would rather not have to deal with ○ *When she is confronted with a political hot potato such as abortion or tightening the gun laws, she is not beyond voicing her opinion.*

potatoes

small potatoes something that is not important or significant ○ *While a total tour attendance of around 20,000 is small potatoes by national standards, it is very big in this state.*

potluck

be potluck if a meal at your house will be potluck, you have not planned it or prepared any special food ○ *"We'll just be casual and eat in the kitchen. It's just potluck," Moira said. "Hope you don't mind."*

> A potluck meal or dinner is a meal at which different guests bring different parts of the meal.

★ **take potluck** to make a choice from what is available, although you do not have any knowledge to help you, and so it is a matter of luck whether you get something good ○ *We'd take potluck at whatever restaurants might still be open.* ○ *Travel agencies stuck with hundreds of unsold package vacations are offering great breaks on a potluck basis.*

pound

your pound of flesh something you are entitled to, even though you might not need it and it will cause problems for the people you are getting it from ○ *Banks are quick enough to demand their pound of flesh from the small businesses and other regular customers when overdrafts run a little over the limit.*

≣ This expression comes from Shakespeare's play "The Merchant of Venice" (Act 4, Scene 1). Shylock is owed money by Antonio, and attempts to carry out an agreement which allows him to cut off a pound of Antonio's flesh.

powder

keep your powder dry to be ready to take immediate action in case a situation suddenly gets worse ○ *The only course upon which the government could agree was to move cautiously, keep its powder dry, and await the outcome of events abroad.*

≣ The powder referred to here is gunpowder. The expression comes from a story about the English leader Oliver Cromwell. He is said to have ended a speech to his soldiers, who were about to cross a river and go into battle, by saying: "Put your trust in God, my boys, and keep your powder dry."

powder keg

sit on a powder keg to be in a very dangerous situation, in which something could suddenly go seriously wrong at any time ○ *The Prime Minister was all too aware*

that he was sitting on a powder keg which could explode at any moment.

≣ A powder keg was a small barrel that was used to store gunpowder.

power

more power to someone said to show that you do not oppose what someone is doing but that you do not want to do it yourself ○ *"If he can raise the money, more power to him," she said. "I can't afford to help, though."*

the power behind the throne a person who has all the power and control in an organization or situation, although someone else may appear to rule ○ *She was the real power behind the throne, a strong and single-minded woman manipulating a weaker husband for her own ends.*

powers

★ **the powers that be** the authority or the people who are responsible for something ○ *If the powers that be in the WWE continue to book Del Rio in such a matter, then I can see him becoming a champion much sooner than later.*

practice

★ **practice what you preach** to behave in the way that you encourage other people to behave ○ *Blundell practiced what he preached; having declared himself to be a Kenyan, he was the first British-born resident to apply for Kenyan citizenship.*

praise

damn with faint praise to say something about someone that sounds nice but that shows that you do not really have a high opinion of them ○ *In recent months he has consistently damned the government with faint praise, but earlier this week he issued an appeal for continuity.*

≣ This expression was first used by the English writer Alexander Pope in his

"Epistle to Dr. Arbuthnot" (1735): "Damn with faint praise, assent with civil leer, And, without sneering, teach the rest to sneer."

praises

★ **sing the praises of someone or something** to praise someone or something in an enthusiastic way ○ *This may sound like we're singing our own praises here, but I honestly think most people find our music irresistible.*

prayer

someone does not have a prayer of doing something said when you think that it is impossible for someone to achieve something ○ *He did not seem to have a prayer of regaining the world title.*

pregnant

you can't be half pregnant used to express the idea that you must commit yourself fully to a definite plan of action, rather than changing your mind or making different proposals ○ *You can't be half pregnant," he says. "You either have a government-managed program or you have a private solution."*

premium

at a premium not easily available, and so having a high price ○ *Quality storage space is at a premium – it's not like they can just throw works of art in a warehouse somewhere.*

put a premium on something to consider something very important and valuable ○ *We put a premium on personal integrity, teamwork, problem solving and winning.*

press

a full-court press a situation in which people are making a lot of effort and putting a lot of pressure on something or someone in order to get a particular result ○ *The administration's full-court press on economic remedies also includes moves by the Treasury Secretary.*

In basketball, a full-court press is where the defensive players stay close to the attacking players over the whole area of the court, rather than just in front of their own basket.

★ **get a bad press** to be repeatedly criticized, especially in the newspapers, on television, or on radio ○ *So-called "arranged marriages," common in many cultures, tend to get a bad press in the West.*

pretty

sit pretty to be in a good, safe, or comfortable situation ○ *When the war started, they thought they were sitting pretty, because they had all that surplus grain.*

price

★ **at any price** even if unpleasant things happen as a result of your actions ○ *There's likely to be more violence from rebel groups that are determined to stop the peace process at any price.*

★ **at a price**
1 if something can be obtained at a price, it is very expensive ○ *Guests can always find a meal of sorts in the hotel restaurant, but at a price.*
2 if you get something you want at a price, you get it but you have to accept something unpleasant as well ○ *Fame comes at a price.*

★ **everyone has their price** or **every man has his price** used to suggest that everyone can be persuaded to do something dishonest or immoral, if they are offered a large enough amount of money ○ *While it may not be true that every man has his price, there are always those who have.*

a price on someone's head a reward for capturing or killing someone ○ *He's on America's Most Wanted list, with a price on his head.*

the price is right said to mean the cost

of something is reasonable ○ *Although it doesn't have a remote control, the price is right for this portable speaker and it earns our recommendation.*

pricks

kick against the pricks *(mainly British, literary, old-fashioned)* to show your opposition to people in authority ○ *Kicking against the pricks when you're 30 or 40 or more strikes me as a better test of one's convictions.*

> This expression occurs in the Bible (Acts 9:5). It refers to cattle kicking out when people try to move them along by poking them with sticks.

pride

★ **swallow your pride** to decide to do something even though it is shameful or embarrassing, and you would prefer not to ○ *However, if political compulsions demand, he can swallow his pride and ally himself with his political enemies.*

print

★ **the fine print** or **the small print**
the part of a contract, agreement, or advertisement which contains important legal information, often in very small writing ○ *Patients who thought they were fully covered are being hit by huge bills because they did not read the small print on their insurance forms.*

prisoners

take no prisoners to carry out a plan or an action in a very forceful and determined way, without caring if you harm or upset other people ○ *You will have to fight for what you want and what you believe in and you should assume the attitude that you're taking no prisoners.*

production

make a (big) production of something to do something in a complicated or exaggerated way, when it could be done much more simply ○ *He made a production of brushing his hands clean on his pant legs.*

> A production here is something such as a play or a musical.

profile

★ **a high profile** if someone has a high profile, people notice them and what they do ○ *He will be thinking about his future now that he has such a high profile in the cycling world.* ○ *She works three days a week in a high-profile job as communications director for a top advertising agency.*

★ **keep a low profile** to avoid doing things that will make people notice you ○ *Sonoma County's agricultural commissioner kept a low profile Monday following her arrest over the weekend on suspicion of drunk driving.*

proof

the proof of the pudding is in the eating used to emphasize that something new can only be judged to be good or bad after it has been tried or used ○ *A year after the changes were implemented, perhaps we can now apply the old saying that "the proof of the pudding is in the eating."*

> In this expression, "proof" means the testing of something rather than establishing that it is true. The idea is that the best way to test the quality of a pudding is to taste it rather than admire its appearance.

public

★ **air your dirty laundry in public** or **wash your dirty linen in public**
to talk about unpleasant or personal matters in front of other people, when most people consider that such things should be private ○ *We shouldn't wash our dirty laundry in public and if I was in his position, I'd say nothing at all.*

go public
1 to make something known to everyone, for example, through the media or on the Internet ○ *Johnson has gone public with allegations about Smith's past.*
2 If a company goes public, it changes from being privately owned to being traded on a stock exchange, by offering shares for sale ○ *Facebook may go public as early as 2012, a member of its Board of Directors has revealed.*

pulp

beat someone to a pulp to injure someone very badly by hitting them repeatedly ○ *Motorists were pulled from their cars, beaten and kicked to a pulp, and left to die in the road.*

pump

★ **prime the pump** (*journalism*) to take action to help something succeed or grow, usually by spending money on it ○ *Spring is the time when the government primes the pump to help farmers prepare their fields.*

≡ To prime a water pump means to pump it until it is full of water and all the air has been forced out, so that it is ready to be used.

punch

★ **pack a punch** to have a very powerful effect ○ *Arthur Miller's classic play "Death of a Salesman" still packs a punch.*
pleased as punch very pleased ○ *Branfoot announced he was as pleased as punch with his team's performance.*

≡ "Punch" is a character from traditional "Punch and Judy" puppet shows, who enjoys making trouble for people. The puppet usually has a big grin.

punches

★ **not pull your punches** or
pull no punches to speak very honestly and directly about something even if it upsets people ○ *He had never lied to me in the past and he didn't pull his punches now. He told me that in his opinion, Robin would be dead in nine months.*

≡ If boxers pull their punches, they do not hit their opponent as hard as they could do.

roll with the punches to not allow difficulties or criticism to discourage you or affect you badly ○ *He has impressed all sides by his ability to negotiate and willingness to roll with the punches.*

≡ If boxers roll with the punches, they move their head and body backwards, away from their opponent's punch.

puppy

puppy love romantic love between children or teenagers that is not expected to last ○ *It was just puppy love, nothing serious.*

≡ This idiom may be comparing the young people to puppy dogs, or could refer to the deep affection puppies seem to feel for their carers.

purposes

at cross purposes if two people are at cross purposes, there is a misunderstanding between them because they think they are talking about or trying to do the same thing as each other, but they are actually talking about or trying to do different things ○ *They had been talking at cross purposes earlier, Enron realized. The Hungarian hadn't been offering him a slice of the deal at all.*

purse

★ **hold the purse strings** to control the way that money is spent in a particular family, organization, or country ○ *Six out of ten women think that financial institutions treat them like simpletons, even though they usually hold the domestic purse strings.*

push

get the push to summon enough enthusiasm or force to do something
○ *Will you ask him why we continue to run up the middle when it is obvious our offensive line can't get the push?*

★ **when push comes to shove** or **if push comes to shove** when a situation reaches a critical point and you must make a decision on how to progress

○ *They knew they could sit back, and when push came to shove I'd do all the work.*

putty

putty in your hands someone who will do anything you ask or tell them to do ○ *I was completely in awe of him, I was putty in his hands.*

Putty is a thick paste that is used to secure glass in window frames.

Qq

quantity

★ **an unknown quantity** a thing or person that you know very little about ○ *She had known Max for some years now, but he was still pretty much an unknown quantity.*

quarters

close quarters a small, crowded space ○ *The miners have been stuck in an underground mine in close quarters since August 5.*

question

★ **beg the question**

1 to make people want to ask a particular question ○ *Hopewell's success begs the question, why aren't more companies doing the same?*

2 (*formal*) to suggest that another, more important problem has not been dealt with ○ *The New York Times stated that "the warming of the earth's climate is no longer in dispute," somewhat begging the question of whether or not that warming is a greenhouse effect or, indeed, necessarily part of a continuing long-range trend.*

This is a rough translation of the Latin expression *petitio principii*, a technical term used in logic to describe a situation in which the truth of something is assumed before it has been proved.

★ **a question mark** doubt or uncertainty

○ *Multi-party democracy has arrived – albeit with many question marks about its eventual form.*

quick

cut someone to the quick to make someone very upset ○ *That tone of hers always cut him to the quick.*

The quick is the very sensitive flesh under the fingernails or toenails.

quick as a flash very quickly ○ *Harrison responded as quick as a flash.*

quiet

quiet as a lamb very quiet, calm or gentle ○ *She's fine, quiet as a lamb. You really mustn't worry.*

quiet as a mouse very quiet or silent ○ *We were quiet as mice, hiding in there.*

quits

call it quits to decide to stop doing something or stop being involved in something ○ *There is a disco called the Club Coqui, which stays open until the last customer is ready to call it quits.*

quote

★ **quote, unquote** said before or after a particular word or phrase that has been used when you do not think that it is accurate or suitable ○ *"Even though I'm this big, huge superstar quote unquote, I have family problems, insecurities about my body,"* she says.

Rr

rabbit

★ **pull a rabbit out of the hat**
(*journalism*) to unexpectedly do
something that solves a problem or helps
you to achieve something ○ *I cannot pull a
rabbit out of a hat every time I go into the
boxing ring. All I can do is do my best.*

> This expression refers to a traditional
> magician's trick, in which a rabbit is
> produced mysteriously out of an
> apparently empty hat.

race

★ **a race against time** a situation in
which you have a very short time to finish
a task and have to work very quickly ○ *The
paramedics were in a race against time to treat
a six-year-old girl suffering with breathing
difficulties in Cranston, Rhode Island.*

rack

on the rack in a state of anxiety, distress,
or difficulty ○ *They put us on the rack when
we were 2-1 up but we came back well and it
was great to win with such a late goal.*

> The rack was an instrument of torture
> that was used in the past. Prisoners
> were tied to the rack, and their arms
> and legs were stretched until they
> confessed or told secrets, or died.

rack and ruin something that is going
to rack and ruin is falling into a very bad
condition, because nobody is looking
after it or dealing properly with it ○ *The
country is going to rack and ruin under this
government.*

> The old-fashioned spelling of "rack" –
> "wrack" means the same as "wreck,"
> something that has been destroyed.

radar

be on someone's radar to have the
attention of someone, as a goal or as a
matter that needs to be dealt with
○ *Bruce LeVell said the position is on his
radar, but his priority right now is the
November election.*

drop off the radar to be forgotten or
ignored because people's attention has
moved to something more important
○ *Stories in the news drop off the radar with
people after a couple of weeks.*

under the radar happening or going
on in secret, or without being noticed or
detected. ○ *Chicago has had a season that
has flown under the radar for the most part
and now the Bears will be in the playoffs.*

> Radar is the system of radio waves
> used to find the position and track the
> movement of aircraft. When a plane or
> other moving object is on the radar, it
> is visible. When it drops off the radar, it
> can no longer be detected.

rag doll

like a rag doll used to describe a
situation in which someone or
something has no power or strength and
someone or something else completely
controls them ○ *Suddenly, his knees gave
way and he collapsed like a rag doll.*

> The literal meaning of "rag doll" is a
> child's toy, a soft doll made of fabric
> and stuffed like a pillow.

ragged

run someone ragged to make
someone do so much that they get
extremely tired ○ *He tends to produce his*

best football before half-time, though often coming back to run defenders ragged in the closing minutes.

rags

★ **rags to riches** used to describe the life of someone who was very poor when they were young, and who later became very rich and successful ○ *His life sounds to me like the classic rags to riches story. He married some money, I gather, but he made a lot more himself.*

rail

★ **the third rail** something that is dangerous to deal with, or that many people argue about ○ *Social Security became known as the "third rail" of politics, a taboo to be addressed by politicians only at the risk of becoming a social outcast*

   The third rail of an electric train is the one that carries the electric current and that will instantly kill anyone who falls on it.

rails

★ **go off the rails**
1 to start behaving in an unacceptable or strange way ○ *Our family was so happy until our daughter went off the rails. She dropped out of school at 15, ran away from home, and now lives on the street.*
2 to start to go wrong ○ *By the spring, the project seemed to be going off the rails. No major sponsor had come forward with the extra $1 million or so needed.*

rain

come rain or shine in whatever circumstances, regardless of the weather or other problems ○ *He plays golf, come rain or shine, every Monday.*
it never rains but it pours said when you notice that when one bad thing happens, other bad things often happen too and make the situation worse ○ *And after all that, the cellar floods. It never rains, but it pours.*

take a rain check to refuse an offer or invitation politely, or say that you would like to accept it, but at a different time ○ *She says she'd like to take a rain check on it and do it in May.*

   This expression refers to baseball. If a baseball game is canceled because of rain, people are entitled to see another game by showing their original ticket or receipt. This ticket is called a rain check.

rainbows

chase rainbows to waste your time trying to get something that you can never have ○ *Kemp could see why there had been no clear verdict, and why the police were having difficulty finding proof; they might as well be chasing rainbows.*

ranch

bet the ranch to spend all the money that you have in order to achieve something, and risk losing it if you fail ○ *We thought that if we could do it, it would give us an important lead over our competition in future years. We've taken risks before and so we bet the ranch.*
meanwhile, back at the ranch used to introduce a slightly different but related subject to the one you are discussing ○ *American jobs have been flowing to other rising economic powers. Meanwhile, back at the ranch, American job opportunities are requiring new skills and more education.*

   This expression was probably inspired by Western movies, in which the action regularly shifted from a ranch to some other place.

rank

pull rank to make unfair use of your power or position to make people do what you want ○ *The Federal Government threatened to pull rank and override the states with its own legislation.*

rank and file the ordinary members of an organization, rather than the management ○ *The union's rank and file will vote on the contract Oct. 15.* ○ *I expect rank-and-file soldiers to accept whatever rule is imposed on them, if they expect to continue in the military.*

ranks

A rank of soldiers is a line of them standing side by side.

★ **break ranks** to disobey the instructions of a group or organization of which you are a member, and express your own opinion ○ *Would you break ranks with your party and vote against the president's tax bill?*

When soldiers break ranks, they stop standing in a line and move apart.

★ **close ranks** to support the other members of a group totally and oppose any criticism or attacks from outside ○ *Malaysian Cabinet ministers have closed ranks behind Prime Minister Mahathir Mohamad, saying there was no question of his stepping down.*

When soldiers close ranks, they stand closer together so that it is hard for anyone to break through the line.

ransom

★ **hold someone for ransom** to use your power or influence to force someone to do something they do not want to do ○ *But who are the powerful men at the Bundesbank who have the power to hold Europe for ransom?*

a king's ransom → see **king**

rap

"Rap" is slang for a criminal charge.

beat the rap to escape the blame or punishment for a crime or other bad action ○ *The state, in fact, tried to prosecute him over child labor violations, and he beat the rap.*

take the rap to accept the blame or responsibility for something that has been done badly or has gone wrong, even if it is not your fault ○ *He had tried, and failed, to get someone to take the rap for a corruption scandal.*

rat

look like a drowned rat to be very wet, for example, because you have been caught in the rain or because your hair is wet ○ *By the time I got there I looked like a drowned rat.*

★ **the rat race** a job or way of life in which people compete aggressively with each other in order to be successful ○ *I had to get out of the rat race for a while and take a look at the real world again.*

★ **smell a rat** to suspect that something is wrong in a particular situation, for example, that someone is trying to deceive you or harm you ○ *If only I'd used my head, I'd have smelled a rat right away and never touched the proposition.*

ray

a ray of sunshine someone or something that makes you feel better because there is something positive and refreshing about them ○ *I am looking forward to the wedding, it's the one ray of sunshine for the future.*

razor

a razor's edge a situation that may change at any time and that is possibly dangerous ○ *If my patience was wearing thin in the build-up to this match, it's now a razor's edge.*

reality

★ **a reality check** an analysis of a situation or idea to see if it is realistic or possible ○ *People need a swift reality check on what life is really like after retirement.*

reap

you reap what you sow used to emphasize the idea that everything that happens is a result of things that you have done in the past ○ *It seems to me that if we create areas of such bleakness and social deprivation we should expect to reap what we sow.*

This is based on a quotation from the Bible (Galatians 6:7). It says that whatever you plant, that is what you will harvest (or, in other words, if you behave well, good things will happen to you, and if you behave badly, bad things will happen to you).

rearguard

★ **fight a rearguard action** to try hard to stop something happening, without much hope of success ○ *National telephone companies are fighting a rearguard action against competition from beyond their frontiers.*

The rearguard of a retreating army is a unit which separates from the rest and acts as a defense while the rest of the army is getting away.

record

★ **off the record** used for saying that you do not want anyone to report what you have said ○ *That's off the record. Don't go repeating what I've said, you hear.*

★ **on the record** used for saying that you are willing for people to report and repeat what you are saying ○ *We are on the record as saying we will protect our friends in the war zone, and we mean that.*

★ **set the record straight** to correct a mistake or misunderstanding ○ *But a company seeing wrong information about itself on a report can have a frustrating time setting the record straight.*

red

★ **in the red** owing money to someone or to another organization ○ *The company was already in the red to the extent of more than three million dollars.*

This expression comes from the practice in the past of using red ink to fill in entries on the debit side of a book of accounts.

red as a beet having a very red face, for example because you are very hot or very embarrassed ○ *He turned as red as beet when I told him.*

a red letter day a day when something very important or exciting happens ○ *Back in 1986 Jim had his first picture published in Wildlife Magazine. "That was a real red letter day for me!" he confesses.*

In the past, important feast days and saints' days were printed in red in some calendars.

★ **see red** to suddenly become very angry or annoyed because of something that has been said or done ○ *The programs so far have simply reinforced negative stereotype images of young black people. It makes me see red.*

This is a reference to the traditional belief that the color red makes bulls angry. In bullfighting, the matador waves a red cape to make the bull charge.

red-handed

★ **catch someone red-handed** to catch someone while they are doing something illegal or wrong ○ *In fact, the burglar wasn't inside the house, but on the roof, and was caught red-handed by the police.*

The reference here is to a guilty person whose hands are covered in blood.

reign

★ **a reign of terror** a period during which there is a lot of violence and killing, especially by people who are in positions of power ○ *The president last night* *dismissed the government, accusing it of having unleashed a reign of terror against its political opponents.*

The original Reign of Terror was during the French Revolution between April 1793 and July 1794, when many thousands were put to death by the government.

rein

The reference in these expressions is to a rider using the reins to control a horse.

★ **give someone free rein** to give someone all the freedom they want or need to do something ○ *He was given free rein to manage the cavalry as he wished.*

★ **keep a tight rein on someone or something** to control someone or something firmly ○ *The recession has forced people to keep a very tight rein on their finances when on vacation.*

rest

the rest is history → see **history**

rhyme

without rhyme or reason happening without any logical or obvious reason ○ *Cuts are being made without rhyme or reason. The only motive is to save money to meet budget targets.*

rich

rich as Croesus very rich ○ *He may be nearly as rich as Croesus, but that's still not rich enough for him.*

Croesus was the ruler of Lydia, a kingdom in Asia Minor, in the 6th century BC. He was famous for being very rich.

strike it rich to suddenly earn or win a large amount of money ○ *I've been thinking, prospecting might be just what we've been looking for: a quick way to strike it rich.*

riddles

speak in riddles to not say clearly and directly what you mean ○ *For several days, he dropped enigmatic clues to Ann, and spoke in riddles about his unpredictable absences of the past months.*

ride

★ **a free ride** a situation in which someone gets some benefit from a situation without putting any effort into achieving it themselves ○ *I never wanted anyone to think I was getting a free ride or special treatment from the boss.*

go along for the ride to decide to join in an activity without doing it seriously or getting deeply involved in it ○ *Your boyfriend is not likely to be serious about anything this week except having a good time. Go along for the ride.*

★ **a rough ride** a situation in which you have a lot of problems and it is very difficult for you to achieve something ○ *The past two years have been a rough ride, Paterson acknowledged Wednesday, with the nation facing the longest economic downturn since the Great Depression.*

★ **take someone for a ride** to deceive or cheat someone ○ *You've been taken for a ride. Why did you give him five thousand francs?*

This expression comes from gangsters' slang. When gangsters "took someone for a ride," they took them away in a car in order to kidnap them or kill them.

right

right as rain feeling well or healthy again after an illness or injury ○ *We put a bandage on his knee, gave him a cookie and a glass of milk and he was right as rain.*

rights

bragging rights a reason to be proud or boastful about something ○ *The companies are competing for bragging rights*

as the nation's largest aircraft carrier.
by rights according to what is fair, expected, or allowed ○ *They don't have a majority, so by rights they weren't entitled to bring the motion forward.*

ringer

★ **a dead ringer for someone** someone who looks or sounds exactly like another person ○ *An ordinary guy from Baltimore, Dave Kovic is extraordinary in one respect: he's a dead ringer for the US President.*

The word "ringer" may originally have come from a name for dishonest traders at fairs who sold brass rings, pretending they were gold. In horse racing, a "ringer" is a horse that has been dishonestly substituted for another in a race.

rings

run rings around someone to be much better at a particular activity than someone else, and be able to beat or outwit them ○ *Mentally, he can still run rings around men half his age.*

ringside

a ringside seat an excellent and clear view of what is happening somewhere ○ *The first US presidential election for which I had a ringside seat was the one that brought John F. Kennedy to office over 30 years ago.*

In boxing, the ringside seats are the seats that are closest to the ring and have the best view.

riot

read the riot act to angrily tell someone off for having done something stupid or wrong ○ *The president read the riot act to his party, warning those who sought to preserve the old system that power was already slipping from their grasp.*

The Riot Act was a law passed in Britain in 1715. It made it an offense for a group of twelve or more people to refuse to break up and leave if someone in authority read them the relevant section of the Act.

★ **run riot**
1 to get out of control ○ *There should be no parts of Baltimore that are no-go areas, where gangs run riot terrorizing the innocent while the police stay safely away.*
2 if something such as imagination or speculation runs riot, it expresses itself or spreads in an uncontrolled way ○ *We have no proof and when there is no proof, rumor runs riot.*

In hunting, if the hounds run riot, they follow the scents of other animals rather than the one they are supposed to be chasing.

rip

★ **let it rip** to do or proceed with something without restraint ○ *With a 20 mph wind at his back, Daly uncorked his patented backswing that points to the ground as if he were swinging a fishing pole, and let it rip.*

rise

get a rise out of someone to deliberately make someone angry by teasing them or making fun of them ○ *Johnson stopped bothering him once he saw he couldn't get a rise out of him.*

The reference in this expression is to a fish rising to the surface of the water to take the bait.

ritz

put on the Ritz to spend a lot of money in order to have a very enjoyable time ○ *Arlington High School seniors put on the ritz last night for their annual senior prom.*

This expression may come from the chain of expensive hotels called Ritz.

river

sell someone down the river to betray someone or do something that harms them in order to gain an advantage for yourself ○ *He has been sold down the river by the people who were supposed to protect him. It had a devastating effect on his health.*

> This is a reference to slaveholders on the Mississippi river selling unwanted slaves to other slaveholders further down the river, where the conditions were harsher.

road

★ **down the road** after a particular amount of time ○ *Twenty-five years down the road from independence, we have to start making some new priorities.*

★ **hit the road** to begin a journey ○ *Urban commuters are having to hit the road earlier to be sure of beating the jams and finding a parking space.*

the road to hell is paved with good intentions it is not enough for someone to make plans or promises, but they must also do those things ○ *The road to hell is paved with good intentions, and there are many, many jars of vitamin tablets which have been started but never finished.*

> To pave a path or road means to cover it using flat stones called paving stones. The word "pavement" is derived from this word. This expression was used by the writer Samuel Johnson and is mentioned in his biography in an entry dated 16 April 1775, in the form "hell is paved with good intentions." The idea is that good intentions do not guarantee a good outcome.

take the high road to follow the course of action that is the most moral or most correct and that is least likely to harm or upset other people ○ *US*

diplomats say the president is likely to take the high road in his statements about trade.*

rock

between a rock and a hard place in a difficult situation where you have to choose between two equally unpleasant courses of action ○ *We're caught between a rock and a hard place. Either we spend two months planning the operation and end up being late, or we come in right now and risk making mistakes.*

★ **hit rock bottom**
1 to be at an extremely low level and be unable go any lower ○ *The auto industry slumped to one of its blackest days yesterday as new car sales hit rock bottom.*
2 to be in a hopeless or difficult situation which makes you feel very depressed ○ *When my girlfriend asked me to move out of our apartment and end our relationship, I hit rock bottom.*

> This expression comes from mining, and refers to the layer of rock that is reached once the supply of minerals being taken from the mine has been used up.

rocker

off your rocker (informal) crazy ○ *Mrs. Stevens will think I'm off my rocker handing out my money like that before the bankruptcy business is even settled.*

rocket

not rocket science very easy to learn or understand ○ *In 1981, it didn't take long for our people at CBS to learn these techniques. As I'd told Sauter, this isn't rocket science.*

rocks

on the rocks experiencing difficulties and likely to end or fail ○ *Their marriage was on the rocks, but they had determined not to divorce until the children were grown up.*

The image here is of a ship that is stuck on rocks.

rod

spare the rod and spoil the child
(old-fashioned) said to mean that if you fail to punish a child that behaves badly, the child's behavior will be worse generally ○ *We need to remember, "Spare the rod and spoil the child." It is time to stop being so politically correct and afraid of instilling common decency.*

This expression is sometimes used with the first phrase only because it is so common and people understand what is meant. The expression is inspired by verses in the Bible.

roll

★ **be on a roll** to be in a situation where things are going very well for you, and you are making a lot of progress ○ *We're on a roll and we're winning, which gives the players that extra belief in themselves.*

This expression probably comes from surfing.

be rolling in it (informal) to be very rich ○ *She's only 25 and she's rolling in it.*

Rome

fiddle while Rome burns to do nothing or spend your time on unimportant things when you have very serious issues or problems to deal with ○ *Fighting with one another over small details is like fiddling while Rome burns: it is a distraction from the main issue.*

There is a story that the Emperor Nero set fire to Rome, and then played his lyre and sang as he watched the flames. Afterwards he denied this and blamed the Christians for the destruction.

Rome was not built in a day used to reassure someone that it takes a long time to do a job or task properly, and they should not rush it or expect to do it quickly ○ *I know Rome wasn't built in a day but I don't want to wait 200 years.*

when in Rome used to express the idea that people should follow the customs of the people they are visiting or living with ○ *We had a leisurely lunch, followed by a little sleep - when in Rome!*

This was probably first used by St. Ambrose (died 397 AD) in answer to a question about whether religious fasting should take place on the day set aside in Milan or the day used in Rome. A fuller form of the expression is "When in Rome, do as the Romans do."

roof

★ **go through the roof**
1 if the level of something such as the price of a product goes through the roof, it suddenly increases very rapidly ○ *House prices were going through the roof.*
2 to suddenly become very angry, and usually show your anger by shouting at someone ○ *I admitted I had ordered a racing car, and found myself in terrible trouble. He went through the roof!*

★ **raise the roof** to make a very loud noise, for example, by cheering, singing, or shouting ○ *Best audience I've ever had in my life – they practically raised the roof.*

a roof over someone's head a place for someone to live ○ *This new facility will put a roof over the heads of some homeless men and women in Minnehaha County.*

rooftops

shout something from the rooftops to let a lot of people know about something that you are particularly angry or excited about ○ *I would love to be able to shout our score from the rooftops.*

room

★ **a smoke-filled room** if a political or business decision is made in a smoke-filled room, it is made by a small group of people in a private meeting, rather than in a more democratic or open way ○ *Richards doesn't think that a return to the smoke-filled room, in which a few bosses make the decision, would be possible.*

≣ This was first used to refer to the suite in the Blackstone Hotel in Chicago where Warren Harding was chosen as the Republican presidential candidate in 1920.

roost

★ **rule the roost** to be the most powerful and important person in a group ○ *In Germany, scientists will be found at the top of many manufacturing companies; in Britain, accountants rule the roost.*

≣ This expression seems to refer to the dominant rooster in a chicken coop. However, "rule the roost" may have developed from the earlier expression "rule the roast," which refers to the head of the household who carves and serves the meat.

root

★ **root and branch** if something is changed root and branch, it is changed completely, so that none of the old or traditional parts remain ○ *These measures should change our economic system root and branch.*

≣ In 1641 the Root and Branch Bill abolishing the government of the church by bishops was presented to the English Parliament. Those who supported the bill were known as "root-and-branch men," and the term has been used to refer to reform ever since.

★ **take root** to become established or begin to develop ○ *The idea of starting up his own picture library began to take root.*

roots

put down roots
1 to make a place your home, for

example, by taking part in activities or making a lot of friends there ○ *Servicemen and women are seldom in the same place long enough to put down roots and buy their own home.*

2 if something puts down roots somewhere, it becomes firmly established there, so that it is likely to last and to be successful in the future ○ *Not only did the party increase its share of the poll but it also put down roots in areas where it had previously been weak or even non-existent.*

rope

give someone enough rope to hang themselves to give someone the freedom to do something in the way they want to do it, usually in the hope that they will fail or become weak by doing it the wrong way ○ *The King has simply given the politicians enough rope to hang themselves: once the party system has been discredited by political in-fighting, he will present himself once again as an absolute ruler.*

ropes

★ **learn the ropes** to learn how to do a particular job or task ○ *By the time he was 34, he had learned the ropes of the jewelry trade.*

≣ The origin of this expression is from sailing ships, where the sailors had to get to know the complicated system of ropes that made up the rigging.

★ **on the ropes** very close to failing or being defeated ○ *The Denver-based developer has been on the ropes because of depressed housing markets in Denver, Texas and Arizona.*

≣ The image here is of a boxer who has been pushed back against the ropes around the edge of the ring.

show someone the ropes to show

someone how to do a particular job or task ○ *We had a patrol out on the border, breaking in some young soldiers, showing them the ropes.*

The origin of this expression is from sailing ships, where the sailors had to get to know the complicated system of ropes that made up the rigging.

roses

come up smelling like roses or **come up smelling of roses** to be in a better or stronger situation than before, after experiencing a difficult situation ○ *Ellis, who was fired on Monday, has come up smelling like roses. He has been taken on by a rival company and his financial package is even healthier.*

everything is coming up roses used about someone who is having a lot of success and everything is going well for them ○ *For Rachel Ashwell, everything's coming up roses both in her home and her working life.*

This was the title of a song from the musical "Gypsy" (1959), with words by Stephen Sondheim.

rote

by rote without thought, understanding or sincerity. This expression usually follows verbs of learning, doing, and speaking. ○ *After waiting on scores of people a night, many waiters end up saying things by rote, and "enjoy" is certainly one of them.* ○ *Education experts have criticized learning by rote, since it doesn't teach children to think for themselves.*

rough

★ **rough and ready**
1 done in a hurry, and so basic, or not very exact ○ *The rough and ready method used to limit total costs worked reasonably well.*
2 not polite or well educated ○ *At first the*

rough and ready sailors did not know what to make of the young cleric.

★ **rough and tumble** a situation in which the people involved try hard to get what they want, and do not worry about upsetting or harming others ○ *Whoever expected leaders in the rough and tumble of electoral politics to be nice or fair?*

Originally, a rough and tumble was a boxing match in which there were no rules or restrictions.

take the rough with the smooth to be willing to accept both the unpleasant and the pleasant aspects of something ○ *You have to take the rough with the smooth. I never promised there would be no risk.*

roughshod

★ **ride roughshod over someone** to pay no attention to what someone wants, or make decisions without considering their feelings or interests ○ *Bosses nowadays seem to think they can ride roughshod over unions and I like to see them fighting back.*

In the past, a roughshod horse had nail heads sticking out from its shoes, so it would not slip on icy roads. These shoes could cause terrible injuries if the horse was ridden over a person in a battle or by accident.

roulette

★ **play Russian roulette** to do something that is very dangerous because it involves big risks ○ *America's space agency has been accused of mismanagement and playing Russian roulette in launching some of its missions.*

If someone plays Russian roulette, they fire a revolver containing only one bullet at their head without knowing whether the bullet will be released or not.

row

★ **in a row** if something happens several times in a row, it happens that number of times without a break ○ *It was the team's fifth win in a row, a team record.*

a tough row to hoe a situation that is very difficult to deal with ○ *I think, however, that in a criminal prosecution against the police, the prosecutor has a very tough row to hoe.*

rub

don't rub it in (*spoken*) used to say that someone should not draw attention to something that is unpleasant or embarrassing for you ○ *Of course too much good fortune could give rise to someone else's envy, so don't rub it in by boasting.*

★ **there's the rub** used when there is a problem or contradiction that is difficult or impossible to deal with ○ *"I am definitely not part of the club. They think I am this ferocious feminist who doesn't approve of them." And there's the rub. Women are much more likely to imagine they are being criticized even when they are not.*

≣ This is from the well-known speech that begins "to be or not to be" in Shakespeare's play "Hamlet," act 3 scene 1, when Hamlet is wondering whether or not to commit suicide: "To die, to sleep; To sleep, perchance to dream. Ay there's the rub; For in that sleep of death what dreams may come..."

Rubicon

cross the Rubicon to make an important decision that cannot be changed and that will have very important consequences ○ *Today the Irish government has crossed the Rubicon in favor of the Euro.*

≣ The Rubicon was a small river that separated Roman Italy from Gaul, the province ruled by Julius Caesar. Caesar

≣ crossed the Rubicon in 49 BC, invaded Roman Italy, and started a civil war. "The die is cast" is based on the same incident.

rug

★ **pull the rug from under someone's feet** to suddenly stop helping and supporting someone ○ *Every time we have been close to saving the shipyard, the Government has pulled the rug from under our feet.*

sweep something under the rug to try to forget about something and hide it because you find it embarrassing or shameful ○ *By sweeping the wrongdoing under the rug, executives seek to avoid being accused of mismanagement by directors and shareholders.*

rule

★ **a rule of thumb** a general rule about something that you can be confident will be right in most cases ○ *A good rule of thumb for any type of studio photography is to use no more light sources than are strictly necessary.*

≣ This expression probably dates back to the use of the first joint of the thumb as a unit of measurement.

rules

★ **bend the rules** to do something that is not normally allowed, either to help someone else or for your own advantage ○ *The river authorities said they were willing to bend the rules for us and allowed us to go through the first lock.*

run

a dry run or
a test run or
a trial run a trial or test procedure that you carry out in order to see if a plan or process will work properly ○ *Before we started we did a test run, checking out all the streets and offices we would use, and*

planning our escape route.

★ **give someone a run for their money** to put up a very strong challenge in a contest which someone else is expected to win fairly easily ○ *The British team gave the host side a run for its money to finish a close second in the team competition.*

have someone on the run to be in a stronger position than your opponent, so that you can control their actions and defeat them ○ *It is clear that the opposition thinks it has him on the run.*

in the long run or
over the long run after or taking account of a long period of time ○ *We should look at not just who would be better for this district but who would be better in the long run for the nation.*

runaround

give someone the runaround to deliberately try to mislead or confuse someone and not tell them the truth about something which they need or want to know ○ *In early August, someone close could give you the runaround, especially where it concerns money or other joint matters.*

running

★ **be in the running** to have a good chance of getting a job or winning a prize ○ *The US needs a win tonight to still be in the running for the gold.*

▤ If a horse is "in the running," it has a good chance of winning a race.

rush

a mad rush an uncontrolled movement of people attempting to get something that there is not enough of ○ *Once the gates opened, there was a mad rush for the closest seats.*

Ss

saber

★ **saber-rattling** a situation in which someone is behaving very aggressively and making threats, often of military action, although it is not certain how serious they are or whether they will actually carry out their threats ○ *After more than a week of saber-rattling, the two countries have agreed to talk about their differences.*

A saber is a heavy sword with a curved blade that was used in the past by soldiers on horseback.

sack

hit the sack to go to bed ○ *It was raining and we were tired, so we only half-unpacked the car and then hit the sack.*

In the past, people sometimes used sacks and hay as bedding.

saddle

in the saddle in charge of the affairs of a particular country, or making the important decisions in an organization ○ *It is his bad luck to be in the saddle when his country has to decide which road it is now going to follow.*

tall in the saddle or **high in the saddle** showing that you are successful in your behavior and your attitude ○ *Robinson stood tall in the saddle and aimed his darts accurately.*

safe

better safe than sorry said when you want to encourage a course of action that is careful rather than risky ○ *These security measures seem tough, but better safe than sorry.*

★ **play it safe** to avoid any risks ○ *The pilot decided that Christchurch was too far away, and played it safe, landing at Wellington.*

safety

★ **there is safety in numbers** when danger is present it is safer to be in a group than to be alone ○ *If you walk to or from school, do so with other students as there is safety in numbers.*

sailing

smooth sailing easy to do or achieve ○ *Once I got used to the diet it was smooth sailing. I lost 20 pounds over a four-month period and the weight loss has been maintained.*

"Smooth sailing" is sailing in favorable conditions, without any difficulties.

sails

trim your sails to change your behavior to deal with a difficult situation, for example, by limiting your demands, needs, or expectations ○ *Mr. Lee, for his part, has already begun trimming his sails in preparation for dealing with the new government.*

To trim sails means to adjust them according to the strength and direction of the wind.

salad

someone's salad days (literary) the time when someone was young and inexperienced ○ *The Grand Hotel did not seem to have changed since her salad days.*

This is a quotation from Shakespeare's "Antony and Cleopatra" (Act 1, Scene 5), when Cleopatra is talking about her youth: "My salad days, When I was green in judgment."

saloon

the last chance saloon for someone the final opportunity for someone to succeed in what they are doing ○ *The boxers understand one thing clearly. As far as the world title goes, Saturday is the last chance saloon for both of them.*

salt

★ **no one worth their salt would do something** used to say that no one who is good at their job would consider doing a particular thing ○ *No player worth his salt wants to play in the minor leagues.*

> In the past, salt was expensive and rare. Roman soldiers were paid a "salarium" or salt money, so they could buy salt and stay healthy.

★ **rub salt into the wound** to make something even worse for someone, for example, by reminding them of their failures or faults or by increasing their difficulties ○ *Compensation paid to criminals is rubbing salt into the wounds of victims of serious crimes.*

the salt of the earth a person or people whom you admire for their honesty and reliability ○ *These are good people, rather rough-and-ready, but the salt of the earth.*

> This expression comes from the Bible, when Jesus tells his followers that they are the salt that gives the earth its flavor. (Matthew 5:13)

take something with a grain of salt
or
take something with a pinch of salt to not rely on something, such as a piece of information, because it may not be accurate or true ○ *You have to take these questionnaire results with a pinch of salt because respondents in such surveys tend to give the answers they feel they should.*

A pinch of salt or a grain of salt is a small amount of salt held between your thumb and your first finger. Some people believe that this expression refers to the King of Pontus, Mithridates VI, who lived in the first century BC. It is said that he made himself immune to poison by swallowing small amounts of it with a grain of salt. However, other people think that it is a medieval English expression, which suggests that you need to be suspicious of unlikely stories in the same way that you need salt with food.

sand

be built on sand to not have a strong or a proper basis, and therefore to be likely to fail or come to an end ○ *He moved into the newspaper business in the Seventies. It was an empire built on sand. The newspapers folded, and by 1981 he was bankrupt.*

> This expression relates to a story in the Bible (Matthew 7:24-27), where Jesus compares the people who follow his teachings to a wise man, who built his house on rock. When floods came, the house built on rock remained standing, while others collapsed.

sands

shifting sands a situation that keeps changing and is therefore difficult to deal with ○ *Even his critics in the West have acknowledged his shrewd tactical skills in the shifting sands of Arab politics.*

sandwich

someone is one sandwich short of a picnic used about someone who is very stupid or is behaving very strangely. This expression is usually used humorously. ○ *His daughter confirmed that her father was definitely one sandwich short of a picnic.*

sardines

be packed like sardines to be fitted tightly into a small space and therefore to be unable to move around easily ○ *The people are in appalling conditions. They're packed like sardines on the ship. They can barely move so the sanitary conditions are very, very bad.*

≋ The image here is of canned sardines
≋ that have been tightly packed.

sauce

what's sauce for the goose is sauce for the gander → see **goose**

saying

it goes without saying something is so obvious that it does not need to be said or explained ○ *And of course it goes without saying that if there's anything you should need while you're out here, please don't hesitate to call me here at the embassy.*

scales

the scales have fallen from someone's eyes *(literary)* used when someone suddenly realizes the truth about something after a long period of not understanding it or of being deceived about it ○ *The scales have finally fallen from his eyes and he realizes that he's made a dreadful mistake.*

≋ This is a reference to the Bible story of
≋ Saul, who became blind after he had a
≋ vision of God on the road to Damascus
≋ (Acts 9:18). Saul became a Christian
≋ after a follower of Jesus restored his
≋ sight. The Bible says that at the
≋ moment when Saul's sight was
≋ restored, it was as if scales had
≋ suddenly fallen from his eyes.

scene

★ **on the scene** at the place where something is happening ○ *Austin police are on the scene of a shooting near William Cannon Drive.*

★ **set the scene for something**

1 *(journalism)* to briefly tell people what they need to know about a subject or topic, so that they can understand what is going to happen or be said next ○ *To set the scene for this latest program exploring the improvement in East-West relations, here's Kevin Connolly from Moscow.*

2 to create the conditions in which a particular event is likely to happen ○ *The first hour's play set the scene for a superbly entertaining day of world-class tennis.*

scenes

★ **behind the scenes** in private or in secret, rather than publicly ○ *The President's remarks put in the public arena a debate which has been going on behind the scenes for months.* ○ *The debate was postponed for a third time after another day of intensive behind-the-scenes negotiations.*

≋ This refers to the scenes or scenery
≋ used on the stage in the theater, and
≋ was originally used to refer to those
≋ events in a play that took place off-
≋ stage.

scent

throw someone off the scent to deliberately confuse or deceive someone who is trying to find out the truth about something, by making them believe something that is not true ○ *The murderer tried to throw the cops off the scent by claiming that he saw another man attacking the woman.*

≋ This is a reference to hounds that get
≋ distracted from the trail of an animal
≋ they are hunting because of another
≋ smell.

school

★ **of the old school** having traditional ideas and values, and being fairly old-fashioned ○ *As a builder of the old school, he did not always see eye to eye with* designers of new houses. ○ *She is very much an old-school nurse and her outlook leads to clashes with other staff*

the school of hard knocks a very difficult or unpleasant life ○ *He graduated from the school of hard knocks as well – most of his family perished in the war.*

This is being contrasted with a formal academic education and the qualifications obtained by studying at a school or college. A similar phrase sometimes used is "the University of Life."

school of thought a particular set of opinions about a subject, when there are many different views ○ *There is also the school of thought that teams should play hard all the time.*

science

blind someone with science to tell someone about something in a complex or technical way so that they have great difficulty in understanding it ○ *As a teenage, amateur photographer, I learned all the technical jargon so I could impress people by blinding them with science.*

score

★ **know the score** to know what the real facts of a situation are and how they affect you, even though you may not like them ○ *Taylor knows the score now, and what will happen if he fails.*

★ **settle a score** or
settle an old score to take revenge for something that someone has done to you in the past ○ *The ethnic groups turned on each other to settle old scores, leaving millions dead.*

scratch

★ **something or someone is not up to scratch** used about something or someone that is not as good as they ought to be ○ *Athletes have no one to blame but themselves if their performances are not up to scratch.*

In the past, boxers started a fight with their left feet on a line drawn on the ground, known as the scratch. When a boxer was knocked down, they were allowed thirty seconds' rest before coming "up to the scratch" once more. A boxer who was not at the line in time lost the fight.

★ **start from scratch** to create something completely new, rather than adding to something that already exists ○ *She moved to a strange place where she had to make new friends and start a new life from scratch.*

In the past, the starting line for races was often a line scratched in the earth.

screw

have a screw loose *(informal)* to be slightly crazy ○ *My sister looked at me as if I had a screw loose.*

The image is of a piece of machinery that needs to be adjusted or repaired.

screws

put the screws on someone to use pressure or threats to make someone do what you want ○ *They had to put the screws on Harper. So far, he was the only person who might know something.*

This is a reference to a method of torture called the thumbscrew; see the explanation at "tighten the screws on someone."

tighten the screws on someone to increase the pressure on someone to make them do what you want ○ *NATO is tightening the screws on the president and piling on the pressure.*

These expressions are a reference to a method of torture called the thumbscrew. The prisoner's thumbs were pressed between two bars of iron which were then tightened by means of a screw.

scum

★ **the scum of the earth** the very lowest or worst sort of person. This expression is usually meant to be insulting. ○ *Animal and child abusers are the true scum of the earth. They are so low that every single one of them would need to stand on a ladder to kiss a snake.*

sea

at sea

★ **all at sea** very confused by a situation; unable to understand a situation ○ *When he was in prison, he knew at least where he stood. Now that he's been released, he's all at sea.*

≣ The reference here is to a ship or a boat that has gotten lost.

★ **a sea change** *(literary)* a complete change in someone's attitudes or behavior ○ *Supermarkets have a huge influence on what we eat and will continue to do so until there is a sea change in political thinking on food.*

≣ This phrase is taken from act 1 scene 2 of Shakespeare's play "The Tempest"(1611), which begins with a storm at sea and is a tale of magic and transformation: "Full fathom five thy father lies; Of his bones are coral made: Those are pearls that were his eyes: Nothing of him that doth fade, But doth suffer a sea-change Into something rich and strange."

seams

The seams of a piece of clothing are the places where the separate pieces of cloth used to make it are stitched together.

★ **burst at the seams** to be completely full of people or things ○ *If your shed is bursting at the seams or you can't get your car into the garage because of the clutter, it's time to get organized.*

come apart at the seams

1 to be in a very bad state and about to fail ○ *Teachers have given a warning that the public school system is in danger of coming apart at the seams because of cuts in government funding.*

2 to behave in a strange or illogical way, because you are under severe mental strain ○ *He stood for a moment, breathing deeply; he was coming apart at the seams, something he had never thought would happen to him.*

season

★ **open season on someone or something** when a lot of people are criticizing or attacking someone or something ○ *It seems that, as far as the media are concerned, it's open season on the first family.*

≣ In hunting, the open season is the period of the year when it is legal to hunt particular types of animals or birds.

seat

fly by the seat of your pants to do something difficult or dangerous using only your instincts, because you lack the right kind of experience or information about it ○ *The truth is that neither experts nor mothers know as much as each might wish; to a great extent, all of us fly by the seat of our pants and try to learn quickly from experience.*

≣ If you fly an aircraft by the seat of your pants, you do not use maps or instruments.

★ **in the hot seat** in a position where you have to make important or difficult decisions, or answer difficult questions ○ *The club was formed in 1900 and since 1902 they have had only seven managers. Syd King was the longest-serving with 30 years in the hot seat from 1902.*

★ **take a back seat**

1 to allow other people to have all the power, importance, or responsibility ○ *You will be aware that there are some situations when it is wise to take a back seat and some where it is appropriate to fight for your, and others', rights.*

2 if one thing takes a back seat to another, people give the first thing less attention because they think that it is less important or less interesting than the other thing ○ *Dr. McLaren's own private life takes a back seat to the problems and difficulties of his patients.*

security

a security blanket something that provides someone with a feeling of safety and comfort when they are in a situation that worries them or makes them nervous ○ *To small children, teachers are security blankets – loved, respected, trusted.*

A young child's security blanket is a piece of cloth or clothing that the child holds and often chews in order to feel comforted.

seed

go to seed

1 to allow yourself to become out of shape, messy, or fat as you grow older ○ *Once he had carried a lot of muscle but now he was going to seed.*

2 to become dirty and neglected because of lack of care ○ *The report painted a grim picture of an America going to seed, its bridges and roads falling apart, its national parks neglected.*

When vegetables such as lettuce go to seed, they produce flowers and seeds, and are no longer fit to eat..

seed corn resources or people that will produce benefits in the future rather than immediately ○ *I regard the teachers as the people who are planting the seed corn for the future and therefore I regard their work as crucially important.*

A farmer's seed corn is the grain that is used for planting rather than being sold or eaten.

seeds

★ **sow the seeds of something** or **plant the seeds of something** to start the process that causes a particular problem or benefit to develop ○ *Shortly after that came foreign armies, foreign settlers and foreign apartheid, which planted the seeds of today's crises in Africa.*

send

★ **send someone packing** to tell someone very forcefully or in an unsympathetic way to leave a place, job or position ○ *We had an idyllic life in the country until I decided I wanted to live alone for the first time in my life and I sent my boyfriend packing.*

sense

a sixth sense knowledge or understanding about something that does not seem to come through the ordinary five senses ○ *Maggie Hardin has a sixth sense about people's ailments.*

shade

put someone in the shade to be so impressive that you make another person or thing seem unimportant by comparison ○ *Although now in her seventies, Joan Collins always stuns the crowds with her chic outfits and still manages to put younger women in the shade.*

Shade here means the shadow or darkness produced by blocking the light.

shades

shades of someone or something said when someone or something reminds you of another person or thing ○ *Andie MacDowell stars in the bizarre mystery thriller Ruby Cairo, as the wife of* *a crook who has faked his death (shades of The Third Man, perhaps?).*

≡ "Shade" is an old word for "ghost."

shadow

afraid of your own shadow very timid or nervous ○ *They're all afraid of their own shadows. Can't say I blame them. After all, this is a police state.*

★ **cast a long shadow over something** to have an influence over something, usually a bad one, that lasts for a long time ○ *Cancer has cast its long shadow over almost every family in the country.*

★ **a shadow of someone's or something's former self** said of someone or something that you think is much less powerful or capable than they used to be ○ *Kevin dreaded going downhill as a football player. He hated the thought of ending up a shadow of his former self.*

shakes

in two shakes of a sheep's tail (old-fashioned, spoken) very soon or very quickly ○ *I'll be back in two shakes of a sheep's tail.*

no great shakes ineffective, useless, or of poor quality ○ *This restaurant is no great shakes gastronomically, but the portions are huge.*

≡ This expression probably refers to shaking dice and getting a low score, although there are other possible explanations.

shape

whip something into shape

★ **get something into shape** to use whatever methods are necessary to change or improve something, so that it is in the condition that you want it to be in ○ *After a successful career at the Italian central bank, few people doubt his ability to whip the economy into shape.*

shape up or ship out said to or about someone who should start behaving in a more reasonable or responsible way, or else they should leave the place where they are or give up what they are doing ○ *The message to every player in the team is clear – shape up or ship out.*

shave

have a close shave to very nearly have an accident or disaster or to very nearly suffer a defeat ○ *Gingrich had a close shave in the 1990 general election.*

shebang

the whole shebang (informal) everything; the most complete version of something ○ *And if history rings true, the winner of that match will win the whole shebang.*

≡ No one knows the exact origins of the word "shebang," which only occurs in this expression.

sheep

★ **the black sheep** or **the black sheep of the family** someone who is very different from the other people in their family or group and who is considered bad or worthless by them ○ *My aunt was very famous in those days, but because she was the black sheep of the family I was never encouraged to talk about her.*

≡ Black sheep are less valuable than white sheep since their wool cannot be dyed. In addition, people used to associate the color black with evil and wrongdoing.

separate the sheep from the goats to examine a group of things or people and decide which ones are good and which are bad ○ *It is getting harder and harder to separate the sheep from the goats among the 4,000 or so titles for children that are published every year.*

≡ The Bible says that on the Day of Judgment, Jesus will divide His sheep from the goats (Matthew 25:32). The sheep represent those who are going to heaven, and the goats represent those who are going to hell.

someone might as well be hanged for a sheep as a lamb (British) used to say that someone will suffer or be punished whatever they do, so they might as well do something really bad if they can get some enjoyment or profit from it ○ *This seductive thought process – I might as well be hanged for a sheep as a lamb – is a trap that awaits all dieters. After succumbing to one cookie you feel such a failure you consume the whole package.*

For a long time in the past in England, the penalty for sheep stealing was death.

sheet

start with a clean sheet to be allowed to forget previous debts or mistakes, and so be given a new chance to succeed at something ○ *The Christmas break has erased unhappy memories and allowed the government to start the new year with a clean sheet.*

sheets

★ **three sheets to the wind** (old-fashioned) extremely drunk ○ *He wouldn't stand a chance playing against me even if I were three sheets to the wind.*

This old expression comes from sailing. A boat with three sheets to the wind (that is, not properly secured) would lurch, much as a drunken sailor would.

shelf

on the shelf not currently active, engaged, or being used ○ *Gaiter said he pushed to re-establish the team after it sat on the shelf for a few years.*
shelf life the length of time that something will last ○ *A large proportion of small businesses have a short shelf life.*

shell

★ **come out of your shell** to become less shy, and more talkative and friendly ○ *She used to be very timid and shy but I think she's come out of her shell.*
play a shell game to deliberately deceive people, for example, by changing things or pretending to change things, in order to gain an advantage ○ *The union accused the mine owners of playing a shell game, planning to open mines in the future with the intention of hiring non-union miners.*

The shell game is an old confidence trick. An object is hidden under one of three cups, which are then moved out of their original order. The victim bets on where the object is, and typically gets it wrong. The trick may have become known as the shell game because it was originally done with walnut shells rather than cups.

shine

take the shine off something to make something less enjoyable than it should be ○ *There are two factors which may take the shine off the immediate euphoria following the end of the coup.*
take a shine to someone (old-fashioned) to like someone a lot from the very first time that you meet them ○ *Laura took a shine to her at the interview and offered her the job on the spot.*

ship

abandon a sinking ship to leave an organization or cause that is about to fail completely ○ *When the company's director resigned, CEOs of rival companies accused him of abandoning a sinking ship.*
★ **jump ship** to leave an organization or cause, either because you think it is about to fail or because you want to join a rival organization ○ *I think that if WWE does not start utilizing Christian in say a year,*

then he should jump ship to TNA.

> If sailors jump ship, they leave their ship without permission and do not return.

run a tight ship to keep firm control of the way your business or organization is run, so that it is well organized and efficient ○ *Andy, our team coach, is very organized and confident. He runs a tight ship and he does a great job.*

when someone's ship comes in when someone becomes rich and successful. People use this expression without really expecting that it will happen. ○ *When my ship comes in, I'll buy a big house in the country.*

> This is a reference to a merchant's ship returning home with a heavy load of cargo.

shirt

give someone the shirt off your back to be willing to do anything to help someone, even if it would be a great loss to you ○ *"He was such a good caring man, he would help anybody out, give the shirt off his back," James said.*

keep your shirt on to calm down and not be angry or impatient ○ *"For heaven's sake, hurry up, Pete!" – "All right. Keep your shirt on! I'm just coming."*

lose your shirt to lose all your money on a bad investment or bet ○ *If you play cards with these guys, you can lose your shirt.*

a stuffed shirt someone in an important position who behaves in a very formal or pompous way ○ *His seminars work because he keeps things simple. He walks around talking like an ordinary person, rather than a stuffed shirt.*

> This refers to a shirt being displayed on a mannequin in a clothing store. The mannequin is hollow and has no use apart from filling the space occupied by the shirt.

shoe

drop the other shoe to complete a task by doing the second and final part of it ○ *Last week, TimeWarner Inc. dropped the other shoe in its two-step $13.86 billion acquisition of Warner Communications Inc.*

if the shoe fits used to tell someone that unpleasant or critical remarks that have been made about them are probably true or fair. The usual British expression is **if the cap fits**. ○ *Although I trained as an architect, I have always been interested in interior design too. So, when people saw my work and said "You're an interior designer," I thought "If the shoe fits."*

the shoe is on the other foot a situation has changed completely, so that the people who were previously in a better position are now in a worse one, while the people who were previously in a worse position are now in a better one ○ *I'm in the job. You may have assisted along the way, but as far as I know you're not in a position to remove me. The shoe is now on the other foot.*

> Until the end of the 18th century, shoes could be worn on either foot, as cobblers did not make "right" and "left" shoes. If a person found that one of their shoes hurt their foot, they could try wearing it on their other foot to see if it felt better that way.

wait for the other shoe to drop to expect an event, usually a bad one, to result from something that has already happened ○ *Back then, everybody was waiting for the other shoe to drop. Everybody was always waiting for us to fail.*

> The idea in this expression is that you almost never hear only one footstep; another usually follows.

shoes

fill someone's shoes to do someone's job or hold their position as well as they did ○ *It'll take a good man to fill our old boss's shoes.*

goody-two-shoes someone who tries to impress people in authority by doing everything correctly and being morally very good ○ *The movie centers on a high school goody two-shoes who gets in with a bad crowd.*

★ **put yourself in someone's shoes** to make an effort to imagine how you would feel or act if you were in the same situation as a particular person ○ *You should be kinder when considering others, and put yourself in their shoes once in a while.*

shake in your shoes to be very frightened or anxious about something that is about to happen ○ *The prospect of having to give evidence against him in court made the witnesses shake in their shoes.*

someone wouldn't like to be in another person's shoes used about someone who would not like to be in the same situation as a particular person ○ *He hasn't made any friends and has upset a lot of powerful people. I wouldn't like to be in his shoes if he comes back to work.*

★ **step into someone's shoes** to take over someone's job or position ○ *In America, if a president resigns or dies in office, the vice-president steps into his shoes.*

shoestring

★ **on a shoestring** using very little money ○ *Newly divorced with two children to raise, she was living on a shoestring.* ○ *"Douchebag" is quite accomplished for a movie that was shot on a shoestring.*

  The reference here is to the very small amount of money that is needed to buy shoestrings, also called shoelaces.

shoo-in

"Shoo-in" is sometimes spelled "shoe-in."

be a shoo-in for something to be certain to win something, such as an

election or a contest ○ *The president looks as though he's a shoo-in for another four years.*

shooting, shootin'

sure as shooting or
sure as shootin' very certainly; without doubt or mistake ○ *Sure as shooting, the man's car was found in a nearby field, as Guidry had predicted.*

  People often pronounce this expression in the informal way, without a 'g' sound on the end of "shooting," and this reflects the rural origin of the saying.

shop

close up shop to be forced to close your business, for example, because of difficult economic conditions ○ *Unless business picks up soon, some of the 245 foreign-owned banks in Switzerland may have to close up shop.*

set up shop to start a business or start doing business ○ *Vendors set up shop in showcase buildings in the center of the grounds.*

talk shop to talk about work to other people who do the same type of work, in a way that is boring for other people to hear ○ *Although I get on well with my colleagues, if you hang around together all the time you just end up talking shop, which gets boring.*

shopping

a shopping list a list of demands or requirements that someone wants to get from a particular person or organization ○ *Mr. Baker presented a shopping list of additional help the United States was requiring from its allies.*

short

have someone by the short and curlies to have someone completely in your power ○ *The unions' chief negotiator last night said: "We had the company by the short and curlies."*

In this expression, "short and curlies" may refer to a person's pubic hair, to hair on the back of their neck, or to the hair in their beard.

sell someone short to fail to provide someone with all the things that they think you ought to provide ○ *The president accused his former aides of failing to support him, of selling him short.*

The reference here is to someone being cheated by being given less of something than they have paid for.

sell yourself short to be modest about your achievements and good qualities, so that other people do not realize just how good you are ○ *Be confident in your ideas and ability, and don't sell yourself short.*

shot

a big shot an important or powerful person. This expression is always used disapprovingly. ○ *He's now a big shot in some bank, and thinks he can do what he wants.*

a cheap shot a remark or action meant to injure someone in a way that most people disapprove of ○ *The newpapers published what I think is an incredibly cheap shot at teachers today.*

by a long shot used to add emphasis to a statement, especially a negative statement or one that contains a superlative ○ *We have to know what is going on, and we don't, not yet, not by a long shot.*

do something like a shot to do something immediately, because you are very eager to do it or because something forces you to do it ○ *If I won the lottery, I would give up my job like a shot.*

★ **fire a warning shot across someone's bows** or
fire a shot across someone's bows to do something that shows that you are prepared to oppose someone strongly if they do not stop or change what they are

doing ○ *Spain's agriculture minister departed from his prepared speech to fire a shot across Norway's bows.*

The bows are the front part of a ship.

★ **give something your best shot** to try as hard as you can to achieve something, even though you know how difficult it is ○ *I gave it my best shot, but I wasn't quite good enough to win.*

a long shot
1 a way of solving a difficulty or problem that, although it has little chance of success, is still worth trying ○ *You could try to find her. It's a long shot but you could look in the phone book.*
2 something that is very unlikely to happen ○ *Observers say a deal between the White House and Congress is a long shot in an election year, when both political parties are trying to get the upper hand.*

The reference here is to someone shooting at a target from a very long distance.

★ **a shot in the arm** help and encouragement at a time when you badly need it ○ *The remaining problems can be dealt with in weeks, and to risk further delay would be to deny the world economy a desperately needed shot in the arm.*

A "shot" is an injection, in this case an injection of a drug that stimulates you.

someone's best shot at something someone's best chance of achieving something ○ *Mazankowski and other analysts say Canada's best shot at economic recovery is continued growth in the United States.*

shotgun

ride shotgun to sit in the front passenger seat of a car ○ *While at the track, winners will get to ride shotgun with Mario Andretti in a two-seat Indy car.*

This expression comes from the days of stage coaches, when a man with a shotgun sat next to the driver for protection.

a shotgun wedding

1 a wedding that takes place because the bride is pregnant ○ *It certainly wasn't a shotgun wedding, but their courtship was pretty damn fast.*

2 a merger or agreement that comes about quickly, out of necessity ○ *Hotel owners say the merger was a shotgun wedding which improperly ended the franchise.*

The image suggested by this expression is of the father of the bride threatening the groom with a shotgun if he doesn't agree to marry.

shots

★ **call the shots** to make all the important decisions in an organization or situation ○ *Is the military really the power behind the President now? Who really calls the shots?*

This may refer to someone shooting and saying which part of the target they intend to hit. Alternatively, it may refer to a pool player saying which ball they intend to hit or which pocket they intend to hit it into.

shoulder

come straight from the shoulder to be direct and completely honest ○ *His opinions about top politicians in Washington and New York come straight from the shoulder. "The president," he says, "was out of touch with reality."*

In boxing, a blow that is straight from the shoulder is a direct and powerful blow, delivered with a straight arm.

★ **give someone the cold shoulder** to deliberately ignore someone ○ *He gave me the cold shoulder at the party; he didn't talk to me at all.*

A shoulder is a cut of meat that includes the upper part of the animal's front leg. This expression refers to a medieval practice where important guests were given roast meat. Less important people were only given cold meat left over from previous meals.

put your shoulder to the wheel to put a great deal of effort into a difficult task ○ *These hard-working and decent people are prepared to put their shoulders to the wheel, to build a better society.*

In the days when people traveled in carriages or carts on roads that often got very muddy, people would help free vehicles that were stuck by leaning against a wheel and pushing.

★ **a shoulder to cry on** someone you can rely on to give you emotional support when you are upset or anxious ○ *If you ever need someone to hold your hand or a shoulder to cry on, we're here for you, buddy.*

★ **stand shoulder to shoulder** to work cooperatively with and support someone else in order to achieve a common aim ○ *President Obama told South Korea that the US stands shoulder to shoulder with its Asian ally after North Korea's attack.*

shoulders

★ **broad shoulders** an ability to bear a lot of responsibility or difficulty ○ *While Ella-Tina carries the show on her broad shoulders, she is well matched by supporting performers.*

show

The show referred to in the following expressions is a theatrical performance.

get the show on the road to put a plan or an idea into action ○ *He checked his watch. "Shouldn't we get this show on the road, now that Rolfe's here?"*

keep the show on the road to ensure that a plan or an idea continues to operate successfully ○ *The government is* going to have to find something to offer the unions during these talks if it is to keep the show on the road.

★ **run the show** to be in control of an organization, event, or situation ○ *The fear is that you have on paper the restoration of democracy, but in reality the military still run the show.*

★ **show and tell** an occasion when someone presents information about something and talks about it ○ *Children learned how different aspects of law enforcement work through show and tell.* ○ *There are show-and-tell talks about numerous subjects, including Florida's venomous snakes and large reptile invaders.*

The origin of this expression is a school activity for young children called show and tell, in which a child brings an interesting item to school and tells the other children about it.

★ **steal the show** to get more attention or praise than the other people or things in a show or other event ○ *It was the Chinese swimmers who stole the show on the first day of competition. They set new Asian records in almost every race.*

★ **stop the show** to give an outstanding performance in a show or other event ○ *Twelve-year-old Reggie Jackson stopped the show last night, singing "America the Beautiful."* ○ *She got a standing ovation for her show-stopping number at the concert yesterday evening.*

showers

send someone to the showers to disqualify someone from a game or exclude them from an activity, because of their bad behavior or poor performance ○ *Within the first 15 minutes, four players had been sent to the showers for fighting.*

In baseball and other sports, players who are sent off cannot return to the field and so can take a shower before the game is finished.

shrift

★ **get short shrift** to be treated very rudely or to receive very little attention ○ *Employees' complaints are getting short shrift.*

"Shrift" is an old word meaning confession to a priest. In the past, condemned criminals were allowed only a few minutes to make their confession before they were executed.

shuffle

get lost in the shuffle to not be noticed and have no attention paid to you ○ *He worries campaign finance reform will get lost in the shuffle of White House priorities.*

When decks of cards are properly shuffled, it is impossible to know where a particular card is.

sick

sick as a dog very ill or very upset ○ *In the children's story The Chocolate Wedding, the main character, Lulu, eats 16 chocolate eggs and is as sick as a dog.*

side

★ **be on the safe side** to do something as a precaution, although it is unlikely to be necessary ○ *I reserved the car for an extra half-hour, just to be on the safe side.*

be on your side to give you an advantage and help you to achieve something ○ *Having time and money on your side always helps, of course.*

laugh out of the other side of your mouth → see mouth

let someone's side down (mainly British) to disappoint people by doing something badly or by doing something that people do not approve of ○ *My presence would not have changed anything, but I felt I had let our side down by not being around when the Opposition outfoxed us.*

A side is one of the teams in a game or competition.

★ **look on the bright side** to try to be cheerful about a bad situation by concentrating on the few good things in it or by thinking about how it could have been even worse ○ *I tried to look on the bright side, to be grateful that I was healthy. I didn't talk to other people at all about my disastrous relationship with my boyfriend.*

on the side of the angels → see **angels**

sunny side up

1 (*journalism*) bright and cheerful ○ *It's not always easy to be sunny side up.*

2 used to describe a fried egg that has been cooked on one side only and not turned over in the pan ○ *Nicole cooked his eggs the way he liked them – sunny side up with a drizzle of melted butter on top.*

sides

talk out of both sides of your mouth → see **mouth**

two sides of the same coin or **opposite sides of the same coin** two opposite aspects of the same situation or idea ○ *He says he draws no line between tragedy and comedy. "I've always felt that they are inseparable, that they are two sides of the same coin."*

sight

★ **at first sight** used to describe your first impression of someone or something, usually to indicate that this first impression was wrong or incomplete ○ *Nothing is ever quite as good or quite as bad as it looks at first sight.*

look a sight (*informal*) to look messy, ridiculous, etc. ○ *By the time we got to the restaurant, I was soaking wet and I must have looked a sight.*

★ **lose sight of something** to forget or ignore an important aspect of something because you have other things to think about ○ *As so often happened, Peter, Tommy and Henry had totally lost sight of their real objective.*

out of sight, out of mind used to say that it is easy to forget about someone or something, or to stop caring about them, when you have not seen them for a long time ○ *My boyfriend and I broke up when he went to work in China – it was a case of out of sight, out of mind.*

a sight for sore eyes someone or something that you are very happy to see ○ *A slow start and a strong finish as the Broncos squeak into the playoffs. Wouldn't that be a sight for sore eyes?*

sights

The sights on a weapon such as a rifle are the part that helps you to aim it more accurately.

★ **have something in your sights** to be aiming or trying hard to achieve something, and to have a good chance of success ○ *I am studying at a top university, with good job prospects firmly in my sights.*

This expression is often used more literally to say that someone is looking at a target through the sights of a gun.

★ **set your sights on something** to decide that you want something and to try very hard to get it ○ *Although she came from a family of bankers, Flora set her sights on a career in medicine.*

This expression is also used literally to say that someone is looking at a target through the sights of a gun.

signed

★ **signed and sealed**

★ **signed, sealed and delivered** official and unable to be changed ○ *Well, the agreement is signed and sealed, and there's nothing you can do or say about it.*

In the past, documents were "sealed" with wax into which a special mark or design was pressed using a device called a seal. The mark or design in the wax proved that the document was authentic and had not been opened.

silk

you can't make a silk purse out of a sow's ear said to emphasize that it is impossible to make something really successful or of high quality out of something that is unsuccessful or of poor quality ○ *Well, this just goes to show that you can't make a silk purse out of a sow's ear. It's a truly awful novel, and even when you throw famous stars at it, you can't make it into a great movie.*

silver

born with a silver spoon in your mouth born into a very rich family and having a privileged upbringing. This expression is usually used to show resentment or disapproval. ○ *Samantha was born with a silver spoon in her mouth; there's always someone to pay her bills if her inheritance isn't enough.*

This expression goes back to the 17th century. The reference is to babies from wealthy families being fed using silver spoons.

hand someone something on a silver platter → see **platter**

sing

sing the same tune or **sing the same song**
1 to continue to express the same ideas or opinions that you have expressed before ○ *The president keeps singing the same tune he's been singing for years, which presumably he believes.*
2 if a group of people are singing the same tune, they are all expressing the same opinions about something ○ *Everyone was singing the same tune – one politician after another stood up to declare that there was only one solution to the crisis.*

sink

leave someone to sink or swim to leave someone to do something on their own, with their success or failure depending entirely on their own efforts or abilities ○ *The sad part is that many of these wounded soldiers have been left to sink or swim on their own after serving their country.*

sitting

★ **do something in one sitting** to not stop doing something until you have finished it ○ *She can easily go through a box of chocolates in one sitting.*

six

★ **deep six someone or something** → see **deep**
six of one and half a dozen of the other said when you think that both of two people, situations or possible courses of action are equally bad or equally good ○ *To me it was six of one and half a dozen of the other. They were both at fault.*

size

★ **cut someone down to size** to do or say something to someone who is behaving arrogantly, to show them that they are less important or impressive than they think they are ○ *It may be that people are drawn to work in journalism because of the chance to cut everyone else down to size.*

try something on for size to consider something carefully in order to decide whether you believe it or to try using something in order to decide whether you think that it is good ○ *"Jarvis killed Mr. Rownall?" he said slowly, trying on the idea for size and seeming to find it plausible.*

skeleton

★ **have a skeleton in the closet** to keep secret something that would be scandalous or embarrassing for you if other people knew about it ○ *But* *everybody's got secrets, haven't they? Everybody has a skeleton in the closet.*

skid

be on skid row to have lost everything in your life, usually because of addiction, alcohol, or emotional problems ○ *Gamblers can get through huge amounts of money. They spend their savings, then the mortgage payments stop. It's a downhill spiral and soon they're on Skid Row.*

Skid row is used to refer a poor part of a city where many drunks and homeless people live.

skids

★ **be on the skids** or
hit the skids doing badly and very likely to fail ○ *My marriage was on the skids.*
put the skids to something or someone or
put the skids on something or someone to cause something or someone to do badly or fail ○ *Two new witnesses in the murder case have put the skids to the accused man's alibi.*

skies

praise someone or something to the skies to praise someone or something a lot ○ *If you are a famous athlete, you have to get used to hearing yourself praised to the skies but only minutes later reading about how you are a disaster.*

skin

★ **do something by the skin of your teeth** to just manage to do something, although you very nearly fail ○ *Boston won the title by the skin of their teeth.*

This expression seems to come from the book of Job in the Bible, although its meaning has completely changed. Job loses everything and then says "I am escaped with the skin of my teeth" (Job 19:20), meaning that the skin of his teeth is all he has left.

get under someone's skin
1 to annoy or worry someone ○ *The continuing criticism of his behavior is getting under his skin a little bit.*
2 to cause someone to feel interest or affection ○ *After a slow start, the film gets under your skin because of its affection for its characters and sympathy with the frustrations of small-town life.*
3 to try to find out how someone feels and thinks, so that you are able to understand them better ○ *It is only through getting right under the skin of your colleagues and loved ones that you will be able to relate to them as equals.*

it's no skin off someone's nose
(informal) used to say that someone does not have to worry about something bad that has happened because it only affects or harms other people, or because it is not their responsibility ○ *When I heard she got fired, I thought, it's no skin off my nose. She's not what you'd call a friend, and losing a lousy job like that's no big deal, is it?*

jump out of your skin to receive a sudden unpleasant shock or surprise ○ *When I heard gunshots, I jumped out of my skin.*

make your skin crawl to make you feel disgust ○ *He gave a laugh that made my skin crawl.*

★ **save your own skin** to try to save yourself from something dangerous or unpleasant, often without caring what happens to anyone else ○ *The government is trying to save its own skin rather than trying to help the victims of the disaster.*

★ **skin and bone(s)** very thin, because of lack of food or serious illness ○ *Many villages are deserted. In one we found nomads looking for water. They were skin and bones. They had no food.*

★ **a thick skin** an ability to not be upset by criticism ○ *A woman politician needs a thick skin.*

★ **a thin skin** a tendency to be easily

upset by criticism ○ *He has a thin skin and lacks determination – he's certainly not cut out to be a journalist.*

sky

blow something sky-high to do or say something that completely destroys something, such as someone's hopes or beliefs ○ *All our hopes, plans and dreams have just been blown sky-high.*

out of a clear blue sky completely unexpectedly ○ *Out of a clear blue sky and after 34 months of successive increases, unemployment has dropped by 2%.*

This expression compares an unexpected event to a bolt of lightning from a blue sky. The expressions "out of the blue" and "a bolt from the blue" are based on a similar idea.

★ **the sky's the limit** said when you think it is possible that someone or something will be very successful ○ *"How much are you hoping to make for this charity of yours?" "Well, lots hopefully. I mean the sky's the limit."*

slack

cut someone some slack to make things slightly easier for someone than you normally would, because of their special circumstances or situation ○ *When you're new at a job, colleagues and bosses cut you a little slack. They forgive minor mistakes because you're new.*

★ **take up the slack** or
pick up the slack to start making full use of all of the resources or potential of, for example, an industry, economy, or organization ○ *Losing one of our best players was tough. However, the rest of the team came together and picked up the slack.*

If you take up the slack in a rope, you tighten it.

slam

★ **a slam dunk** a big success that is achieved easily or that is sure to be

achieved ○ *The race has long been considered a slam dunk for Barney Frank, but now it's getting some attention.*

This expression comes from basketball, where a slam dunk is a basket scored by jumping high in the air and throwing the ball down through the basket.

slap

★ **a slap in the face** a situation in which someone upsets you by insulting you or appearing to reject you ○ *The daughter of a murdered terrorist victim said that it is a slap in the face when convicted terrorist killers are being treated like national heroes.*

a slap on the wrist a very light punishment or reprimand ○ *Other than a few slaps on the wrist, the General went unpunished.*

slate

In the past, people used pieces of slate for writing on. Storekeepers would write customers' debts on their slates, and wipe them clean when the debts were paid.

a clean slate an opportunity to succeed without some bad event from the past interfering ○ *They wanted to make sure that when the new director took over he or she would have a clean slate.*

★ **wipe the slate clean**
1 to get rid of an existing system so that you can replace it with a new one ○ *There's a strong desire among the public to wipe the slate clean and to call for early presidential and legislative elections.*
2 to earn enough money to pay off your debts, so that you no longer owe money to anyone ○ *Over a decade he wiped the firm's slate clean of debt and brought it into healthy profit.*
3 to be punished for something wrong that you have done, or to make amends for it by your good behavior, so that you

can start your life again without feeling guilty about it ○ *Serving a prison sentence makes some people believe they have wiped the slate clean.*

sleep

★ **not lose any sleep over something** to not worry about something at all ○ *I'd like to have a little more money – who wouldn't – but I won't lose any sleep over it.*

sleep on it to wait until the next day to make a decision, so that you have some time to consider it carefully ○ *Don't make any promises today. We'll talk about it tomorrow when you've had a chance to sleep on it.*

sleeve

★ **have something up your sleeve** to have a secret idea or plan which you can use to gain an advantage over other people ○ *The company's strategy for improvement is simple, according to Mr. Pearse: "We've got nothing fancy up our sleeves. We just have to be better."*

> If someone wanted to cheat at cards, they could hide a good card up their sleeve to use at an appropriate time.

laugh up your sleeve (*mainly British*) to be secretly amused by something, for example, because someone has done something very badly, or because you know something that nobody else knows. This expression is usually used to show disapproval. ○ *He wondered just how smugly she was laughing up her sleeve at his ineptitude.*

> The image here is of someone trying to hide the fact that they are laughing by putting their hand or arm in front of their mouth.

sleeves

roll up your sleeves to get ready to work hard, often as part of a group of people ○ *He was very much a team player, rolling up his sleeves and getting down to work.*

slings

the slings and arrows of something the unpleasant things that happen to you that are not your fault ○ *She was very ill at that time, which reduced her ability to cope with the slings and arrows of life.*

> This is a quotation from a speech in Shakespeare's play "Hamlet," where Hamlet is considering whether or not to kill himself: "To be, or not to be - that is the question; Whether 'tis nobler in the mind to suffer The slings and arrows of outrageous fortune, Or to take arms against a sea of troubles, And by opposing end them?" (Act 3, Scene 1)

slip

a slip of the tongue or
a slip of the pen something that you said or wrote by mistake ○ *The interviewer asked Mr. Clarke about the time he said that The Mirror was read by morons. Mr. Clarke replied that the comment was a slip of the tongue. He added: "I meant to say it was written by morons."*

there is many a slip twixt cup and lip (*literary*) used to express the idea that a plan may easily go wrong before it is completed, and you can never be sure of what will happen ○ *Joe must be a hot favorite to win in Biloxi, but there's many a slip twixt cup and lip.*

> "Twixt" is an old-fashioned word meaning "between."

slippery

slippery as an eel used to describe someone whom it is very difficult to catch, or from whom it is very difficult to get the information that you want ○ *His opponent in the boxing ring was as slippery as an eel, as cunning as a fox and as quick as lightning.*

slope

★ **a slippery slope** a course of action that

cannot be stopped and that will lead to failure or serious trouble ○ *These young people are already on the slippery slope to criminality.*

small

make someone feel small or **make someone look small** to deliberately say or do something that makes someone look or feel stupid, especially in front of other people. ○ *He made me feel small, like an idiot.* ○ *I could see he was going to do whatever he could to make me look small.*

smoke

blow smoke to deliberately confuse or mislead someone in order to deceive them ○ *It was time to see if Sam was just blowing smoke or if he actually had some useful information for us.*

★ **go up in smoke** to fail or end without anything being achieved ○ *But with just eight minutes to go, their dreams of glory went up in smoke. Atlanta scored twice within minutes and went way ahead.*

send out smoke signals to give an indication of your views or intentions, often in an unclear or vague form which then needs to be interpreted ○ *I'll tell you exactly what I think we ought to do, but what kind of smoke signals ought to be sent by the White House is up to them to figure out.*

≡ Smoke signals are columns of smoke which were used to send messages over long distances by Native American tribes.

smoke and mirrors things that are intended to deceive or confuse people ○ *The president claims that his economic plan is free of the smoke and mirrors that have characterized earlier budget plans.*

≡ Magicians sometimes use smoke and mirrors when they are performing tricks, in order to confuse or deceive people.

where there's smoke there's fire or **there's no smoke without fire** used to say that if people are saying something bad about someone, what they are saying is probably true or partly true ○ *I was incredibly upset by the story. It was the main item on the news and people were bound to think where there's smoke there's fire.*

smooth

★ **smooth as silk** extremely smooth, easy, or free from disturbance ○ *The six speed automatic was smooth as silk, even when pushed hard.*

snail

★ **at a snail's pace** very slowly, often too slowly ○ *The economy grew at a snail's pace in the first three months of this year.*

snake

a snake in the grass someone that you strongly dislike and disapprove of because, although they pretend to be your friend, they are actually your enemy and betray you ○ *He's just a snake in the grass. You can't trust that guy.*

≡ This phrase was first used by the Roman poet Virgil in his work "The Eclogues" to refer to a hidden danger.

snake oil something that someone is trying to sell you or make you believe in when you think it is false and is not to be trusted ○ *He said he was in the oil business. He just omitted to say it was the snake oil business.*

≡ Snake oil was a substance typically made from the plant snakeroot. Dishonest salesmen tried to persuade people to buy it, claiming that it was a medicine that would cure their illnesses.

snooze

you snooze, you lose (*informal*) said to mean if you are not paying attention

you may miss a good opportunity
○ *Do your shopping now while there are good deals: remember, you snooze, you lose.*

snow

a snow job lies and exaggerations, intended to deceive or flatter someone. ○ *They have the experience to know the difference between getting information and getting a snow job.*

be able to sell snow to an Eskimo to be so persuasive that you could conceivable sell something to people that they already have plenty of. You can also talk about **selling ice to Eskimos**. ○ *He could sell anything -- even snow to an Eskimo!*

"Eskimo" is an old-fashioned word for the Inuit people of the Arctic regions of North America.

snowball

not a snowball's chance in hell
➜ see **chance**

snug

be as snug as a bug in a rug *(old-fashioned)* to be in a very comfortable situation ○ *Jamieson sat down beside McKinnon. "Ideal working conditions, you said. Snug as a bug in a rug, one might say."*

soap

no soap used to indicate that you have tried to do something but that you have failed ○ *I looked everywhere for him, then finally I went home. I called him at home this morning. No soap.*

sober

sober as a judge *(old-fashioned)* used to emphasize that someone is not drunk ○ *"Have you been drinking?" the policeman asked. Les looked up at him and shook his head. "No. Sober as a judge, officer."*

sock

sock it to someone to achieve a major

victory or advantage over someone ○ *After all, the last time UCLA socked it to the Burnt Orange in Austin, the head coach was run out of town.*

socks

someone or something will knock your socks off said when you think that someone or something is very good and impressive ○ *This band will knock your socks off!*

song

★ **go for a song** to be sold for an unexpectedly low price ○ *I bought this rug from a second-hand shop. I couldn't resist it when I saw it – it was going for a song.*

This expression may be a reference to printed song sheets, which were very cheap. Alternatively, it may refer to small amounts of money that passers-by give to someone who is singing in the street.

make a song and dance about something to react in a very anxious, excited, or angry way to something that is not important ○ *Jan made a great song and dance about the change of plan at first, but she calmed down soon enough.*

sing the same song ➜ see **sing**

sorrows

drown your sorrows to drink a lot of alcohol in order to forget something sad or upsetting that has happened to you ○ *His girlfriend has just dumped him so he's gone off to the club to drown his sorrows.*

soul

bare your soul to someone to tell someone all the thoughts and feelings that are most important to you ○ *We all need someone we can bare our souls to, someone we can confide in.*

a living soul any person at all. This expression is usually used with a negative. ○ *He is HIV Positive, which he has been for ten years, and he hasn't told a living soul.*

★ **sell your soul for something** to do whatever you need to in order to get what you want, even if it involves abandoning your principles or doing something you consider wrong ○ *They have sold their soul to the devil; they do anything for money.*

There are many stories about people who sold their souls to the devil in return for wealth, success, or pleasure. The most famous is about Dr. Faustus, whose story was first told in a book published in Germany in 1587, and later told by writers such as the English writer Marlowe and the German poet Goethe.

sound

sound as a bell in a very good condition and very reliable ○ *The doctor says that grandpa's heart is sound as a bell.*

"Sound" in this expression means whole and undamaged. A bell that has a crack in it will not ring clearly.

soup

in the soup in trouble ○ *She has a knack of landing herself right in the soup.*

south

★ **go south** to fail or stop working ○ *His hopes of a professional singing career went south long ago.*

space

★ **breathing space** a time during which there are no problems expected, allowing someone to rest or do something important ○ *A loan from the IMF has given the country some breathing space to adopt the needed reforms.*

spade

call a spade a spade to speak honestly and directly about something, especially if it is controversial or embarrassing, rather than being careful about what you say ○ *I'm not at all secretive, and I'm not afraid to call a spade a spade.*

In a play by the Ancient Greek dramatist Menander, one of the characters says "I call a fig a fig, and a spade a spade."

spades

★ **have something in spades** to have a lot of something ○ *This Kentucky band have got talent in spades.*

sparks

sparks fly

1 if sparks fly between two people, they discuss something in an angry or excited way ○ *From what I have seen of this TV discussion program, the presenters are not afraid to tackle serious issues or let the sparks fly when necessary.*

2 used to describe a situation or relationship that is very exciting ○ *Whenever two such temperamental artists meet, you know sparks will fly.*

species

an endangered species something that is under threat and that may not continue to exist ○ *Family owned and operated businesses seem to be an endangered species.*

The literal meaning of "endangered species" is a type of plant or animal that is almost extinct, usually because human activity has destroyed its living conditions.

speed

bring someone up to speed to give someone all the latest information about something ○ *I guess I should bring you up to speed on what's happened since I came to see you yesterday.*

bring something up to speed to make something reach its highest level of efficiency ○ *The fear is that the system will not be cheap to bring up to speed.*

spick

| "Spick" is sometimes spelled "spic." |

spick and span very clean, neat, and tidy ○ *When she arrived, she found Ann dusting the furniture, making sure the house was spick and span.*

This expression has developed from an old-fashioned expression "spick and span-new," meaning "very new." "Spick" probably came from a Dutch word meaning "new," and "span-new" meant "completely new."

spin

in a spin so angry, confused, or excited that you cannot act sensibly or concentrate on what you are doing ○ *This news came right out of the blue and it's left me in a spin.*

If a plane goes into a spin, it goes out of control and falls very rapidly toward the ground in a spiraling movement.

spit

be the spitting image of someone if one person is the spitting image of another person, the first person looks exactly like the second ○ *Sam is the spitting image of his father. He's tall and dark, just like his dad.*

The origin of this expression is uncertain, but it may have developed from "spirit and image." If one person was the spirit and image of another, they were alike both in character and physical appearance.

spit and polish used to talk about a place that is very clean or that is being made very clean ○ *The bar, which had been open for two months now, was all spit and polish.*

splash

★ **make a splash** to attract a lot of attention because of something successful that you do or by the way you behave on a particular occasion ○ *She made quite a splash at the party with her outspoken views and colorful and expensive clothes.*

spleen

vent your spleen to express your anger about something ○ *The meeting gave angry staff members the chance to vent their spleen.*

An early system of medicine believed that the spleen was the seat of anger in the body, so "venting" the spleen allowed the anger to escape.

spoon

★ **a greasy spoon** a cheap restaurant that is not particularly clean ○ *We grabbed lunch at a greasy spoon downtown.*

spot

★ **be on the spot** to be in the place where something that you are talking about is actually happening ○ *Ironically, the first that reporters on the spot knew about the release of Mr. Mann was when they heard a news flash on a local radio station.* ○ *The Austrian government has dispatched a group of experts to Thailand to begin an on-the-spot investigation.*

★ **a blind spot** something that you do not understand or know anything about, although you feel that perhaps you should ○ *Computers are a blind spot with me.*

★ **do something on the spot** to do something immediately ○ *Watch out for sales staff who say you'll get a special discount or prize if you sign on the spot.*

★ **have a soft spot for someone** to like or care about someone a lot ○ *It looked to me as if Tom had a soft spot for Emily.*

hit the spot to be very good and to succeed in pleasing people ○ *The company's new ad really hits the spot.*

★ **put someone on the spot** to put

someone in a difficult situation which they cannot avoid, for example, by making them answer awkward questions ○ *You shouldn't have asked Gary whether he's asked Linda to marry him. You put him on the spot and that's very unfair.*

spots

hit the high spots to give attention only to the most important parts ○ *There is enough information here to sink a ship, so we are only going to hit the high spots.*

spring

no spring chicken someone who is no longer young. This expression is often used when you think someone's appearance or behavior is surprising for their age. ○ *At 85, he is no spring chicken, but Enrico Cuccia is busier than ever.*

≡ A spring chicken was a young chicken that was ready to be eaten in the spring time, as opposed to an older bird.

spur

★ **do something on the spur of the moment** to do something suddenly and without planning it in advance ○ *He had decided on the spur of the moment to make the trip south to Vegas.* ○ *Judges currently cannot reflect in their sentencing the difference between a planned killing and a spur-of-the-moment emotional crime.*

square

★ **be back to square one** to have failed completely in what you were trying to do, so that now you have to start again ○ *So we are back to square one. Their costly intervention has been for nothing, a carefully-constructed peace process lies in ruins.*

≡ This expression may refer to board games where the players move counters along a series of squares, and sometimes have to start again at the beginning.

on the square honest ○ *Are you sure this guy's on the square?*

≡ This expression probably comes from the use of a square, a measuring device used to check that a right angle is completely accurate.

squeeze

put the squeeze on someone or something to create difficulty or pressure for someone or something ○ *The recession has put the squeeze on hotel and rental car taxes.*

somebody's main squeeze someone's boyfriend or girlfriend ○ *Keira arrived with her new main squeeze, Liam.*

★ **a tight squeeze** a place in which there is little room to move ○ *Six people can fit round this table. Seven is a tight squeeze.*

stab

★ **make a stab at something**

★ **take a stab at something** to try to do or achieve something in a casual or not very determined way ○ *Companies including Ford have taken a stab at made-to-order automobiles over the years.*

★ **a stab in the dark** an action undertaken or a guess made when you don't have very much information ○ *A vote for Rayne Brown is like taking a stab in the dark: You are not quite sure what is going to happen.*

stack

blow your stack to become very angry with someone and shout at them ○ *My father really blew his stack over this.*

someone would swear on a stack of Bibles said when someone wishes to emphasize that what they are saying is true and could not be mistaken or false ○ *Even with a letter from your employer swearing on a stack of bibles that he intends to employ you for life, getting a mortgage today is not easy.*

stage

★ **set the stage for something** to make preparations so that something can happen ○ *Jamaica's prime minister set the stage for a snap election this month by announcing candidates for his People's National Party.*

stake

at stake in danger of being lost or changed in an undesirable way ○ *Political control of both houses of Congress is at stake in next month's elections.*

have a stake in something to own a part of something, or to be affected by what happens to it ○ *The governor faced an audience of men and women who have a stake in the future of downtown Holyoke.*

stakes

★ **pull up stakes**

★ **pull stakes** to leave a job, home, or situation and go somewhere else ○ *There's little doubt that Downtown would lose some of its swagger were Saks Fifth Avenue to pull up stakes and move to, say, Ross Park Mall.*

The stakes referred to here are the stakes that hold down a tent.

stamp

put your stamp on something to do something that clearly shows your influence on something ○ *As the eatery's owner and executive chef, Portillo gets to put her stamp on a variety of dishes.*

stand

★ **stand up and be counted** to state publicly your support for or rejection of something, especially when this is difficult or controversial ○ *We must have the courage to stand up and be counted on this issue.*

standard

★ **the standard bearer of something** someone who acts as the leader or representative of a particular organization or group of people ○ *Inevitably, the public perception of her is that of a standard bearer for women jockeys.*

A standard is a flag with badges or symbols on it, which represent a person or organization. In the past, a standard bearer was the person who led an army into battle carrying a standard.

stars

have stars in your eyes to be very hopeful and excited about things that you expect to happen to you in the future. This expression is often used to suggest that someone is naive and that their hopes are unlikely to come true. ○ *We had stars in our eyes last weekend. Now we understand the reality of the situation.*

★ **reach for the stars** to be very ambitious and try hard to achieve something, even though it may be very difficult ○ *If you're ready to move on in your career, keep your feet firmly on the ground while reaching for the stars!*

starters

for starters (*informal*) used to emphasize the first and most important reason for something ○ *There are a few things that make Anderson a standout among other entrepreneurs. For starters, he's only 16.*

state

★ **state of the art** having the most modern and advanced features or technology ○ *The press release describes the new surgery center as state of the art.* ○ *Using state-of-the-art technology, this device instantly measures the distance you walk.*

★ **the state of play** the current situation ○ *Ben Willmott gives you the state of play on marijuana and the law.*

steam

> The following expressions refer to the use of steam to provide power for a machine, especially a steam engine.

do something under your own steam to do something on your own, without help from anyone else ○ *He left the group convinced he could do better under his own steam.*

go full steam ahead to start to carry out a particular project in a thorough and determined way ○ *The prime minister declared it was full steam ahead for a fourth term of government.*

go somewhere under your own steam to make your own travel arrangements, rather than letting someone else organize them for you ○ *Most hotels organize tours to inland beauty spots, but car rental is cheap enough to consider taking off into the hills under your own steam.*

★ **let off steam** or

blow off steam to do or say something that helps you to get rid of your strong feelings about something ○ *I was so upset that I pulled the car over to the side of the road, got out, and took a long walk. I just had to let off steam.*

> The reference here is to steam escaping noisily from the safety valve of a steam engine.

pick up steam to start to become stronger or more active ○ *Boskin said the economy should pick up steam next year.*

run out of steam to become weaker or less active, and often to stop completely ○ *The US is in a triple dip of recession. The promised recovery ran out of steam, the economy is slowing sharply and consumer spending is falling.*

step

one step ahead in a position of advantage over an opponent, competitor, or pursuer. You can also talk about being **one jump ahead**. See **jump**. ○ *Once you are able to give your customers what they are looking for you are already one step ahead of the competition in terms of making yourself the undisputed authority in your niche.*

steroids

on steroids expressed or done to an exaggerated degree ○ *It isn't just a gallery, it's an art institution on steroids.*

> Steroids are drugs that some athletes take, often illegally, in order to give them more energy and improve their performance.

stew

in a stew (old-fashioned) very worried about something ○ *He's been in a stew ever since he took that phone call early this morning.*

stick

carry a big stick to have a lot of power, and therefore be able to get what you want ○ *The company carries a big stick. Over the past 107 years it has built itself up into the biggest brand in the world and now controls 44% of the global market.*

> This expression comes from a saying that became widely known through a speech made by Theodore Roosevelt in 1903: "There is a homely old adage which runs, 'Speak softly and carry a big stick; you will go far.'"

★ **get on the stick** to start making an effort and taking action to achieve something ○ *She and Whitman need to get on the stick with their advertising.*

get the short end of the stick to end up in a worse position than other people in a particular situation, although this is not your fault ○ *As usual it's the consumer who gets the short end of the stick.*

get the wrong end of the stick to completely misunderstand something

○ *People are so easily confused, and so often get the wrong end of the stick.*

have more things than you can shake a stick at to have a very large number of a particular thing ○ *My daughter has more pairs of shoes than you can shake a stick at.*

make something stick to make something successful or effective ○ *The 49ers jumped to a 14-0 lead in the first quarter, then tried to make it stick for almost 50 minutes.*

a stick in the mud a person who does not like doing new things or having fun ○ *Maybe Microsoft isn't the stick in the mud we've learned to whine about and this is the beginning of some big changes.*

★ **a stick to beat someone with** something that can be used to cause embarrassment or difficulty for someone ○ *Surprisingly, the opposition, usually eager to find any stick to beat the government with, is refusing to comment on the affair.*

stiff

be as stiff as a board to have a very stiff body ○ *When you start to do yoga, you can gain flexibility very quickly – even if you are as stiff as a board at your first session.*

sting

★ **something has a sting in the tail** used about a remark or proposal that seems welcome or pleasing at first but that contains an unpleasant part at the end ○ *The agreement had a sting in the tail. It said that the entire aid package would be suspended if the country did not make progress on the economic front.*

≡ This is a reference to a scorpion, which is small and looks harmless, but has a poisonous stinger in its tail.

take the sting out of something to make something less unpleasant or painful ○ *The most serious situation can be viewed with humor and that always helps to take the sting out of hard facts.*

stitch

a stitch in time or
a stitch in time saves nine used to emphasize that it is better to deal with a problem in its early stages, in order to prevent it getting worse ○ *The saying "a stitch in time saves nine" is never more true than with a boat's paintwork: one must be immediately ready to touch up the chips that occur in order to prevent a bigger job later.*

stitches

someone or something has you in stitches used about someone or something that makes you laugh a lot ○ *The outrageous comedienne plans to have the north of England in stitches when she performs at the Liverpool Festival of Comedy.*

stomach

★ **not have the stomach for something** to be unable to bear something because it is so shocking ○ *I don't have the stomach for horror movies.*

★ **turn your stomach** to make you sick or disgusted ○ *Staying in a hotel that will turn your stomach is not a fun experience and can be prevented if these simple steps are followed.*

stone

★ **leave no stone unturned** to consider or try every possible way of doing something ○ *In the difficult weeks ahead, we'll leave no stone unturned in our search for a peaceful solution to the crisis.*

a rolling stone gathers no moss used to say that if a person keeps moving from one place to another, they will not get many friends or possessions ○ *He said that a rolling stone gathers no moss, that I'd never have a family if I spent my life touring with the band. I was determined to prove him wrong.*

something is not set in stone used to say that something such as an agreement, policy or rule is not permanent and that it can be changed ○ *Promises made two or three years before an election are not set in stone and can be changed.*

★ **a stone's throw from somewhere** very close to a particular place ○ *Burke found employment and rented a house a stone's throw from his new office.*

stool

a stool pigeon (old-fashioned) a spy or someone who secretly gives information to the police ○ *Despite taking the vow of silence, several mob members have turned stool pigeon.*

> The original meaning of stool pigeon was a wooden pigeon mounted on a stool that was used as a decoy (a model to deceive real pigeons).

stops

★ **pull out all the stops** to do everything you possibly can to make something happen in the way that you want it to ○ *The administration has pulled out all the stops to try and ensure an election victory.*

> On a church organ, the stops are the knobs that you pull or push in order to control the type of sound that comes out of the pipes. The organ plays loudest when all the stops are out.

storage

put something into cold storage to delay doing something or dealing with something, usually because other more important things need your attention or because you are not ready to do it ○ *The author's illness means that he has put completion of his fourth novel into cold storage.*

storm

ride out the storm to succeed in surviving a very difficult period ○ *It's going to be a difficult few months, but if we work together we can ride out the storm.*

★ **take somewhere by storm** to be very successful or popular in a particular place, and to make a good impression on people there ○ *The film has taken America by storm.*

> This expression originally meant to capture something such as a fort or a military position by means of a sudden, violent attack.

★ **weather the storm** to survive a difficult situation or period without being seriously harmed or very badly affected by it ○ *The company has weathered the storm of the current recession better than most. As car sales have plummeted, it's seen its share of the market actually increase.*

story

to make a long story short said when you are only going to mention the final result or point of a complicated account of something, without giving any further details ○ *I met Paul at a party two years ago – he was the most handsome man I'd ever seen – and, to make a long story short, we're getting married next year.*

the story of my life said to mean that a recent, bad experience has happened to you many times before ○ *This was the story of my life; liking guys who were emotionally not available.*

stove

★ **slave over a hot stove** to spend a lot of time and effort cooking ○ *Despite wracking my brains and slaving over a hot stove, my husband still complained of lassitude and loss of appetite.*

straight

★ **keep someone on the straight and narrow** to help someone to live an honest, decent life and prevent them from doing immoral or illegal things ○ *Our goal is to keep these vulnerable young people on the straight and narrow.*

"Straight" was originally "strait," which meant "narrow." The expression probably refers to a passage in the Bible: "Because strait is the gate, and narrow is the way which leads to life, and there are few that find it." (Matthew 7:14)

straight as an arrow

1 completely honest ○ *Tom's not the devious type – he's as straight as an arrow.* **2** very straight ○ *The streets are lined up, straight as an arrow, along the left bank of the Guadiana estuary.*

straw

draw the short straw to be chosen from a number of people to perform a task or duty that nobody else wants to do ○ *Jim drew the short straw: he had to drive forty miles to the airport at midnight to pick up Elizabeth.*

This expression comes from the practice of using pieces of straw to decide who will win or lose. One person holds several pieces of straw in their hand with the ends poking out. Each person in the group takes a piece of straw and the person with the shortest piece loses.

★ **the last straw** the latest in a series of unpleasant or difficult events that makes you feel that you cannot tolerate a situation any longer ○ *Mr. Elton was already distraught over his mother's death. When his wife asked him for a divorce, it was the last straw.*

a straw man

1 a person who is used to represent a more important person for an unpleasant task ○ *The director frequently employs straw men to dismiss principled arguments.* **2** a person or matter that is not important but is presented as being important ○ *Political and economic commentators send armies of straw men*

our way every day.

the straw that breaks the camel's back the latest in a series of unpleasant or difficult events that makes you feel that you cannot tolerate a situation any longer ○ *Last week, I broke my wrist skateboarding for the second time. That was the straw that broke the camel's back. My dad has told me to give up the sport.*

The reference here is to an animal that is already carrying a great deal on its back and that collapses when one more thing is added.

straws

draw straws to decide who will have to do something unpleasant by choosing pieces of straw of different lengths ○ *That Sunday morning, we were snowbound, so we drew straws to see who would go out for food.*

grasp at straws to rely on ideas, hopes, or methods that are unlikely to be successful, because you are desperate and cannot think of anything else to try ○ *This extraordinary speech was made by a man grasping at straws to gain much-desired publicity.*

The image here is of a drowning person who is desperately trying to grab hold of anything to save himself or herself, even a straw.

streak

talk a blue streak to talk a lot and very fast ○ *Although I'm usually shy, that night I talked a blue streak from the moment I arrived at the party.*

This expression refers to a blue streak of lightning flashing quickly across the sky.

stream

★ **against the stream** opposite to the usual or most popular way of doing something. You can also talk about going

against the grain. ○ *At a time when so many people are repeating the same ideas, Arkoun's is one of few voices that go against the stream.*

street

★ **on easy street** in an easy and comfortable situation ○ *Hernandez explained how once he broke the line of scrimmage, he felt like he was on easy street.*

something is right up your street (*mainly British*) used about something that is exactly the kind of thing you like or know about. Americans use the expression **up your alley**. See **alley** ○ *Actor Roy Barraclough has taken on a role that's right up his street, as Sherlock Holmes' bumbling sidekick Watson.*

stretch

★ **by any stretch (of the imagination)** used with a negative statement to give it strong emphasis ○ *They aren't a great team by any stretch, but they do a couple of things really well.*

stride

★ **hit your stride** or
get into your stride to start to do something easily and confidently, after being slow and uncertain at the beginning ○ *The administration is getting into its stride and seems, for the moment, to be fulfilling its promises.*

off your stride not doing something as well as you usually do it ○ *The game began well, but we started making mistakes and the goal really knocked the players off their stride.*

take something in stride to deal with a difficult situation calmly and successfully ○ *Ridley didn't start shouting, or anything like that. In fact, right until the end he seemed to be taking it all in stride.*

strikes

In baseball, a "strike" is a legal pitch of the ball that the batter fails to hit. The batter is out after three strikes.

three strikes against someone or something three factors that make it impossible for someone or something to be successful ○ *He said to me, "Listen, you've got three strikes against you. You're poor, you're uneducated and you're homeless."*

three strikes and you're out used to characterize a policy or law, according to which people who commit three offenses are punished very severely, even if the individual offenses are not very serious ○ *California has recently introduced a law known as three strikes and you're out, meaning that after a third conviction, you are put in prison.*

string

have another string to your bow to have more than one useful skill, ability, or thing that you can use in case you are unsuccessful with the first skill, ability, or thing. In this expression, "bow" is pronounced with the same vowel sound as the word "show." ○ *Stephanie has another string to her bow. Before her career in interior design, she was a photographer.*

Archers used to carry a spare bowstring in case the first one broke.

have someone on a string to make someone do whatever you want, because you control them completely ○ *For the rest of his life he had her on a string, spending her money and controlling every aspect of her life.*

strings

★ **pull strings** to get something you want, not by your own merit but by using your friendships with powerful and influential people. This expression is usually used in a disapproving way. ○ *Many of Anna's colleagues felt that she was pulling strings to advance her career.*

★ **pull the strings** to control everything that another person or an organization does ○ *Having engineered many of these political changes and pulled the strings from* behind the stage, he now feels it's his due, as it were, to become national leader.

≣ The image here is of a puppet that is controlled by means of strings.

★ **with no strings attached** used when you want to emphasize that an offer or agreement has no unpleasant conditions that must be accepted ○ *This is an extremely generous offer, which comes with no strings attached. I think that we should accept.*

with strings attached used when an offer or agreement has unpleasant conditions that must be accepted ○ *The charity has a very strict rule that it refuses to accept any donations with strings attached.*

stripes

earn your stripes to show that you deserve your job, rank, or position ○ *The Jamisons don't have professional culinary credentials but have earned their stripes through decades of kitchen work.*

≣ This expression comes from the military, where the number of stripes on the sleeves of a uniform is an indication of rank.

strokes

in broad strokes in general terms rather than in detail ○ *The speech will lay out in broad strokes the two candidates' differing approaches towards how best to stimulate the economy.*

≣ The image here is of an artist painting a picture roughly or quickly.

different strokes for different folks people are different, and some individuals or groups have different needs and wants from others ○ *The federal government has always been respectful of local customs in local communities, and therefore you had different strokes for different folks.*

strong

strong as an ox extremely strong ○ *Big Beppe, as everybody calls him, is enormous and as strong as an ox.*

stubborn

stubborn as a mule determined to do what you want and unwilling to change your mind, often in a way that annoys other people ○ *He is, without question, a man of his word, but he can certainly be stubborn as a mule.*

stuff

★ **strut your stuff** to do something that you know you are good at in a proud and confident way in order to impress other people ○ *He was the type of guy who liked to show off and strut his stuff.*

stuffing

knock the stuffing out of someone to destroy someone's energy and self-confidence, and leave them feeling weak and nervous ○ *The opposition knocked the stuffing out of us early on and we never got into the game.*

stump

★ **on the stump** traveling to different places and speaking to voters in order to get their support ○ *Despite his falling popularity, the president braved it on the stump today.*

≣ This expression comes from politicians using tree stumps as platforms when giving a speech in the open air.

style

cramp someone's style to prevent someone from behaving freely in the way that they want ○ *Like many women with good jobs, independent spirits and high standards, she believes marriage would cramp her style.*

like something is going out of style with a great deal of energy or effort; excessively ○ *She's pregnant and she's taking prenatal vitamins like they're going out of style.*

sucker

there's a sucker born every minute
said to mean that there are many people
who will believe anything and can be
easily deceived ○ *Hundreds of people give
confidential information away to callers –
as they say, there's a sucker born every
minute.*

> Most people attribute this saying to
> the 19th century entertainer and
> promoter P. T. Barnum, but there is no
> good evidence that he said it.

suit

> The following expressions refer to the
> four suits in a deck of cards: diamonds,
> hearts, clubs, and spades.

★ **follow suit** to do the same thing that
someone else has just done ○ *If Tim
decided to have pancakes for breakfast, Pam
would follow suit.*

> If you follow suit in a card game, you
> play a card of the same suit as the
> previous player.

something is someone's strong suit
or
something is someone's long suit
used to say that someone is good at
something, or knows a lot about it,
which gives them an advantage ○ *Taking
care of children is not her strong suit. She's
definitely a career woman.*

> If a large number of a player's cards
> belong to a particular suit, you can call
> that suit their strong suit or long suit.

summer

an Indian summer a period of great
success late in your life or career, often
after a period of not being successful
○ *The recent revival in international fashion
is proving an Indian summer for Mr. Rabanne,
better known for his perfumes in the Seventies
and Eighties.*

> An Indian summer is a period of
> unusually warm sunny weather during
> the autumn.

supper

sing for your supper *(old-fashioned)* to
have to do a particular job before you are
allowed to do or have something that
you want ○ *"You're going to have to sing for
your supper," said the organizer. "While the
guests are eating, I want you to sit at the end
of the table and perform for us."*

sure

sure as shooting or
sure as shootin' → see **shooting**

surface

★ **scratch the surface of something**
to deal with or experience only a small
part of something ○ *Officials say they've
only scratched the surface of the city's
political corruption.*

swallow

**one swallow doesn't make a
summer** *(mainly British)* used to express
the idea that although something good
has happened, the situation may not
continue to be good, and you cannot rely
on it ○ *Sales are up by 1%, which is a vast
improvement on the last six months. One
swallow, however, doesn't make a summer
and business could still be better.*

> Swallows here are barn swallows, a
> type of bird. The reference here is to
> the arrival of swallows in Europe at the
> beginning of summer, after spending
> the winter further south.

swan

someone's swan song a last
performance, or the last thing that
someone does in a particular job
○ *Saturday night was the club's swan song.
After the final band on stage played its final
song, Cafe Metropolis closed its doors.*

This expression developed from a belief that a dying swan sings.

swear

swear up and down → see **up**

sweat

do something by the sweat of your brow (*literary*) to do something through hard physical work, without any help from anyone else ○ *Most people are no longer earning their bread by the sweat of their brow.*

in a cold sweat very frightened, anxious, or embarrassed ○ *It was a terrifying experience, a nightmare. I still come out in a cold sweat thinking about it.*

sweep

a clean sweep
1 a very thorough job that leaves nothing undone or uncertain ○ *The new governor's clean sweep replaced all but two of the department's advisors.*
2 a series of easy victories ○ *The USA has made a clean sweep of all five titles in the Women's Gymnastics event.*

sweetness

sweetness and light a happy, friendly mood or atmosphere ○ *We haven't been winning, so it's not all sweetness and light at the club at the moment.*

swing

★ **be in full swing** to be operating fully or to have already been happening for some time, rather than just having started ○ *Twelve days after Hurricane Andrew left its trail of destruction and misery across South Florida, officials say recovery efforts are at last in full swing.*

get into the swing of something to get used to something and to start doing it well or start enjoying it ○ *I assumed everything would be okay once I got into the swing of college but I had no idea how lonely I would be.*

sword

★ **a double-edged sword** something that has both a good and a bad side ○ *The strong currency is a double-edged sword. It helps the nation's banks, but it also raises the costs of exports for car and electronics manufacturers.*

have the Sword of Damocles hanging over your head to be in a situation in which something very bad could happen to you at any time ○ *As a Grand Prix driver you have the Sword of Damocles hanging over your head at every moment.*

This expression comes from a Greek legend. Dionysius, the ruler of Syracuse, was annoyed by Damocles, who kept flattering him and saying how much he admired him. Dionysius invited Damocles to a feast, and asked him to sit in his own seat. When Damocles looked up during the feast, he noticed a sword hanging by a single thread above his head, and so he could no longer enjoy the feast. The sword symbolized the dangers and fears that rulers have, in addition to all the privileges.

swords

beat swords into plowshares to try to stop war or conflict, and to use the resources and technology of warfare to do other things to improve people's lives ○ *For Ukrainians, beating swords into plowshares and turning rocket plants into car factories is an economic necessity.*

A plowshare is one of the blades on a plow. This expression may come from the Bible (Isaiah 2:4), which says that people should make their swords into plowshares; they should stop fighting wars, and start working together productively.

cross swords with someone to disagree and argue with someone, or oppose them ○ *These two politicians* *have crossed swords on many occasions.*

system

★ **get something out of your system**
to say or do something that you have
been wanting to say or do for a long time,
and therefore begin to feel less worried or
angry about it ○ *If something awful
happens to you at least you can write about
it. I'm sure you feel better if you get it out of
your system.*

systems

it's all systems go said when
everything is happening or ready to
happen with a particular project or
activity ○ *Work started on the indoor sports
arena at the beginning of the year and it's
now all systems go, with a huge team of
builders working on the project.*

This expression became popular as a
result of its use during the launch of
spacecraft in the United Sates in the
1960s and 1970s. It indicated that the
spacecraft was functioning correctly
and was ready for takeoff.

Tt

tab

★ **pick up the tab** to pay a bill or pay the costs of something, especially something that you are not responsible for ○ *Pollard picked up the tab for dinner.*

★ **run up a tab** to do things that cause you to owe a lot of money ○ *The Council has run up a tab of at least $100,000 – and counting – in legal fees.*

These expressions use the sense of "tab" that means an account or bill that can be used to keep a record of what someone spends.

table

drink someone under the table to drink much more alcohol than someone else can without getting drunk ○ *Donna is the only person I know who can drink me under the table.*

under the table in a secret, dishonest way ○ *Some staff made deals under the table with freight companies by charging extra money for express delivery when sometimes the express service did not exist.*

★ **put something on the table** to present something, such as a proposal, plan or offer, formally to other people, so that it can be discussed and agreed on ○ *The United States said Europe must put a new offer on the table to save the talks.*

tables

★ **turn the tables on someone** to do something to change a situation so that you gain an advantage over someone or cause them problems, following a time when they had the advantages or caused problems for you ○ *The governor has turned the tables on his many enemies and has given them something to worry about for a change.*

The image here is of a player in a game such as chess turning the board through 180 degrees, so that the situations of the two players are reversed.

tabs

★ **keep tabs on someone** to make sure that you always know where someone is and what they are doing, often in order to control them ○ *The FBI kept close tabs on the novelist, at times opening his mail and recording his conversations.*

This expression uses the sense of "tab" that means an account or bill that can be used to keep a record of what someone spends.

tail

chase your own tail or
chase your tail to spend a lot of time and energy doing something, but achieving nothing ○ *It feels great to be making some progress on this project at last, and not just chasing my own tail.*

go off with your tail between your legs to go away feeling very ashamed and embarrassed because of a defeat or a foolish mistake that you have made ○ *I ran out of money, lost my job, my house, my girlfriend. I came home to Sydney with my tail between my legs, absolutely broke and shattered.*

★ **on someone's tail** following someone closely, often chasing them ○ *Juarez entered the finishing lap with Zadrobilek right on his tail. Only three kilometers remained.*

the tail end of something the very last part of something ○ *He's at the tail end of his career and he's looking forward to retirement.*

the tail wags the dog used to describe a situation in which a small or unimportant part of something is becoming too important and is controlling the whole thing ○ *To avoid the impression of the tail wagging the dog, the prime minister cannot be seen to be giving in to the wishes of a minority party.*

turn tail to turn and run away from someone or something because you are frightened of them ○ *Rebels were forced back from position after position until they turned tail and fled.*

tale

live to tell the tale to survive a dangerous or frightening experience ○ *Michael Sproule was attacked by a shark. He lived to tell the tale but underwent emergency surgery for multiple injuries.*

something tells its own tale (mainly British) used about something that reveals the truth about a particular situation ○ *The fact that we originally booked for only one night but ended up staying eight tells its own tale. We can't recommend the hotel highly enough.*

tales

★ **tall tales** stories or statements that are difficult to believe because they are so exaggerated or unlikely ○ *Pollard was described as someone whose rich imagination and keen intellect were convincing; some of his college chums believed his tall tales.*

"Tall" used to be used to describe language that was considered extremely formal or exaggerated.

tell tales to tell lies or reveal secrets about someone, so that they get into trouble ○ *She had no right to tell tales to his mother!*

talk

someone is all talk or **someone is all talk and no action** used about someone who talks about

doing something without ever doing it ○ *No wonder people no longer believe a word he says. He's all talk and no action. No matter what he promises, nobody will be able to trust him.*

talk the talk to talk about a subject or situation with confidence, but not actually do anything. This expression is often used in combination with **walk the walk**. ○ *Most people just like to talk the talk when it comes to saving money and streamlining government. One woman had the personal courage to walk the walk.*

tall

★ **walk tall** to behave with confidence and authority ○ *If there is any soldier who is ready to fight enemies abroad, it is one who is strong enough to walk tall in the face of discrimination at home.*

tangent

go off on a tangent to start saying or thinking something that is not directly connected with what you were saying or thinking before ○ *Our teacher occasionally goes off on a tangent, talking about things totally unrelated to our textbooks or the curriculum.*

In geometry, a tangent is a straight line that touches a curve at one point but does not cross it.

tank

someone or something is built like a tank used about someone is very big and strong, or something has been made very well and very solidly, and will last for a long time ○ *Nick's built like a tank and lots of people are afraid of him when they first meet him, but he's actually a really friendly, gentle guy.*

tap

★ **on tap**

1 available and ready for immediate use ○ *The enterprise agency's close links with both the university and several business* institutions provides local businesses with a wealth of knowledge on tap.

2 scheduled to happen very soon ○ *More military and medical experiments are on tap for Atlantis astronauts today.*

If a drink such as beer is available on tap, it is kept in a barrel fitted with a tap, so it can be drawn off as required.

tape

★ **red tape** official rules and procedures that seem complicated and unnecessary and that cause delay ○ *Two lawyers have written a book in a bid to help people cut through the red tape when dealing with immigration and nationality laws.*

Lawyers and government officials used to tie documents together with red or pink tape.

tar

tar and feather someone to publicly criticize someone and cause embarrassment for them ○ *Many critics are eager to tar and feather the big banks and mortgage companies for tossing so many people out of their homes.*

This expression comes from an old form of punishment, in which a person was first coated with tar and then with feathers.

target

be shooting for the same target if two people are shooting for the same target, they are in agreement about what they are trying to achieve together ○ *We'll only succeed if we're both shooting for the same target.*

task

take someone to task to criticize someone strongly for something they have done ○ *One day she took me to task for never using her name when I was talking to her.*

taste

someone or something is an acquired taste used about someone or something that is not immediately attractive or enjoyable, but that you may start to like later ○ *While political art may be an acquired taste, at least one local gallery has made a specialty of tackling issues such as racism and homelessness.*

something leaves a bad taste in your mouth or
something leaves a nasty taste in your mouth said about something that someone does makes you feel angry or disgusted with them because it was a very unpleasant thing to do ○ *Some people are abusive in stores, in buses and on trains. They seem to think it is fun. For the victim it leaves a nasty taste in the mouth.*

tea

someone would not do something for all the tea in China said to emphasize that someone definitely does not want to do something ○ *He would not change his job for all the tea in China.*

In the past, all tea came from China.

tee

★ **to a tee** or
to a T perfectly, or in exactly the right way ○ *His job suits him to a tee.*

T stands for "tittle," a small mark in printing such as the dot over an i. The expression refers to writing being very clear and exactly right.

teeth

armed to the teeth having or carrying a lot of weapons or very effective weapons ○ *The police are grossly underpaid and underequipped while the criminals are armed to the teeth with the latest weapons.*

★ **cut your teeth doing something** to do something new that gives you experience and helps you learn how to do more advanced or complicated things ○ *Dennis cut his teeth with theater roles before taking on parts in TV series and films.*

≡ When a child cuts a tooth, the tooth ≡ begins to appear through the gum.

fed up to the teeth with something annoyed or tired because something has been happening for a long time and you think it should be stopped or changed ○ *I've always supported the Republican Party but I'm fed up to the teeth with them at the moment.*

★ **get your teeth into something** to become deeply involved with something and do it with a lot of energy and enthusiasm ○ *Half the trouble is having nothing interesting to do. We've not had a project to get our teeth into for weeks.*

★ **gnashing of teeth** overreacting or expressing concern about something in an excessive way ○ *Much wailing and gnashing of teeth followed the recent release of the Pew Forum's survey of Americans' religious knowledge.*

≡ The phrases "weeping and gnashing of ≡ teeth" and "wailing and gnashing of ≡ teeth" both appear several times in the ≡ Bible in descriptions of the people who ≡ are sent to hell.

grind your teeth to be very angry or frustrated about something, but feel that you cannot say or do anything about it ○ *Lucy appeared to think this over for a moment and then walked away, grinding her teeth in frustration.*

★ **grit your teeth** to decide to continue even though the situation you are in is very difficult ○ *He says that there are no simple solutions and that it will be hard work, but we just have to grit our teeth and get on with it.*

kick someone in the teeth to unexpectedly treat someone very badly and unfairly ○ *The union expected that the*

proposal would be given favorable treatment: "Instead we have been kicked in the teeth."

lie through your teeth to tell very obvious lies while appearing not to be embarrassed about this ○ *It's clear that the government are lying through their teeth.*

like pulling teeth very difficult to do ○ *Getting this information out of him was like pulling teeth.*

≡ When a dentist pulls someone's tooth, ≡ they pull it out of their gum. In the ≡ past, this was done without ≡ anesthetic and so it was difficult and ≡ painful.

set your teeth on edge if something sets your teeth on edge, you find it extremely irritating or unpleasant ○ *His casual arrogance never failed to set my teeth on edge.*

show your teeth to show that you are capable of fighting or defending yourself ○ *We need to show our teeth if we are going to overturn the county's plan to build new houses in our town.*

something has teeth used about something, such as an organization or a law, that has the necessary authority or power to make people obey it ○ *The prison operates under a contract that has teeth – financial penalties can be imposed and it's independently monitored.*

teething

★ **teething troubles** small problems in the early stages of a new project, or when a new product first becomes available ○ *The company conceded there have been teething troubles with the new system but said that these were now being corrected.*

tell

tell someone where to get off to tell someone in a rude and forceful way that you cannot accept what they are saying or doing ○ *If somebody said that to me, I'd tell them where to get off.*

tempest

a tempest in a teapot something that is not important but that people are making a lot of unnecessary fuss about ○ *"It's a tempest in a teapot," he said of the controversy over the painting.*

tent

a big tent an organization, group or area of activity that includes a wide range of opinions, beliefs or styles ○ *"We're a big tent, with opinions from all sides," said the channel's spokesman.*

tenterhooks

on tenterhooks very nervous or excited, because you are eager to know what is going to happen ○ *"It was a good match wasn't it? Very exciting." "Yes, we were on tenterhooks."*

In the past, when cloth had been woven, it was stretched on a frame called a tenter and held in place by hooks. The person's emotional state is being compared to the tension in the cloth.

territory

something goes with the territory used about something that often occurs in a particular kind of situation or activity, and so you have to be prepared for it ○ *People often point me out and ask me for pictures and autographs, but that goes with the territory. I chose to become an actor and I'm not going to complain about that.*

test

★ **something has stood the test of time** used about something that has proved its value and has not failed or has not gone out of fashion since it first appeared ○ *Since it began manufacturing in 1933, Gossen has built easy-to-use, reliable equipment that has stood the test of time.*

tether

★ **at the end of your tether** feeling desperate because you are in a difficult situation and you do not know how to deal with it. An equivalent expression is **at the end of your rope**. ○ *She was at the end of her tether. She needed someone she could talk to, someone she could trust.*

A tether is a length of rope, used for tying animals up. The image is of an animal which cannot move very far because it is tied to something with a tether.

that

that's that or
that takes care of that used to show that you are finished with a subject, or that everything necessary has been done ○ *We always make sure to revisit the problem when we're both calmer and talk and apologize. That's what you do. You work it out, you move past it, and that's that.*

there

★ **be there for someone** to always be ready to listen to someone's problems and to help and support them ○ *Jimmy's a good friend to me – he's always been there for me with support and advice.*

someone is not all there used about someone who is not very intelligent, or who is slightly mentally ill ○ *You could tell that she wasn't all there. You could see it in her eyes.*

thick

★ **do something through thick and thin** to continue doing something even when the situation makes it very difficult for you ○ *I'll love you through thick and thin, no matter what happens.*

This comes from a hunting expression "through thicket and thin wood." A thicket is a small group of trees or bushes which are growing closely together.

★ **in the thick of it** deeply involved in a particular activity or situation ○ *A fight* broke out in the bar and he suddenly found himself in the thick of it.

lay it on thick to exaggerate something such as a statement, an experience, or an emotion, in order to impress people ○ *Sue was laying it on a little thick when she said that Tom was the best dancer she'd ever seen.*

thick as thieves if two or more people are as thick as thieves, they are very friendly with each other ○ *Jones and Cook have known each other since the age of ten – they're thick as thieves.*

thick as a board *(mainly British)* very stupid. Americans use the expression **dumb as a post**. ○ *She has a backbone, she isn't as thick as a board and she shows loyalty toward her father.*

thin

spread yourself too thin to try to do a lot of different things at the same time, with the result that you cannot do any of them properly ○ *The company grew too fast and spread itself too thin across too many diverse areas.*

thin as a rail extremely thin ○ *She's as thin as a rail, but she can drive the ball 260-270 yards.*

thing

★ **do your own thing** to live or behave in the way you want to, without paying attention to convention and without depending on other people ○ *Her parents let her do her own thing as long as she keeps in touch by phone to say she is okay.*

★ **one thing led to another** said, when you are giving an account of something, to mean that you do not think you need to give any details of events, because they happened in an obvious way ○ *Elsa got in with the wrong crowd of people. They were bad news. One thing led to another and she started shoplifting.*

thorn

★ **a thorn in someone's side** someone or something that continually annoys or causes trouble for someone else ○ *She has become a thorn in the side of the government since publishing a number of reports pointing out that public cash was being mishandled.*

This refers to a passage in the Bible (2 Corinthians 12:7), in which St. Paul says that the Devil gave him an illness (or a "thorn in his flesh") to make him suffer, and to stop him from becoming too proud.

thread

hang by a thread to be very likely to fail soon ○ *It's clear that the ceasefire is hanging by a thread and may be broken at any time.*

someone's life hangs by a thread used when someone is seriously ill and is very likely to die soon ○ *The baby was delivered by emergency Caesarean and the life of her mother hung by a thread.*

This expression may relate to the story of the Sword of Damocles: see the explanation at "sword."

throat

cut your own throat to make a mistake by doing something which is going to result in disaster for you ○ *I think the union is cutting its own throat because, if the company can't reduce its costs, then even more jobs will be lost.*

grab something by the throat to make a determined attempt to control, defeat, or deal with something ○ *Instead of being passive and waiting for things to happen, you must get out there and grab life by the throat.*

jump down someone's throat to react to something someone has said in a very impatient, angry, and unpleasant way ○ *Even if I just asked her how she was, she'd jump down my throat, as if I were interrogating her.*

★ **ram something down someone's throat** to try to force someone to accept, believe, or learn something against their will ○ *When I was a kid, my parents rammed religion down my throat.*

something grabs you by the throat used about something that is so powerful, interesting, or exciting that you are forced to pay attention to it ○ *Fifty years after it was made, the film still grabs you by the throat.*

something sticks in your throat

1 used about something makes you annoyed or impatient ○ *It sticks in my throat that politicians think that they still have something to tell the rest of us about morality.*

2 used when you cannot say a particular word, or you dislike saying it, because it does not express your real feelings or because it makes you feel uncomfortable ○ *She found it impossible to utter the usual terms of maternal endearment: words such as "darling" or "pet" stuck in her throat.*

throats

★ **be at each other's throats** if two people or groups are at each other's throats, they are continually arguing or fighting ○ *He and Stevens didn't get along; they'd been at each other's throats for years.*

throes

★ **in the throes of something** busy doing or deeply involved in something, especially something difficult or unpleasant ○ *The newspaper's future looks bleak. It's in the throes of a four-month-old strike and is losing nearly a million dollars a day.*

throttle

do something at full throttle to do something with all your energy and effort ○ *She's a high-powered businesswoman who always goes at things at full throttle.*

If an engine is operating at full throttle, it is operating at its maximum speed.

thumb

★ **be under someone's thumb** be under the control or influence of another person ○ *Ian was completely under his wife's thumb. She controlled the money, told him what to do and wouldn't allow him to have any friends of his own.*

have a green thumb to be very good at gardening ○ *She had a green thumb and, using only instinct and loads of manure, casually grew huge crops of fruit.*

someone or something sticks out like a sore thumb used about someone or something that is very noticeable because they are very different from the other people or things around them ○ *"First impressions are very important," says Baines. "You don't want a new house to stick out like a sore thumb; it should blend into its surroundings."*

thumbs

be all thumbs to do something with your hands in a clumsy way and keep making mistakes while you are doing it ○ *Can you open this packet for me? I'm all thumbs today.*

★ **give something the thumbs down** or

give the thumbs down to something to show that you do not approve of something, such as a plan, a suggestion, or an activity, and are not willing to accept it ○ *Out of 58,000 replies to the questionnaire, 79 per cent gave the thumbs down to the proposal.*

A thumbs down or a thumbs-down sign is a sign that you make by pointing your thumb downwards in order to show dissatisfaction or disagreement, or to show that things are going badly. In ancient Rome, a signal in which the thumb was bent down was used at the games to tell a victorious gladiator not to kill his opponent.

★ **give something the thumbs up** or **give the thumbs up to something** to show that you approve of something, such as a plan, a suggestion, or an activity, and are willing to accept it ○ *A big US oil company has given the thumbs up to the president's energy plan.*

A thumbs up or a thumbs-up sign is a sign that you make by pointing your thumb upwards in order to show satisfaction or agreement, or to show that everything is all right. In ancient Rome, a signal in which the thumb was straight was used at the games to tell a victorious gladiator to kill his opponent.

twiddle your thumbs to waste your time and achieve nothing because you have nothing to do ○ *Graduates who have invested time and their parents' money to go to college do not want to sit twiddling their thumbs.*

thunder

steal someone's thunder to stop someone from getting attention or praise by doing something better than them or doing something before them ○ *He's a very insecure boss – he's always afraid that his staff might steal his thunder.*

This expression may come from an incident in the early 18th century. A British playwright, John Dennis, invented a new way of making the sound of thunder for his play "Appius and Virginia." However, the play was unsuccessful and soon closed. Soon afterwards, Dennis went to see a production of "Macbeth" by another company and found that they had stolen his idea for making thunder sounds. He is said to have jumped up and accused them of stealing his thunder.

ticket

just the ticket exactly what is wanted or needed ○ *Our news website is just the ticket if you're sitting on a train on your way to work.*

a one-way ticket to something something that is certain to lead to a particular situation or state, usually an undesirable or unpleasant one ○ *Having strong feelings for someone when those feelings aren't returned is a one-way ticket to unhappiness.*

tide

★ **stem the tide of something** to get control of something bad that is happening on a large scale, and stop it ○ *The authorities seem powerless to stem the tide of violence.*

swim against the tide to do or say something that is the opposite of what most other people are doing or saying ○ *Adenauer generally appeared to be swimming against the tide in international politics.*

tight

★ **sit tight** to wait and see how a difficult situation develops before taking any action ○ *In a recession, the message is that those who want to sell their houses should sit tight for a couple of years if they can.*

tightrope

★ **walk a tightrope** to be in a difficult situation where you must be very careful about what you do or say, because you are trying to satisfy opposing groups ○ *He is walking a tightrope between the young activists and the more traditional elements within the democracy movement.*

time

★ **be living on borrowed time** to not be expected to survive for much longer ○ *From this moment onwards, this government is living on borrowed time.*

big time used to emphasize the

importance or extent of something that is happening ○ *With a little luck we could make this plan work, and work big time.*

★ **buy time** to increase the time available for something to happen ○ *This procedure won't cure the illness, but it will buy time while patients learn to change their lifestyles.*

★ **have time on your hands** to have a lot of free time and not know what to do with it ○ *Children need discipline and planned activities. If they have too much time on their hands, they can get into trouble.*

★ **hit the big time** to become very famous and successful ○ *The fashion designer hit the big time in 1935, when he was chosen to design the Duchess of Gloucester's wedding dress.*

in no time very quickly or very soon ○ *You're going to be OK, buddy. We'll get some back-up out here and you'll be on your way to the hospital in no time.*

★ **kill time** to not do anything new or decisive, because you are waiting to see how a situation will develop ○ *We feel we're just killing time until our new boss arrives.*

★ **play for time** to try to delay doing or saying something definite until you have decided what is the best course of action to take ○ *He poured himself a drink, playing for time, giving himself a moment to think before he answered her question.*

someone would not give someone the time of day said when someone strongly dislikes or disapproves of someone and wants to have nothing to do with them ○ *She adored Jack, but he wouldn't give her the time of day.*

tin

have a tin ear for something to be unable to appreciate or understand music or something else that you can hear ○ *For a playwright specializing in characters who use the vernacular, he has a tin ear for dialogue.*

a tin god someone who thinks they are much more important and powerful than they really are ○ *The history of the country is littered with tin gods and dictators attempting to dominate national life.*

tip

★ **just the tip of the iceberg** something that is part of a very large problem or a very serious situation, although other aspects of the problem or situation may not yet be obvious ○ *We get about 2,000 complaints every year but this is just the tip of the iceberg. Many more people just suffer in silence.*

Only a very small part of an iceberg can be seen above the water. About nine-tenths of it is below the surface.

something is on the tip of your tongue said when you are sure you know something, such as a word, an answer, or a name, but you cannot remember it at the moment ○ *I know the answer to this question. No, no, don't tell me. Oh, it's on the tip of my tongue.*

something was on the tip of your tongue said when you really wanted to make a remark or ask a question about something, but you decided not to ○ *"Do you know anything about this?" he asked after a while. It was on the tip of my tongue to tell him what I'd seen but, in the end, I said nothing.*

tip the scales

★ **tip the balance** to produce one result in a particular situation where, before, two possible results seemed equally likely ○ *As the election looms, the two main parties appear so evenly matched that just one issue could tip the balance.*

tire

a spare tire a noticeable circle of fat around someone's waist ○ *A spare tire is developing around her middle, and she knows she needs to go on a diet.*

tit

tit for tat an action that is intended to harm someone who has harmed you ○ *Too often, people are focused less on real dialogue, and more on giving tit for tat, or scoring points.* ○ *There has been an appeal for peace and an end to tit-for-tat violence.*

toast

someone or something is toast (*informal*) used about someone or something that is dead, finished, or no longer important or powerful ○ *"Hit your sales targets next year or you're toast," my manager told me.*

today

here today, gone tomorrow used to describe someone or something that is only present for a short time. You often use this expression to suggest that this is a bad thing. ○ *Most gang members live day to day and their philosophy is "Here today, gone tomorrow."*

toe

dip your toe in the water or **dip a toe in the water** to start doing something that you have not done before in a slow and careful way because you are not sure if you will like it or if it will be successful ○ *After years of selling her jewelry through fashion stores, she finally dipped a toe in the water and opened her own jewelry store in Pittsburgh.*

go toe to toe with someone to fight, argue, or compete with someone fiercely and directly ○ *They're confident that the company is now strong enough to go toe to toe with its rivals.*

toes

★ **on your toes** alert and ready for anything that might happen ○ *Our new boss has kept us on our toes right from the moment she took over the job.* ○ *"You have to be on your toes 24/7. People are out to take your money, take your vehicle, they don't care," said Rich Marella of New Jersey.*

make your toes curl to make you feel very embarrassed for someone else ○ *There are moments of tenderness and some very funny scenes in Nigel Charnock's direction. And there are scenes, too, that make your toes curl.* ○ *Movies about famous explorers rarely work, as some recent toe-curling efforts show.*

★ **step on someone's toes** to offend someone by criticizing the way they do something or by interfering in something that is their responsibility ○ *Women often feel ridiculously inhibited and duty-bound not to antagonize the men they work with or tread on too many toes.*

toll

take its toll to have an undesirable effect, usually after a long period ○ *The downturn in the economy has taken its toll on many in this community.*

Tom

every Tom, Dick, and Harry any person, even an ordinary person with no special skills or qualities ○ *This hotel used to be exclusive. Nowadays they let in every Tom, Dick and Harry.*

All of these names used to be very common, and so they began to be used to refer to ordinary people in general.

tomorrow

like there's no tomorrow without thinking about the results of your behavior ○ *In the last property boom, the banks lent to developers like there was no tomorrow.*

tomorrow is another day said to emphasize that although you have just had a bad experience, you are confident or hopeful that your life will be much better in the future ○ *Everything went wrong. I didn't play well. However, tomorrow is another day.*

ton

come down on someone like a ton of bricks to speak very angrily to someone because they have done something wrong or to punish them severely ○ *If you make even the tiniest mistake, they all come down on you like a ton of bricks.*

like a ton of bricks very suddenly and dramatically ○ *The reality of the situation hit her like a ton of bricks.*

tongue

★ **bite your tongue** to not say a particular thing, even though you want to, because it would be the wrong thing to say at the time, or because you are waiting for a better time to speak ○ *I wanted to tell him how much I would miss him, but I bit my tongue.*

find your tongue to begin to talk, when you have previously been too shy or frightened to say anything ○ *After a long silence, Tom eventually found his tongue.*

get your tongue around something to pronounce a name, word or phrase correctly ○ *When my brother was little, he couldn't get his tongue around the word "bicycle"; it always came out as "bi-ci-click."*

give someone a tongue-lashing to speak harshly or angrily to someone about something that they have done ○ *The President of the EU Commission was given a tongue-lashing from Mr. Major and told to drop his objections to a world trade deal.*

hold your tongue to be silent or to stop speaking ○ *Murphy and Lynch managed to keep the news quiet but it wasn't easy, Lynch claims – even though she held her tongue all summer.*

speak with a forked tongue to lie or deliberately mislead people ○ *He speaks with a forked tongue. I don't trust him and I don't like him.*

The reference here is to snakes, which often have forked tongues and are not considered to be trustworthy. This expression is popularly believed to have begun with American Indians.

★ **tongue in cheek** used to describe a remark or a piece of writing that is meant to be funny and ironic, and is not meant to be taken seriously ○ *I think people are taking all this more seriously than we intended. It was supposed to be tongue in cheek.*

tongues

tongues are wagging used when people are gossiping as a result of someone's behavior ○ *They spent an evening together at his Knightsbridge flat. He said they talked and played cards but added: "No doubt tongues will be wagging."*

tools

the tools of the trade the skills and equipment that you need to do your job properly ○ *As a pianist, Grace's fingers were the tools of her trade.*

tooth

be long in the tooth to be getting old ○ *"Why don't you enroll in the college and take a course?" "Aren't I a bit long in the tooth to start being an undergraduate?"*

This expression refers to the fact that you can judge the age of a horse by looking at its teeth. As horses get older, their teeth look longer because their gums are receding.

fight tooth and nail to make a determined effort to keep or get something, when other people are trying to take it away from you or prevent you from having it ○ *The prime minister let it be known that she would fight tooth and nail to stay in office.*

★ **have a sweet tooth** to like eating things that are sugary or taste sweet ○ *She has a sweet tooth; she can't resist*

chocolate cake and peppermint creams.
red in tooth and claw *(literary)*
behaving competitively and ruthlessly
○ *The company's pursuit of self-interest in the market sphere was painted as ruthless, red in tooth and claw.*

> This is a quotation from the poem "In Memoriam" (1850) by the English poet Alfred, Lord Tennyson. (Part 56, stanza 4)

top

at the top of the heap or
at the top of the pile → see **heap**
→ see **pile**
blow your top to become very angry with someone and shout at them ○ *I never asked her personal questions because, for some reason, she'd always blow her top and tell me I was being nosy.*
★ **from top to bottom** very thoroughly ○ *She cleaned the house from top to bottom.*
★ **from top to toe** used to talk about the whole of someone's body ○ *She was trembling from top to toe.*
get on top of you to make you feel anxious and that you are not managing a situation well because there is too much work or too many problems ○ *Most of us are irritable or bad-tempered when things get on top of us.*
off the top of your head → see **head**
★ **on top of something** dealing with a difficult task or a situation successfully ○ *With two young children and a full-time job, I'm so busy that I'm not keeping on top of the housework.*
on top of the world → see **world**
★ **over the top** extreme and exaggerated. This expression is usually used disapprovingly. ○ *I'm sorry. I realize now that I was a bit over the top, accusing you of being a traitor.*

> During the First World War, "to go over the top" meant to climb out of the trenches and run into no-man's land in order to attack the enemy.

push someone over the top in a competition or contest, if something pushes someone over the top, it results in them winning ○ *The advertising campaign pushed the company over the top, allowing them to replace their rivals as the number-one soft drink in supermarkets.*

torch

> The torch referred to in these expressions is a long stick with burning material at one end which provides a light. This kind of torch is sometimes used in processions or parades.

carry a torch for someone to be in love with someone who does not love you, or who is already involved with another person ○ *What makes a woman so special that a man will carry a torch for her all his life?*
carry the torch for something to support something, such as a political party or a particular belief, very strongly and try to persuade other people to support it too ○ *This group carries the torch for the millions of people who demonstrated against the regime, and the thousands who died.*
pass the torch to someone to give leadership or responsibility to someone else, usually someone younger ○ *It's time for him to retire and pass the torch to someone else.*

toss-up

★ **it's a toss-up** used when two or more courses of action seem equally likely to succeed or fail, or two or more things are equally likely to happen ○ *It's a toss-up whether oil prices will go up or down over the days ahead.*

> When you toss a coin, there is an equal chance that the coin will land heads or tails.

totem pole

low on the totem pole having little or no importance ○ *Usually, consumer confidence ranks low on the totem pole of economic reports.*

★ **the low man on the totem pole** the person in an organization or group with the lowest status ○ *In my family, when it comes to any DIY project, I am the low man on the totem pole.*

A totem pole is a pole on which certain Native American peoples carve representations of their totems, which are animals with spiritual significance. The idea is that those higher up on the pole are more important.

touch

★ **do something at the touch of a button** to do something very easily and quickly, usually because of new technology ○ *Specially trained staff will be able to trace obscene and threatening calls at the touch of a button, and pass the information to police.*

★ **the common touch** the quality that some people in a position of power have of being able to understand how ordinary people think and feel and of being able to communicate with them ○ *Yudhoyono is seen as a politician with the common touch, who sings, writes poetry and plays guitar in a band.*

★ **it's touch and go** you cannot be certain whether something will happen or not ○ *I thought I was going to win the race, but it was still touch and go.*

lose your touch to lose your ability to do something well ○ *Then, Falcone lost his touch. His funds, which he had been managing successfully for years, plunged as the economy slowed.*

★ **someone is a soft touch** used when it is easy to make someone do what you want, or to make them agree with you ○ *Pamela was always a soft touch when*

Michael needed some cash.

To touch a person for money means to approach them and persuade them to let you have some money as a loan or a gift.

tough

hang tough to persist in a determined way when there is a lot of difficulty or resistance ○ *The Wildcats' offense reached full steam and were able to hang tough in the final two sets.*

tough as nails having a strong and independent character ○ *He was a very easy-going type of person in a large group, but across a negotiating table, he was tough as nails.*

tough as shoe leather difficult to chew and swallow ○ *The meat in the stew was as tough as shoe leather.*

towel

★ **throw in the towel** to stop trying to do something, because you know that you cannot succeed ○ *It seemed, initially, as if the police had thrown in the towel and were planning to abandon the investigation, but the following day the interviews resumed.*

In boxing, a fighter's trainer sometimes throws a towel or sponge into the ring as a signal of defeat in order to stop the fight before there are any more injuries.

tower

★ **a tower of strength** someone who gives you a lot of help or support during a difficult period of your life ○ *In her terrible sadness she has found Charles to be a tower of strength.*

town

go to town on something to deal with something with a lot of enthusiasm or energy ○ *They really went to town on the decorations for the party.*

out on the town in a public place of

entertainment, such as a restaurant, club, or theater ○ *A gossip columnist reported seeing them out on the town as "a nice cozy item."*

paint the town red to go out and enjoy yourself ○ *Let's go out and paint the town red!*

▤ This expression is said to have originated in the Wild West. It may have been used to describe groups of Native Americans setting fire to towns. Another possibility is that it referred to cowboys threatening to "paint the town red" with the blood of anyone who tried to stop their drunken behavior.

traces

kick over the traces to pay no attention to rules and conventions, and behave exactly as you want to ○ *Young people always want to kick over the traces, refusing to accept old values without question.*

▤ When a horse pulling a cart or carriage kicks over the traces, it steps over the side straps attached to its harness, so it can no longer be controlled effectively by the driver.

track

★ **the fast track to something** the quickest way of achieving something ○ *Like many of his classmates, Chris Urwin believes a university degree will be the fast track to corporate success.* ○ *The company offers fast-track promotion schemes for promising young executives.*

▤ A track here is a running track or racing track.

★ **have the inside track** to have an advantage, such as special knowledge about something ○ *Denver has the inside track among 10 sites being considered for the airline's new $1 billion maintenance facility.*

▤ On a racing track, the inside track is the shortest, and so the competitors want to use it in order to take advantage of this fact.

★ **keep track of something or someone** to make sure that you have accurate and up-to-date information about something or someone all the time ○ *I could never keep track of all the visitors to the mansion.*

★ **lose track of someone or something** to no longer know where someone or something is or what is happening to them ○ *You may wonder how the administrators of this fund can lose track of $20 million meant to help the poorest citizens.*

★ **off the beaten track** if a place is off the beaten track, it is isolated and quiet, because it is far from large cities or their centers, and so few people go there or live there ○ *The village is sufficiently off the beaten track to deter all but a few tourists.*

▤ A track here is a footpath or narrow road.

★ **on the right track** acting or progressing in a way that is likely to result in success ○ *Guests are returning to our hotel in increasing numbers – a sure sign that we are on the right track.*

★ **on the wrong track** acting or progressing in a way that is likely to result in failure ○ *Polls show that around 55 percent of voters believe the country is headed on the wrong track.*

★ **a track record** the reputation that a person, a company, or a product has, which is based on all their successes and failures in the past ○ *This corporation has a high-quality management team with a good track record.*

▤ An athlete's track record is a record of the performances he or she has achieved.

tracks

come from the wrong side of the tracks to come from a poor, unfashionable, and lower-class area of town ○ *Here are two sisters who come from the wrong side of the tracks in Los Angeles and have come to dominate the world of women's tennis.*

≣ Railroad tracks sometimes mark boundaries between different parts of a town, for example, between richer and poorer areas.

★ **cover your tracks** to hide or destroy evidence of your identity or actions, because you want to keep them secret ○ *The killer may have returned to the scene of the crime to cover his tracks.*

≣ Tracks here are footprints.

make tracks to leave the place where you are, usually in a hurry ○ *Webb looked at the bar clock. "Ten past nine. We must make tracks or we'll be late for the meeting."*

≣ In this expression, "tracks" are footprints.

★ **stop someone in their tracks** or **stop someone dead in their tracks** to make someone suddenly stop moving or doing something because they are very surprised, impressed, or frightened ○ *The sound of gunfire stopped them dead in their tracks.*

★ **stop something in its tracks** or **stop something dead in its tracks** to make something, such as a process or an activity, immediately stop continuing or developing ○ *Fresno Police say they've stopped a large car theft operation dead in its tracks.*

trail

★ **blaze a trail** to be the first person to do or discover something new and important, which will make it easier for other people to do something similar in the future ○ *The party is blazing a trail for*

the advancement of women in politics. ○ *A trailblazer in the treatment of mental illness, Bateman has served as a psychiatrist, administrator and teacher.*

≣ New trails or routes through forests were often marked by "blazing," which involved making white marks called "blazes" on tree trunks, usually by chipping off a piece of bark.

trap

★ **fall into the trap of doing something** to make a very common mistake, or one that is very easy to make ○ *School administrators often fall into the trap of thinking that discipline problems, not unsatisfying education, are the cause of low levels of achievement among pupils.*

traveler

a fellow traveler someone who is not a member of an organization but who supports its aims and ideas ○ *She was a supporter of McCormick and is a fellow traveler in the same school of thought.*

≣ This term was used in the 20th century to refer to people who were sympathetic to Communism and it is often used today with negative connotations.

tree

bark up the wrong tree to follow the wrong course of action because your beliefs or ideas about something are incorrect ○ *If you plan to become a writer because it will make you lots of money, you're barking up the wrong tree.*

≣ This expression comes from raccoon hunting, which takes place at night. Dogs that are trained to show where raccoons are hiding by barking sometimes indicate the wrong tree.

out of your tree (*informal*) crazy or behaving very strangely, sometimes as a result of drinking alcohol ○ *It was obvious* *they had been drinking. They were both out of their tree.*

★ **up a tree** in a difficult situation ○ *Here are ten rules to remember while hunting deer that won't leave you up a tree.*

trees

something does not grow on trees used about something that is very rare and difficult to obtain ○ *Mitchell will not be replaced in a hurry: managers with his expertise do not grow on trees.*

trial

★ **a trial balloon** an idea or plan that is suggested in order to find out about public opinion on a subject that causes many arguments ○ *The administration has not officially released details of the economic plan, although numerous trial balloons have been floated and hints have been dropped.*

≡ Balloons were formerly used to find out about weather conditions.

trick

★ **do the trick** to achieve the result that you want ○ *If these self-help remedies don't do the trick, consult a qualified homoeopath.*

it's the oldest trick in the book said when you want to suggest that people should have expected something dishonest or unfair that someone has done because it is a very common or obvious thing to do ○ *Well, that's the oldest trick in the book – to blame someone else for your problems.*

★ **not miss a trick** to always know what is happening and take advantage of every situation ○ *My assistant, Eileen, has a good eye for detail and never misses a trick.*

≡ The reference here is to a player winning every trick in a card game such as whist or bridge.

use every trick in the book to do everything you can think of in order to succeed in something ○ *Companies are using every trick in the book to stay one step*

ahead of their competitors.

tricks

★ **be up to your old tricks** to be behaving in a dishonest or foolish way that is typical of you ○ *They're up to their old tricks of promising one thing and doing the opposite.*

trigger

trigger happy too willing to use guns or react with violence ○ *The use of tasers is widespread among police departments, but critics worry the devices have made officers trigger happy.*

trim

in fighting trim in very good condition ○ *The company needs to be in fighting trim for the next decade, when domestic competition may increase.*

≡ A boxer who is in fighting trim is fit and ready to fight.

trooper

swear like a trooper to use a lot of swearwords ○ *Mo was rude and abusive and swore like a trooper.*

≡ A trooper is a soldier.

trowel

★ **lay something on with a trowel** to apply something thickly or do something to excess ○ *She wrote in her memoir that she knew how to get what she wanted: "When it comes to flattery, lay it on with a trowel."*

truck

big enough to drive a truck through or

[...] that you can drive a truck through used to suggest that an argument, proposal, contract, or something similar has a serious weakness or fault in it ○ *They aim to establish clear rules without loopholes that you can drive a truck through.*

★ **have no truck with something** to

strongly disapprove of something and refuse to become involved with it ○ *Smith stated clearly that his party will have no truck with any extremist attitudes or views.*

> "Truck" in this expression has an older meaning that refers to trading goods by bartering. "To have no truck with someone" literally means to have no dealings with them.

true

ring true if a statement or a promise rings true, it seems to be true or sincere ○ *He said he was sorry for upsetting me but his apology just didn't ring true.*

trump

play your trump card to do something unexpected that gives you a definite advantage over other people ○ *If she wished, she could threaten to play her trump card, publishing an autobiography of embarrassing disclosures.*

> In card games such as whist and bridge, one of the four suits is chosen as trump for each hand. Cards of that suit then rank higher than cards of the other three suits.

★ **a trump card** something that gives you a definite advantage over other people ○ *Only two days into the strike, the distribution of goods was suffering: and that, ultimately is the rail workers' trump card.*

trumps

★ **come up trumps** or
turn up trumps
1 to achieve an unexpectedly good result ○ *Sylvester Stallone came up trumps at the US box office with his movie Cliffhanger.*
2 to unexpectedly help someone with a problems ○ *In moments of crisis for me, you always come up trumps!*

> In card games such as whist and bridge, one of the four suits is chosen as trumps for each hand. Cards of that suit then rank higher than cards of the

other three suits. The reference here is to a player drawing a trump from the pack.

truth

★ **be economical with the truth** to deceive people by deliberately not telling them the whole truth about something. People use this expression when they want to suggest that someone is being dishonest, but do not actually want to accuse them of lying. ○ *She asked repeated questions but only received answers which were at best economical with the truth, at worst deliberately designed to deceive.*

tubes

be going down the tubes or
go down the tubes → see **down**

tune

carry a tune to sing the notes of a song properly ○ *I'm not a trained singer, but I can carry a tune.*

★ **call the tune** to be in control of a situation and make all the important decisions ○ *My husband spends lots of money on his hobbies but moans when I want to buy anything. He thinks he has the right to call the tune as he earns more money than I do.*

> This expression comes from the proverb "he who pays the piper calls the tune."

★ **change your tune** to express a different opinion about something or someone from the one you had expressed before ○ *He had maintained for many years that the Earl was dead. But these days he has changed his tune.*

dance to someone's tune to do whatever someone wants or tells you to do, usually without questioning them or hesitating. This expression is often used to criticize someone for allowing themselves to be controlled in this way. ○ *Supermarkets buy huge quantities of meat* *from farmers, but at the lowest possible price. So farmers have, unfortunately, been forced to dance to their tune.*

sing a different tune

1 to express ideas or opinions that are in complete contrast to the ones which you were expressing a short time ago ○ *She declared herself at peak fitness. Just 24 hours later, she was singing a different tune after losing badly in her match against Williams. "I wasn't prepared," she said. "And I was suffering from jet lag."*

2 if a group of people are singing a different tune, they are all expressing different opinions about something ○ *The problem of homelessness is great enough without two Government departments singing different tunes.*

sing the same tune → see **sing**

tunnel

★ **have tunnel vision** to focus all your energy and skill on the task that is most important to you and ignore things that other people might consider important ○ *They always say that you have to have tunnel vision to be a champion. You can't have any outside distractions at all.*

> Tunnel vision is a medical condition in which someone can only see things that are immediately in front of them, and cannot see things that are to the side.

turkey

cold turkey if someone stops something cold turkey or goes cold turkey, they completely and suddenly stop doing something or using something that they are used to do or use frequently ○ *The hardest part was having to give up coffee cold turkey, but I feel much better for it now.*

> This phrase may have originated from "talk cold turkey." See **talk turkey**, below.

talk turkey to discuss something in an honest, direct and serious way ○ *Suddenly government and industry are talking turkey. Last month the Prime Minister promised a partnership to improve the climate for business.*

> This expression is said to have its origin in a story about a white man who went hunting with a Native American. They caught several wild turkeys and some other birds. After the trip the white man divided the birds unfairly, keeping the turkeys for himself and giving the Native American the less tasty birds. The Native American protested, saying he wanted to "talk turkey."

a turkey shoot a battle or other conflict in which one side is so much stronger or better armed than the other that the weaker side has no chance at all. This expression is usually used to suggest that the situation is unfair. ○ *After weeks of bombing, it was a one-sided battle. The fighting stopped earlier than expected partly because of public disquiet at the "turkey-shoot."*

> A turkey shoot is an occasion when people hunt turkeys, which are very easy to shoot.

turn

★ **at every turn** if something happens at every turn, it happens very frequently or continuously, and usually prevents you from doing what you want to do ○ *Although the government has had a coherent economic plan, parliament has set out to block it at every turn.*

turtle

turn turtle if a boat turns turtle, it turns upside down when it is in the water ○ *The dinghy nearly turned turtle twice, but I managed to keep her upright.*

> Turtles are helpless when they are turned onto their backs.

twain

never the twain shall meet or
ne'er the twain shall meet *(literary)*
used to suggest that there are so many
differences between two groups of
people or two groups of things that
people believe that they can never exist
together in the same place or situation
○ *The education system is notorious for
separating the sciences and the humanities.
This academic "ne'er the twain shall meet"
policy unfortunately does not always reflect
the needs of the real world.*

> "Twain" is an old-fashioned word
> meaning two. This is a quotation from
> "The Ballad of East and West" (1889) by
> the English poet Rudyard Kipling: "Oh,
> East is East, and West is West, and
> never the twain shall meet."

two

be two of a kind to be two very similar
people ○ *We're two of a kind, Ed. That's
probably why our friendship's lasted this long.*
it takes two to tango a situation or
argument involves two people and they
are both therefore responsible for it ○ *I've
tried everything to stop our marriage falling
apart. But it takes two to tango and, so far,
my husband has made no effort to save our
relationship.*

> This is the title of a song by Hoffman
> and Manning, written in 1952.

★ **put two and two together** to
correctly guess the truth about
something from the information that
you have ○ *It's not going to be long before
the police put two and two together and come
looking for you.*

typhoid

Typhoid Mary a person who brings bad
luck or disaster wherever he or she goes,
and so is avoided by others ○ *These clients
were considered akin to Typhoid Mary among
private bankers.*

> Historically, Typhoid Mary was a cook
> who spread the disease typhoid to
> several hospitals that she worked in,
> though she never became ill herself.

Uu

ugly

★ **ugly as sin** extremely ugly and unattractive ○ *This car is just plain ugly as sin.*

unglued

come unglued

1 to lose control of your emotions and to behave in a strange or crazy way ○ *She had apparently come unglued since losing her job.*

2 to fail ○ *Their marriage finally came unglued.*

up

★ **on the up and up**

1 honest or legal ○ *If you're honest and on the up and up, I'll be able to tell it, feel it. If you're hiding something, I can tell that too.*

2 becoming very successful and doing well ○ *Their career path has flattened out slightly rather than still being on the up and up.*

swear up and down to insist that you are telling the truth ○ *He'd sworn up and down he was going to get the cash and bring it right back.*

★ **up and coming** likely to be successful in the future ○ *He was one of our very up and coming young ministers and I feel he had a great future in front of him.*

★ **up and running** working or functioning successfully after a good start ○ *We've invested in the people, tools, and technology to get your system up and running quickly and keep it that way.*

upstairs

kick someone upstairs to give someone a job or position which appears to have a higher status but actually has less power or influence ○ *The radicals kicked him upstairs to the ceremonial job of president.*

use

it's no use crying over spilled milk → see **milk**

Vv

vacuum

★ **in a vacuum** separately from the things that you would expect something to be connected with ○ *Such decisions do not occur in a political vacuum, but have serious political implications both at home and abroad.*

variety

variety is the spice of life used to express the idea that doing and seeing a lot of different things makes life more enjoyable and interesting ○ *It is important to vary the training program so that boredom is avoided. Exercise should be fun and variety is the spice of life.*

veil

draw a veil over something to deliberately not talk about something or give any details, because you want to keep it private or because it is embarrassing ○ *Most of us have something in our past career over which we choose to draw a veil.*

▤ A veil is a piece of cloth used by a woman to cover her face.

victor

to the victor go the spoils or **to the victor belong the spoils** (*literary*) said to mean whoever wins a contest, election, or war gains control over many things that belonged to the loser ○ *We believe that anyone who's qualified and out-performed the others – to the victor belong the spoils.*

▤ "Spoils" are things taken in a war by the winner from the loser.

view

a bird's-eye view a clear impression of what is happening ○ *When I was a Congressional staffer I got a bird's-eye view of the way politicians encourage people to believe in dreams.*

★ **take a dim view of something** to disapprove of something ○ *Back in 1989 he took a dim view of lotteries, and wrote to a proposer: "I do not support your proposal for a lottery and would wish not to be involved at this stage."*

a worm's eye view an impression of what is happening in a situation from the point of view of someone who has a low status, or is considered inferior in some way ○ *They were considered to be leaders who, for the most part, "were complete fools, with a worm's eye view of the world and a poor understanding of their jobs."*

villain

★ **the villain of the piece** the person who is responsible for all the trouble or all the problems in a situation ○ *If he is indeed the villain of the piece, as the police claim he is, he should have been more carefully watched.*

▤ In this expression, the "piece" is a play.

vine

wither on the vine or **die on the vine** (*literary*) to die or gradually come to an end ○ *I talked to senior citizens and ordinary people all over this state who are worried that the American dream is dying on the vine.*

violet

a shrinking violet a person who is very shy and timid ○ *None of the women he paints could be described as shrinking violets.*

In the past, violets were considered to be a symbol of modesty, because of their small size and the fact that the flowers remain hidden among the leaves until they open.

volumes

★ **speak volumes** to reveal or imply a lot about a situation ○ *What you wear speaks volumes, and it can lie, too.*

≡ In this expression, a "volume" is a book.

Ww

wad

someone has shot their wad
someone has done everything they can
or spent all their money to achieve
something but has failed, and now can
do nothing else to achieve their aims
○ *They shot their wad in the first part of the
game and didn't score in the second half.*

This expression is based on one of the
informal meanings of wad, which is "a
bundle of money."

wagon

be on the wagon to have stopped
drinking alcohol ○ *He was an alcoholic, but
he's been on the wagon for more than 10
years.*

Originally the expression was "on the
water wagon" or "water cart." Water
carts were horse-drawn carts used for
transporting water or for sprinkling
the streets. If someone was "on the
wagon," they were drinking water and
not alcohol.

**hitch your wagon to someone or
something** to try to become more
successful by forming a relationship with
someone or something that is already
successful ○ *The increasing power of the
Pacific rim provides a reason why Russia
should not hitch its wagon too closely to
America.*

This is a quotation from the essay
"Civilization" (1870) by the American
writer Ralph Waldo Emerson: "Now
that is the wisdom of a man, in every
instance of his labor, to hitch his
wagon to a star, and see his chore
done by the gods themselves."

wagons

circle the wagons to unite with the
other people in a group in order to
protect yourselves and fight whoever is
attacking you ○ *Some African-Americans
who initially opposed Thomas because of his
politics are circling the wagons to support
him because of his race.*

According to some Wild West stories,
when wagon trains were attacked by
Native Americans, the settlers drove
the wagons into a circle in order to
defend themselves better.

wake

The wake of a ship is the trail of white
foaming water behind it.

★ **in something's wake** if an event
leaves an unpleasant situation in its
wake, that situation happens after that
event or is caused by it ○ *A deadly cloud of
gas swept along the valleys north of Lake
Nyos in western Cameroon, leaving a trail of
death and devastation in its wake.*

★ **in the wake of something** happening
after an earlier event, especially an
unpleasant one, often as a result of it
○ *Local taxi drivers say they are acting more
cautiously in the wake of a murder of one of
their own in Sacramento early Monday
morning.*

wake-up

★ **a wake-up call** an event that shocks
people into taking action about a difficult
or dangerous situation ○ *The jury said the
damages were intended to send a wake-up
call to the firm and other big companies that
sexual harassment would not be tolerated.*

If you have a wake-up call, you arrange for someone to telephone you at a certain time in the morning so that you are sure to wake up at that time.

walk

take a walk to go away or to stop interfering ○ *The Coastguard broke in almost immediately, asking if we required any assistance. "Tell him to take a walk," said Steve.*

a walk in the park something that is very easy ○ *I thought marriage was tough, but that's a walk in the park compared to golf.*

★ **walk tall** → see **tall**

walk the walk (*informal*) to act in a way that matches the things that you say ○ *But the time has come for Mr. Coleman to prove that he can walk the walk to the same level as he can talk the talk.*

wall

drive someone up the wall to annoy someone a lot ○ *He's so uncooperative - he's beginning to drive me up the wall.*

★ **go to the wall** to take extreme and determined action in order to succeed ○ *"The committee will go to the wall on women's rights," she said.*

hit the wall to reach a point where you cannot go any further or achieve any more ○ *To ensure their businesses do not hit the wall, operators must ensure their financial management is strong and streamlined.*

nail someone to the wall to make someone suffer, because you are very angry with them ○ *If he could not pay off his debt, they would nail him to the wall.*

★ **off the wall** unusual, unconventional, or eccentric ○ *The new channel is so off the wall and unlike anything we see at the moment that you really have to watch it to appreciate how it will be.* ○ *At other times the band plays a kind of off-the-wall lounge music, a kind of soundtrack to a hip science fiction movie.*

This may be a reference to a shot in a game such as squash or handball, where the ball bounces off the wall at an unexpected angle.

someone will go to the wall for someone or something used about someone who is prepared to suffer on behalf of a person or a principle that they support strongly ○ *Above all, he prizes loyalty. He'll go to the wall for someone or something he believes in.*

One explanation for this expression is that it refers to someone who is trapped with their back to a wall and no way of escape. Another explanation is that it refers to medieval chapels in which healthy people used to stand, but which had seats around the walls for sick people. A third explanation is that it refers to someone standing in front of a wall before being executed by a firing squad.

★ **the writing is on the wall** or **the handwriting is on the wall** said when you have noticed things that strongly suggest that a situation is going to become difficult or unpleasant ○ *The writing is clearly on the wall. If we do nothing about it, we will only have ourselves to blame.*

This expression comes from a Bible story (Daniel 5) in which a mysterious hand appears and writes a message on the wall, announcing that Belshazzar's kingdom will soon come to an end.

wallop

pack a wallop to be very powerful, effective, or forceful ○ *Despite numerous health problems, Lewis still packs a wallop in his stage show.*

A wallop is a powerful blow.

walls

climb the walls to feel very frustrated, nervous, or anxious ○ *I'm climbing the* *walls now because I haven't got a job. I have been searching hard for six months without success.*

walls have ears said to warn someone that they should be careful about what they are saying because people might be listening ○ *Take care. This place is like a village. Assume all walls have ears.*

war

a war of nerves → see **nerves**

★ **a war of words** a situation in which two people or groups of people argue or criticize each other because they strongly disagree about a particular issue ○ *A war of words has blown up over who is to blame for a confrontation between police and fans outside the venue.*

warpath

on the warpath very angry and getting ready for a fight or quarrel ○ *St. Vincent and Grenadines' biggest businessmen are on the warpath after claims that foreign nationals are trying to con them out of thousands of dollars.*

Native Americans were said to be "on the warpath" when they were on an expedition to attack their enemies. The warpath was the path or route that they took.

warts

★ **warts and all** used for describing someone or something as they are, including all their faults ○ *Judith would not be the first wife to have gotten the measure of her husband and decided that he is still the man for her, warts and all.*

The 17th century English leader Oliver Cromwell is said to have told an artist who was painting his portrait that he did not wish to be flattered: "Remark all these roughnesses, pimples, warts, and everything as you see me, otherwise I will never pay a farthing for it."

wash

everything will come out in the wash said to reassure someone that everything will be all right ○ *That will be the end of that. Everything will come out in the wash – I promise you.*

something will come out in the wash used as a warning that people will eventually find out the truth about something ○ *It will make great listening at his trial. Everything will come out in the wash, and Flashman will deserve it all.*

waste

lay waste to something (literary) to completely destroy something ○ *In less than ten years this destructive beetle has laid waste to millions of ash trees in several states and Canada.*

watch

★ **on someone's watch** during a period when someone is in a position of power, and is therefore considered to be responsible for what happens ○ *Mistakes were made on my watch, and accordingly I believe my decision to retire, while painful, is appropriate.*

When someone such as a soldier is on watch, they have been ordered to remain alert, usually while others sleep, so that they can warn of danger or an attack.

water

★ **be dead in the water** to have failed and to have little hope of success in the future ○ *People are not spending money: they're not buying houses; they're not going into stores. This economy is dead in the water.*

The image here is of a sailboat that cannot move because there is no wind.

blow something out of the water to destroy something completely, suddenly, and violently. ○ *The government is in a state of paralysis. Its main economic and* foreign policies have been blown out of the water.

> The image here is of a ship that is completely destroyed by a missile or torpedo.

in deep water in a difficult or awkward situation ○ *You certainly seem to be in deep water and doing your utmost to reverse the negative trends of the past couple of months or so.*

★ **in hot water** in a situation in which you have done something wrong and people are angry with you ○ *Debbie is in hot water when Rick discovers her attempt to sabotage his relationship with Sarah.*

like water off a duck's back if criticism is like water off a duck's back, it is not having any effect at all on the person being criticized ○ *Every time you discipline him he will smile sweetly so that you may think your rebukes are streaming away like water off a duck's back.*

> The feathers on a duck's back are covered with an oily substance that keeps them from absorbing water so that it flows straight off them.

★ **pour cold water on something** or **throw cold water on something** to point out all the problems of an idea or plan, rather than sharing other people's enthusiasm for it ○ *They poured cold water on the French proposal for a peace conference involving both the EU and the UN.*

★ **something does not hold water** used to suggest that a theory or an argument cannot possibly be true or right ○ *They make it clear that the governor's argument does not hold water.*

★ **test the water** or **test the waters** to try to find out what the reaction to an idea or plan might be before taking action to put it into effect ○ *I was a bit sceptical. I decided to test the water before committing the complete management team.*

★ **tread water** to be in an unsatisfactory situation where you are not progressing, but are just continuing doing the same things ○ *I could either tread water until I was promoted, which looked to be a few years away, or I could change what I was doing.*

> When swimmers tread water, they move their arms and legs in order to keep their head above the water without actually making progress in any direction.

water over the dam or **water under the bridge** used for describing an event or situation that happened in the past and so is no longer worth thinking about or worrying about ○ *Mr. Bruce said that he was relieved it was over and that he regarded his time in jail as water under the bridge.*

waterfront

cover the waterfront to cover a very wide range of things, or cover every aspect of something ○ *We have five employees looking after this whole project. They cover the entire waterfront: oil, real estate, high-tech, and everything else.*

Waterloo

meet your Waterloo to suffer a very severe defeat or failure, especially one that causes you to finally give up what you are trying to do ○ *At the foot of cliff I met my Waterloo. The face of the cliff rose sheer above us, and it was clear even to me that we would not be able to climb it.*

> In 1815, the French leader Napoleon suffered his final defeat at the Battle of Waterloo in Belgium.

waters

muddy the waters to deliberately try to make a situation or an issue more confusing and complicated than it really is ○ *This ruling seems only to have muddied the waters. It seems a bit confusing and we are seeking clarification.*

still waters run deep used about someone who seems to be unemotional or who is hard to get to know is in fact interesting and complex ○ *He's extremely shy and withdrawn, though it may be that still waters run very deep.*

troubled waters a difficult or delicate situation ○ *Last month the company ran into troubled waters, and it is now facing bankruptcy.*

test the waters → see **water**

wave

catch the wave to seize an opportunity that is presented to you, especially an opportunity to do something new ○ *With mid-term elections on the horizon, politicians are hoping to catch the wave of rising discontent.*

≡ Surfers need to catch a wave just as it breaks in order to ride it successfully.

wavelength

★ **on the same wavelength** if two people are on the same wavelength, they understand each other well because they share the same attitudes, interests, and opinions ○ *We could complete each other's sentences because we were on the same wavelength.*

≡ A radio program cannot be heard unless the radio is tuned to the correct wavelength.

waves

★ **make waves** to disturb a situation by changing things or by challenging the way things are done, often in a way that improves the situation ○ *Maathai has a history of making waves. In 1971 she became the first woman in East and Central Africa to earn a PhD.*

way

★ **the easy way out** doing what is easiest for yourself in a difficult situation,

rather than dealing with the problem properly ○ *It is the easy way out to blame others for our failure, and this is bad practice.*

go back a long way or

go way back to have been friends or associates for a very long time ○ *We go back a long way, and she's always kept in touch, always been there for me.*

★ **look the other way** to deliberately ignore something unpleasant, immoral, or illegal that is happening when you should be trying to deal with it or stop it from happening ○ *Stolen goods are sold unashamedly in broad daylight but you tend to look the other way and mind your own business.*

★ **pave the way for something** to make it easier for another thing to happen ○ *A peace agreement last year paved the way for this week's elections.*

rub someone the wrong way to annoy someone a great deal ○ *Ella had an uncommon knack of rubbing everyone the wrong way.*

≡ Cats do not like having their fur rubbed "the wrong way," that is in the opposite direction to the way it naturally grows.

someone can't [...] their way out of a paper bag said to mean that someone is very bad at a particular activity. This expression can be used with many different action verbs. ○ *We've already shown you that they are no use to you as allies. They couldn't fight their way out of a paper bag.* ○ *Some of the cast couldn't act their way out of a paper bag.*

ways

cut both ways to have two different effects, usually one good and one bad ○ *Revenge cuts both ways in the Israeli-Palestinian conflict, with attacks by either side leading to retaliation.*

★ **mend your ways** to stop behaving badly or illegally and improve your behavior ○ *He seemed to accept his* sentence meekly, promising to work hard in prison and to mend his ways.

set in your ways having very fixed habits and ideas that you are unlikely or unwilling to change ○ *Try not to become set in your ways. It's very easy to develop personal routines and not to accept that other people have other ways of doing things.*

wayside

★ **fall by the wayside**

1 to fail in something you were doing and give up trying to achieve success in it ○ *The average player's lifespan at the top is five years. You either play well, deal with the pressure, or you fall by the wayside.*

2 if an activity has fallen by the wayside, people have stopped doing it and forgotten about it ○ *Each year our birthday parties grow more and more polite. We still have a birthday cake and give presents, but dancing seems to have fallen by the wayside.*

This expression comes from the story of the sower (= a person who plants seeds) told by Jesus in the Bible (Mark 4:4). The seed that falls by the wayside represents the people who do not pay attention to Jesus's teachings.

wazoo

★ **up the wazoo** or
out the wazoo (*informal*) to a great extent or in huge quantity ○ *He received endorsements up the wazoo and nobody seemed to be concerned with his entrenchment in the world of payday lending or shady real estate deals.*

wear

wear and tear damage to something that is expected from its normal use ○ *The company does not accept liability for normal wear and tear to baggage, for example damage to straps and handles.*

weather

make heavy weather of something to make an activity or task much more difficult or take more time than it needs to ○ *To an outsider, though, the surprising thing is not that Spain's conservatives are inching ahead but that they are making such heavy weather of it.*

Ships were said to make heavy weather when they handled badly and were difficult to control in rough seas.

★ **under the weather** not feeling very well ○ *If you're feeling a bit under the weather but can't work out what's wrong, try our DIY guide to self-diagnosis.*

web

a tangled web something that is very confused and difficult to understand ○ *It is sometimes difficult to cut through the tangled web of government information in order to know the benefits you can claim.*

wedge

★ **drive a wedge between people** to cause bad feelings between two people who are close in order to weaken their relationship ○ *I did try to reassure her, but that only seemed to irritate her more. That made me upset, and I started to feel Toby was driving a wedge between us.*

the thin end of the wedge the beginning of something that seems harmless or unimportant at present but is likely to become important, serious, or harmful in the future ○ *I think it's the thin end of the wedge when you have armed police permanently on patrol around a city.*

weight

★ **carry weight** to be respected and able to influence people ○ *El Tiempo is Colombia's leading newspaper. Its opinions carry considerable weight in the country.*

carry the weight of the world on your shoulders to have many troubles or responsibilities ○ *You look as if you're carrying the weight of the world on those lovely shoulders.*

This expression may be a reference to

Atlas, a giant in Greek mythology, who was punished by Zeus by being made to carry the heavens on his shoulders, and who is often portrayed with the world on his back.

dead weight something or someone that makes change or progress extremely difficult ○ *The Los Angeles Angels were carrying around a lot of dead weight this season, and that's not a good thing when you're trying to run the bases.*

★ **pull your weight** to work as hard as everyone else who is involved in the same task or activity ○ *Your performance will be judged by the performance of your team, and you cannot afford to carry members who are not pulling their weight.*

throw your weight around to behave aggressively and use your authority over other people more forcefully than you need to ○ *Jonathon Rose, defending, told the jury: "My client is the sort of person who likes to throw his weight around after he's been watching football with the boys."*

★ **throw your weight behind someone or something** to do everything you can to support a person, plan, or campaign ○ *The U.S. government is promising now to throw its weight behind the peace negotiations.*

worth your weight in gold very useful, helpful, or valuable ○ *Successful television is about having ideas. People with ideas are worth their weight in gold.*

west

go west (old-fashioned) to die ○ *When he went west, he wanted to be remembered.*

The sun "goes west" when it sinks below the horizon in the west at the end of the day. The comparison between going west and dying has been used in many different languages and cultures for many centuries. For example, people sometimes associate this expression with Native Americans,

who used to say that a dying person went west to meet the sinking sun.

whack

★ **out of whack** not working properly; out of order ○ *The overwhelming sense among so many Americans is that the relationship between government and the governed has gotten out of whack.*

whale

have a whale of a time to enjoy yourself a lot ○ *I had a whale of a time in Birmingham.*

wheat

separate the wheat from the chaff to decide which things or people in a group are good or necessary, and which are not ○ *The reality is often blurred by the propaganda. It is becoming more and more difficult to separate the wheat from the chaff.*

The "chaff" is the outer part of wheat that has been separated from the grain. In the Bible (Matthew 3:12; Luke 3:17), John the Baptist uses the image of someone separating the wheat from the chaff to describe how Jesus will separate those who go to heaven from those who go to hell.

wheel

a big wheel someone who has an important and powerful position in an organization or society ○ *They flew Robin to New York, where George's uncle was a big wheel at Memorial Hospital.*

reinvent the wheel to work on an idea or project that you consider new or different, when it is really no better than something that already exists ○ *Learn from Scandinavia. We have created foundations for other countries to follow. Each country's organization does not need to reinvent the wheel.*

the squeaky wheel gets the grease said to mean someone who complains often or loudly will get the attention they want ○ *I've sent numerous letters to the town officials because the squeaky wheel gets the grease.*

a third wheel someone who is unwanted and unimportant in a situation ○ *Women really do suffer more as widows. The fifth woman at a couples dinner party is a third wheel.*

≡ A third wheel on a bicycle would be unnecessary.

wheels

grease the wheels to help things to run smoothly and successfully ○ *Credit cards greased the wheels of the consumer boom by allowing us to buy what we want, when we want.*

set the wheels in motion to do what is necessary to start carrying out an important plan or project ○ *I have set the wheels in motion to sell my place: the sooner I get out of this neighborhood, the better.*

spin your wheels to fail to do or achieve anything satisfactory ○ *He is not getting anywhere. He's just spinning his wheels.*

the wheels are turning used when a process or situation is continuing to develop and progress ○ *The wheels are turning on plans to convert the building into a bookstore.*

wheels within wheels a situation that is very complicated because many different things, which influence one another, are involved in it ○ *Our culture is more complex than he knows. Wheels within wheels. Hierarchies.*

≡ This expression comes from the Bible: "The wheels looked the same. They looked like a wheel within a wheel." (Ezekiel 1:16)

whip

crack the whip to make people work very hard and treat them strictly and perhaps harshly ○ *They run the school, I don't. They crack the whip and I have to jump to it.*

have the whip hand or
hold the whip hand to have more power than the other people involved in a situation, and so have an advantage or control over them ○ *The biggest party in Congress should have the whip hand in decision-making.*

whirl

give something a whirl to try something in order to see whether you like it or think you can be successful doing it ○ *Why not give acupuncture a whirl?*

whirlwind

reap the whirlwind *(literary)* to suffer now because of mistakes that were made in the past ○ *We are reaping the whirlwind from parents who grew up in the sixties, and who themselves were encouraged to question everything.*

≡ This is a quotation from the Bible (Hosea 8:7). It refers to the punishment of the Israelites for disobeying God. It says that they have planted the wind, and that they will now harvest a whirlwind (= a storm).

whisker

be within a whisker of something to be almost a particular amount ○ *Unemployment, at 6.4 per cent of the workforce, is now within a whisker of the rate at which inflation has often started to climb.*

by a whisker if you succeed in doing something by a whisker, you almost fail. If you fail to do something by a whisker, you almost succeed. ○ *At the end we lost by a whisker and I feel terribly disappointed.*

★ **come within a whisker of doing something** to nearly succeed in doing something. ○ *He came within a whisker of scoring a spectacular goal.*

whistle

★ **blow the whistle on someone or something** to tell the authorities about something secret or illegal, or someone who is doing something illegal, dishonest, or immoral because you feel strongly that what they are doing is wrong and they should be stopped ○ *Members of Queensland coastal communities are being asked to blow the whistle on activities that damage the marine environment.* ○ *The department needs to protect whistle-blowers, health professionals who want and care to make a change in the system.*

In games such as football, the referee blows a whistle to stop play when a player has committed a foul.

someone can whistle for something said rudely to mean that you will not give something to someone ○ *She refused to open her books to the auditors, closed the show and told the city it could whistle for its money.*

There was an old superstition among sailors that they could make the wind blow by whistling.

white

white as a sheet or
white as a ghost very pale and frightened ○ *There was another truckdriver who pulled in in front of me, who it affected badly. She was as white as a sheet.*

white as snow very white in color ○ *When it's warm enough to go bare-legged but your skin's as white as snow, a fake tan's the answer.*

whiter than white used for describing someone whose actions are always honest and moral. You usually use this expression when you are referring to doubts about the person's character or behavior, or when you are being ironic and trying to suggest that the person is less honest or moral than they appear to

be. ○ *He is prepared to forgive Atherton's deceit this time, but it has left him in no doubt that his behavior must be whiter than white in future.*

whys

the whys and wherefores the reasons for something ○ *Even successful bosses need to be queried about the whys and wherefores of their actions.*

"Wherefore" is an old-fashioned word meaning "for what" or "why."

wilderness

★ **in the wilderness** used for describing a part of someone's career when they are inactive and ignored, and do not have an influential role ○ *He is delighted to get another chance to represent his country after a period in the wilderness.*

a voice crying in the wilderness or **a lone voice in the wilderness** someone who is pointing out the dangers in a situation or the truth about it, but nobody is paying any attention ○ *For years, he was a lone voice in the wilderness, and a lot of it came across as self-serving. But I'll tell you, the man was right.*

This is from the Bible (Matthew 3:3), and refers to John the Baptist who preached the coming of the Messiah but was often ignored.

wildfire

★ **spread like wildfire** to very quickly reach or affect a lot of people ○ *When final confirmation of his release came, the news spread like wildfire.*

This expression may refer to the way fires that start in the countryside spread very quickly and are difficult to control.

willies

give you the willies to make you feel

very nervous or frightened ○ *Living on the mountainside is enough to give anyone the willies – especially when the wolves howl like the wind at night.*

wind

blow in the wind to be thought about and discussed, but not decided upon or resolved ○ *The agreement blowing in the wind at Montreal signalled a change in business conditions, and du Pont decided to jump in.*

★ **get wind of something** to get to know about a plan or information, often when other people did not want you to ○ *I want nothing said about this until I give the word. I don't want the public, and especially not the press, to get wind of it at this stage.*

This expression refers to animals being able to smell hunters or other animals when they are some way off, because the smell is carried to them on the wind.

gone with the wind gone forever ○ *It is really sad to know that the sacredness of marriage is all but gone with the wind this time.*

"Gone With the Wind" is the title of a 1936 novel, later made into a movie, about the Civil War. It deals with the fact that the war completely changed the way of life in the South.

in the wind likely to happen ○ *Change is in the wind and this team will alter as the year unfolds.*

it's an ill wind or
it's an ill wind that blows nobody any good used to express the idea that unpleasant events and difficult situations often have unexpected good effects for someone ○ *It's an ill wind, of course, and what is bad for the oil companies is good for the consumer and inflation.*

like the wind very quickly ○ *Out on the water, the boat goes like the wind.*

sail close to the wind to take a risk by doing or saying something that may get you into trouble ○ *Max warned her she was sailing dangerously close to the wind and risked prosecution.*

If someone sails a boat too close to the wind, they try to sail in the direction from which the wind is blowing, and may stop or capsize as a result.

a second wind the strength or motivation to go on and succeed in what you are doing when you are tired or unsuccessful ○ *It was great tennis and it was fun. I got a second wind midway through the fourth set.*

If runners who are out of breath get their "second wind," their breathing becomes easier and they are able to continue.

see which way the wind is blowing or
see how the wind is blowing to understand or realize how a situation is developing and use this in deciding what to do ○ *He wasn't one to make pronouncements before he had seen which way the wind was blowing.*

spit in the wind to waste your time by trying to do something that has little or no chance of success ○ *But the idea that you can talk about a single currency today is to spit in the wind of economic reality.*

take the wind out of someone's sail or
take the wind out of someone's sails to make someone feel much less confident in what they are doing or saying ○ *We hit a bad patch after losing in the semi-final. The effort and disappointment took the wind out of our sails for a while.*

twisting in the wind or
swinging in the wind left in a very difficult and weak position, often by people who hope to gain advantage from this for themselves ○ *Any global*

settlement with Knauf, to be considered truly global, cannot leave those victims twisting in the wind.

windmills

tilt at windmills to waste your time on problems or issues that in other people's opinion are not really problems at all ○ *I have spent my life tilting at windmills. Will I never learn?*

This expression refers to the novel "Don Quixote" (1605) by the Spanish writer Cervantes, in which Don Quixote sees some windmills, thinks that they are giants, and tries to attack them.

window

★ **go out the window** or
fly out the window if a plan or a particular way of thinking or behaving goes out the window, it disappears completely ○ *Three years later she met Mick, and her good intentions flew out the window.*

wing

do something on a wing and a prayer to do something in the hope that you will succeed, even though you do not have the proper resources for it, or are not properly equipped or prepared ○ *Whatever the cause, large parts of the government seem to be running on a wing and a prayer.*

This is the title of a song by H. Adamson, written in 1943, which referred to the emergency landing of an aircraft: "Tho' there's one motor gone, we can still carry on, Comin' In On A Wing And A Pray'r."

★ **take someone under your wing** to protect someone and make sure that they are all right ○ *I let him tag along because he had not been too well recently. I took him under my wing and looked after him.*

The image here is of a hen gathering her chicks under her wing.

under the wing of someone in a situation in which someone controls you or takes responsibility for you ○ *If their problems are picked up at school and they come under the wing of an educational psychologist, they may be found a place in a special school.*

The image here is of a hen gathering her chicks under her wing.

wings

★ **clip someone's wings** to limit someone's freedom to do what they want ○ *The opposition has been trying to clip his wings by making his actions and his appointments subject to parliamentary approval.*

People sometimes clip the wings of captive birds to prevent them from flying away.

★ **spread your wings** to do something new that is more ambitious than anything you have done before ○ *I've always had a very strong musical direction and I was able to really flourish and spread my wings.*

try your wings to try to do something new to see if you can succeed ○ *He was very eager to try his wings and be a deputy on his own.*

★ **wait in the wings** to wait for an opportunity to take action, especially to take over another person's job or position ○ *He was one of a number of young, up and coming American players who were waiting in the wings for the next Major Championship.*

In a theater, the wings are the hidden areas to the left and right of a stage, where the actors wait before going on to the stage.

wink

not sleep a wink or
not get a wink of sleep to not be able

to go to sleep ❍ *This was my first Grand Prix win of the season and I was so excited I couldn't sleep a wink that night.*

winks

forty winks (old-fashioned) a short sleep or rest ❍ *There's nothing like forty winks to ease away the tension and stresses of a hard day.*

wire

★ **down to the wire** until the last possible moment ❍ *As Congress worked down to the wire to reach a compromise, the president lectured a group of White House interns on the budget crisis.*

get in under the wire to get in somewhere or do something at the last possible moment ❍ *On first reading it looks like they'll get in under the wire because they have a US partner on the team.*

≡ The "wire" here is an imaginary one that the horses pass under at the end of a race. A horse that gets in "under the wire" just manages to beat another horse and finish in one of the winning places.

a live wire someone who is very lively and energetic ❍ *She is a wonderful girl, a real live wire and full of fun.*

≡ A live wire is an electric wire or cable that has an electric current running through it.

wires

get your wires crossed to be mistaken about what someone else means or thinks ❍ *Despite her tone of voice, she still looked vaguely confused. He began to wonder if they'd got their wires crossed.*

witless

scare someone witless to make someone very frightened or worried ❍ *The door used to blow open and scare me witless.*

wits

★ **at your wits' end** very worried and desperate about something and not knowing what to do about it ❍ *People are at their wits' end about crime and they want to do something. They want action.*

collect your wits or

gather your wits (literary) to make an effort to control yourself and become calm again, after you have had a frightening or shocking experience ❍ *For a moment all he knew was the shocked terror of being left in a hail of gunfire; then he collected his wits, scrambled up and fled.*

have to have your wits about you or

have to keep your wits about you or

need your wits about you to need to be alert and ready to take action in a difficult or new situation ❍ *You've got to have your wits about you when you're driving a car.*

pit your wits against someone to use your intelligence to try to defeat someone ❍ *He has to pit his wits against an adversary who is cool, clever, cunning and desperate not to be caught.*

scare someone out of their wits or

scare the wits out of someone to make someone very frightened or worried ❍ *The tree crashed through the conservatory and set off all the alarms, which joined with the sound of the gale to scare me out of my wits.*

wives

★ **an old wives' tale** a commonly held belief that is based on traditional ideas, often ones that have been proved to be incorrect or inaccurate ❍ *My mother used to tell me to feed a cold and starve a fever. Is it just an old wives' tale?*

wolf

★ **cry wolf** to continually ask for help when it is not needed, or warn about danger when it does not really exist, so that people stop believing you and will not help you when it is really necessary ○ *Knowing when to order an evacuation is crucial. If it is issued too early, the storm could veer off in another direction, then officials could be accused of crying wolf and future orders might not be taken seriously.*

In one of Aesop's fables, a little boy who looks after sheep amuses himself by calling for help and making the villagers rush to rescue him when in fact there is no danger. One day a wolf comes and attacks the sheep, but the villagers do not believe him when he calls for help, and the sheep are all killed.

keep the wolf from the door to provide you with enough money to live on ○ *Your pension will keep the wolf from the door, but for a comfortable old age you need to make maximum use of the financial choices now open to you.*

For many centuries in the past, wolves were symbols of hunger.

a lone wolf someone who is independent and likes doing things on their own, rather than doing them with other people ○ *Among his peers, he is something of a lone wolf.*

a wolf in sheep's clothing someone who appears harmless or ordinary, but is really very dangerous or powerful ○ *A Muncy-area man described as "the worst type of predator - a classic wolf in sheep's clothing" was sentenced Thursday to 35 to 70 years in state prison.*

In one of Aesop's fables, a wolf wraps itself in a fleece and manages to get into a sheepfold without being noticed. It then attacks the sheep and eats them. This image is also used in the Bible (Matthew 7:15), where people are advised to beware of false teachers of God's word; they may appear harmless, but in fact they are dangerous and destructive.

wolves

throw someone to the wolves to allow someone to be criticized severely or treated roughly, and not try to protect them ○ *What I fear most is the thought of being released into the general prison population. I don't know what will happen if they throw me to the wolves.*

wonder

a one-day wonder or
a nine-day wonder something or someone that is interesting, exciting, or successful for only a very short time, and does not have any lasting value ○ *If the goal was simply to make people aware of environmental problems it was a great success. The fear of environmentalists, though, is that this may prove to be a one-day wonder.*

"A nine-day wonder" may be related to the Catholic "Novena" festivals, which last for nine days.

wood

dead wood someone or something that is no longer useful or effective in a particular organization or situation ○ *Now is the time for the dead wood at the top of the organization to be cut away.*

knock on wood said when you hope that a situation will continue to be good and that you will not have any bad luck ○ *She's never even been to the doctor, knock on wood. She's a healthy happy child and anyone can see that.*

This expression may come from the ancient belief that good spirits lived in trees and people used to tap on them to ask the spirits for help or protection. Alternatively, it may be related to the Christian practice of touching a rosary or crucifix. People sometimes actually touch or knock on a wooden surface as they say this.

woods

★ **not out of the woods** still having difficulties with something or still in a bad condition ○ *One economist warns the nation's economy is not out of the woods yet, that there has to be concern about financial shocks coming from abroad.*

⋮ This may come from the proverb "Don't halloo till you are out of the wood," which is a warning not to celebrate something before you have actually achieved your aim.

not set the woods on fire to not be very exciting or successful ○ *The Mississippi defense has not been setting the woods on fire this year.*

woodwork

come out of the woodwork to suddenly start publicly doing something or saying something, when previously you did nothing or kept quiet ○ *People are starting to come out of the woodwork to talk about fraudulent practices in the industry.*

wool

★ **dyed-in-the-wool** used to describe a supporter of a particular philosophy or a member of a particular group to suggest that they have very strong beliefs or feelings about that philosophy or group, and are unlikely ever to change ○ *Mr. Purves has made Hong Kong his home for the past 38 years but he remains a dyed-in-the-wool Scotsman.*

⋮ In medieval times, wool was often dyed before it was spun and woven. This meant that color was more evenly distributed in the wool, and lasted longer.

pull the wool over someone's eyes to try to deceive someone in order to get an advantage over them ○ *"I just told them I was ten years younger than I really was," says Liliana, speaking yesterday about how she pulled the wool over the medical profession's eyes.*

⋮ In the past, wigs for men were sometimes called "wool" because they looked like a sheep's fleece. It was easy to pull wigs over people's eyes, either as a joke or in order to rob them.

word

★ **a dirty word** something that someone disapproves of and does not want to have anything to do with ○ *At the root of their problems was the misplaced belief that good products sell themselves. Marketing became a dirty word at the company.*

★ **from the word go** from the very beginning of an activity ○ *Right from the word go, many of the players looked out of breath and out of their depth.*

get a word in edgewise to manage to say something even though someone else is talking so much ○ *For heaven's sake, Sue, will you let me get a word in edgewise!*

not breathe a word to not tell anyone about something ○ *Don't breathe a word of this to anyone.*

someone's word is law used to emphasize that everyone in an organization or group has to obey someone, even if this is unreasonable. ○ *His father was the kind of parent who saw no reason to discuss anything with his son; his word was law.*

a word in someone's ear a situation in which you speak to someone quietly and privately about a delicate or difficult matter ○ *I'll go and see him. It won't be official, mind. Just a word in his ear over lunch.*

words

★ **eat your words** to be proved to be wrong when you have given an opinion about something ○ *England made Denmark eat their words with a brilliant victory in the European championship. The Danish coach had criticized England prior to their semi-final clash.*

famous last words said when you want to suggest that your claim that something will definitely happen in a certain way will be proved wrong ○ *"All under control," said Bertie. "Famous last words," added Idris with a wide grin.*

in words of one syllable as simply and clearly as possible. You often use this expression to suggest that the person you are talking to is stupid or slow to understand something. ○ *I'm sure I don't have to spell things out in words of one syllable to you.*

★ **lost for words** or

at a loss for words so amazed, shocked, or moved by something that you do not know what to say or how to express your feelings in words ○ *I had the feeling they were all waiting for me to say something. But for the first time in my life I felt at a loss for words.*

★ **not mince your words** to state an opinion clearly and directly, even though you know that some people will not like what you are saying ○ *She did not mince her words when she came to the platform to demand a vote of no confidence in the president.*

put words into someone's mouth to try to make someone give opinions or make statements which they have never actually given or made ○ *You're trying to get me to say things! You're putting words into my mouth which have got nothing to do with me or my book!*

take the words out of someone's mouth to say the thing that someone was just about to say ○ *"Well, it's been amazing," she said in closing. "You took the words right out of my mouth, Lisa."*

work

★ **do someone's dirty work** to do something unpleasant or difficult on someone's behalf because they do not want to do it themselves ○ *He's always got other people to do his dirty work for him.*

★ **have your work cut out** to have a very big problem to deal with that you will not find easy to do. ○ *The Prime Minister has his work cut out for him as most analysts see little chance of resolving the constitutional crisis.*

make short work of something to achieve or complete something with little effort ○ *The other team made short work of us in the second contest.*

a piece of work a very surprising, unusual, or impressive person ○ *Her next role is to play the most highly decorated policewoman in New York City. She's a real piece of work – very controversial.*

works

★ **gum up the works** to make something more difficult to do, or to make a process less efficient ○ *Nothing will gum up the works of claims more than having inconsistent data from many sources.*

★ **in the works** being planned or in progress. ○ *The Office of Development for the city says that a shopping center is in the works.*

the works or

the whole works said after mentioning a number of things, to mean many other things of the same kind ○ *Amazing place he's got there – squash courts, swimming pool, jacuzzi, the works.*

world

come down in the world or

go down in the world (old-fashioned) to have less money than you had before and now have a lower social status ○ *Young women of middle class families which had come down in the world also found work in the upper ranges of domestic service.*

come up in the world or

go up in the world (old-fashioned) to have more money than you had before and now have a higher social status ○ *A well brought-up young man: he was said to have been an ordinary worker who had come up in the world.*

dead to the world sleeping very deeply ○ *Sarah was dead to the world and would probably sleep for twelve hours.*

it's a small world or

small world said to express your surprise when you unexpectedly meet someone you know in an unusual place, or you learn that two people you know actually know each other as well ○ *I'm only just recovering from the surprise of running into you like this. Small world.*

not long for this world likely to die soon ○ *Peter asked Jan to become his assistant earlier that year, perhaps knowing that he was not long for this world. When he died in June, Jan became chairman.*

not set the world on fire to not be exciting and to be unlikely to be very successful ○ *Munton is a good batter, but hardly likely to set the world of baseball on fire.*

★ **on top of the world** extremely happy ○ *When she came back from that vacation she was so happy, on top of the world.*

★ **out of this world** very good or impressive ○ *The show was really good. The music was great and the costumes were out of this world.*

think the world of someone to like and admire someone very much or be very fond of them ○ *He is an involved and caring father, and Sam thinks the world of him.*

the world is your oyster said when you want to suggest that someone has the opportunity to achieve great success in their life ○ *You've got a wonderful watershed in your life, Johnny. You're young, you've got a lot of opportunity. The world is your oyster.*

This expression suggests that success can be taken from the world in the same way that pearls can be taken from oysters. This idea was used by Shakespeare in "The Merry Wives Of Windsor": "Why, then the world's mine oyster, Which I with sword will open." (Act 2, Scene 2)

worlds

★ **the best of both worlds** all the benefits and advantages of two different things, without any of the problems or disadvantages ○ *These locations combine the best of both worlds. They're in the town yet close to beautiful mountains and state parks.*

★ **the worst of both worlds** all the problems and disadvantages of two different things without any of the benefits and advantages ○ *Fans got the worst of both worlds: higher prices and more low-quality football.*

worm

the worm has turned used when someone who has tolerated a lot of bad treatment from other people without complaining unexpectedly changes their behavior and starts to behave in a more forceful way ○ *Then my mother came home and started bossing us around. She said, "The worm has turned. Things are going to be different around here."*

worms

★ **a can of worms** or

a bag of worms a situation that is much more complicated, unpleasant, or difficult than it seems at first ○ *Now we have uncovered a can of worms in which there has not only been shameful abuse of power, but a failure of moral authority of the worst kind.*

worried

worried sick extremely worried ○ *Where have you been? I've been worried sick about you.*

worse

★ **the worse for wear** looking tired or in a bad state, especially because you have been working hard or drinking a lot of alcohol ○ *He turned up at important functions two hours late and noticeably the worse for wear.*

worst

the worst of both worlds → see **worlds**

wounds

★ **lick your wounds** to feel sorry for yourself after being thoroughly defeated or humiliated ○ *Five games in to the regular season, the win-less Buffalo Bills are licking their wounds, and preparing in earnest for the rest of the season.*

≡ Some animals, such as cats, lick their wounds when they are injured.

open old wounds to remind people of an unpleasant or embarrassing experience in the past that they would rather forget about ○ *But that afternoon my world was overturned. Ted's diagnosis had opened old wounds and I no longer felt secure.*

wraps

★ **keep something under wraps** to keep something secret and not reveal it to anyone ○ *The official report has been kept under wraps for months by legal objections from pharmaceutical companies.*

take the wraps off something to tell people about something such as a proposal or a new product for the first time ○ *Later this year, Porsche will take the wraps off their Ferrari-bashing 911 Turbo.*

wrench

throw a wrench into the works or **throw a monkey wrench into the works** to cause problems that prevent something from happening in the way that it was planned ○ *When Elton was robbed it threw a monkey wrench into the works.*

wringer

go through the wringer or **be put through the wringer** to go through a very difficult period or situation that upsets you greatly and makes you ill or unhappy ○ *I felt as though I'd been through the wringer. My life seemed a wreck.*

Yy

yards

the whole nine yards everything;
the fullest amount or extent possible
○ *I went down on one knee, proposed to her
at sunrise, the whole nine yards.*

There are many theories about the
origin of this expression. It may refer to
the amount of cement, nine cubic
yards, which is contained in a cement-
mixer truck.

yesterday

not born yesterday not as naive or as
easily deceived as people seem to
think ○ *He was rewarded with a
disbelieving smirk. "Now you really do
sound like my father. I wasn't born
yesterday, you know."*

yonder

into the wild blue yonder or
into the wide blue yonder
(literary) on a journey to a faraway
place that is unfamiliar or mysterious
○ *Sailing into the wide blue yonder,
Colin discovers his very own Treasure
Island.*

Zz

zero-sum

a zero-sum game a situation in which if one person gains an advantage, someone else involved must suffer an equivalent disadvantage ○ *In New York people pursue money, which is not a zero-sum game. No one has to lose money for you to make money.*

A zero-sum game is one in which the winnings and losses of all the players add up to zero.

zone

be in the zone to be performing particularly well ○ *I remember riding back to the stables on a rising tide of emotion and hugging my dad. By now I was in the zone and brimming with confidence.*

zoo

it's a zoo the situation is chaotic and noisy ○ *"It's a zoo," said boater Garth Clouster of Anderson. "When all the crazies get out there and the water gets real choppy."*